THE DISAPPEARANCE OF GOD

THE DISAPPEARANCE OF GOD

FIVE NINETEENTH-CENTURY WRITERS

ᪧ ᪧ ᪧ ᪧ

J. HILLIS MILLER

THE BELKNAP PRESS OF
HARVARD UNIVERSITY PRESS

Cambridge, Massachusetts, and London, England

1975

Library of Congress Catalog Card Number 75-24626
ISBN 0-674-21101-4
Printed in the United States of America

TO DOROTHY

Preface to the Edition of 1975

Things thought too long can be no longer thought. — W. B. Yeats, "The Gyres"

The Disappearance of God is now twelve years old and can stand or fall on its own without any further help from me. Rereading it, in order to write this preface, I have felt its independence. I am no longer quite the same person I was when I wrote it, and I would not write it in quite the same way today.

On the other hand, I find myself still more or less in agreement with the interpretations I proposed of my five authors. I am, somewhat intransigently, perhaps most still in agreement where my readings have been most challenged. Matthew Arnold is no doubt a key figure in Victorian England. He still seems to me most important in the subversions of his irony and in his courageous recording of what was most negative in his spiritual experience. He remained for the most part heroically willing to report the finding of an absence, a lack, where he would like to have found some solid standing ground or to have received some rejuvenating spark from heaven. The authenticity of Gerard Manley Hopkins' work and life still seem to me to lie in the way they embody, in the word and in the flesh, certain contradictions within his version of Catholicism. Were I writing these two essays again I would relate the negative aspect of Arnold and the unresolved tension in Hopkins more elaborately to their explicit theories of language. This would mean more discussion of the admirable theological books of Arnold's later years and more discussion of Hopkins' early etymological notes as well as of his treatment of the theme of language in "The Wreck of the Deutschland." My sense of all five writers has, nevertheless, not changed greatly.

Far more problematic are the methodological presuppositions which formed, so to speak, the scaffolding of the book. To change the metaphor, these presuppositions were the machinery allowing

expression of the insights, such as they are, into the writings of
these authors. I still believe that the aim of criticism is to get inside
the works criticized and to convey as intimate a sense as possible
of what goes on there. This requires what might be called "gen-
erosity," a willingness to accept what one finds in an author and
to go all the way with him. I would still agree with Georges Poulet
and others that criticism is an extension of the act of reading, an
allegory or figure for reading. I believe even more strongly than I
did when I wrote the preface for the paperback edition of this
book (reprinted here along with the original preface) that literary
criticism is an international enterprise. If only to avoid laborious
duplication of the work of others, critics of English and American
authors should know as much as possible of Continental as well
as of Anglo-American criticism. The delay, for instance, in making
available to those who do not read Russian the best recent Russian
criticism — for example, that of Mikhail Bakhtin — has been unfortunate. I should see this now, however, as much less a matter
of creating some eclectic "methodology," combining the strategies
of many countries and schools, than as enabling what is after all
in the case of each critic a more or less idiosyncratic enterprise.
Each genuine act of criticism, like each act of reading, is to a
considerable degree unique and to a considerable degree lonely.
One is, however, perhaps best helped in becoming oneself by
knowing the widest variety of other selves, and, in criticism,
what one most needs as a model or stimulus for a particular work
of interpretation may come from unexpectedly distant sources.

If "participation" and "inwardness" still seem the chief requirements of valid literary criticism, I am much less certain
that this intimacy is to be defined as the identification of the mind
of the critic with the mind of the author. Nor am I sure that the
aim of criticism is properly to be described as the most exact
delineation of the consciousness of the author. Much is gained
by these assumptions. They encourage elimination of the peripheral and concentration on the fundamental. They provide a way
to unify and concentrate a critical essay. They give the critic
the sense that he has a solid foundation, an origin, and a goal
for his work. There can be no doubt that the act of reading gives
the reader the powerful sense that he is encountering, through
the words, another mind. Terms descriptive of consciousness and

of interpersonal relations may be indispensable to criticism. It could be, nevertheless, that all these securities are based on a fiction. They may be based, that is, on a figurative transference of terms from psychology and social relations to the realm of literature. Such terms may apply in literature not literally but by an "as if." When we read a novel by Trollope or a poem by Browning it is "as if" we were encountering another mind or knowing another mind from within. It may be that the "consciousness of the author" is an illusion or phantasm generated by the words on the page. This phantasm may have nothing necessarily to do with the actual mind of the person who once put those words down on paper. This is a familiar notion now in discussions of the "narrator" in prose fiction, but it may have a wider relevance. Consciousness, in literature at least, may be a function of language, a fictive appearance generated by language, rather than something language describes or reflects.

It could be argued that the question of whether the term "consciousness" in criticism is to be taken literally or figuratively is trivial. It is enough if the hypothesis works to achieve the inwardness and economy requisite in good criticism. The difficulty is that, like all such "presuppositions" or "hypotheses," the notion of consciousness in criticism begs all sorts of questions. These questions may possibly be at stake in the work being criticized. If so, they might better be left open, whatever the cost in making criticism more difficult and more problematic.

The word "hypothesis," it will be remembered, means etymologically "to place under." Perhaps there is no literary criticism which does not base itself on hypothetical fictions. All criticism must hypothecate or pledge something which remains its own (rather than belonging to the work in question). Only in this way can it take possession of the work and build its structure of interpretation on that heterogenous base, partly its own and partly the work's. If this is so, one would like to know it for sure and would like to be sure, in a given piece of criticism, what has been hypothesized or hypothecated.

The form of the essays in *The Disappearance of God* follows naturally from the hypothesis of consciousness. These essays tend to assume that the mind of any author is unitary, single, "monological." From that unified mind everything in the author's writing comes, and to it everything returns or may be returned. The "dialectical" method of criticism is justified by this assumption. Though multiplicity and even self-contradiction are present in the work of any author, that apparent heterogeneity can be arranged in a natural sequence. This begins with a starting place in some act of self-awareness. It leads through an itinerary of adventures of the spirit in its encounters with the world to a final stage which is a genuine goal. This endpoint is in fact the starting point of self-consciousness raised to a higher level, and so the essay comes full circle. The presupposition of consciousness is the origin, goal, and underlying ground giving shape, coherence, and limits to the reading.

Latent in this procedure is an implicit spatialization of literature and of criticism. Consciousness is a homogeneous inner realm. The critical essay moves from place to place within that inner space on a journey of exploration which has an intrinsic beginning and ending. There is an inn in the morning and another inn at night where the knight-errant of criticism may rest. Moreover, the critic remains "at home" within a homogeneous space, however multifarious may be the thematic elements he encounters in a given writer. Time becomes spatialized or a category of space, an aspect of the unified consciousness of the author.

Such criticism, finally, tends to project its system of assumptions back on literary history or on history as such. The concepts of origin, end, and underlying ground were probably borrowed from theories of history in the first place. They are familiar as the key assumptions of the "metaphysical" view of history, for example, in Hegel's *Philosophy of History*. Such criticism tends to assume that there was a *Zeitgeist*. Within this "consciousness of the age" the mind of each individual writer was bathed as in a limiting or even determining milieu. From this it is but a step to seeing the sequence of literary periods as related to one another dialectically, in the same way that the "stages" in the spiritual journey of a single author are related. Each period "progresses" beyond the last in a kind of *Aufhebung*, a simultaneous canceling, preserving, and elevating. The "death of God" and the "recovery of immanence" in the twentieth century are, for example, seen as "going beyond" the "disappearance of God." This tends to imply that there is a grand goal for all history or for literary

history. It is unclear, however, whether this is an actually attainable goal or only a sort of vanishing point on the horizon.
It might even turn out to be a stage of enlightenment making
literature no longer possible or necessary.

All these notions about literature, about criticism, and about
history follow almost inevitably from the generative assumption
that the aim of criticism is to identify one's mind with the mind
of the author being criticized. These notions form an interdependent
system, each element implying all the others and necessary to
them in its turn.

As I began by saying, I believe that valid insights into the
authors discussed in *The Disappearance of God* were enabled or at
any rate not inhibited by the method of criticism used there.
Perhaps the scaffolding of method is less important than the
readings it facilitates. Having constructed the building, one can
dismantle the scaffolding. One wonders, however, if the scaffolding
can really be distinguished from the building in this way. One
wonders, in short, whether the assumption of a unified consciousness in each author may not to some degree have predetermined
the results of the interpretation. The questions about the nature
of the mind, about literature, and about history, begged by this
assumption, may in one way or another be an issue in the works of
Emily Bronte, Thomas De Quincey, and the rest. Perhaps there
could be a criticism which, without getting bogged down in endless preliminary methodological minutiae, would nevertheless keep
these questions open.

Such a criticism might leave room for the possibility that in
literature fictive minds are generated by language rather than
language being the mirror of a pre-existing mind. Such a criticism
might be more concerned with language as such in literature.
It would study that play of figures which challenges any mimetic
reading, even a reading which sees each work as mimetic of the
mind that fathered it. For such a criticism time rather than space
would be seen as the constitutive dimension of literature. To
substitute time for space would put the possibility of discontinuity
or heterogeneity in place of the assumption of homogeneity. As a
paradigm for the generation of meaning in literature it would
replace the relation of reflector and reflected inside a mirroring
mind with the relation of sign to sign across the gap of time. Such

a criticism would entertain the possibility that a work of literature, rather than having a single mind at its origin, may be dialogical. Such a work would have two or more implied generative sources; it could not, therefore, be reduced to a single, coherent, all-inclusive reading. The interpretation of such a work might reach the impasse of two incompatible readings, both arising from the text itself. Such a text would be "undecidable," "unreadable." This alternative criticism would, finally, see literary history not as progressive or teleological but as permutations of possibilities inherent in the finite repertoire of concepts, figures, and narrative patterns possessed "from the beginning" by our Western family of languages. A later stage is as likely to be regressive as progressive in relation to a given earlier stage. In poetry, as in criticism or in philosophical insight, it may be impossible to do more than periodically reach again in different ways pinnacles already scaled by the earliest writers in our tradition.

To substitute language for consciousness, figurative for literal, intraliterary for mimetic generation of meaning, time for space, the possibility of the dialogical for the assumption of the mono-logical, a permutative for a progressive theory of literary history, would no doubt lead to different procedures of criticism. Doubtless these would have their own tendency to predetermine the results of criticism, for "questions," as we know, "are remarks," that is, already answers. Whether a criticism keeping such possibilities open would necessarily forgo those virtues of orderliness, of penetration, and of proximity to the texts which to me seem present in the essays of *The Disappearance of God* remains to be seen. In any case, it is toward such a criticism that I, along with some others, am now working, if only because "things thought too long can be no longer thought" and because one needs to put in question one's earlier work in order to make possible the new. As Wallace Stevens says, "one of the motives in writing is renewal." This need for renewal does not, however, obscure my sense that it may be the methodological assumptions of *The Disappearance of God* which made possible what is accomplished there.

The relation between a critic's method and his results may not, however, be so straightforward. At any rate, it appears that the relation between my present work and that of over a decade ago is more than simply negative. It may be in the nature of literature that investigations of it initiated according to a given hypothesis will lead, if carried far enough, to insights which call that hypothesis into question. Such insights, it seems to me, are already present in one way or another in *The Disappearance of God*. The interpretations are not wholly consistent with the critical presuppositions that motivated them. I shall leave it to the reader to find these inconsistencies for himself. Such self-subverting insights might be the analogue in literature and in criticism for Gödel's incompleteness theorem. According to that theorem, any formal system will lead ultimately to conclusions which cannot be encompassed within its original assumptions. Such conclusions are neither provable nor unprovable, neither true nor false. The specific forms this might take in literature and in criticism would be worth investigating. They would no doubt have something to do with the problems I have been discussing in this new preface and something also to do with those aspects of *The Disappearance of God* which implicitly question its own overt assumptions about literature and about criticism.

J. H. M.

Calhoun College, Yale University
May 31, 1975

Preface to the Paperback Edition

This book is an investigation into the work of five nineteenth-century writers, an approach to a description of the spiritual history of the period, and an attempt to use a certain kind of literary criticism as a means of doing these two things. Even in the brief time since the book was first published this kind of criticism has become better known in America, through translations, reviews, and other commentaries, as well as through its influence on critical practice. Now it appears possible that European ways of doing criticism, whether that of the so-called "Geneva School," or that of the more recent structuralist critics in Paris, may present themselves to Americans as alternatives to the new criticism or to archetypal criticism. The happiest result would be the creation of another indigenous criticism, one assimilating the advances of European criticism in the past twenty years but re-shaping these to our peculiarly American experience of literature and its powers.

I now look upon the spiritual situation described in *The Disappearance of God* as part of a development leading from romanticism to twentieth-century writers like Yeats, Stevens, and William Carlos Williams. These poets, as I have tried to show in another book,[1] grow out of romanticism but go beyond it. This growth goes by way of the nihilism which is covert in the nineteenth-century English novel and becomes explicit in the work of Conrad. In nihilism the disappearance of God becomes the death of God, which is a different thing entirely. This death is the presupposition of much twentieth-century literature.

J. H. M.

The Johns Hopkins University
May 23, 1965

[1] *Poets of Reality: Six Twentieth-Century Writers* (Cambridge, Mass.: The Belknap Press of Harvard University Press, 1965).

Preface

For a writer, as for a musician or a painter, the multiplicity of works provides that variation of circumstances which makes it possible to discern, by a sort of experimentation, the permanent traits of character. — Marcel Proust[1]

Literary criticism may focus on a single poem, play, or novel, on the total body of a writer's work, or on the unity made up of all the writings of an age. These contexts are like three concentric circles, each containing the next smaller and forming its milieu. The entire work of a poet is the atmosphere in which his poems live, just as all his writings are bathed in the ambient presence of a period of history. Though a critic may confine himself to one or another of the circles of criticism, the comprehension of literature takes place through a constant narrowing and expansion of the focus of attention, from the single work of an author, to the whole body of his works, to the spirit of the age, and back again in a contraction and dilation which is the living motion of interpretation.

Literature is a form of consciousness, and literary criticism is the analysis of this form in all its varieties. Though literature is made of words, these words embody states of mind and make them available to others. The comprehension of literature is a process of what Gabriel Marcel calls "intersubjectivity." Criticism demands above all that gift of participation, that power to put oneself within the life of another person, which Keats called negative capability. If literature is a form of consciousness the task of the critic is to identify himself with the subjectivity expressed in the words, to relive that life from the inside, and to constitute it anew in his criticism.

Though the distinguishing traits of an author's genius may be present in each of his creations, just as every work bears the mark of its age, those traits are usually recognized only with difficulty

[1] Marcel Proust, *Pastiches et mélanges* (Paris: Gallimard, 1937), p. 107; my translation.

in a single work. The structure of consciousness expressed in a poem or novel is like that "inscape" which Gerard Manley Hopkins says is present in every example of a given species, but usually "detached to the mind" [2] only through repetition. Repetition "gives the visible law: looked at in any one instance it flies." [3] Each chapter in this book attempts to identify the "inscape" of an author, to detach from the body of his writings that organizing form which presides over the elaboration of each of his works. My presupposition is that all an author's writings form a living unity, just as each individual work is a life within that larger life, and my method is the one recommended by Proust and Hopkins: the juxtaposition of diverse works in order to identify the "novel and unique beauty" [4] which is their common essence.

Though literature is a form of consciousness, consciousness is always consciousness *of* something. A work of literature is the act whereby a mind takes possession of space, time, nature, or other minds. Each of these is a dimension of literature. Literature may also express a relation of the self to God. I have chosen to approach five writers from a theological perspective because in De Quincey, Browning, Emily Brontë, Arnold, and Hopkins theological experience is most important and determines everything else. My primary concern has been the identification of the "novel beauty" of each, not the description of similarities between them, though similarities do exist. Prolonged immersion in the work of each writer, in an attempt to discover his "inscape," has come before any attempt to make statements about resonances or echoes from writer to writer. My introductory chapter was written last. It describes the atmosphere in which all five writers lived. In this there is no assumption of historical determinism. The relations between the general consciousness and particular minds can never be accounted for on the model of cause and effect in the material world. The metaphor of organism and environment is better, but in literature the organism creates the environment as much as it is created by it. The source of historical generalizations can be nothing but affirmations made by particular men, just as the or-

[2] Humphry House and Graham Storey, eds., *The Journals and Papers of Gerard Manley Hopkins* (London: Oxford University Press, 1959), p. 289.
[3] Hopkins, *Journals*, p. 139.
[4] Marcel Proust, "La prisonnière," *À la recherche du temps perdu*, XII (Paris: Gallimard, 1949), 219.

ganizing form of a writer's work exists only as it is embodied in particular works. The chapters here assembled stay chiefly in the second circle of criticism, but they also make that expansion and contraction to the larger and smaller circles which is the systole and diastole of criticism.

ළ❧

Acknowledgments

A few sentences in Chapter VI have been taken from my essay, "The Creation of the Self in Gerard Manley Hopkins," *ELH*, XXII (1955), 293–319, and are used by permission of The Johns Hopkins Press and the editors of *ELH*. Some passages in Chapters I, III, V, and VI have been published in my essay, "The Theme of the Disappearance of God in Victorian Poetry," *Victorian Studies*, VI (1963), 207–227.

The writing of much of this book was made possible by a year's leave of absence from The Johns Hopkins University and a fellowship from the John Simon Guggenheim Memorial Foundation. For both of these I wish to express my gratitude.

ළ❧

Method of Citation

Where a book is frequently quoted in a chapter I have identified it in an initial footnote, have indicated the abbreviation to be used, and have thereafter put the references to that book in parentheses after quotations. The abbreviation is in each case followed by the page number, or the volume and page number, of the quotation. In cases where a single book or edition is cited very frequently in a chapter, after the first citation only page numbers or volume and page numbers are given.

CONTENTS

THE DISAPPEARANCE OF GOD

⊷ I ⊷

Introduction

Post-medieval literature records, among other things, the gradual withdrawal of God from the world. This book studies five members of an important group of nineteenth- and twentieth-century writers who represent the culmination of a long process. De Quincey, Browning, Arnold, Hopkins, and Emily Brontë all begin in the situation of the characters in *Vanity Fair*. They are "a set of people living without God in the world." [1]

Such a situation must not be misunderstood. It does not mean blank atheism, the "God is dead" of Nietzsche as it is often interpreted. God still lives, but, as Hölderlin said, he lives "above our heads, up there in a different world." [2] Arthur Hugh Clough expresses perfectly this paradoxical belief in a God of whose existence there is no immediate evidence:

> That there are beings above us, I believe,
> And when we lift up holy hands of prayer,
> I will not say they will not give us aid. [3]

He will not say the gods do not care for man, but neither will he say they do. For such a man God exists, but he is out of reach.

There was a time when things were different, when it seemed that God dwelt in the human world. In that time "the Word was there, was very near at least, on the tip of everybody's tongue, any one might have hit upon it." [4] But for Kafka and for other writers who belong to his spiritual family the Word now is no-

---

[1] W. M. Thackeray, *Letters and Private Papers,* ed. G. N. Ray, II (Cambridge, Mass., 1945), 309.

[2] Friedrich Hölderlin, "*Brod und Wein.* An Heinze," *Sämtliche Werke,* IV (Berlin, 1923), 123: "Zwar leben die Götter, / Aber über dem Haupt droben in anderer Welt."

[3] H. F. Lowry, A. L. P. Norrington, and F. L. Mulhauser, eds., *The Poems of Arthur Hugh Clough* (London, 1951), p. 409.

[4] Franz Kafka, *Gesammelte Schriften,* V (New York: Schocken Books, 1946), p. 259: ". . . und jenes Wort war da, war zumindest nahe, schwebte auf der Zungenspitze, jeder konnte es erfahren . . ." I have quoted the translation of Willa and Edwin Muir, *The Great Wall of China* (New York: Schocken Books, 1946), pp. 46, 47.

where to be found. The lines of connection between us and God have broken down, or God himself has slipped away from the places where he used to be. He no longer inheres in the world as the force binding together all men and all things. As a result the nineteenth and twentieth centuries seem to many writers a time when God is no more present and not yet again present, and can only be experienced negatively, as a terrifying absence. In this time of the no longer and not yet, man is "Wandering between two worlds, one dead,/The other powerless to be born." [5] His situation is essentially one of disconnection: disconnection between man and nature, between man and man, even between man and himself. Only if God would return or if we could somehow reach him might our broken world be unified again. But this has not yet happened. God keeps himself hidden. There seems to be no way to re-establish connection. In our time "there is a goal, but no way; what we call the way is only wavering." [6]

Such has been the spiritual situation for many Western writers during the last hundred and fifty years. This situation has a special quality in each country, and, within each country, each writer who finds God absent expresses this absence in a unique form. The writers studied in this book are five examples of the nineteenth-century English way of experiencing the disappearance of God. Different as are their heritages, and different as are their spiritual adventures, their starting points are strikingly similar, and therefore they may be distinguished from other Victorian writers whose initial situations are different.

How did this situation come about? In the Presocratic philosophers, in the earliest books of the Old Testament, perhaps even in archaic Egyptian sculpture, modern scholars see evidence that our culture, at its beginnings, experienced the divine power as immediately present in nature, in society, and in each man's heart. [7]

[5] C. B. Tinker and H. F. Lowry, eds., *The Poetical Works of Matthew Arnold* (London, 1950), p. 302.

[6] Franz Kafka, *Gesammelte Werke*, VIII (New York: Schocken Books, 1953), p. 42: "Es gibt ein Ziel, aber keinen Weg; was wir Weg nennen, ist Zögern"; trans., *The Great Wall*, p. 283.

[7] Martin Heidegger is of course the champion of this interpretation of the Presocratics. See especially *Holzwege* (Frankfurt am Main, 1950), pp. 296–343, and *Vorträge und Aufsätze* (Pfullingen, 1954), pp. 207–282. For this interpretation of the Old Testament see Jacob Taubes, "From Cult to Culture," *Partisan Review*, XXI (1954), 387–400, Oskar Goldberg, *Die Wirklichkeit der Hebraër* (Berlin, 1925), and chapter XXVIII of Thomas Mann's *Doktor Faustus* (Stockholm, 1947). For

So Moses saw God in the burning bush, and so Parmenides and Heraclitus are philosopher-poets of total immanence. And even though the central tradition of Western civilization, in later Judaism, in Platonism, and in Christianity, defines God as transcending his creation, the miracle of the Incarnation brought God back to earth, so that once more he walked among us as he had before the fall, when history had not yet begun. Christ was the mediator joining a fallen world and a distant God. The daily re-enactment of the Incarnation on all the altars of Christendom was the manifestation and guarantee of communion. God, man, nature, and language participated in each other and were at one in the Eucharist. The words of the sacrament brought about the transubstantiation of the natural elements into the body and blood of Christ, and in partaking of these the members of the Christian community were assimilated to one another and to God. But the communion service was only the most manifest form of the presence of God throughout the world. Nature and human history were full of symbols and types of divine truth. Each page of the book of nature was written by God and was another revelation of God by God. Created things were not merely signs pointing to something which remained off at a distance, separated from them. The Eucharist was the archetype of the divine analogy whereby created things participated in the supernatural reality they signified. Poetry in turn was, in one way or another, modeled on sacramental or scriptural language. The words of the poem incarnated the things they named, just as the words of the Mass shared in the transformation they evoked. The symbols and metaphors of poetry were no mere inventions of the poets. They were borrowed from the divine analogies of nature. Poetry was meaningful in the same way as nature itself — by a communion of the verbal symbols with the reality they named.

The history of modern literature is in part the history of the splitting apart of this communion. This splitting apart has been matched by a similar dispersal of the cultural unity of man, God, nature, and language. It is not possible to explain why this fragmentation has come about. A great historical transformation remains mysterious, just as does the homogeneity of the culture of

Egyptian sculpture see Claude Vigée, *Les artistes de la faim* (Paris, 1960), pp. 40–42.

a single age. We can neither explain why people stop feeling and believing in an old way, nor why a new way of feeling and believing appears simultaneously in widely separated individuals. The attempt to establish the genesis of historical change usually reveals more about the presuppositions of the historian than about cause and effect relations in the events themselves. To a Marxist economic and social changes produce ideological changes. To a man like Yeats the rise of a materialist civilization has itself been governed by occult spiritual forces turning the gyres of history. It may be that the disappearance of God has been caused not so much by man's turning his back on God, as by a strange withdrawal of God himself. It certainly has seemed so to many modern writers.

It is therefore impossible to describe the coming into existence of modern times on the model of physical change. We cannot construct an orderly system of events, each causing the next in line. All we can say is that a whole set of changes, both spiritual and material, happened more or less simultaneously, like a great wave breaking on the shore, and that by the nineteenth century the starting place for a writer was likely to be the isolation and destitution of Matthew Arnold or of the early Hopkins.

The transformations making up this wave can be identified easily enough even though the question of which causes which can never be answered. In the social and material worlds there are all those changes associated with the rise of science and technology: industrialization, the increasing predominance of the middle class, the gradual breakdown of the old hierarchical class structure, the building of great cities. The specific conditions of life in the city express most concretely the new mode of existence which is coming into being for industrialized man. From Wordsworth and Coleridge through Arnold, Baudelaire, and Hopkins to T. S. Eliot and Apollinaire there is an increasing dominance in poetry of the image of the city. The poets tend to see the city as a vast agglomeration of bricks and people, in which "all is seared with trade; bleared, smeared with toil;/And wears man's smudge and shares man's smell." [8] Life in the city is even more important for the novel, which might be defined as the art form called into being to deal with the conditions of urbanized life. In dozens of Victorian novels, supremely in Dickens, there is dramatized the new life of

[8] Gerard Manley Hopkins, *Poems*, third ed. (New York, 1948), p. 70.

man in the city — the dirt and soot and bad smells, the murk of
fog and smoke, the somber prisons crowded with inmates, the dark
rooms wholly cut off from one another, as if they were far underground, the labyrinthine streets, the crowds of people passing
through these streets or over the bridges, each as isolated from all
the others as if he were living on a desert island, the living death
of the poor clerk chained to a meaningless job, the dark river
flowing muddily through the city, adding more dirt than it carries
away, and offering a fearful temptation to the homeless and the
lost.

The industrialization and urbanization of man means the progressive transformation of the world. Everything is changed from
its natural state into something useful or meaningful to man.
Everywhere the world mirrors back to man his own image, and
nowhere can he make vivifying contact with what is not human.
Even the fog is not a natural fog, rolling in from the sea, but is
half soot and smoke. The city is the literal representation of the
progressive humanization of the world. And where is there room
for God in the city? Though it is impossible to tell whether man
has excluded God by building the great cities, or whether the
cities have been built because God has disappeared, in any case
the two go together. Life in the city is the way in which many
men have experienced most directly what it means to live without
God in the world.

Along with these social and material changes have gone other
more spiritual transformations. Paralleling the development of
urban, technologized life there has been a gradual dissipation of
the medieval symbolism of participation. Many scholars have studied the breaking of the circle, the untuning of the sky, the change
from the closed world to the infinite universe which slowly destroyed the polyphonic harmony of microcosm and macrocosm.[9]
In that old harmony man, society, nature, and language mirrored
one another, like so many voices in a madrigal or fugue. The idea
of the Incarnation was the ultimate basis for this harmony. But it

[9] See A. O. Lovejoy, *The Great Chain of Being* (Cambridge, Mass., 1936), M. H.
Nicolson, *The Breaking of the Circle* (Evanston, Ill., 1950; rev. ed., New York,
1960), Alexandre Koyré, *From the Closed World to the Infinite Universe* (Baltimore,
1957), E. R. Wasserman, *The Subtler Language* (Baltimore, 1959), and John Hol-
lander, *The Untuning of the Sky; Ideas of Music in English Poetry* (Princeton,
N.J., 1961).

was precisely belief in the Incarnation which gradually died out of the European consciousness. The Reformation, if not immediately, certainly in its ultimate effects, meant a weakening of belief in the sacrament of communion. Instead of being the literal transubstantiation of bread and wine into the body and blood of Christ, the Eucharist came more and more to be seen in the Zwinglian or Calvinistic manner. To these reformers the bread and wine are mere signs commemorating the historical fact that Christ was once, long ago, present on earth: "This do in remembrance of me." Instead of being a sharing in the immediate presence of Christ, the communion service becomes the expression of an absence. For Gerard Manley Hopkins, in the middle nineteenth century, the chief attraction of Catholicism is the doctrine of the Real Presence. This and this alone, says Hopkins, will destroy the "sordidness" of the world, and Protestantism offers no escape from this sordidness.[10]

As Claude Vigée has suggested,[11] the Protestant reinterpretation of the Eucharist parallels exactly a similar transformation in literature. The old symbolism of analogical participation is gradually replaced by the modern poetic symbolism of reference at a distance. Like the Zwinglian Eucharist such symbols designate an absence, not a presence. They point to something which remains somewhere else, unpossessed and unattainable. Mallarmé, with his poetry of "the absence of all bouquets," or of "the notion of an object, escaping, which fails to be," [12] is merely the climax of a long evolution in modern literature. In this evolution words have been gradually hollowed out, and have lost their substantial participation in material or spiritual reality. Just as the modern city is the creation of a set of people living without God in the world, so modern literature betrays in its very form the absence of God. God has become a *Deus absconditus,* hidden somewhere behind the silence of infinite spaces, and our literary symbols can only make the most distant allusions to him, or to the natural world which used to be his abiding place and home.

In this perspective we can see the special importance of baroque

[10] *Further Letters* (London, 1956), pp. 17, 92, 226, 227.

[11] *Les artistes de la faim,* pp. 51–60.

[12] Stéphane Mallarmé, *Oeuvres complètes,* éd. de la Pléiade (Paris, 1945), pp. 368, 647: "l'absente de tous bouquets"; "la notion d'un objet, échappant, qui fait défaut."

poetry. Baroque poetry in France, Italy, and Spain, like the architecture, painting, and sculpture of the period, is characterized by
a constant multiplication of motifs, all unstable, all in motion, all
melting into one another, and all revealing themselves as an insubstantial décor, a kind of theatrical surface detached from any
solid reality. In such poetry natural objects twist, curve, and distort themselves as if to express a violent effort to reach something
which remains beyond them. A great flood of metaphors and symbols, doubling one another to infinity, strives desperately to say
what a single phrase of the old poetry, in its calm possession of
its spiritual meaning, could say in a moment. Baroque poetry
represents a violent effort by the human imagination to keep open
the avenues of communication between man and God. It tries to
express, in a language which is visibly disintegrating and becoming empty, a divine reality which is in the very act of disappearing
from the world. In baroque poetry we can witness the crucial
moment of the change from a poetry of presence to a poetry of
allusion and absence. In the High Renaissance, God is both transcendent and immanent, and in many writers there is an intuition
of nature as everywhere inhabited by God. There is a turn toward
panpsychism, even to pantheism, as in Giordano Bruno. But the
God within nature and the God beyond nature gradually separate
from one another, and by the eighteenth century we have the
watchmaker God, maker of a universe which is a perfect machine,
and therefore no longer needs his presence. Baroque art is the
expression of the moment of this separation, just as, in nineteenth-
century England, Evangelicalism and the Catholic revival are belated attempts to stop the "melancholy, long, withdrawing roar"
of the sea of faith.[13]

When the old system of symbols binding man to God has finally
evaporated man finds himself alone and in spiritual poverty. Modern times begin when man confronts his isolation, his separation
from everything outside himself. Again the causal relation is reversible. It would be just as plausible to say that the rediscovery
or redefinition of subjective consciousness caused the death of
medieval symbolism as to say that the latter caused the former, or

---

[13] Arnold's phrases, of course, in "Dover Beach"; see Ford K. Brown, *Fathers of
the Victorians: The Age of Wilberforce* (Cambridge, 1961) for a detailed history
of the Evangelical revival and its gradual deterioration.

that both were caused by the building of cities and the technologizing of man. In any case modern thought has been increasingly dominated by the presupposition that each man is locked in the prison of his consciousness. From Montaigne to Descartes and Locke, on down through associationism, idealism, and romanticism to the phenomenology and existentialism of today, the assumption has been that man must start with the inner experience of the isolated self. Whether this experience is thought of as consciousness, the *Cogito* of Descartes, or as feelings and sense impressions, the sensations of Locke, or as a living center, the *punctum saliens* of Jean Paul, or as the paradoxical freedom of Sartre, in all the stages of modern thought the interior states of the self are a beginning which in some sense can never be transcended.

This limitation to private experience is an assumption of modern literature no less than of modern philosophy. The relation between the philosophy of F. H. Bradley and the early poetry of T. S. Eliot is a good example of this mirroring of philosophy by literature. Eliot quotes in the footnotes to "The Waste Land" Bradley's eloquent expression of the theory of subjective limitation,[14] and this passage is echoed in a climactic passage of "The Waste Land" itself. It is a passage in which the inturned repetition of the word "key" expresses all the pathos of the reflexive isolation of consciousness:

> I have heard the key
> Turn in the door once and turn once only
> We think of the key, each in his prison
> Thinking of the key, each confirms a prison . . .[15]

Much modern writing has been a dramatization in existential terms of the consequences of this kind of subjectivism. One great theme of modern literature is the sense of isolation, of alienation, brought about by man's new situation. We are alienated from God; we have alienated ourselves from nature; we are alienated from our fellow men; and, finally, we are alienated from ourselves, the buried life we never seem able to reach. The result is a radical sense of inner nothingness. Most of the great works of nineteenth-

---

[14] F. H. Bradley, *Appearance and Reality* (London, 1908), p. 346.
[15] T. S. Eliot, *The Complete Poems and Plays: 1909–1950* (New York, 1952), p. 49, quoted with permission of the publishers, Harcourt, Brace and World, and Faber and Faber.

century literature have at their centers a character who is in doubt
about his own identity and asks, "How can I find something outside myself which will tell me who I am, and give me a place in
society and in the universe?" In eighteenth-century English literature too, for example in *Tom Jones,* the hero is initially in doubt
about his identity, but it usually turns out in the end that there is
a place waiting for him in a stable society. In eighteenth-century
England the stability of the social order, sustained by divine Providence, is a guarantee of the stability of selfhood. For some writers
at least God is still immanent in society. But in nineteenth-century
literature the protagonist is usually in the condition of the central
character of Kierkegaard's *Repetition.* "My life," says Kierkegaard's hero, "has been brought to an *impasse.* I loathe existence
. . . One sticks one's finger into the soil to tell by the smell in
what land one is: I stick my finger into existence — it smells of
nothing. Where am I? Who am I? How came I here? What is this
thing called the world? What does this word mean? Who is it that
has lured me into the world? Why was I not consulted, why not
made acquainted with its manners and customs . . . ? How did
I obtain an interest in this big enterprise they call reality? Why
should I have an interest in it? Is it not a voluntary concern? And
if I am to be compelled to take part in it, where is the director?
I should like to make a remark to him. Is there no director?
Whither shall I turn with my complaint?" [16]

"Where is the director?" Subjectivism, like urbanization and
the failure of medieval symbolism, leads man back to an experience of the absence of God. But the rediscovery of the autonomy
of consciousness is associated with one more all-important quality
of modern times: the appearance of the historical sense. And here
too it is impossible to establish causal priority. Surely the sense of
history is one of the causes of the experience of existential isolation, but withdrawal into the privacy of consciousness can also
lead to an awareness of historical contingency.

The central factor in historicism is an assumption of the relativity of any particular life or culture. Man in a time of historicism
knows too much to believe that his selfhood can be limited without loss to the categories of a single culture or a single system of
thought. In the midst of one culture he is aware of all the other

[16] S. Kierkegaard, *Repetition,* trans. Walter Lowrie (Princeton, N.J., 1946), p. 114.

possible attitudes toward life. These tend to cancel one another out and leave him with a mere empty sense of infinite potentiality. He is aware of the arbitrariness of any belief or culture, of the process of growth and decay in civilizations, of the apparent dependence of beliefs, values, and language on material determinants: climate, mode of agriculture or manufacture. The attitude of historicism accompanies the failure of tradition, the failure of symbolic language, the failure of all the intermediaries between man and God. This may lead to a philosophy of perspectivism, such as we find in Spengler, in Henri Focillon, or even in Wallace Stevens, when he shows us so eloquently that there are at least thirteen ways of looking at a blackbird. And if thirteen why not thirty-three, or three hundred and thirteen — any number? No one way of looking at the world is perfect or complete. So rather than seeking some absolute perspective we should yield ourselves to a mobile existence, an existence in which we take up as many "life-attitudes," one by one, as we can.

Historicism does not mean merely an awareness of the contradictory diversity of cultures and attitudes. The ancient world had that. The modern historical sense means rather the loss of faith in the possibility of ever discovering the right and true culture, the right and true philosophy or religion. St. Augustine was aware that the city of the world is a Babel of conflicting cultures. But he opposed to this the city of God, and his own certainty that the Christian view is the correct one. The modern historicist, however, doubts the absolute validity of any world view or philosophy. Wilhelm Dilthey begins his *Weltanschauungslehre* with a strong affirmation of the irreconcilable antinomy between the search made by metaphysicians for the true structure of the world, and the intransigent relativism of the historical consciousness.[17] Dilthey speaks as a calm and rational philosopher describing the facts. But as it is lived from the inside the attitude of historicism can be less pleasant and neat. As lived, historicism can mean the anguish of feeling that one is forced to carry on one's life in terms of a mockery of masks and hollow gestures. To Matthew Arnold it seems that a sense of history undermines our culture, until all seems artificial and sham. To be a victim of "the modern spirit"

[17] See Wilhelm Dilthey, *Weltanschauungslehre, Gesammelte Schriften*, VIII (Leipzig and Berlin, 1931), pp. 3, 6.

means to be forced to conduct oneself according to inherited institutions, beliefs, laws, and customs which no longer seem at all appropriate to actual conditions, and it means doubt of the possibility of ever finding the proper form of life.[18]

Historicism, which begins as an interest in the past, ends by transforming man's sense of the present. As time wears on toward the twentieth century, and especially after the destructive cataclysm of the First World War, this sense of the artificiality of our culture is changed into an even more disquieting certainty that not just the outer form of our civilization, but civilization itself, is doomed to go the way of all the cultures of the past. This is the terrible truth expressed by Paul Valéry in a famous essay written soon after the war. Like Babylon, Nineveh, and Elam, our civilization will become mere heaps of broken artifacts, fragments whose very use, it may be, will have been forgotten.[19]

To think of our civilization as doomed to be reduced to ruins is also in some sense to think of it as already in pieces, for if it is so fragile, what real solidity does it have even now? W. B. Yeats describes this sense of catastrophe in some of his most powerful lines, lines full of our century's rage for destruction, terror of destruction. He speaks, in "Meru," of an urge in human nature to reject and demolish everything factitious, everything manmade, all "manifold illusion," in order to come at last into "the desolation of reality." [20]

This opposition between the illusion of culture and the desolation of reality is the very essence of historicism. Reality is conceived of as gross, heavy, and meaningless, the desert of the world before man. But the values which man has created by transforming the world into his own image are mere subjective illusions. They exist only as fragile forms of consciousness, ready at any moment to evaporate, leaving man face to face once more with the desolation of reality. Culture in all its forms is the insubstantial foam upon a great ocean of shapeless matter.

Historicism and the rise of subjectivistic philosophies are intimately related. What once seemed objective fact, God and his angels, with all the harmonious structure depending therefrom,

[18] See Matthew Arnold, *Works,* III (London, 1903), 174, and *Poetical Works,* p. 239.
[19] See Paul Valéry, "La crise de l'esprit," *Oeuvres,* IV (Paris, 1934), pp. 13, 14.
[20] W. B. Yeats, *Collected Poems* (New York, 1953), p. 287.

is now transformed into a figment of man's imagination. And this cultural change is once more mirrored in literature. The change from traditional literature to a modern genre like the novel can be defined as a moving of once objective worlds of myth and romance into the subjective consciousness of man.[21] To Don Quixote the windmills are giants, to Emma Bovary Rodolphe is the fulfilment of her romantic dreams, and for Henry James the novel presents not facts but someone's interpretation of them. The ideal world still exists, but only as a form of consciousness, not as an objective fact. The drama has all been moved within the minds of the characters, and the world as it is in itself is by implication unattainable or of no significance. Love, honor, God himself exist, but only because someone believes in them. Historicism, like perspectivism, transforms God into a human creation. And as soon as a man sees God in this way he is effectively cut off from the living God of faith. The God of Abraham, Isaac, and Jacob is turned into a mere temporary "value" like all the rest. Historicism, like all the other qualities of life in modern times, brings us back to the absence of God. Life in the city, the breakup of medieval symbolism, the imprisoning of man in his consciousness, the appearance of the historical sense — each of these is another way in which modern man has experienced the disappearance of God, and taken together all form the background against which De Quincey, Arnold, Browning, Hopkins, and Emily Brontë must be seen if we are to understand them.

Though the spiritual adventure of each of these writers is unique, nevertheless they all belong to the same family, and can be distinguished as a group from other reactions to the disappearance of God, as well as from those writers for whom God has not disappeared at all. The writers studied here rejected or were excluded from certain ways of dealing with the loss of God. For some Victorians God was still present. Some lamented the fading of God. Some noted the fading, but did not at all lament. For example, there have been the atheistical humanists. These, like Marx, Feuerbach, or Sartre, have been able to say: "There is no God. Therefore let us rejoice, for we are free to make our own city of man." George Eliot's religion of humanity moves in this

[21] See José Ortega y Gasset, "The Nature of the Novel," trans. Evelyn Rugg and Diego Marín, *Hudson Review*, X (1957), 11–42.

direction, as does the humanism of John Stuart Mill, and the less theoretical Trollope is able to accept his isolation from God and to create in his novels a purely human world of intersubjective relations. Related to this attitude but more God-centered is the pious acquiescence of Tennyson, so like the pious acquiescence of thousands of his countrymen. Tennyson could accept the withdrawal of God as an unfathomable mystery, and say: "So be it. It is God's will. I still believe, though I cannot see. And I have faith that God will be waiting for me when I have crossed the bar." [22] Or it has been possible for some writers to accept a theory of human life as role-playing, as the exploration of one or another of the infinite diversity of ways to organize the world by living in it. Such a strategy has been tried by writers as different from one another as Ortega y Gasset, Dilthey, Santayana, Nietzsche, and Gide. At the opposite extreme there have been those writers for whom the absence of God has been experienced as a positive thing, the *néant* of Mallarmé. For such writers the transcendence of God has reversed its polarity and has turned into a devouring darkness, the frightening reality of a positive rather than empty nothingness. From Baudelaire, Rimbaud, and Lautréamont, through Nietzsche, Conrad, and Mann, to such contemporary writers as Maurice Blanchot, Georges Bataille, or Samuel Beckett there has been a continuous tradition of this diabolical nihilism, this Prometheanism of the depths. For these writers God in his absence turns into a destructive power, the heart of darkness.

Humanism, perspectivism, nihilism, pious acceptance — each of these has been a possible reaction to the absence of God. But the five writers studied here all belong to another tradition: romanticism. The romantics still believe in God, and they find his absence intolerable. At all costs they must attempt to re-establish communication. They too begin in destitution, abandoned by God. All the traditional means of mediation have broken down, and romanticism therefore defines the artist as the creator or discoverer of hitherto unapprehended symbols, symbols which establish a new relation, across the gap, between man and God. The artist is the man who goes out into the empty space between man and

[22] See Walter E. Houghton, *The Victorian Frame of Mind* (New Haven, Conn., 1957), pp. 93–180, for an excellent discussion of the paradoxical Victorian combination of faith and awareness that the articles of faith can no longer be satisfactorily proved.

God and takes the enormous risk of attempting to create in that vacancy a new fabric of connections between man and the divine power. The romantic artist is a maker or discoverer of the radically new, rather than the imitator of what is already known. In the new world the arts are, as Shelley said, the "mediators" between earth and heaven,[23] and the new archetype of human nature is neither the prophet receiving revelation, nor the prince obeying or disobeying divine law. The new type of man is the romantic artist, the man who in the absence of a given world must create his own. The central assumption of romanticism is the idea that the isolated individual, through poetry, can accomplish the "unheard of work," [24] that is, create through his own efforts a marvelous harmony of words which will integrate man, nature, and God.

But the romantic project can also fail of accomplishment, and, accordingly, there appears a new, peculiarly romantic, mode of tragedy. It may be the tragedy of the failure of the work of art, its inability to hold in its frail bounds the divine spark which it tries to catch and preserve for man. Or it may be the tragedy of the evanescence of the artwork: it reaches its goal but for a moment and then drops back. Or it may be the tragedy of the Faustian artist whose error is the defiant creation of an autonomous work of art, a work which attempts to fill the emptiness left by the disappearance of God. All this tradition of the romantic artist as tragic hero is admirably recapitulated and dramatized in Thomas Mann's *Doktor Faustus*.

Many Victorian poets inherit the romantic conception of poetry, but such poets differ in one essential way from their predecessors. Almost all the romantic poets begin with the sense that there is a hidden spiritual force in nature. The problem is to reach it, for the old ways have failed, and though it is present in nature, and in the depths of man's consciousness, it is not immediately possessed by man. But the writers studied here precisely do *not* begin with this sense of what Wordsworth has called "A motion and a spirit, that impels/All thinking things, all objects of all thought,/ And rolls through all things." [25] The spiritual power, for them, is altogether beyond the world. De Quincey, though he is a con-

[23] See "Prometheus Unbound," III, iii, 49–60.

[24] Rimbaud's phrase, *Oeuvres complètes, éd. de la Pléiade* (Paris, 1946), p. 176: "l'oeuvre inouïe."

[25] "Tintern Abbey," ll. 100–102.

temporary of Wordsworth and Coleridge, betrays himself as a man of the Victorian age by his inability to experience a Wordsworthian presence in nature. The literary strategy of De Quincey, and of the Victorians who come after him, must consequently be more extreme, more extravagant, as the gap between man and the divine power seems greater.

Though their situations are more desperate, the writers discussed here all attempt, like the romantics, to bring God back to earth as a benign power inherent in the self, in nature, and in the human community. Other Victorian writers belong to this tradition and might have been included here, but I have chosen five who seem to me among the most important. Taken together they suggest a spectrum of variations within a single tradition. Each of the following chapters is intended to be a full exploration of the writings of one of these authors, an exploration which has its own independent unity, and does not depend on the generalizing perspectives of this introductory chapter. The latter have imposed themselves only gradually as I have come to see similarities between authors who are in many ways dissimilar. Every poetic universe is unique and ultimately incommensurable with any other. Each has its own special tone and atmosphere. The spiritual wrestling of Hopkins in "Carrion Comfort," for example, is quite unlike the passive resignation of Arnold. Nevertheless, the writings of De Quincey, Browning, Emily Brontë, Arnold, and Hopkins, in spite of their differences, can be seen as responses to similar spiritual situations. Each of these writers goes beyond his initial situation, but for all five the absence of God is, in one way or another, a starting place and presupposition.

This book, then, is an attempt to trace the courses of five spiritual adventures, each different from the others and yet bound to them by many echoes and similarities. These adventures might be defined as so many heroic attempts to recover immanence in a world of transcendence. In studying them I have been guided by the assumption that each work by an author gives us a new glimpse of an underlying vital unity, a unity of the kind so eloquently defined by De Quincey in a passage from the "Suspiria de Profundis": "The fleeting accidents of a man's life, and its external shows, may indeed be irrelate and incongruous; but the organising principles which fuse into harmony, and gather about fixed predetermined centres, whatever heterogeneous elements life may have accumulated from without, will not permit the grandeur of human unity greatly to be violated . . ." [26]

The unity of a human life, like the unity of the writings which express it, is not something fixed and unchanging. A human life is a dynamic process which moves through various phases, while returning often to earlier ones, in the search for a full comprehension of its "organizing principles." Only through development can the nature of those principles be gradually revealed, for they cannot be completely expressed in any single form. The sequence of sections in each of my chapters corresponds to this dynamic motion of life. The sequence is not so much chronological as dialectical. Each section tries to identify the meaning of one mode of experience in the writer. Such a form of experience constitutes a relation to the world which may recur again and again throughout the writer's work. The sections in each chapter lead in a progressive unfolding from some starting place of fundamental need, some special orientation of desire, to a final stage of triumphant attainment or resigned defeat.

[26] Thomas De Quincey, *Collected Writings*, ed. David Masson, XIII (London, 1897), 347.

❧ II ❧

Thomas De Quincey

About the close of my sixth year, suddenly the first chapter of my life came to a violent termination; that chapter which, even within the gates of re-covered Paradise, might merit a remembrance. . . . *"Life is Finished! Finished it is!"* was the hidden meaning that, half-unconsciously to myself, lurked within my sighs . . .[1]

For De Quincey, self-awareness is generated by "the sudden revela-tion that *all is lost*" (XIII, 338). Conscious life begins at the mo-ment when life is finished.

Before this revelation De Quincey has been happy, so happy that even in Paradise regained such happiness would be worth re-membering. This happiness was the joy of a complete repose in a perfect love between two persons: "The peace, the rest, the central security which belong to love that is past all understanding — these could return no more. Such a love, so unfathomable — such a peace, so unvexed by storms, or the fear of storms — had brooded over those four latter years of my infancy, which brought me into special relations to my eldest sister . . ." (I, 29). Such a peaceful love was an island of bliss in the midst of the disordered flux of the world. It was like "some mysterious parenthesis in the current of life, 'self-withdrawn into a wondrous depth' " (I, 55).

As a human relation the love between De Quincey and his sister was the immediate possession of two persons by one another. De Quincey also felt that he participated, through his sister, in the presence of God's universal love. This immanence of a diffused love, both human and divine, gave to him, as to Arnold later in "The Buried Life," the power to go outside himself and speak his most secret feelings. Currents of love and communication flowed like light between De Quincey and his sister, and, by reflection

[1] Thomas De Quincey, *Collected Writings*, ed. David Masson, 14 vols., I (London, 1896, 1897), 28. Further references to this edition are by volume and page numbers in parentheses after each text.

from her, to and from God. So he apostrophizes his sister in his *Autobiography*: "That lamp of Paradise was, for myself, kindled by reflection from the living light which burned so steadfastly in thee; and never but to thee, never again since *thy* departure, had I power or temptation, courage or desire, to utter the feelings which possessed me" (I, 36).

But just because De Quincey was so happy, he did not know he was happy. So perfect was his joy that he could not make that least movement of withdrawal, the act of reflection which would have been necessary to make him aware of himself and of his state. His happiness was a "happy interval of heaven-born ignorance" (I, 35). Not knowing he was happy, he was, in a sense, *not* happy. Or, rather, his joy was essentially different from self-conscious pleasure. De Quincey distinguishes between "happiness" and "rapture." Happiness he has had in early childhood — a state of complete repose, in which there were no conflicts, no contrasts, no division into subject and object. "Rapture," on the other hand, is a reflective happiness, a happiness which knows it is happy. Such an awareness of joy is only possible if there is something against which joy can be set, as white is set against black. Constant in De Quincey is the notion that we can know only through antagonism, or rather through the deep attraction of antagonists for one another. This produces a union of opposites, each relieving the other and making it visible. "Rapture" is, accordingly, just that mode of happiness in which joy is known through the co-presence of its opposite:

. . . raptures are modes of *troubled* pleasure. (I, 29)

. . . the rapture of life (or anything which by approach can merit that name) does not arise, unless as perfect music arises, music of Mozart or Beethoven, by the confluence of the mighty and terrific discords with the subtile concords. Not by contrast, or as reciprocal foils, do these elements act, — which is the feeble conception of many, — but by union. . . . without a basis of the dreadful there is no perfect rapture. (XIII, 350, 351)

The death of De Quincey's sister turns his heaven into hell, and reveals the abysmal depths of human life. At the same moment he is made aware for the first time of the heavenly heights he has lost. Only after the death of his sister can De Quincey have that "vision of life" which anticipates Baudelaire in its intuition of the double simultaneous postulation of human existence toward heavenly joy and infernal misery: "The horror of life mixed itself already in earliest youth with the heavenly sweetness of life" (XIII, 350).

Now that he knows death, even his happiest moments will be troubled, troubled by his dim foretaste or "prelibation" of their inevitable end. They will be "rapture," not true happiness. There are many passages in which De Quincey describes the power of prophetic anticipation to change homogeneous "happiness" into the troubled chiaroscuro of "rapture":

. . . that grief which one in a hundred has sensibility enough to gather from the sad retrospect of life in its closing stage for *me* shed its dews as a prelibation upon the fountains of life whilst yet sparkling to the morning sun. (XIII, 350)

I lived under the constant presence of a feeling which only [Shakespere] (so far as I am aware) has ever noticed; viz. that merely the excess of my happiness made me jealous of its ability to last, and in that extent less capable of enjoying it; that, in fact, the prelibation of my tears, as a homage to its fragility, was drawn forth by my very sense that my felicity was too exquisite. (XII, 176)

The death of De Quincey's sister colors all his existence thereafter. It is made the center of the original *Suspiria de Profundis*, in passages later modified for the *Autobiography*; it is re-experienced again and again, as in the death of little Kate Wordsworth or of De Quincey's own eldest son; and it reappears in more or less disguised form throughout his narrative writings, as in the death of the wife in "The Household Wreck" (XII, 157 ff.), or in the death of the girl whom De Quincey watches with paralyzed horror in "The Vision of Sudden Death" (XIII, 300 ff.). Moreover, the death of his sister, repeated in the loss of Ann, the pariah girl who befriends him in London, is the central event of *The Confessions of an English Opium-Eater*. This loss is the key to De Quincey's opium dreams, reappearing there in manifold forms, "split into a thousand fantastic variations" (III, 444). Indeed, the dream of the loss of Ann forms the emotional climax of the "Confessions": ". . . and at last, with the sense that all was lost, female forms, and the features that were worth all the world to me; and but a moment allowed — and clasped hands, with heart-breaking partings, and then — everlasting farewells!" (III, 446).

"Everlasting farewells!" — the death of De Quincey's sister introduces him to the first of "Our Ladies of Sorrow": *"Mater Lachrymarum,* Our Lady of Tears . . . she . . . that night and day raves and moans, calling for vanished faces" (XIII, 365). This death is more than merely his introduction to the adult world of tears. The experience of his sister's death is a complex spiritual event, in which several changes happen simultaneously to transform his inner and outer worlds. All these changes result from the breaking apart of what had been an indissoluble unity.

Before, De Quincey, his sister, and the divine love which he possessed through her formed a charmed circle of warmth and intimacy. He was not aware of any distance because he was in close touch with everything around him. He was ignorant of anything beyond his mysterious parenthesis in the current of life. He was not aware of himself because self and world interpenetrated one another and overlapped. There was no problem of communication, for his feelings were understood by his sister almost before they were spoken.

With his sister's death, all this is changed. With her disappearance disappears the mediator who had bound him to God and the world. Three things then happen simultaneously. God withdraws to an infinite distance, and all sense of his immanent presence is lost. At the same time De Quincey becomes aware of the infinity of space and time. God has withdrawn to a place outside of all space, and to a time before and after time, and the wind of his departure makes apparent the immeasurable extent of the creation. Finally, the disappearance of God and the manifestation of space and time bring about the initial moment of self-awareness. Until now the self has been diffused into its surroundings. Now it contracts to a point and sinks into the solitude of itself. Just as the awareness of happiness is only possible when heavenly sweetness and infernal horror are married, so awareness of self is not possible until the self draws into itself and sets itself against the surrounding world. It then becomes "a dim lotus of human consciousness, finding itself afloat upon the bosom of waters without a shore" (XII, 158). Finding itself so, it first becomes aware of "that inner world, that world of secret self-consciousness, in which each of us lives a second life apart and with himself alone, collateral to his other life, or life which he lives in common with others." [2] "That is a world," says De Quincey, "in which every man, the very meanest, is a solitary presence, and cannot admit the fellowship even of that one amongst all his fellow-creatures whom he loves the most and perhaps regards as his other self" (Page, I, 304). This speck of vague consciousness in the midst of an alien immensity is altogether unable to communicate its feelings to those around it. After his sister's death De Quincey suffers "the burden of the Incommunicable" (III, 315).

The withdrawal of God from the world, the discovery of the infinity of space and time, the awareness of the self as a solitary point — all these motifs are present in De Quincey's description of his visit to the room where his sister's body lies. He discovers that the bed has been moved, and instead of his sister's face, he finds himself confronting for the first time the limitless depths of space: ". . . turning round, I sought my sister's face. But the bed had been moved, and the back was now turned towards myself. Nothing met my eyes but one large window, wide open, through which the sun of midsummer at mid-day was showering down torrents of splendour. The weather was dry, the sky was cloudless, the blue depths seemed the express types of infinity . . ." (I, 38).

Infinity of space, but also infinity of time, for at the same moment as he sees the fathomless blue depths of the empty sky, he hears the solemn Memnonian wind which seems to blow from before time. This wind is an audible symbol of eternity, just as the sky is a visible symbol of the infinity of space: ". . . and, whilst I stood, a solemn wind began to blow — the saddest that ear ever heard. It was a wind that might have swept the fields of mortality for a thousand centuries. Many times since, upon summer days, when the sun is about the hottest, I have remarked the same wind arising and uttering the same hollow, solemn, Memnonian, but saintly swell: it is in this world the one great audible symbol of eternity" (I, 41, 42).

This infinity of space and eternity of time are precisely an infinity and eternity of the unavailability of God. Though the Memnon head in the British Museum "wears upon its lips a smile co-extensive with all time and all space, an Æonian smile of gra-

---

[2] H. A. Page, *Thomas De Quincey: His Life and Writings*, 2 vols., I (London, 1877), 304. These volumes will be cited hereafter as "Page." H. A. Page is the pseudonym of Alexander H. Japp.

cious love and Panlike mystery, the most diffusive and pathetically divine that the hand of man has created" (I, 41), nevertheless this universal presence of God in time and space is experienced as an absence. The Memnon head is mentioned again in De Quincey's essay on the "System of the Heavens as Revealed by Lord Rosse's Telescopes," and there too it symbolizes "the diffusive love, not such as rises and falls upon waves of life and mortality, not such as sinks and swells by undulations of time, but a procession — an emanation from some mystery of endless dawn" (VIII, 17). The Memnon head expresses the constant flowing of God's love into the infinite spaces of the creation, in an endlessly renewed beginning. But in the astronomical essay the Memnon head is mentioned only to be replaced by the vision of another sort of sublimity: the horrid head in the nebula in Orion, with its cleft skull and its expression of infinite cruelty and revenge (VIII, 17–21). The Memnon head and the frightful face in the nebula are both valid symbols of the astronomical infinites of space and time. It may be that God is present in the world, but he has hidden himself, as if with secret malice, and the climax of De Quincey's experience in his sister's room is the direct apprehension of a God who plays hide and seek with man, and always withdraws into a further deep of space and time as we approach closer to his throne: ". . . instantly a trance fell upon me. A vault seemed to open in the zenith of the far blue sky, a shaft which ran up for ever. I, in spirit, rose as if on billows that also ran up the shaft for ever; and the billows seemed to pursue the throne of God; but *that* also ran before us and fled away continually. The flight and pursuit seemed to go on for ever and ever. Frost gathering frost, some Sarsar wind of death, seemed to repel me; some mighty relation between God and death dimly struggled to evolve itself from the dreadful antagonism between them" (I, 42).

The Memnonian wind of God's diffusive love gives way to the Sarsar wind of death, and there seems to be some secret and mysterious relation between them. Even if they are not identical, the death of De Quincey's sister has transformed the one into the other, and that transformation has made him aware of his solitude in the midst of the infinite fields of space and time. In these fields God is unattainable, if not absent. What was an indissoluble unity has been fragmented.

When this fragmentation has occurred there is nothing for a
man to do but to sink back on the center of himself, and, as the
last link attaching him to God and the world is broken, to heave
one sigh and acquiesce in silence to the irrevocable fact that all is
lost. This sigh is the last outward exhalation of a spirit which is
about to contract and become wholly enclosed in the abyss of itself. It is a sigh from the depths, one of the "suspiria de profundis,"
the final inarticulate attempt to communicate the incommunicable
before the outcast withdraws into dumb and hopeless misery. This
sigh appears many times in De Quincey's writings. It always accompanies the recognition that "life is finished," and we may say
that it is the denouement of the first stage of De Quincey's spiritual
adventure:

. . . I sank away in a hopelessness that was immeasurable from all effort at
explanation. . . . a solitary word, which I attempted to mould upon my lips,
died away into a sigh . . . (III, 315, 316)

Yes, a long, long sigh — a deep, deep sigh; that is the natural language by
which the overcharged heart utters forth the woe that else would break it. I
sighed — O how profoundly! But that did not give me the power to move.
(XII, 185)

The sentiment which attends the sudden revelation that *all is lost* silently
is gathered up into the heart; it is too deep for gestures or for words; and no
part of it passes to the outside. . . . The voice perishes; the gestures are
frozen; and the spirit of man flies back upon its own centre. I, at least, upon
seeing those awful gates closed and hung with draperies of woe, as for a death
already past, spoke not, nor started, nor groaned. One profound sigh ascended
from my heart, and I was silent for days. (XIII, 338)

ह

As soon as De Quincey is aware of himself as a separate being
his life is already finished. The door back into the Paradise of
childhood has been locked, the key taken away, and he is "shut out
for ever" (I, 43). He is *outside,* a solitary point of consciousness
surrounded by infinite reaches of space and time. These reaches
are organized by no plastic force sweeping through the whole and
orienting it, as a magnet orients its field. The Kirkstone Pass, for
example, does not seem to De Quincey, as all nature seemed to
Wordsworth, the abiding place of "something far more deeply
interfused." Instead, the pass arouses in De Quincey a "feeling of

intense and awful solitude, which is the natural and presiding sentiment — the *religio loci* — that broods for ever over the romantic pass" (II, 310). De Quincey's inability to experience an immanent spiritual principle in nature marks him as a post-romantic, more like Matthew Arnold in this respect than like Wordsworth or Coleridge. The creation for him is a trackless solitude. Sometimes he speaks of the "illimitable growths" (VIII, 16) of astronomical time and space, abysses from which God seems to be absent. Sometimes the image is that of "the wilderness of the barren waters," or of a desert, "the wilderness of the barren sands," each an "eternal spectacle of the infinite" (VIII, 437). In a desert one place is so like every other place that it is impossible ever to "find yourself." You might live for generations in the desert and still not feel at home: "The same thing happens in the desert: one monotonous iteration of sand, sand, sand, unless where some miserable fountain stagnates, forbids all approach to familiarity: nothing is circumstantiated or differenced: travel it for three generations, and you are no nearer to identification of its parts; so that it amounts to travelling through an abstract idea" (VIII, 31).

Sometimes the expression of this infinite disorder is the labyrinthine complexity of a great city, the "nation of London," crowded with people all living in profound isolation from one another: "No man ever was left to himself for the first time in the streets, as yet unknown, of London, but he must have been saddened and mortified, perhaps terrified, by the sense of desertion and utter loneliness which belong to his situation. No loneliness can be like that which weighs upon the heart in the centre of faces never-ending, without voice or utterance for him . . ." (I, 182). The "transient glimpses" of side streets in London, stretching far off into a "murky atmosphere" of "gloom and uncertainty" give De Quincey an increasing sense of the "vastness and illimitable proportions" of the city. He cannot see it all piece by piece, for it is too vast, and yet neither can this "Babylonian confusion" be comprehended from any single point of view. London is an infinite circle, a circle without a center: "We could not traverse the whole circumference of this mighty orb; that was clear; and, therefore, the next best thing was to place ourselves as much as possible in some relation to the spectacles of London, which might answer to the centre. Yet how? That sounded well and metaphysical; but what did it mean if acted upon? What was the centre of London for any purpose whatever . . . ?" (I, 183).

Astronomical space, the wilderness of ocean, a pathless desert, the gloomy and centerless maze of London — the place of lonely exile from Paradise can take all these forms, but the situation of the lost one remains the same. Having been initiated by the first of the Ladies of Sorrow, he is now by an inevitable logic brought into the realm of the second: *"Mater Suspiriorum,* Our Lady of Sighs" (XIII, 366). This second sister broods over all the forlorn exiles of the world, slaves, criminals, and victims of social injustice, "all that are betrayed, and all that are rejected; outcasts by traditionary law, and children of *hereditary* disgrace: . . . the houseless vagrant of every clime" (XIII, 367). Our Lady of Sighs, in short, governs the realm of "the pariah worlds" (XIII, 369).[3] The worlds of the pariahs are plural, we may assume, because every *isolato* lives in his own world. His archetype is Ahasuerus, the "Wandering Jew," or, in his German name, "der ewige Jude," the "everlasting Jew" (I, 43), for the infinity of his exile is both temporal and spatial. It is an *everlasting wandering.* Having been excluded from happiness, he can do nothing but wander hopelessly seeking some fortuitous return of that happiness. He can find nothing within himself or without which gives him a goal or a sense of direction. But though he has no reason to go in one direction rather than another, he cannot keep still. It is "as if some overmastering fiend, some instinct of migration, sorrowful but irresistible, were driving [him] forth to wander like the unhappy Io of the Grecian mythus, some oestrus of hidden persecution [bidding him] fly when no man pursue[s]" (III, 338). De Quincey's own youthful wanderings in Wales are the objective expression of

---

[3] "Pariah" is a favorite word of De Quincey's, and of special interest to him are the histories of outcasts and victims of all sorts. He writes essays on Judas, on Joan of Arc, on Richard Bentley, that outcast among scholars, on "Walking Stewart," and on Edward Irving. His narrative of "The Revolt of the Tartars" describes the epic wanderings of a whole nation of pariahs; "The Spanish Military Nun" is a rollicking picaresque novel in which the pariah triumphs over every obstacle; and De Quincey's "first grand and jubilant sense" of "the immeasurableness of the morally sublime" was given to him by a passage in Phaedrus describing "The Apotheosis of the Slave": "A colossal statue did the Athenians raise to Æsop; and a poor pariah slave they planted upon an everlasting pedestal" (I, 127, 125).

his spiritual exile. Harried by a hidden persecuting force, he moves restlessly from place to place. "Mere accident" (III, 339) leads him to choose one path rather than another.

The life of this wanderer is discontinuous both in space and in time. Since he is in the midst of infinite spaces, or lost in an endless urban labyrinth, all places look alike, and no place is related to any other place. He cannot remember the past because it had no meaning for him, and he cannot anticipate the future. To move from one place to another is immediately to lose what he has just left, and the man who is lost in a strange city has no way of knowing what lies in wait around the next corner. Even if he comes back by chance to the same place he will not recognize it, for everything looks the same, like the "sand, sand, sand" of the desert. In this infinite space of wandering a man could be only a few feet from all he has lost, and yet not know it, so strict is his imprisonment in the present point of time and space. A tiny interval of space or time is as effectual a gulf as centuries or millions of miles, and two people might walk for years in the same city without reaching one of the rare and accidental "*nodes* of intersection" (XI, 331) which must sooner or later occur:

This is felt generally to be the most distressing form of human blindness — the case when accident brings two fraternal hearts, yearning for re-union, into almost touching neighbourhood, and then in a moment after, by the difference, perhaps, of three inches in space, or three seconds in time, will separate them again, unconscious of their brief neighbourhood, perhaps for ever. (I, 312)

If she lived, doubtless we must have been sometimes in search of each other, at the very same moment, through the mighty labyrinths of London; perhaps even within a few feet of each other — a barrier no wider, in a London street, often amounting in the end to a separation for eternity! (III, 375)

The wanderer in the endless labyrinth of the world can never find what he seeks, never turn a corner and find himself face to face with his dead sister or the lost Ann. Even if he makes brief friendships and finds brief havens, he is doomed to suffer again and again the loss of love and the failure of communication. But the experience of "everlasting wandering" has led to an advance in knowledge over the moment when De Quincey first stood by the body of his sister, and looked into the infinite depths of the empty sky. Then he discovered infinity as something exterior to himself, and his spirit withdrew upon itself and contracted to a point. Gradually, through the experience of wandering, he comes to discover that the infinity is also within, and that his inner spiritual depths are the exact mirror of the empty sky, or the desert, or the labyrinth of London. The external infinity in which he moves from place to place in perpetual errancy is echoed by an equal infinity within the mind.

The exploration of the outer space of the pariah worlds turns out to be at the same time an act of self-discovery, the exploration of inner space. Finding out the nature of the world he lives in, the pariah also beholds a vision of "the infinity which lurks in a human spirit," "the absolutely infinite influxes of feeling or combinations of feeling that vary the thoughts of man" (XI, 80). In a splendid passage in the "System of the Heavens as Revealed by Lord Rosse's Telescopes," De Quincey explains how the infinity of astronomical space and time is the mirror image of "the infinity of the world within" (X, 49). The former is visible only as the reflex and objective correlative of the latter:

Great is the mystery of Space, greater is the mystery of Time. Either mystery grows upon man as man himself grows; and either seems to be a function of the godlike which is in man. In reality, the depths and the heights which are in man, the depths by which he searches, the heights by which he aspires, are but projected and made objective externally in the three dimensions of space which are outside of him. He trembles at the abyss into which his bodily eyes look down, or look up; not knowing that abyss to be, not always consciously suspecting it to be, but by an instinct written in his prophetic heart feeling it to be, boding it to be, fearing it to be, and sometimes hoping it to be, the mirror to a mightier abyss that will one day be expanded in himself. (VIII, 15)

Just as inner space shares the infinity of outer space, so it shares also its disorganization. The representation of De Quincey's inner world is the fourteen and more volumes of his collected work.[4]

[4] Students of De Quincey's writings have shown that a great many passages in his work are translations or close adaptations of one source or another. (For the most recent and complete of such studies see Albert Goldman, "Sources for the Writings of Thomas De Quincey" [Columbia University Dissertation, 1961]. Mr. Goldman's findings will soon be published by Southern Illinois University Press as a book entitled *The Mine and the Mint: Sources for the Writings of Thomas De Quincey*.) De Quincey, however, shows a remarkable ability to assimilate what he borrows into his own style and view of things, and it often seems to be the configurations of his own inner world which guide his borrowings, as, for example, a passage from John Paul Richter (to be discussed later) enters into

His work is the exact image of the space of wandering — sky or desert or, most exactly, enormous city. For De Quincey is, as Baudelaire saw, "essentiellement digressif." [5] To read an essay by De Quincey is to experience a strange and exasperating sense of disorientation. The essay will begin boldly with a statement of subject, and sometimes even with an outline of the course to be followed. Everything seems admirably clear and logical. But as we read on we become aware that we have insensibly wandered away from the predicted course and are miles away from it, pursuing voluminously a theme which has only the most distant connection with the nominal subject of the essay. We draw ourselves up short in a kind of dizzy amazement. Yet if we look back over the pages we have just read we can find no place where the thread of connection was broken. One thing has led to another as easily as a man turns a corner in the city, and yet two or three such turns have led us so far away from the original vista that it is hopeless to try to get back. De Quincey's most characteristic essays get longer and longer without establishing an over-all pattern, and finally trickle off into digressive irrelevances, like a stream dispersing itself in sand. Rare is the work of his which pursues its announced course and reaches its predicted goal.

Sometimes De Quincey justifies this digressiveness, and makes it the very law of the work to be lawless, as when he speaks of his autobiography as "a work confessedly rambling, and whose very duty lies in the pleasant paths of vagrancy" (I, 316). More often De Quincey himself is unwittingly beguiled into wandering, and notices only when it is too late that he has left his ostensible subject far behind and has no hope of finishing it in the space at his disposal. The records of the moments when he realizes he has gone astray are strewn through his work:

But I am insensibly wandering beyond the limits assigned me. (XIV, 129)

But our growing exorbitance from our limits warns us to desist. (VI, 135)

We find a difficulty in pursuing this subject without greatly exceeding the just limits. (V, 236)

De Quincey's imagination and becomes the expression of an important aspect of his own thought.
[5] *Oeuvres complètes, éd. de la Pléiade* (Paris, 1958), p. 480.

For De Quincey there *is* no subject with just limits, a finite goal which may be seen from the beginning, and pursued through a logical train of thought. The realm of his essays is, like London itself, a space of infinite wandering. Just as it is impossible to say of astronomical space whether we "look down, or look up" into it, so there is a consistent ambiguity in De Quincey's descriptions of his mental space. The divine presence has withdrawn, or made itself invisible, so it is impossible for him ever to know whether he is going toward God or away from him. Neither inside the mental space nor outside it is there any manifest power which gives it a structure. Since he is an infinite distance from God, he is just as close to the devil, and any other point is up or down from here, just as any direction is both right and wrong. Since there is no sense of orientation, there is no evident reason to write about one subject rather than another. There is a large measure of fortuitousness in De Quincey's choice of subjects. He writes an essay about Pope, or Josephus, or Matthew Hill's system of the education of boys, not because these subjects interest him more than others, or are a means to attain the goal of his life-work, but simply because some editor asks him, or because a new book falls by accident under his eye. In his youth De Quincey planned a great work, to be called, after an unfinished work of Spinoza's, *De Emendatione Humani Intellectûs* (III, 431). This work was to mark a turning point in man's conquest of his inner space. Instead of finishing this project De Quincey frittered away his talent for forty years writing miscellaneous periodical essays. The establishment of an all-embracing organization proved to be impossible. In his mental realm as in his objective milieu nothing is connected to anything else, though everything dwells crowded together like the inhabitants of London. Or, rather, everything *is* related to everything else, but in random and fortuitous ways. To De Quincey "all things . . . appear to be related to all" (X, 115). He always prides himself on his gift "for feeling in a moment the secret analogies or parallelisms that connect things else apparently remote" (III, 332). This very power of analogy leads him to wander. If A makes him think of B, which has some slender connection to it, and B leads to C, and so on, then in a few sentences he can by insensible gradations be led far afield from his original subject. For example, De Quincey writes an essay ostensibly on Charles Lamb (V, 215 ff.), but Lamb leads to Hazlitt, Hazlitt to Southey, then Southey reminds him of Joan of Arc, and soon we find ourselves in the midst of a discussion which is only very remotely connected with the original subject. We often find De Quincey writing long digressive footnotes which for several pages crowd out the main text. Sometimes there are footnotes to the footnotes! The essays slip away imperceptibly from their goal because they exist in an infinite plenum which is without magnetic field. The pulls in all directions from the present equilibrium are equally strong. Anything can lead to anything else. In such a situation a man is necessarily guilty of "*levity* — the simple fact of being unballasted by any sufficient weight of plan or settled purpose to present a counterpoise to the slightest momentum this way or that, arising from any impulse of accident or personal caprice. When there is no resistance, a breath of air will be sufficient to determine the motion" (X, 36).

Ballasted by no plan, living in a mental space which has no pattern of its own, De Quincey seems condemned to a spiritual vagrancy which is made visible and objective by his literal wanderings in Wales and London. Just as he will find the lost Ann, if at all, by chance, so in his mental vagabondage he will intersect with the truth only by accident, by "wandering into truth" (XIV, 306). Crossing the right path as a man lost in the city might unwittingly cross the street leading to his goal, De Quincey will not know he has made a "node of intersection" with the truth. Driven by his fatal levity, he will persist in his endless wandering: "Where the erroneous path has wandered in all directions, has returned upon itself perpetually, and crossed the field of inquiry with its mazes in every direction, doubtless the path of truth will often intersect it, and perhaps for a short distance coincide with it; but that in this coincidence it receives no impulse or determination from that with which it coincides will appear from the self-determining force which will soon carry it out of the same direction as inevitably as it entered it" (X, 78).

Only a divine mind, it seems, could avoid this fate. For God sees the whole expanse of time and space in a single instant. Like light in the old theory, he is everywhere at once. His mental calculations are also instantaneous. To suppose that God must travel through a series of syllogisms to reach a conclusion would be a profane limitation of his power: "God must not proceed by steps and the fragmentary knowledge of accretion; in which case at starting he has all the intermediate notices as so many bars between himself and the conclusion, and even at the penultimate or antepenultimate act he is still short of the truth. God must *see*; he must *intuit,* so to speak; and all truth must reach him simultaneously, first and last, without succession of time or partition of acts: just as light, before that theory had been refuted by the Satellites of Jupiter, was held not to be propagated in time, but to be here and there at one and the same indivisible instant" (X, 103).

Man, alas, cannot *see*. He is doomed to remain in one place in space and in one moment of time. If he possesses with his body at least his own location in space, he possesses even less of time, that "greater mystery." For the present moment, as we search it out, contracts to a mathematical point and dissolves into nothingness under the encroachments of past and future. Even that nothing, the infinitely thin slice of time which is the true present, is fleeting with infinite velocity away from us, and plunging into the dead world of what has been and is no more:

You see, therefore, how narrow, how incalculably narrow, is the true and actual present. Of that time which we call the present, hardly a hundredth part but belongs either to a past which has fled, or to a future which is still on the wing. It has perished, or it is not born. It was, or it is not. Yet even this approximation to the truth is *infinitely* false. For again sub-divide that solitary drop, which only was found to represent the present, into a lower series of similar fractions, and the actual present which you arrest measures now but the thirty-sixth-millionth of an hour; and so by infinite declensions the true and very present, in which only we live and enjoy, will vanish into a mote of a mote, distinguishable only by a heavenly vision. . . . The time which *is* contracts into a mathematic point; and even that point perishes a thousand times before we can utter its birth. (XIII, 360, 361)

Man would be satisfied only by a divine multiplicity and simultaneity of experience. He would be the *homme-dieu* of whom Baudelaire speaks (*Oeuvres complètes,* p. 462). But this hunger for infinity cannot, so it seems, be assuaged. Standing in his tiny place in space, and on his mote's mote of time, man looks at the multitudes of things which exist outside that point, and is tortured by "a miserable distraction of choice" (X, 40). He is even

excluded from the depths of his own nature, depths "stretching
. . . far below his power to fathom." [6] For he can think only
one thought at a time. His thought must all be "carried on dis-
cursively; that is, *discurrendo*, — by running about to the right
and the left, laying the separate notices together, and thence
mediately deriving some third apprehension" (X, 103). He would
know everything, and know it all at once. Desiring immediacy,
he is doomed to the mediate. As he surveys the inexhaustible possibilities from which he is excluded, a kind of madness seizes him,
a madness of desire to be everywhere at once. This madness makes
it impossible for him to enjoy the little bit of time and space he
actually possesses. Wanting everything, he has nothing at all, and
he now realizes the full torment of the plight of the pariah. It
is the torment of the finite being who can apprehend, but not
possess, the infinite riches which lie within him and without:

Here, said I, are one hundred thousand books, the worst of them capable
of giving me some pleasure and instruction; and before I can have had time
to extract the honey from one-twentieth of this hive, in all likelihood I shall
be summoned away. . . . I protest to you that I speak of as real a case of
suffering as ever can have existed. And it soon increased; for the same panic
seized upon me with respect to the works of art. I found that I had no chance
of hearing the twenty-five thousandth part of the music that had been produced. And so of other arts. Nor was this all; for, happening to say to myself, one night as I entered a long street, "I shall never see the one thousandth
part of the people who are living in this single street," it occurred to me that
every man and woman was a most interesting book, if one knew how to read
them. Here opened upon me a new world of misery; for, if books and works
of art existed by millions, men existed by hundreds of millions. . . . Nay, my
madness took yet a higher flight; for I considered that I stood on a little
isthmus of time which connected the two great worlds, the past and the future.
I stood in equal relation to both; I asked for admittance to one as much as
to the other. . . . In short, I never turned my thoughts this way but I fell
into a downright midsummer madness. I could not enjoy what I had, —
craving for that which I had not, and could not have; [and] was thirsty, like
Tantalus, in the midst of waters . . . (X, 38–40)

ह

. . . in an hour, O heavens! what a revulsion! what a resurrection, from its
lowest depths, of the inner spirit! what an apocalypse of the world within
me! (III, 381)

[6] A. H. Japp, ed., *The Posthumous Works of Thomas De Quincey*, 2 vols., I
(London, 1891), 27. These volumes will be cited hereafter as "Post. Wks."

Well might De Quincey say, "O just, subtle, and all-conquer-
ing opium!" (III, 395). Like Coleridge, he is one of those rare
spirits who are "preconformed to its power," one of those "whose
nervous sensibilities vibrate to their profoundest depths under the
first touch of the angelic poison" (V, 210). The magic of opium
lies precisely in its power to stir a man to his depths, and to put
him in immediate possession of every last corner of his own mental space: "It is in the faculty of mental vision, it is in the increased power of dealing with the shadowy and the dark, that
the characteristic virtue of opium lies" (V, 211). Before, he was a
finite point in the midst of infinite unavailable riches. Now that
point expands to fill up every place in the infinity. Opium reveals
an "abyss of divine enjoyment" (III, 381).

This enjoyment is, literally, divine, for the opium-eater has
God's ubiquity in time and space. Before, he suffered the discontinuity of the man lost in a labyrinth, the man who knows
only his present place and has no idea what lies before or behind.
Now he is in all places at once, and he connects all those places
effortlessly in a perfect continuity. Before, he was conscious of
himself as separate from the spectacle he beheld. Now self and
world, seer and seen, are identical. De Quincey possesses the whole
expanse of space with all its multitudinous contents: ". . . many
a time it has happened to me on a summer night — when I have
been seated at an open window, from which I could overlook the
sea at a mile below me, and could at the same time command a
view of some great town standing on a different radius of my
circular prospect, but at nearly the same distance — that from
sunset to sunrise, all through the hours of night, I have continued
motionless, as if frozen, without consciousness of myself as of an
object anywise distinct from the multiform scene which I contemplated from above" (III, 394, 395).

Before the revelation of the powers of opium, activity and
repose were both equally bad. Repose would have meant acquiescence in his isolation, and activity, his frenzied wandering in
the labyrinth, like a rat in a maze, was the very evidence of his
sad state. Now infinite activity and infinite repose are not incompatible. Possessing all, he does not need to do anything to
reach it, but possessing all, he enjoys also the infinite activities of
that all. He has, like God, a perfect harmony and equilibrium

of all his forces, for "a nature truly divine must be *in equilibrio* as to all qualities" (VIII, 226). Opium, unlike wine, introduces among the mental faculties "the most exquisite order, legislation, and harmony" (III, 383). It is as though his mind were the ocean which he beholds, swayed with an everlasting gentle agitation, and the world, the contents of the mind, were the city which he sees in the other direction, but at a distance, so that its turmoil and suffering are tranquilized and reduced to order. He does not distinguish himself from the scene he beholds, ocean and city, and the two together form not so much the symbols as the direct expressions of the mind and the contents of the mind, the totality of the creation absorbed and reduced to a harmony which reconciles infinite activities and infinite repose:

> The scene itself was somewhat typical of what took place in such a reverie. The town of Liverpool represented the earth, with its sorrows and its graves left behind, yet not out of sight, nor wholly forgotten. The ocean, in everlasting but gentle agitation, yet brooded over by dove-like calm, might not unfitly typify the mind, and the mood which then swayed it. For it seemed to me as if then first I stood at a distance aloof from the uproar of life; as if the tumult, the fever, and the strife, were suspended . . . Here were the hopes which blossom in the paths of life, reconciled with the peace which is in the grave; motions of the intellect as unwearied as the heavens, yet for all anxieties a halcyon calm; tranquillity that seemed no product of inertia, but as if resulting from mighty and equal antagonisms; infinite activities, infinite repose. (III, 395)

The opium-eater, having triumphed over space, finally even triumphs over the greater mystery of time. After his sister's death, De Quincey was tormented by the memory of the happiness he had lost. Opium brings back the total past of the dreamer as an immediate and simultaneous possession, in all the freshness of its happening. Not one experience or fleeting sensation is ever lost. All lie hidden in the depths of the human spirit, layer upon layer, waiting to be resurrected:

> What else than a natural and mighty palimpsest is the human brain? . . . Everlasting layers of ideas, images, feelings, have fallen upon your brain softly as light. Each succession has seemed to bury all that went before. And yet, in reality, not one has been extinguished. . . . Yes, reader, countless are the mysterious handwritings of grief or joy which have inscribed themselves successively upon the palimpsest of your brain; and, like the annual leaves of aboriginal forests, or the undissolving snows on the Himalaya, or light falling

upon light, the endless strata have covered up each other in forgetfulness. But by the hour of death, but by fever, but by the searchings of opium, all these can revive in strength. They are not dead, but sleeping. (XIII, 346, 348)

The countless images of the buried past have inscribed themselves *successively* on the brain, and it seems as if their resurrection too will be successive. De Quincey more than once emphasizes the processional character of dreams, the way they consist of an endless succession of images following one another, as parts of a theatrical procession are substituted for one another on a vast stage:

Perhaps you are aware of that power in the eye of many children by which in darkness they project a vast theatre of phantasmagorical figures moving forwards or backwards between their bed-curtains and the chamber-walls. (Post. Wks., I, 7)

. . . at night, when I lay awake in bed, vast processions moved along continually in mournful pomp; friezes of never-ending stories . . . (III, 434)

In such dreams or waking visions, as on a long summer afternoon whose seeming endlessness expresses astronomical distances, "Time becomes the expounder of Space" (III, 293). The succession of figures in the time of the dream expresses the way they exist side by side in space, each taking up its own volume, and each separate from all the others. But in the climax of the opium dream the succession of events in time, and the mutual exclusion of places in space, is forgotten and transcended. The dreamer beholds a space in which all things are coexistent and harmoniously interrelated, without ceasing to be distinct, and this space of copresence becomes the emblem of simultaneity. The dreamer sees as an instantaneous vision in space all the events which have been gathering successively in his brain, layer upon layer, during his life. In such dreams, as in the visions of drowning men, space becomes the expounder of time, and in this spatialized time the dreamer possesses his total past in a single instant:

. . . a chorus, &c., of elaborate harmony displayed before me, as in a piece of arras-work, the whole of my past life — not as if recalled by an act of memory, but as if present and incarnated in the music . . . (III, 391)

. . . she saw in a moment her whole life, clothed in its forgotten incidents, arranged before her as in a mirror, not successively, but simultaneously; and she had a faculty developed as suddenly for comprehending the whole and every part. (III, 435)

. . . immediately a mighty theatre expanded within her brain. In a moment, in the twinkling of an eye, every act, every design of her past life, lived again, arraying themselves not as a succession, but as parts of a coexistence. . . . her consciousness became omnipresent at one moment to every feature in the infinite review. (XIII, 347, 348)

Omnipresence in space, simultaneity of all times, complete disappearance of the separation of the scene and its beholder — opium seems to have granted to the finite solitary a repossession of the infinity from which he has been excluded. Even the happiness of childhood is recaptured. When De Quincey gets back all his own past, he gets back even his lost sister. "O just and righteous opium!" he exclaims, "that . . . , 'from the anarchy of dreaming sleep,' callest into sunny light the faces of long-buried beauties, and the blessed household countenances, cleansed from the 'dishonours of the grave' " (III, 395, 396). If he recovers his sister, and that happy time, may he not even recover the lost God whom he possessed through his sister? The faculty of dreaming, so puissantly released by opium, is the avenue by which man possesses more than the infinite depths of his own spirit and the infinity of external time and space. In dreams man communicates also with the shadowy eternities which lie below all life, and sleep in the bosom of God. "The machinery for dreaming planted in the human brain," says De Quincey, "was not planted for nothing. That faculty, in alliance with the mystery of darkness, is the one great tube through which man communicates with the shadowy. And the dreaming organ, in connexion with the heart, the eye, and the ear, composes the magnificent apparatus which forces the infinite into the chambers of a human brain, and throws dark reflections from eternities below all life upon the mirrors of that mysterious *camera obscura* — the sleeping mind" (XIII, 355). In another affirmation of this principle De Quincey claims that opium opens even the gates of heaven: ". . . thou hast the keys of Paradise, O just, subtle, and mighty opium!" (III, 396).

The possibility of regaining Paradise has been revealed by the "artificial paradise" of opium. Opium dreams show that the imagination naturally "seeks the illimitable; dissolves the definite; translates the finite into the infinite" (X, 444). It might be possible to control those powers of the mind which tend toward the infinite. If they could be released voluntarily, it would be possible to approach toward the permanent possession of the Paradise regained momentarily in opium dreams. All of De Quincey's writing, in one way or another, is modeled on the characteristics of his dreams. In writing it is not a question of the dreams themselves, but of the deliberate representation of them, or of something like them, in words.

❧

The first almost insuperable problem is the fact that a piece of writing is a sequence of words which follow one another in time as we read them. It would seem impossible to make words imitate the simultaneity of dreams. Music, however, suggests the escape from this impasse.

De Quincey, I have shown, experiences the total resurrection of his past when he is listening to some elaborate piece of music. Music has the power to generate this experience because, like the dreams themselves, it is a kind of spatialized time. The whole of a piece of music exists potentially in the first notes, and this whole in effect merely unrolls, "as in a piece of arras-work," what was there already furled up in the initial melody. Any moment of the music, by its multiple relations to the whole, is a kind of miniature of the whole. Music is the very model of a use of time to transcend time. It proceeds by repetition with variation, echo, reverberation, by exhaustive permutations and combinations of a certain fundamental pattern which persists throughout. Music constantly circles back on itself. Its aim is not to go in a straight line from one place to another, but to achieve the most complete exfoliation of its primitive germ. While listening to a piece of music we have the sense of being within a musical or aural space which the sounds create. This space is altogether filled up by the music, and this filling up is a vital oscillation, always changing and yet always the same, a dynamic equilibrium of opposing forces which keep one another in harmonious movement. The listener is diffused throughout the musical space and copresent to all parts of it at once, and all these parts interpenetrate one another in the closest intimacy, as in the "ten thousand forms of self-conflicting musical passion" present in the "elaborate music of Mozart" — "the preparation pregnant with the future; the remote corre-

spondence; the questions, as it were, which to a deep musical sense
are asked in one passage and answered in another; the iteration
and ingemination of a given effect, moving through subtle variations that sometimes disguise the theme, sometimes fitfully reveal it, sometimes throw it out tumultuously to the blaze of
daylight . . ." (X, 136).

The experience of music is proof that it is possible for something existing in time to possess those characteristics of simultaneity and omnipresence which make opium dreams a glimpse of
Paradise. In the various styles in which De Quincey writes, he always seeks to achieve in one way or another the characteristics of
music. Those characteristics are also the basis of his judgments
of other writers, and even of his political theory and vision of history. In all these areas perhaps the most persistent motif is
De Quincey's praise of continuity and his distaste for breaks,
blank places, hiatuses. His favorite phrase for discontinuity, *"per
saltum,"* always implies a powerful disapproval, a mixture of
metaphysical and moral distaste for the "fractured and discontinuous" (V, 232). His harshest condemnation of a revolutionary
change in history is to say: "It was a movement *per saltum,* beyond
all that history has recorded" (XIV, 240). In the same way the
evolution of a word, like the evolution of history, should be
continuous: ". . . no word can ever deviate from its first meaning *per saltum*: each successive stage of meaning must always have
been determined by that which preceded" (X, 430). De Quincey
distinguishes, on these grounds, between the mind of Professor
Wilson and the mind of Charles Lamb: ". . . Professor Wilson's
mind is, in its movement and style of feeling, eminently diffusive
— Lamb's discontinuous and abrupt" (III, 88). The worst thing
he can find to say against Pope is that "all his thinking proceeded
by insulated and discontinuous jets" (XI, 62), so that "dismal
rents, chasms, hiatuses, gaped and grinned" in *The Essay on Man*
(XI, 123). Hazlitt is criticized for the same fault: "Hazlitt was
not eloquent, because he was discontinuous. No man can be eloquent whose thoughts are abrupt, insulated, capricious, and . . .
non-sequacious" (V, 231). The man who jumps from one place to
another, and leaves an empty space between, is not playing the
game, and his enterprise can come to no good. Each man must
go, like the lace-maker, with the utmost care over every bit of

the space between "here" and "there," connecting every point with every other point, and never for a moment allowing the thread to break. If necessary he must go over the same area repeatedly, recapitulating it, seeing it from slightly different angles, making sure he has not missed anything. He must be certain he is "filling up all those chasms which else are likely to remain as permanent disfigurations of [the] work" (III, 226). De Quincey does not seek a linear continuity, or even the two-dimensional continuity which is suggested by the metaphor of lace-making. No, his own metaphor of "chasms" is best. He is surrounded by a four-dimensional continuum, and must create a continuous web or network of relations which will fill up with an uninterrupted integument the whole of this multi-dimensional space-time.

Baudelaire, in *Les paradis artificiels,* recognizes that this desire to occupy space, rather than to go in a straight line from one place to another, is the real cause of De Quincey's digressiveness. Describing the wandering circumlocutions of De Quincey's style, he says: "De Quincey's thought is not merely sinuous; the word is not strong enough: it is naturally spiral." In De Quincey, as in Baudelaire himself, the image of this spiral movement is the thyrsus.[7] The nominal subject is the dry peeled stick at the center which holds things together and gives them a linear direction. The stick is there only for the sake of the flowers, leaves, and blossoms, the digressive meanderings which go about and about the shaft, and give it a three-dimensional volume. Only if De Quincey's style is digressive can it fill up space and avoid shrinking to a desiccated line and paradigm of death. All this is said very eloquently by De Quincey himself in a passage in the first version of the "Suspiria":

... the whole course of this narrative resembles, and was meant to resemble, a *caduceus* wreathed about with meandering ornaments, or the shaft of a tree's stem hung round and surmounted with some vagrant parasitical plant. The mere medical subject of the opium answers to the dry withered pole, which shoots all the rings of the flowering plants, and seems to do so by some dexterity of its own; whereas, in fact, the plant and its tendrils have curled

[7] See Baudelaire, *Oeuvres complètes,* p. 550: ". . . cette pensée est le thyrse. . . . Le sujet n'a pas d'autre valeur que celle d'un bâton sec et nu; mais les rubans, les pampres et les fleurs peuvent être, par leurs entrelacements folâtres, une richesse précieuse pour les yeux. La pensée de De Quincey n'est pas seulement sinueuse; le mot n'est pas assez fort: elle est naturellement spirale." See also p. 480.

round the sullen cylinder by mere luxuriance of *theirs*. . . . The true object in my "Opium Confessions" is not the naked physiological theme — on the contrary, *that* is the ugly pole . . . but those wandering musical variations upon the theme — those parasitical thoughts, feelings, digressions, which climb up with bells and blossoms round about the arid stock; ramble away from it at times with perhaps too rank a luxuriance; but at the same time, by the eternal interest attached to the *subjects* of these digressions, no matter what were the execution, spread a glory over incidents that for themselves would be — less than nothing.[8]

The image of the caduceus describes exactly the way De Quincey's sentences gradually traverse the whole space of a subject by going about and about it, "flying and pursuing, opening and closing, hiding and restoring" (I, 51), as he goes through "manœuvres the most intricate, dances the most elaborate, receding or approaching, round [his] great central sun . . ." (III, 418). In the last quotation, however, the center is not a line, the baton of the thyrsus, but a point, the sun. The thyrsus suggests a little too much a steady motion, however spiral, toward a goal to be wholly expressive of the movement of De Quincey's thought, and it may have been a recognition of this which caused De Quincey to cut the splendid passage on the thyrsus from the revised edition of the "Suspiria." More often when reading De Quincey we have the feeling that all forward movement has stopped for a time, that De Quincey has entered into a new space, and has given up all thought of going beyond it until he has completely filled up the present area by circling around and around in it until every point has been traversed. The image of circling, however, is still too linear. The effect is rather of a slow moving river which has overflowed one barrier and now occupies itself in the remorseless flooding of its new volume, swelling slowly but surely in all directions until finally it reaches the top of its bounds, and can spill over and flow on to another stage in its course. A sentence in the "Confessions" describes this process exactly: "It was as though a cup were gradually filled by the sleepy overflow of some natural fountain, the fulness of the cup expressing symbolically the completeness of the rest: but then, in the next stage of the process, it seemed as though the rush and torrent-like babbling of the redundant waters, when running over from every part of the cup, interrupted the slumber which in their earlier stage of

[8] *Blackwood's Edinburgh Magazine*, LVII (1845), 273.

silent gathering they had so naturally produced" (III, 356). De
Quincey is fascinated by that special kind of lake which is called
a "tarn" — perhaps because of some half-conscious recognition of
the symbolic relation of tarns to his own spiritual experience.
Several times in his writings, usually with only a slight connection
to his subject, De Quincey stops to explain that a tarn is a deep
lake in the mountains which has no proper inlet, but is formed
by the slow seeping down of innumerable springs and rivulets
from the surrounding rocks. These multiple sources have filled
up the cuplike hollow in the hills, and by their constant dripping
keep it full (see IV, 118, 119; XIII, 382, 383). A perfect image for
De Quincey's writing! Often he advances not on one single line,
but on many lines at once, and by this multiple flowing from
many directions toward a single space, gradually fills up that space
to the limit.[9] De Quincey's apparent digressions are simply cir-
cumlocutionary withdrawals by which he gathers more material
and brings it back toward his center, where it forms ultimately
one continuous whole. His description of Coleridge's conversation
applies perfectly to his own writing: "Coleridge, to many people,
. . . seemed to wander; and he seemed then to wander most
when, in fact, his resistance to the wandering instinct was greatest
— viz., when the compass and huge circuit by which his illustra-
tions moved travelled farthest into remote regions before they
began to revolve. Long before this coming round commenced
most people had lost him, and naturally enough supposed that
he had lost himself" (II, 152, 153). But no, the whole discourse
is one "continuity of . . . links" (II, 153), and Coleridge, by his
very habit of making wide sweeps away from his subject, "gathered into focal concentration the largest body of objects, *apparently* disconnected, that any man ever yet, by any magic, could
assemble, or, *having* assembled, could manage" (V, 204).

[9] There is a curious parallel to this motif of the cup or tarn in one aspect of
De Quincey's way of living his own life — a parallel both comic and pathetic, and
at the same time a suggestive emblem of his inner world. De Quincey would rent
a room to work in, and then gradually fill it up with books and papers piled
everywhere in wild disorder, until it was literally impossible to walk from the
door to the desk. Then he would say the room was "snowed up," lock the door,
and move to other lodgings, "leaving his landlady . . . fearfully impressed with
the mysterious sin of meddling with his papers" (Page, I, 363). At his death there
were several of these snowed up rooms, each one a space he had in actual fact
filled up to overflowing!

It does not satisfy the demands of continuity to fill up, however scrupulously, the space where we are now before moving on to the next area. We must always be willing to circle backwards in order to be certain that we have established a firm foundation and a true beginning. De Quincey tells us, for example, that the whole purpose of the "Confessions" is to demonstrate the power of dreams. The dreams were caused by opium. He became an opium-eater because of the "blank desolation" (III, 231) derived from his youthful sufferings in London. Those sufferings were caused by his own "unpardonable folly" (III, 231) in running away from school, and by the wicked irresponsibility of his guardians. He had guardians because his father had died when he was a boy. His whole life hangs together, and in order to have the right to describe his opium dreams in all their splendor, he must begin with his early youth and work up to the dreams by an unbroken "series of steps" (III, 223). When he revises the "Confessions" thirty-five years after their first appearance, it is the early and preliminary part which is most subjected to a process of the "integration of what had been left imperfect, or amplification of what, from the first, had been insufficiently expanded" (III, 219). He must be sure that there is "one uninterrupted bond of unity running through the entire succession of experiences, first and last" (III, 413). In the "Suspiria de Profundis," which is a continuation of the "Confessions," he goes back even further — to the "affliction of childhood" (I, 28), the death of his sister, which is the crucial event of his life and the real beginning of it all.

Perfect continuity is the first quality De Quincey seeks, as he tries to create, in words, a musical space which will match the bliss of his opium dreams. But continuity is not in itself enough. If De Quincey's thought is like a slowly gathering fluid which fills space, this fluid must have the curious property of being able to sustain itself in the void. Perhaps by going back far enough a true beginning can be found which will serve as a firm foundation, but the space to be filled stretches away emptily in all directions. The continuum to be created must sustain itself by its own inner equilibrium, like some frail architectural structure hanging in air. Along with continuity De Quincey always seeks in style, as in life and history, another musical quality: balance. Only the intrinsic harmony of opposing forces will keep the continuum from collapsing, like a house of cards, into "the anarchy of Chaos" (XIV, 166).

The necessity of achieving an equilibrium of opposites is both a psychological and an ontological law. One state cannot be known unless we also know its opposite. This notion (which De Quincey may possibly have learned from John Paul Richter, his favorite German writer[10]) is given the widest extension in De Quincey's thought. It is for him a fundamental law of the mind that "where two ideas are correlates and antagonist forces, they explain themselves and define themselves at the same time; for the one is a rebound from the other" (IX, 328). He twice returns to his experience of the fact that death is more affecting in midsummer, and each time the reason he gives is a version of the law of opposites (III, 443, 444, and I, 38, 39). The same idea is repeatedly employed by De Quincey to justify "chiaroscuro" as a law of poetic style. By the "reciprocal entanglement of darkness in light, and of light in darkness" (XI, 303) both darkness and light are made visible: "the two coming into collision, each exalts the other into stronger relief" (I, 39). When Milton uses architectural words to describe the "primitive simplicities of Paradise" (X, 402, 403) there is no error in poetic tact, for "each image, from reciprocal contradiction, brightens and vivifies the other. The two images act, and react, by strong repulsion and antagonism" (X, 403). The same notion is the basis of De Quincey's most famous critical essay, "On the Knocking at the Gate in Macbeth." The sound of ordinary life commencing with the knocking at the gate first "makes us profoundly sensible" of the depth of evil into which Macbeth and Lady Macbeth have stepped: "All action in any direction is best expounded, measured, and made apprehensible, by reaction" (X, 393).

The motif of opposites in tense equilibrium is more than merely a psychological or epistemological principle for De Quincey. Space and time stretch interminably in all directions, with no strong magnetic field to orient things and hold them in position. If this is the case, a man, a system of thought, or a nation must hold itself up in the void by "a steady, rope-dancer's equilibrium of posture" (XI, 351). In the absence of any given lines

[10] The idea that we know by opposites appears several times in the "Analects" which De Quincey translated from John Paul (XI, 273–293).

of force, "two polar forces of reciprocal antagonism" (IX, 374) must be created, and we must "vibrate equally and indifferently towards either pole" (IV, 396). Only in this way can an area in the infinite space be filled up with an harmonious system which will possess internal principles of self-perpetuation. If one force exists without its opposite to pull it out and make it expand, that solitary force will through sheer inertia contract to a point and be as nothing in the immense neutral space which surrounds it. De Quincey believes that there is a built-in law of compensation in man, in nature, and in history whereby any one power tends to call up its opposite and keep things in balanced motion:

Compensations are everywhere produced or encouraged by nature and by providence . . . (V, 375)

. . . there is a principle of self-restoration in the opposite direction; there is a counter-state of repose, a compensatory state, as in the tides of the sea, which tends continually to re-establish the equipoise. (XI, 380)

But in this world all things re-act; and the very extremity of any force is the seed and nucleus of a counter-agency. (VI, 431)

This principle is applied by De Quincey to the most diverse subjects. Roman civilization "was kept going from the very first by strong reaction and antagonism," and "fell into torpor from the moment when this antagonism ceased to operate" (VI, 435). The French Revolution was in itself neither good nor bad, for "the Revolution, and the resistance to the Revolution, were the two powers that quickened each the other for ultimate good" (XI, 312). In the same way there is a contradictory "anti-proverb" for each proverb. Each is false alone, but if taken with its opposite forms one half of a perfect sphere of truth (X, 436). This metaphor is the basis for De Quincey's elaborate discussion of the English party system. The Whigs and the Tories are both right, and they "are able to exist only by means of their co-existence," for "each party forms one hemisphere; jointly they make up the total sphere" (IX, 373; see also V, 129, 130). All these cases exemplify forces which, "though in perfect opposition, are so far from therefore excluding each other that they cannot exist apart, — each, in fact, exists by and through its antagonist" (IX, 371).

If De Quincey's aim is to fill the largest possible mental space, then it follows that he should seek the most widely separated opposites which he can still manage to keep in pregnant tension. Poetry it is, or poetic prose, which creates the most expanded continuum by oscillating between the most widely distant polar antagonists. De Quincey's descriptions of poetry often contain the idea of an equilibrium of opposing forces combined with the notion that language can, like opium dreams, be a "cloud-scaling swing" (XIII, 339) which will traverse and fill up the whole distance between the lowest deep and the highest height. Poetry is "the science of human passion in all its fluxes and refluxes — in its wondrous depths below depths, and its starry altitudes that ascend to the gates of heaven" (XIV, 117). Accordingly, the "Suspiria de Profundis" is governed by a principle of oscillation between astronomical opposites. In this oscillation descent guarantees ascent: ". . . fast as you reach the lowest point of depression, may you rely on racing up to a starry altitude of corresponding ascent" (XIII, 339). The "Suspiria" is bound together as a space-traversing whole by the very antagonism of the forces between which it swings, "even as a bridge gathers cohesion and strength from the increasing resistance into which it is forced by increasing pressure" (XIII, 339).

క∾

Continuity and the balance of polar opposites are the chief means by which De Quincey hopes to create in words a structure which will match the qualities of music or opium dreams. But there are for De Quincey two very distinct kinds of mental building. One he calls, in a famous distinction, rhetoric, the literature of power; the other logic, the literature of knowledge. It might seem that De Quincey makes this distinction in order to dismiss logic and exalt rhetoric. Only rhetoric is truly musical, truly expansive and ascending, whereas logic is linear, discursive, and creeps horizontally along the ground: "What you owe to Milton is not any knowledge, of which a million separate items are still but a million of advancing steps on the same earthly level; what you owe is *power*, — that is, exercise and expansion to your own latent capacity of sympathy with the infinite, where every pulse and each separate influx is a step upwards, a step ascending as upon a Jacob's ladder from earth to mysterious altitudes above the earth" (XI, 56).

How can language, which after all is a linear series of words, expand itself from its straight line, fill up space, and ascend toward heaven?

De Quincey emphasizes two qualities of rhetoric, both necessary if it is to create a musical structure of words. Whereas logical discourse goes as directly as possible to its goal, rhetoric circles like a dancer around and around its subject, embroidering it with the greatest possible density of decoration, as the baton of a thyrsus is decorated with ribbons and flowers. Rhetoric develops its primitive theme to the utmost, subjecting it to the greatest possible number of "combinations and permutations" (XI, 245), and surrounding it with "cycles and epicycles, . . . vortices, . . . osculating curves" (XI, 245). In this way rhetorical language will have a three-dimensional volume rather than being a mere one-dimensional line. The rhetorician's duty is "to hang upon [his] own thoughts as an object of conscious interest, to play with them, to watch and pursue them through a maze of inversions, evolutions, and harlequin changes" (X, 97), so that he can create a "motion of fancy self-sustained from its own activities" (X, 121).

Expansive circling is not enough to create the literature of power. The circling must be directed. Each sentence must be a permutation of the original germ, for "mere joy that does not linger and reproduce itself in reverberations and endless mirrors is not fitted for poetry" (XI, 301), and in poetry "the elements are nothing without the atmosphere that moulds, and the dynamic forces that combine" (V, 231). "What would the sun be itself," asks De Quincey, "if it were a mere blank orb of fire that did not multiply its splendours through millions of rays refracted and reflected, or if its glory were not endlessly caught, splintered, and thrown back by atmospheric repercussions" (XI, 301). The theme of a work of literature must be like the sun in space, which casts forth innumerable variations of itself, making space one uniform continuum of light.[11] Only thus will each part be a mirror image

---

[11] This principle of variations on a primitive theme will untie one knot in De Quincey's thought. Several times he compares Johnson's style to Burke's. In Johnson, "all the future products, down to the very last, lie secretly wrapped up in

or symbol of the whole. And only if each part is an echo of the whole will the discourse keep from falling apart into separate "showers of scintillation and sparkle" (XI, 119). A discontinuous mode of speech is essentially evanescent. Each part, however brilliant in itself, falls into darkness and is forgotten as soon as it is uttered. Only the reverberative, musical style, which is able "to break up massy chords into running variations" (X, 140), will last, and create in time something analogous to the simultaneous interrelation of parts in space: ". . . in successions . . . where the parts are not fluent, as in a line, but angular, as it were, to each other, not homogeneous, but heterogeneous, not continuous but abrupt, the evanescence is *essential;* both because each part really *has,* in general, but a momentary existence, and still more because, all the parts being unlike, each is imperfect as a representative image of the whole process; whereas in trains which repeat each other the whole exists virtually in each part, and therefore reciprocally each part will be a perfect expression of the whole" (XI, 179). Therefore De Quincey always praises the ornate periodic style, which by its "ample volume of sound and self-revolving rhythmus" (V, 116), "modulating through the whole diatonic scale" (VII, 435), is able to produce an ever-expanding continuity, always changing and yet always the same. In such a style "the two opposite forces of eloquent passion and rhetorical fancy [are] brought into an exquisite equilibrium, — approaching, receding, — attracting, repelling, — blending, separating, — chasing and chased, as in a fugue . . ." (X, 104, 105).

De Quincey's own style at its best achieves just these virtues of "the rhythmical — the continuous — what in French is called the

---

the original germ," whereas in Burke "every separate element in the mysterious process of generation" is "an absolute supervention of new matter, and not a mere uncovering of old, already involved at starting in the primary germ" (V, 134). It would seem that we must choose between these two ways. Yet neither is satisfactory. In Johnson's style there is no movement forward to occupy more mental space. His thought is "purely regressive and analytic" (V, 134). On the other hand, though Burke's thought "grows," it is in danger, because of the absolute novelty introduced, of becoming discontinuous with itself, the worst of sins for De Quincey. Musical reverberation in style is precisely a reconciliation of these incompatibles. In such a style, as in a musical theme and variations, the principal subject contains all the later development in germ. As that development grows, new and unforeseen motifs appear, but these motifs are still in resonance with the principal theme. The musical style moves forward from its beginning. It is a constant exfoliation of novelty out of the same, and reaffirmation of identity in difference.

soutenu" (III, 51). Each sentence in rhetorical prose has two "*moments* (to speak dynamically)": "its external connexion in the first place — how does it arise, upon what movement of the logic or the feeling from the preceding period? and, secondly, its own internal evolution" (V, 90). The law governing both the internal and external moments of a sentence is the same — the reverberation of "the *Idem in alio*" (I, 51). De Quincey's best stylistic effects are achieved by a series of sentences, each one of which is ornate and complex, full of clauses in apposition which repeat one another with slight variation. The sentence is a kind of fugue, and the endless echoes among the clauses make it a little infinity in itself. The sentences have the same resonance among one another as do the phrases within each sentence — with this difference: while each sentence circles around within itself, and does not advance beyond its beginning, the sentences in their sequence build upon one another, and each new sentence is another rung in that Jacob's ladder by which the literature of power reaches up to heaven. De Quincey's style is an exact mirror of his mental space and of his means of dealing with that space. Each sentence is a new volume into which De Quincey flows, expanding in all directions until he has filled it up. Having conquered one space, he is free to proceed to another contiguous one, being careful to relate the two spaces rhythmically to one another. He can occupy more and more space in this way, and reach ultimately heavenly heights, for "nothing is trivial or little which can, by continual summation of its never-ending series, amount finally to any great result" (XIV, 90). If the literature of power is successful, the initial sentences may be "the first links in a series whose last may possibly be at an infinite distance from the beginning" (XIV, 91). A magnificent passage on the subject of style offers one example of this. A splendid defense of splendor, a pompous defense of pomp, it is language as rhetoric and music — continuity, equilibrium, expansion, and reverberation all working together to occupy one more volume of the infinite space:

. . . Lamb had no sense of the rhythmical in prose composition. Rhythmus, or pomp of cadence, or sonorous ascent of clauses, in the structure of sentences, were effects of art as much thrown away upon *him* as the voice of the charmer upon the deaf adder. We ourselves, occupying the very station of polar opposition to that of Lamb, — being as morbidly, perhaps, in the one excess as he in the other, — naturally detected this omission in Lamb's nature at an early stage of our acquaintance. Not the fabled Regulus, with his eyelids torn away, and his uncurtained eyeballs exposed to the noontide glare of a Carthaginian sun, could have shrieked with more anguish of recoil from torture than we from certain sentences and periods in which Lamb perceived no fault at all. *Pomp,* in our apprehension, was an idea of two categories: the *pompous* might be spurious, but it might also be genuine. It is well to love the simple — *we* love it; nor is there any opposition at all between *that* and the very glory of pomp. But, as we once put the case to Lamb, if, as a musician, as the leader of a mighty orchestra, you had this theme offered to you — "Belshazzar the King gave a great feast to a thousand of his lords" — or this, "And, on a certain day, Marcus Cicero stood up, and in a set speech rendered solemn thanks to Caius Cæsar for Quintus Ligarius pardoned, and for Marcus Marcellus restored" — surely no man would deny that, in such a case, simplicity, though in a passive sense not lawfully absent, must stand aside as totally insufficient for the *positive* part. (V, 235)

ॐ

De Quincey has escaped at last from the pariah worlds. Opium dreams have given him the keys of Paradise, and have shown him a mental world of omnipresence, simultaneity, echo, vibration — infinite activities, infinite repose. He has found a way to conquer this inner space voluntarily: the literature of power. Discursive language, which hunts over the field to right and to left, has been mentioned only to be dismissed as too linear and too *low*.

Nevertheless, the fact is that De Quincey wrote a great deal of the "literature of knowledge," and he always prided himself on his impeccability in logic: "I . . . hold myself . . . *inexpugnabilis* upon quillets of logic" (VIII, 255); "In matter of logic I hold myself impeccable; and, to say nothing of my sober days, I defy the devil and all the powers of darkness to get any advantage over me even on those days when I am drunk, in relation to *Barbara, Celarent, Darii,* or *Ferio*" (IX, 34). The last sentence helps explain why De Quincey takes such delight in trying to construct on any subject an elaborate logical network. Logic defends him from the powers of darkness outside, and also from drunkenness, the power of incoherence and vagrancy within. Logic is a kind of indestructible sobriety. The study of Ricardo rouses him from his mental torpor in 1818, and his *Logic of Political Economy* is written in the 1840's, when he has again sunk into intellectual prostration after the deaths of his wife and eldest son. Logic keeps a man from wandering. It is easy to see why. If we can once get our postulates clear, all the rest of the system follows inevitably from those. We are freed from a "miserable distraction of choice." Logic is not a synthetic act, in which "we may readily conceive a thousand different roads for any one mind." It is "an analytical act; and there we cannot conceive of more than one road for a thousand minds" (IX, 26).

Logic seems neatly set in opposition to rhetoric. In De Quincey's descriptions of logical thought, however, there is a curious reversal, in which logical discourse comes to be praised for possessing just those qualities which make the literature of power so precious. In one passage, De Quincey affirms that literature, as a discipline of the mind, is not "self-sufficing." Why? Precisely because it is too *discontinuous!* Our ability to understand or create literature is intermittent, and therefore no appeasement for solitude. In literature we may rise to great tumultuous heights, but there are dreadful sinkings in between. Mathematics is better, and just because it is perfectly *continuous,* for in mathematics "the difficulty is pretty equally dispersed and broken up into a series of steps, no one of which demands any exertion sensibly more intense than the rest, [and] nothing is required of the student beyond that sort of application and coherent attention which, in a sincere student of any standing, may be presumed as a habit already and inveterately established" (X, 14).

In other passages De Quincey praises logic in terms which show it to be exactly analogous to the literature of power. Like rhetoric, logic develops by reverberations, permutations and combinations of a primitive germ. Like rhetoric, logic fills a certain volume of mental space with an elaborate self-sustaining architecture, for an "artifice of logic" (IX, 134) is "an arch that supports itself" (VIII, 279). In logic we must "lay a slow foundation for remote superstructures" through a "painful evolution of principles" (IX, 361), but, once this is successfully done, an "immense train of consequences" (IX, 67) follows as "orderly and symmetrical deductions" (IX, 54), "all [of which] are dependent upon each, and each upon all" (IX, 214), "like so many organs of a complex machine" (IX, 208). The basic principles of a system are like "wellheads": "the rest runs down in a torrent of inferences from these *præcognita*" (IX, 238). A process of logic is the "systematic '*genesis*' of [a] complex truth — the act, namely, of pursuing the growth which gradually carries that truth to its full expansion through all its movements" (IX, 128).

The advantages of a fully developed logical system are its indestructibility and its availability. It has all the qualities of dreams or rhetoric, without their fragility. Any one part of a logical system presupposes all the others. Logical discourse too, it turns out, can be described as a kind of linguistic music, but it is a music which develops itself by an inalterable law. The permanence of Christianity is ensured by the fact that it is a complex system whose parts all imply one another, and chase one another in eternal combinations through the Bible, like the voices of a fugue: ". . . in the grander parts of knowledge, which do not deal much with petty details, nearly all the *building* or constructive ideas . . . lie involved within each other; so that any one of the series, being awakened in the mind, is sufficient . . . to lead backwards or forwards . . . into many of the rest. . . . all parts of the scheme are eternally chasing each other, like the parts of a fugue; they hide themselves in one chapter, only to restore themselves in another; they diverge, only to recombine . . ." (VIII, 278, 281).

Logic has turned out to be strictly analogous to rhetoric. But, it may be objected, surely De Quincey would not claim that logical discourse can move up the Jacob's ladder toward heaven. There is, however, a passage which makes just this claim for geometrical thinking, in spite of De Quincey's assertions elsewhere that logic creeps forever along the ground. In the light of all De Quincey's statements about the expansive and architectural powers of logical thought, it does not seem at all inconsistent that he should claim also that it ascends. If we can just be sure we have the founding principles right, we can build upward upon them a limitless structure in space. Geometry is a "vast aerial synthesis," "towering upwards towards infinity" (IX, 118, 119). It "holds 'acquaintance with the stars' by means of its inevitable and imperishable truth" (IX, 119).

Opium dreams reveal the fact that the infinite powers of the mind match its infinite depths, and give De Quincey a brief possession of the omnipresence and simultaneity of God. Music shows De Quincey that a structure existing in time can possess the same qualities as the dreams, and the two forms of literature, rhetoric and logic, provide the means by which the Paradise regained momentarily in dreams may be systematically assaulted, so that even a God who has withdrawn to an infinite distance may be ultimately recaptured. The space between us and God is not, so it appears, a void. It is a continuous atmosphere, which may be traversed and occupied in various ways. Even if God is infinitely far away we may hope to reach him, for the air goes all the way to heaven, and forms an unbroken connection, however tenuous, between man and God: "Whatever we may swear with our false feigning lips, in our faithful hearts we still believe, and must for ever believe, in fields of air traversing the total gulf between earth and the central heavens. Still, . . . we, in that Sabbatic vision which sometimes is revealed for an hour upon nights like this, ascend with easy steps from the sorrow-stricken fields of earth upwards to the sandals of God" (XIII, 311).

੩੭

A finite power measuring itself against one which is in its nature infinite must be defeated . . . (XIV, 82)

In spite of everything, De Quincey's attempt to create, in language, a human equivalent of God's mode of existence is ultimately a failure. It is a failure not so much because the point of consciousness cannot expand to fill the infinity of space and time, as because the unexpanded point can never be described, or filled up, or traversed from side to side. De Quincey will fail even if he gives up altogether the idea of writing a great work on the Establishment of the Human Intellect, and turns to something modestly small and narrow, like political economy, or the Essenes, or even "the casuistry of Roman meals." Every subject, however small, is inexhaustible.

This is so because any subject can be looked at from an infinite multiplicity of different directions. Each point of view will reveal something novel. It is impossible ever to write the definitive history of any period, not so much because the facts are innumerable, as because the facts can be legitimately combined in an infinite number of different ways. History is like a surface of variegated marble in which we can find an unlimited number of different patterns. Like a dewdrop, or a particle of earth, it is "mysterious and Spinosistically sublime" (VII, 251): "The same historic facts, viewed in different lights, or brought into connexion with other facts, according to endless diversities of permutation and combination, furnish grounds for such eternal successions of new speculations as make the facts themselves virtually new, and virtually endless" (VII, 251).

Since even a finite number of facts can be grouped in endlessly different ways, none of De Quincey's essays can be definitive or exhaustive. Each could be rewritten innumerable times, each time giving a different, but equally valid, arrangement of the material. The material of any subject, however small, is an inexhaustible multiplicity. Any finite entity in time and space is infinitely divisible.

De Quincey has a lively understanding of the abyss that lies in this category of infinite divisibility, and of the power it has to dissolve any subject into "details infinite in number and infinite in littleness," and make it "break down and fritter away into fractions and petty minutiæ" (X, 340). In one of his most hopelessly digressive essays (one in which he digresses by talking about digression),[12] he comes, in the midst of his meanderings, to the subject of divisibility, as if it has been called up by his secret awareness of the reason he is having so much trouble making progress with his theme. Sir William Hamilton leads him to the topic of logic, and logic leads him to the old conundrum of Achilles and the tortoise. In the process of solving the conundrum he indirectly states the principle by which it is wholly impossible for him, though he is swift as Achilles, ever to finish with Sir William — or any other subject. The puzzle of Achilles and the tortoise, says De Quincey, is "one amongst the many confounding consequences which may be deduced from the endless divisibility of space" (V, 332). It may be solved by recognizing that time too is infinitely divisible. The immediate perplexity disappears, but only by revealing a worse. If both time and space are infinitely divisible, then so also are the contents of time and space. If De Quincey wishes to exhaust each subject before moving on to the next, then it is impossible ever to get from one to another, however close together the two may be, for he can never finish enu-

[12] "Sir William Hamilton" (V, 303–351).

merating the infinite number of parts into which even a moment or a drop of dew may be divided. Even if Achilles will catch the tortoise, it is impossible to find words for the infinite degrees of his approach.

It might be objected that, though any subject is infinitely divisible, the mind, like nature itself, is organized in a hierarchy of ever more inclusive genera. An enormous number of details can be included in a universal term, and De Quincey can thereby defeat the infinite divisibility of his subject and make real progress toward his goal. Unfortunately, this is not possible. Not only can any entity be subdivided ad infinitum, but for De Quincey each of its parts is unique, and cannot be satisfactorily subsumed under some more general law. The inexhaustible divisibility of things is a "sublime infinity, like that of ocean, like that of Flora, like that of nature, where no repetitions are endured, no leaf is the copy of another leaf, no absolute identity, and no painful tautologies" (XI, 320). De Quincey repeatedly defends the science of casuistry. For him each moral situation is to some degree idiosyncratic and cannot be reduced to rule. As soon as we recognize this, ethics as a finite system disappears and leaves an "enormous accumulation" of separate details built up "by aggregation of *cases,* by the everlasting depullulation of fresh sprouts and shoots from old boughs" (VIII, 314). Each moral situation varies from all the others, and "the tendency of such variations is, in all states of complex civilisation, to absolute infinity" (VIII, 314).

De Quincey several times accepts the Leibnizian *principium indiscernibilium,* and gives it the widest applicability: "Infinite change, illimitable novelty, inexhaustible difference, these are the foundations upon which nature builds and ratifies her purpose of *individuality* . . . As with external objects, so with human actions: amidst their infinite approximations and affinities, they are separated by circumstances of never-ending diversity". (V, 357, 358, and see X, 129). On the basis of this notion he makes a paradoxical defense of astrology, palmistry, craniology, and the reading of moral character from handwriting (V, 357; XIII, 265–269; XIV, 43, 44). Each man's palm, skull, or handwriting is different from every other man's, just as the stars have a unique configuration at the moment of each man's birth, for no two men are born at exactly the same moment. Therefore palm, skull, or stars may secretly foretell a man's life, but no man's skill is equal to reading these signs. To do so we should have to follow to their uttermost reaches the variation of palms or skulls and the divisibility of time. Palmistry and astrology are true, but palmists and astrologers are frauds.

Endless points of view, infinite divisibility in time and space, uniqueness of the infinitesimal part — each of these would be enough to frustrate De Quincey's attempt to exhaust any subject, however limited. Even this is not all. If De Quincey should by some unimaginable miracle traverse every point of one theme, he would have to face the fact that from there it is possible to go on in an infinite number of further directions. One of the reasons for his trouble with the essay on Sir William Hamilton is the fact that Hamilton "stands in a possible relation to all things" (V, 326). In one amusing passage he describes a public speaker who, having reached the end of one stage of his remarks, is unable to proceed, not so much because he can think of nothing more to say, as because he cannot choose among all the plausible next steps: "His anxiety increases, utter confusion masters him, and he breaks down" (X, 229).

The result of all these modes of inexhaustibility is that no essay of De Quincey's can be satisfactorily finished. It will always be possible to go back and redo it on a larger scale, filling up the gaps which have been inadvertently left, and subdividing into smaller units what has been treated as one entity. Any theme may be infinitely inflated without thereby becoming any thinner. The second version of the "Confessions" is much enlarged from the first, without really covering any more ground. Had De Quincey lived long enough, he could have gone back a third time, enlarging it even more, and so on for ever. Each of his papers, long before it is finished, is like the painting in *The Vicar of Wakefield*: "But stop," cries De Quincey. "This will not do. I must alter the scale of this paper, or else — something will happen which would vex me. The artist who sketched the Vicar of Wakefield's family group, in his zeal for comprehensive fulness of details, enlarged his canvas until he forgot the narrow proportions of the good vicar's house; and the picture, when finished, was too big to enter the front-door of the vicarage" (V, 326).

De Quincey can never stop. All his works are fragments, full of unfilled gaps, failures in scale (in which one part of the paper is in far greater detail than other parts), or incomplete at the end, either with a huddled conclusion, or with no conclusion at all, a meander which ends in the air. Often he seizes hold of himself in the middle of an essay, recapitulating what he has said in order to demonstrate that the diversion is not a diversion, and trying with immense effort to put himself back on the track: "Here let us retrace the course of our speculations, lest the reader should suppose us to be wandering" (X, 225); "But all this, though not unconnected with our general theme, is wide of our immediate purpose. The course of our logic at this point runs in the following order" (X, 235). It is no use. He loses himself again immediately. In one essay, a brief digression, "for hasty purposes" (X, 194), about Greek literature turns into a discussion fifty pages long. He never has time to finish his original outline, and the essay wanders off into a completely peripheral conclusion. Similar disasters occur in other essays. He always fails, not because he has an unfortunate habit of wandering, but because, however straight he goes, he can never exhaust the infinite which lurks in the finite. Each subject must be "followed into endless mazes" (XI, 93).

Neither the rhetorical style nor the logical style is able to conquer this insuperable difficulty. The rhetorical style, the style of musical reverberation, degenerates into a series of sentences, each one of which is a maze, and, in its echoing "labyrinth of clauses" (X, 161), contains its own infinity. In De Quincey there are many such "endless and labyrinthine sentences" (X, 158), "involving clause within clause *ad infinitum*" (X, 149):

But the wild, giddy, fantastic, capricious, incalculable, springing, vaulting, tumbling, dancing, waltzing, caprioling, *pirouetting*, sky-rocketing of the chamois, the harlequin, the Vestris, the storm-loving raven — the raven? no, the lark (for often he ascends "singing up to heaven's gates," but like the lark he dwells upon the earth), — in short, of the Proteus, the Ariel, the Mercury, the monster, John Paul, — can be compared to nothing in heaven or earth, or the waters under the earth, except to the motions of the same faculty as existing in Shakspere. (XI, 266)

It is precisely *because* Achilles will in practice go ahead of the tortoise, when, conformably to a known speculative argument, he ought *not* to go ahead — it is precisely this fact, so surely to be anticipated from all our experience, when confronted with this principle so peremptorily denying the possibility of such a fact — exactly this antinomy it is, — the *will be,* as a physical reality, ranged against the *cannot be,* as apparently a metaphysical law — this downright certainty as matched against this downright impossibility, — which, in default of the Leibnitzian solution, constitutes our perplexity, or, to use a Grecian word still more expressive, which constitutes our *aporia,* that is, our resourcelessness. (V, 350)

Such sentences, each one a "huge fasciculus of cycle and epicycle," a "monster model of sentence, bloated with decomplex intercalations" (X, 150), could go on forever. The possible variations of the principal parts are endless. A series of such "plethoric" sentences will produce a horrible parody of the musical style, a collection of words which, like the ornate, periodical sentences of Dr. Samuel Parr, circle forever without getting anywhere, and ultimately evaporate in their own fume: "There was labour, indeed, and effort enough, preparation without end, and most tortuous circumgyration of periods; but from all this sonorous smithery of harsh words, dark and pompous, nothing adequate emerged, — nothing commensurate, — but simply a voluminous smoke . . ." (V, 12).

An exactly analogous fate awaits the logical style. Logical discourse can get caught up in one of those nodes of intellectual perplexity, in which it alternates between two impossible conclusions. Such an event results in a "logical see-saw" (V, 333) paralleling the endless sentences of the rhetorical style. De Quincey remembers the old conundrum of the Cretan who said all Cretans are liars, resurrects from Jeremy Taylor the story of the man who dreamed all dreams are vain, and suggests his own version in the case of the drunken men who spill more the more they are drunk: "Spilling the whole, they could not have been drunk. *Ergo,* could not have titubated.[13] *Ergo,* could not have spilt. *Ergo,* must have drunk the whole. *Ergo,* were dead drunk. *Ergo,* must have titubated. 'And so round again,' as my lord the bishop pleasantly expresses it, *in secula seculorum*" (V, 335).

If the failure of logic matches the failure of rhetoric on the small scale of a unit of thought, so does it also on the large scale of a complete work. Just as the periodic style is always in danger of degenerating into a "sonorous smithery of harsh words," so none of De Quincey's larger logical efforts reaches its goal. A logical structure will more or less construct itself if we can get the

---

[13] De Quincey's charming word for "the reeling and stumbling of intoxication" (V, 334).

foundation stones firmly established. But this never happens. The big work *De Emendatione Humani Intellectûs* is never begun; the "Dialogues of Three Templars," De Quincey's first large work on political economy, is a broken fragment; and his biggest effort in this mode, *The Logic of Political Economy,* goes over and over the first principles of this science, without establishing them securely enough to permit the author to build the upper stories of his logical architecture. De Quincey's efforts to write the literature of knowledge remain "locked up as by frost, like any Spanish bridge or aqueduct begun upon too great a scale for the resources of the architect" (III, 431). They are memorials "of hopes defeated, of baffled efforts, of materials uselessly accumulated, of foundations laid that were never to support a superstructure, of the grief and the ruin of the architect" (III, 431).

The bold attempt to make out of words an equivalent of the simultaneity and omnipresence of opium dreams has proved to be an utter failure. Instead of perfect continuity, musical reverberation, the filling of space, De Quincey has produced only wretched fragments which refuse to cohere. Instead of expanding outward to conquer infinity with the finite mind, he has discovered in the finite an infinite abyss which can never be crossed or filled. He sinks back into impotent misery, a misery in which the self is once again a solitary point. Now, however, it is a point of consciousness surrounded by the sepulchral wreckage of incomplete creations:

It is as if ivory carvings and elaborate fretwork and fair enamelling should be found with worms and ashes amongst coffins and the wrecks of some forgotten life or some abolished nature. In parts and fractions eternal creations are carried on, but the nexus is wanting, and life and the central principle which should bind together all the parts at the centre, with all its radiations to the circumference, are wanting. Infinite incoherence, ropes of sand, gloomy incapacity of vital pervasion by some one plastic principle, that is the hideous incubus upon my mind always. (Page, I, 325)

ଛ

It is impossible to describe in words the process by which Achilles catches the tortoise. Perhaps in dreams or in real life, which are immediate experience, not mediate language, Achilles *can* catch the tortoise. When language fails, De Quincey must turn back to life — and to opium.

When he does this he begins to discover the true horror of the human condition.

Opium shows the dreamer that the human brain is a palimpsest, that all his past lies waiting to be resurrected. This guarantees the continuity and indestructibility of a man's life. But is it so certain that these are an unequivocal good?

Time flows. Events lying hidden in the future surge up momentarily in the present, and sink back into the past: "The eternal now through the dreadful loom is the overflowing future poured back into the capacious reservoir of the past" (Post. Wks., I, 229). In the moment of coming into being in the present, things evaporate like snowflakes. Man has no power to arrest the passage of time, or to write "one perpetual iteration of *stet., stet.*" (V, 306) down the margin of all time has deleted. The present is a kind of unstanchable hemorrhage, as if beads were dropping endlessly, one by one, from a broken necklace into the unfathomable ocean of the past (X, 275).

Having flowed through the present as evanescent as snowflakes, and as ungraspable as dreams, things falling into the past do not simply drop into an abyss and disappear. They fill up the reservoir of the past, and form themselves into a perdurable block from which man can never escape. The true "villainy of Time" (V, 306) is not the fugitive quality of the present. It is the irreparability of the past. Having once existed, however briefly, in the present, events add themselves to the growing weight of those things which having once existed, can never cease to have been. Over this great mass of things which have been, man has no power whatsoever. The subject of "Savannah-la-mar," one of the "Suspiria," is double. It describes the fugacity of the present, the way the infinitely brief moment is "infinite in its velocity of flight towards death" (XIII, 361). But "death" here does not mean nonexistence. Savannah-la-mar itself is a symbol of the past. It is a great city which God in his anger has removed intact to the bottom of the sea. The city still exists, in all its substantiality, but frozen, paralyzed, dead. It shall not change one iota until judgment day (XIII, 359).

It might seem that this persistence of the past could do no harm. What does it matter if all dead things still exist, so long as they remain safely enclosed, like a city under the sea? But this is not the case. The irremediable presence of the past darkens human life, and reaches out to determine it.

Time for De Quincey is an unbroken causal chain, and a man's whole life is irrevocably determined by certain crucial acts or choices. A man can never know when he may be standing at one of these crossroads, where a wrong step will lead into an endless labyrinth of suffering. In this doctrine of the enormous importance of apparently small acts the influence of the rigorous evangelical-ism of his mother on De Quincey can perhaps be seen. A sense that at every moment each man hangs over a moral abyss, a feeling that he can never foresee all the results of any act, an experience of anticipatory guilt, since any act is bound to be in some degree evil, an exaggerated sense of scrupulous responsibility — all these evangelical motifs are present in De Quincey's vision of time as a causal chain, or as a labyrinth where one false turn will lose us forever:

. . . the consequences of all important actions expand themselves through a series of alternate undulations, expressing successively good and evil, and of this series no summation is possible to a finite intellect. (VIII, 139, and see VIII, 354)

But I speak of literal labyrinths. Now, at Bath, in my labyrinthine child-hood, there *was* such a mystery . . . This mystery I used to visit; and I can assert that no type ever flashed upon my mind so pathetically shadowing out the fatal irretrievability of errors in early life. Turn but once wrong at first entering the inextricable jungle, and all was over; you were ruined; no wan-dering could recover the right path. (VII, 203)

For once again I was preparing to utter an irrevocable word, to enter upon one of those fatally tortuous paths of which the windings can never be un-linked. (III, 347)

What we do now will give its coloring to our whole future life. Each choice determines the others, both before and behind, for if it is true that a wrong choice in the labyrinth long before this moment will have fatally caused our present situation, it is also true that a mistaken turning now will just as irretrievably lose us, and so transform what may have been a happy series of right choices into a sequence leading step by step to disaster. At the very door of heaven there is a wicket gate leading to hell. The chance of making the right turn at all the crossings is infinitesimally small. A man is sure to go wrong *somewhere,* and so ruin the whole series:

In fact, every intricate and untried path in life, where it was from the first a matter of arbitrary choice to enter upon it or avoid it, is effectually a path through a vast Hercynian forest, unexplored and unmapped, where each several turn in your advance leaves you open to new anticipations of what is next to be expected, and consequently open to altered valuations of all that has been already traversed. Even the character of your own absolute experience, past and gone, which (if anything in this world) you might surely answer for as sealed and settled for ever — even this you must submit to hold in suspense, as a thing conditional and contingent upon what is yet to come — liable to have its provisional character affirmed or reversed, according to the new combinations into which it may enter with elements only yet perhaps in the earliest stages of development. (III, 314, 315)

Since time is a chain and a labyrinth it is thereby also a miserable travesty of the musical duration which gives De Quincey the model for his style. The temporal series of events in a man's life is a perfect continuity in which any one crucial event echoes and reverberates down the entire chain in multiple repetitions. What was a tiny act at the beginning returns ultimately, often after apparently disappearing, in a tumultuous cascade of consequences. So, in the "Confessions," De Quincey proposes, as a symbol of "the fatality that must often attend an evil choice" (III, 296), the Whispering Gallery of St. Paul's Cathedral, where "a word or a question, uttered at one end of the gallery in the gentlest of whispers, is reverberated at the other end in peals of thunder" (III, 295, 296). In a similar passage for the "Suspiria," not published until after his death, De Quincey describes the inescapable reverberations of a youthful fault: "Oftentimes an echo goes as it were to sleep: the series of reverberations has died away. Suddenly a second series awakens: this subsides, then a third wakens up. So of actions done in youth. After great tumults all is quieted. You dream that they are over. In a moment, in the twinkling of an eye, on some fatal morning in middle-life the far-off consequences come back upon you. And you say to yourself, 'Oh, Heaven, if I had fifty lives this crime would reappear, as Pelion upon Ossa!'" (Post. Wks., I, 23).

De Quincey is the eternal prisoner of his own past acts. There was only one moment when he was really free, and that was the moment *before* the first crucial act of his life. To remember in aftertimes the moment before he forged the first link in the fatal chain has a special poignancy for him, and many times in his work he returns to that moment, a moment so virginal, so pure, so uncommitted: "No night, I might almost say, of my whole life, remains so profoundly, painfully, and pathetically imprinted on my remembrance as this very one, on which I tried prelusively, as it were, that same road in solitude, and lulled by the sweet carollings of the postilion, which, *after* an interval of ten years, and *through* a period of more than equal duration, it was destined that I should so often traverse in circumstances of happiness too radiant, that for me are burned out for ever" (II, 357). The time when De Quincey first traveled the road which was to be so important to him later seems to have been a moment when he might have turned in any direction. Now the past is irrevocably over, but then the past was the future. From our position of slavery to the past it is pathetic to remember a time when the future was free.

The most painful element in the memory of the "moment before the moment" is not the contrast between our present slavery and our former freedom. It is the contrast between our present knowledge and our former ignorance. De Quincey's youthful sufferings in London were caused by his rash decision to run away from school. That was in turn caused by the death of his father, the harshness of his guardians, De Quincey's pariah nature, and so on. There is never a moment when we are free, but there are moments when we are ignorant, moments when we see for the first time a place which will be the scene of later joys and sorrows, or meet for the first time a person whose life is to be intertwined with our own. The poignancy of our memory of such moments is the contrast between the way they look now, and the way they seemed then. When we first experienced them they had the lightness, the irresponsibility, of all present moments, moments which seem, when they are happening, to be ends in themselves, to pass lightly and inconsequentially, and to "slip away . . . into the noiseless deeps of the Infinite" (III, 344). Now that we see those moments from the perspective of the future we see that this lightness and virginal irresponsibility were a mirage, that each moment was pregnant with the future, weighted down with the series of consequences which followed from it. It would have been dreadful if we could have foreseen those consequences. No man could

bear to see the past not as the past, but as the future, as something
yet to be undergone:

> Heavens! when I look back to the sufferings which I have witnessed or
> heard of, I say, if life could throw open its long suites of chambers to our
> eyes from some station *beforehand,* — if from some secret stand we could
> look *by anticipation* along its vast corridors, and aside into the recesses open-
> ing upon them from either hand halls of tragedy or chambers of retribution, —
> simply in that small wing and no more of the great caravanserai which we
> ourselves shall haunt, . . . — What a recoil we should suffer of horror in our
> estimate of life! . . . The past viewed not *as* the past, but by a spectator who
> steps back ten years deeper into the rear in order that he may regard it as a
> future . . . [is] strangely moving for all who add deep thoughtfulness to deep
> sensibility. (XIII, 351, 352)

Total memory, which in the opium dreams seemed such a victory over time, is in reality defeat by time. The complete revivifica-
tion of our past as an instantaneous experience puts us in the
position of the man who can stand in some early time and see his
whole life prophetically spread out before him. Even if what followed was joy, it was joy destined to end, as all joys must, for all
men must sooner or later take a wrong turning in the labyrinth.
And to remember lost joy is more painful, surely, than to remember a pain that is past. The palimpsest of the human brain contains indelibly our early happiness, and opium dreams bring back
this happiness, but also bring back, and just as necessarily, "the
deep, deep tragedies of infancy, as when the child's hands were un-
linked for ever from his mother's neck, or his lips for ever from his
sister's kisses" (XIII, 349). The brief moments of joy are recovered,
but also the shattering moments of loss, for "these remain lurking
below all, and these lurk to the last" (XIII, 349). To have the
happy past resurrected in all its freshness and immediacy is the
worst suffering of all, for we relive it with the awful foreknowledge
that it will end. Alongside the passages in De Quincey's writings
which celebrate the joyful miracle of the resurrection of the total
past, there are other passages where he speaks eloquently of the
anguish of affective memory. The past, that frozen city under the
sea, causes suffering because we are forced to relive it again and
again in memory — not as it was, but as something we have lost
forever: "Of all curses, that which searches deepest is the violent
revelation through infinite darkness . . . of a happiness or a glory
which once and for ever has perished. Martyrdom it is, and no

less, to revivify by effect of your own, or passively to see revivified, in defiance of your own fierce resistance, the gorgeous spectacles of your visionary morning life, or of your too rapturous noontide, relieved upon a background of funeral darkness. Such poisonous transfigurations, by which the paradise of youthful hours is forced into distilling demoniac misery for ruined nerves, exist for many a profound sensibility" (V, 304, 305; see also I, 387, and Post. Wks., I, 27).

It would be best to forget everything, and to have total recall, "in point of misery to the patient, must be the next bad thing to being a vampire" (V, 313). It is like being a vampire who sucks his own blood, for the man who is cursed with a good memory is "a fiery *heautontimoroumenos* (or self-tormentor)" (V, 305). So De Quincey tries to consign all the past, happy and unhappy, to oblivion. In one place he is even able to say: "Heaven be praised, I have forgotten everything" (I, 387).

Though he tries to forget, De Quincey's "memory is subject to frightful irregularities of spasmodic energy" (V, 313). In a moment, in spite of his resistance, his memory is startled into involuntary life by some tone of voice or scrap of music, and instantaneously his whole past parades before him in a solemn procession, a procession of those he has loved who have died. Time is a musical continuity, and just as a single bar of some symphony or concerto will cause the whole elaborate structure of which it is a part to leap to life in the listener's mind, so a single echo from the past will immediately resurrect it all. When this happens, a man is seized with a blind hatred, a hatred which seems to be generated by the malignity of some unknown enemy who dwells in the depths of himself. The resurrection of the past seems to be an act of secret malice on the part of his memory, and memory, the power which seemed to extend the bliss of opium dreams from space to time, now appears to be the means by which a man becomes a fiery self-tormentor, and turns the knife in his own heart:

And, as regards myself, touch but some particular key of laughter and of echoing music, sound but for a moment one bar of preparation, and immediately the pomps and glory of all that has composed for me the delirious vision of life re-awaken for torment; the orchestras of the earth open simultaneously to my inner ear; and in a moment I behold, forming themselves into solemn groups and processions, and passing over sad phantom stages, all that chiefly I have loved, or in whose behalf chiefly I have abhorred and cursed the grave — all that should *not* have died, yet died the soonest — the brilliant, the noble, the wise, the innocent, the brave, the beautiful. With these dreadful masks, and under the persecution of their malicious beauty, wakens up the worm that gnaws at the heart. Under that corrosion arises a hatred, blind and vague, and incomprehensible even to one's self, as of some unknown snake-like enemy, in some unknown hostile world, brooding with secret power over the fountains of one's own vitality. (V, 305)

ε∾

The dreamer who is endowed with the power of resurrecting the past is a vampire who drinks the fountains of his own vitality, but what of the similar power which dreams have over space? The climax of opium dreams gives the dreamer a sovereign power over both time and space. Though the power over time has reversed itself and has become an instrument of pain, perhaps the power over space will remain unequivocally good.

The dreamer's experience of space undergoes a transformation exactly analogous to the change in his experience of time. This transformation is the most dreadful of all. In *all* its effects, "opium is mysterious; mysterious to the extent, at times, of apparent self-contradiction" (III, 414), and the man who answers its call follows "an unknown, shadowy power, leading [he knows] not whither, and a power that might suddenly change countenance upon this unknown road" (III, 416).

The present moment of time is the medium of our experience of space, as of our experience of the past. Under the magical influence of opium both the present moment of time and the space which we apprehend in that moment are enormously aggrandized. It is no longer a question of the simultaneous repetition of the events of the past in the present instant of time, but of a horrifying expansion of space, and a corresponding amplification of the instant of time in which we perceive that space: "The sense of space, and in the end the sense of time, were both powerfully affected. Buildings, landscapes, &c., were exhibited in proportions so vast as the bodily eye is not fitted to receive. Space swelled, and was amplified to an extent of unutterable and self-repeating infinity. This disturbed me very much less than the vast expansion of time. Sometimes I seemed to have lived for seventy or a hundred years in one night; nay, sometimes had feelings representative of a duration far beyond the limits of any human experience" (III, 435). The present moment, so small as to be almost nothing, and the space which is apprehended in that moment, swell out, under the influence of opium, to be gigantic in extent, for "one minute, nay, without exaggeration, a much less space of time, [can be] stretched out in [our] apprehension of things to a wearisome duration" (IV, 346). What are the contents of this point of consciousness, this brief "space of time" which has now expanded to infinity?

Its contents are, first of all, a "deep-seated anxiety and funereal melancholy, such as are wholly incommunicable by words" (III, 435). This anxiety and melancholy take a specific form: the sense of descending or falling into fathomless depths. Such dreams of infinite expansion show what it means to live in a space which transcends its contents and extends forever in all directions. Such a space De Quincey describes in a passage from John Paul which he twice adapts: "End is there none to the Universe of God? Lo! also THERE IS NO BEGINNING" (VIII, 34; see also XI, 291). If space is endless, so also is time, as in the Ceylonese legend, recalled by De Quincey, in which an angel, once every century, brushes with the hem of his garment, "as dreamily as a moonbeam," a large granite block, all of whose substance must be worn away before time is done (VIII, 370, 371). In opium dreams the helpless dreamer has a direct and personal experience of this double endlessness: "a killing sense of eternity and infinity" (III, 443). To apprehend such "bottomless abysses" (VIII, 370) is to feel oneself falling eternally into them, and this is the form taken by the opium-eater's anxiety and melancholy: "I seemed every night to descend . . . into chasms and sunless abysses, depths below depths, from which it seemed hopeless that I could ever re-ascend. Nor did I, by waking, feel that I *had* re-ascended" (III, 435).

These sunless abysses are not empty. They are filled with the contents of De Quincey's dreams. And whether these dreams are of Roman or of English history, of the palatial architecture of vast cities, of expanses of water, crowds of faces, or, finally, of abhorrent Asiatic, Egyptian, and jungle scenery, there is one quality of the dreams which makes them so horrible: their inexhaustible power of self-reproduction. It is not necessarily the contents of the dreams which are terrifying, but the fact that these materials, whatever they may be, are "split into a thousand fantastic variations" (III, 444). Even a pleasant dream, when "multiplied into ten thousand repetitions," becomes something before which we stand "loathing and fascinated" (III, 443).

This lowest depth of De Quincey's experience might be called "the Piranesi effect," taking the name from the most famous such passage in his writings. This motif appears very often in De Quincey, and is one of the fundamental habits of his mind. It is the power which the mind has to sink into its own infinite abyss, not by emptying itself out, but by becoming trapped in some form of thought or mental experience which is repeated forever. This produces a vertigo like that caused by the endless multiplications of a single face in a hall of mirrors. Versions of the Piranesi effect have been noted at crucial moments of De Quincey's experience, as in the "flight and pursuit" of God's throne in his vision after his sister's death, or in the logical conundrums in which his mind can circle endlessly, or even in his habit of writing footnotes to his footnotes. The motif is most dramatic when it is a repetition which seems to sink deeper and deeper into infinity, as deep opens beneath deep. Infinity is a mere abstract idea. The Piranesi effect bodies it forth and gives it a palpable form. It is De Quincey's most vivid experience of what it means to live in a world where time and space stretch endlessly in any direction, and where God has withdrawn himself to an infinite distance. To remain passively where he is is not to apprehend these infinities at all. It is precisely when he is moving, and even moving rapidly, repeating forever his approach toward infinity, and *still* not catching it, that he most closely approximates with his finite imagination the infinity with which he is surrounded.

De Quincey recalls the play within a play in *Hamlet,* and compares this to a room on whose wall is a picture of the room, on whose wall is a picture of the room, on whose wall is a picture of the room . . . , and says "we might imagine this descent into a life below a life going on *ad infinitum*" (X, 344). In his astronomical essay, he imagines a galaxy which is continually receding further into "aboriginal darkness," but continually being brought into visibility again, in a constantly repeated reappearance. This happens because the light previously diffused is now more concentrated and produces a brighter image (VIII, 22). Elsewhere he defends from the strictures of Maria Edgeworth Milton's line, "And in the lowest deep a lower deep still opens to devour me": ". . . in cases of deep imaginative feeling, no phenomenon is more natural than precisely this never-ending growth of one colossal grandeur chasing and surmounting another, or of abysses that swallowed up abysses" (X, 416). The best expression of the Piranesi effect is a passage in the "Confessions," the passage about Piranesi himself.

De Quincey remembers, from Coleridge's description, Piranesi's "Carceri," those strange engravings which depict monstrous underground prisons, with staircases, balconies, and bridges leading upward and downward in repetitive series, and disappearing above, below, and in all directions in shadowy glooms, where we imagine staircases still climbing or descending without end. These plates express, more graphically than any other work of art, the "killing sense of eternity and infinity," eternity and infinity as the everlasting repetition of the same inability to make progress. A man could climb these staircases interminably, repeating again and again the act of climbing, and still not be any closer to the surface. However fast he might climb, he would, in this "world-without-ending-ness," only be "covering the ground rapidly, and yet not advancing an inch" (VI, 154).

The plate which De Quincey remembers from Coleridge's description expresses the motif of eternal repetition even more dramatically than this. It repeats not only the staircase, but the climber himself. This motif of "endless self-multiplication" (VI, 226) occurs elsewhere in De Quincey, and it always inspires in him a peculiar horror, as when he describes the uncanny "Specter of the Brocken," that apparition of the mists which imitates exactly every movement of the terrified onlooker (I, 51–54), or as when he declares that he would murder his *Doppelgänger* if he should meet him (XI, 460, 461). In another place De Quincey affirms that the apex of "dream-horror" is the multiplication of the self within the self, until innumerable alien natures struggle for mastery there: "But the dream-horror which I speak of is far more frightful. The dreamer finds housed within himself — occupying, as it were, some separate chamber in his brain — holding, perhaps, from that station a secret and detestable commerce with his own heart — some horrid alien nature. What if it were his own nature repeated, — still, if the duality were distinctly perceptible, even that — even this mere numerical double of his own consciousness — might be a curse too mighty to be sustained. But how if the alien nature contradicts his own, fights with it, perplexes and confounds it? How, again, if not one alien nature, but two, but three, but four, but five, are introduced within what once he thought the inviolable sanctuary of himself?" (XIII, 292). Just such a horrid reduplication of the self takes place in the Piranesi engraving, and this doubling of the self added to the doubling of the scene multiplies horror by horror in geometrical progression.[14]

In De Quincey's description, the same staircase is repeated again and again, fading into the upper distance, and again and again we see Piranesi himself, each time a little closer to the top, as Achilles each time is a little closer to the tortoise without ever being able to catch it. In this case it is not victory which awaits the runner, but a plunge into limitless depths. The upper end of each staircase hangs in the void, and if Piranesi should ever reach the top an infinity of climbing will be followed by an infinity of falling. This scene, says De Quincey, is an exact representation of the repetitions of his opium dreams (III, 438, 439).

What is it that the dreamer must repeat forever, in a thousand fantastic variations, which "suddenly re-combine, lock back into startling unity, and restore the original dream" (III, 444)? The content of the dreams is nothing else but the past of the dreamer: ". . . these dreams, and this dream scenery, drew their outlines and materials — their great lights and shadows — from those profound revelations which had been ploughed so deeply into the heart, . . . [and] had been burned into the undying memory by the fierce action of misery" (III, 413). At the lowest depth of De Quincey's experience is the theme of the eternal return. Every act we commit, every thought, every accidental encounter, every shat-

---

[14] The picture which De Quincey describes does not actually exist among Piranesi's "Prisons." It is, as Henri Focillon says, an "interprétation toute subjective," and is apparently based entirely on De Quincey's memory of Coleridge's description. There is no evidence that De Quincey ever actually saw the "Carceri," and no way to tell whether it is Coleridge or De Quincey who has invented an engraving which contains in essence the effect of Piranesi's whole series. (See Henri Focillon, *Giovanni-Battista Piranesi* [Paris, 1918], pp. 301, 302, and see also Aldous Huxley, *Prisons; with the "Carceri" etchings by G. B. Piranesi and a Critical Study by Jean Adhémar* [London, 1949] for a further discussion of the "Carceri" and their influence on nineteenth- and twentieth-century writers, of whom De Quincey is one of the earliest.)

tering loss — all these we are doomed to experience not once, but innumerable times. Each event in our lives will haunt us in the future, and must be re-endured forever, not only in its consequences, but in itself, as it returns in its endlessly spiraling courses.

Even the "first" experience of anything is never really the first, but is only another repetition of something we have done innumerable times before, perhaps in another world. When De Quincey first saw the Lake Country he had a strange sense that he had already seen it, and that it was destined to be the scene of important events in his life. And he had a recurrent dream of a woman standing in grief at a cottage door, a dream which was later fulfilled in reality by his wife, or rather it was once again incarnated in reality, for who knows how often it had happened before? De Quincey's experience of *déjà vu* ties together past, present, and future. The present is suddenly experienced as a mysterious repetition of some half-remembered past, and this lightninglike revelation is a guarantee that the present will be repeated yet again in the future: "What man has not . . . some time hushed his spirit and questioned with himself whether some things seen or obscurely felt, were not anticipated as by mystic foretaste in some far halcyon time, post-natal or ante-natal he knew not; only assuredly he knew that for him past and present and future merged in one awful moment of lightning revelation" (Post. Wks., I, 16).

After this final revelation, the discovery that "the love and the languishing, the ruin and the horror, of this world are but moments — but elements in an eternal circle" (Post. Wks., I, 26, 27), De Quincey is paralyzed. In a number of passages he describes himself as frozen with horror, oppressed as with a great weight of remembrance or guilt, unable to move a muscle, and lying down passively to yield himself to his fate:

> The palsy of doubt and distraction hangs like some guilty weight of dark unfathomed remembrances upon my energies when the signal is flying for *action*. (XIII, 311)

> I . . . had the power, and yet had not the power, to decide it. I had the power, if I could raise myself to will it; and yet again had not the power, for the weight of twenty Atlantics was upon me, or the oppression of inexpiable guilt. (III, 446)[15]

[15] See also III, 316, 433, and H. A. Eaton, *Thomas De Quincey: A Biography* (New York, 1936), p. 127.

The key phrases here are "dark unfathomed remembrances" and "oppression of inexpiable guilt." Faced with an instant call to action, De Quincey cannot move a muscle. He is weighted down by a guilt which is a legacy from the past, an unfathomed remembrance. His crime is simply his "undying memory." He is paralyzed by the call to action because of an indistinct feeling that to act is once more to commit the crime of adding something to the city under the sea, something which is fated, like all the rest, to return again and again. It would be better not to act at all.

This fear of action explains why De Quincey was an eternal procrastinator, and had such great difficulty finishing any work he undertook. Like Coleridge, he was "tainted with the infirmity of leaving works unfinished, and suffering reactions of disgust" (V, 208). He left the works unfinished *because* he suffered reactions of disgust, reactions generated by the sudden awareness that he was adding one more straw to the enormous burden of the past. Halfway through an essay or a letter this recognition would come, a paralyzing nausea would seize him, and the incomplete fragment would be added to the great pile of papers which was gradually filling his room. Just this explanation of his inability to finish anything is given in a letter to Miss Mitford, a letter which describes most vividly "the undecipherable horror that night and day broods over [his] nervous system." But the undecipherable is here deciphered, for De Quincey says that the "dark frenzy of horror" which overspreads the page he is writing and prevents him from going on seems to be a revelation from eternity, an eternity "not coming, but past and irrevocable." This glimpse of the eternity of the irrevocable past generates a violent recoil of disgust. He cannot bear to look at the hateful paper, and sweeps it away into the "chaos of papers" (Page, I, 350) which overflows his room. Only by leaving the paper unfinished will he have any chance to escape its eternal consequences, and the recognition of this causes his frenzy of horror (Page, I, 340).

This horror is the endpoint of De Quincey's long exploration of his plight after the death of his sister and the withdrawal of God. Opium dreams are no permanent escape from suffering. They only make it possible for him to experience the true nature of his situation. He is an infinitesimal speck of consciousness an infinite distance from its own inner depths. Those depths are the mirror image of the external infinities of space and time, astronomical abysses where God is present only as an ungraspable absence, and where the benign Memnon head has been transmuted into the frightful face in the nebula of Orion. Lost in the abysses within and without, his fate, after all his attempts to escape, is to spiral ceaselessly in echoing repetitions of the definitive event in his life: the death of his sister and his exile from Paradise, the "everlasting farewells" with which it all began. Having gone from Our Lady of Tears to Our Lady of Sighs, the *Mater Suspiriorum* who rules over the "Pariah Worlds," it seemed as if it might be possible, in opium dreams or through writing, to create an artificial paradise to replace the lost Paradise of childhood. But the attempt to do this leads De Quincey inevitably into the realm of the most dreadful sister of all, "and *her* name is *Mater Tenebrarum,* — Our Lady of Darkness" (XIII, 368). Under *her* aegis falls the man who has tried to make a tolerable resting place of the Pariah Worlds. He is led deeper and deeper into "utter darkness, as of some suicidal despondency" (III, 435). Hating himself, he is even led to hate and defy the God who seems so cruelly to have turned his face from his innocent victim. Our Lady of Darkness "is the defier of God. She also is the mother of lunacies, and the suggestress of suicides. Deep lie the roots of her power; but narrow is the nation that she rules. For she can approach only those in whom a profound nature has been upheaved by central convulsions; in whom the heart trembles and the brain rocks under conspiracies of tempest from without and tempest from within" (XIII, 368).

Thus perishes De Quincey's attempt to be the "homme-dieu," to create a human equivalent of the perfect equilibrium, simultaneity, and ubiquity of God.

 è

Madonna spoke. . . . "And thou," — turning to the *Mater Tenebrarum,* she said, — "wicked sister, that temptest and hatest, do thou take him . . . See that thy sceptre lie heavy on his head. . . . Banish the frailties of hope; wither the relenting of love; scorch the fountains of tears; curse him as only *thou* canst curse. So shall he be accomplished in the furnace; so shall he see the things that ought *not* to be seen, sights that are abominable, and secrets that are unutterable. So shall he read elder truths, sad truths, grand truths, fearful truths. So shall he rise again *before* he dies. And so shall our commission be accomplished which from God we had, — to plague his heart until we had unfolded the capacities of his spirit." (XIII, 368, 369)

The end of De Quincey's spiritual adventure, strangely enough, is not permanent submission to Our Lady of Darkness. The end is resurrection, reconciliation, peace, escape from the wheel of the eternal return. Having reached the depths of suffering and dereliction, he is suddenly free. He rises again, and *before* he dies. The way down is the way up. But how can this be?

The explanation of how it can be is the subtlest part of De Quincey's thought, and the most difficult to grasp.

God is in perfect equilibrium as to all of his qualities. He is everywhere at all times, and does not need to go through a series of mediate steps to reach any goal. Everything for man is finite and transitory. Everything flows away toward death. "But in God there is nothing finite; but in God there is nothing transitory; but in God there *can* be nothing that tends to death. Therefore it follows that for God there can be no present. The future is the present of God . . ." (XIII, 361). A striking formulation! De Quincey does not say, as do many theologians, that God has a perpetual present of immediacy to all events. God has no present at all, for the present means the infinite velocity of the finite in its flight toward death. God's time is the future, that time when all presents will have flowed into the past. In God's time all time is fulfilled, and the dreadful hemorrhage of time has stopped.

Only such a cessation of motion would satisfy man's longing for peace, for all men have "agreed in tending to peace and absolute repose, as the state in which only a sane constitution of feelings can finally acquiesce" (V, 103). "Peace, then, severe tranquillity, the brooding calm, or γαλήνη of the Greeks, is the final key into which all the storms of passion modulate themselves . . . All tumult is for the sake of rest — tempest, but the harbinger of calm — and suffering, good only as the condition of permanent repose" (V, 106).

How can man find peace? All human life is evil, because even the good ends in suffering and loss. At the moment of a man's birth, if he could foresee his life, "one earliest instinct of fear and horror would darken his spirit" (XIII, 351). The only hope is some happy obliteration of all that pain, and perhaps a resurrection into the peace of God. But just the opposite seems to happen.

Man's suffering is not the condition of permanent repose. It is the condition of ever-renewed suffering. And God's present, which is the future, what of that? The divine future is the moment when all time, having happened, has flowed into the past. Does this mean that God is the apocalypse of the eternal return, that he must endure, in his perpetual future, the eternal happening and rehappening of all the events of time? To die, then, would mean being joined to a God who suffers the eternal repetition not of one finite lifetime of suffering and sorrow, but of the whole mighty pageant of suffering from Adam to the last man. This would be frightful! For God to have nothing that tends to death would mean for God to be the eternal resurrection of all dead things. Could this be the "mighty relation between God and death" which De Quincey glimpsed as he stood by his dead sister?

God does not inflict this worst of evils on man. He is, in spite of appearances, a good God. He decrees that evil and suffering shall come to an end at last. Only good participates in the goodness of God and lasts forever. There is "something perishable in evil," and "what is evil by nature or by origin must be transient" (VIII, 224, 225). De Quincey explains this by his theory of the varying *"aeons"* of things.[16] An *aeon*, he says, is "the duration or cycle of existence which belongs to any object, not individually for itself, but universally in right of its genus . . ." (Hogg, 308). It is a great mistake to assume that the *aeons* of all things are the same, for a direct corollary of this proposition would be the idea of the eternity of evil. On the contrary, everything in the world has its own *aeon*, and is in "harmony with the secret proportions of a heavenly scale" (Hogg, 310). God is like a great master-clock whose mighty revolution is an eternal *aeon*. And all things less than God, all things which are "heterogeneous, — evil mixed with good" (VIII, 225), have their own little circlings marked out on the great clock. The *aeons* of all things less than God are finite, for, since all things less than God are a mixture of good and evil, "the two natures, by their mutual enmity, must enter into a collision which may possibly guarantee the final destruction of the whole compound" (VIII, 225). At the dissolution of a finite entity, compound of good

---

[16] "On the Supposed Scriptural Expression for Eternity," *The Instructor* (January 1853), reprinted in James Hogg, *De Quincey and His Friends* (London, 1895), pp. 295–313. This will be cited hereafter as "Hogg."

and evil, the "fugitive" evil disappears, and the good rises to eternal communion with God, for God is the only entity whose *aeon* lasts forever, world without end:

> I separately, speaking for myself only, profoundly believe that the Scriptures ascribe absolute and metaphysical eternity to one sole Being, *viz.*, to God; and derivatively to all others according to the interest which they can plead in God's favour. Having anchorage in God, innumerable entities may possibly be admitted to a participation in divine *aeon*. But what interest in the favour of God can belong to falsehood, to malignity, to impurity? To invest *them* with aeonian privileges, is in effect, and by its results, to distrust and to insult the Deity. Evil would *not* be evil, if it had that power of self-subsistence which is imputed to it in supposing its aeonian life to be co-eternal with that which crowns and glorifies the good. (Hogg, 312, 313)

This passage is of crucial importance for De Quincey. In the clearest way it provides the rationale for his escape from the apparently inescapable wheel of the eternal return. Armed with this passage we can interpret the full text of De Quincey's sentence about the time of God. "The future," he says, "is the present of God, and to the future it is that he sacrifices the human present" (XIII, 361). The human present is chiefly evil, the evil, most often, of unmerited suffering. Even the good, such as the bliss of innocent childhood, is turned into an evil by the lifelong reverberative echoes of its inevitable loss. But all this evil has its *aeon*, and has been marked out on the divine clock since all eternity. It must come into being, and be repeated for so many times, in its effects and in the memory of the one who suffers it, *in order to be able to die.*

This explains why "Levana and Our Ladies of Sorrow" ends with such an unexpected reversal of the downward spiral. Having descended successively through the more and more gloomy realms of Tears, Sighs, and Darkness, a man is suddenly, at the last moment, raised up. The name of the goddess Levana, who presides over the three ladies of sorrow, means "she who raises aloft." In De Quincey's world a man descends in order that he may be raised up. It is only by having "the capacities of his spirit" "unfolded" through suffering that he can "rise again *before* he dies." So much suffering is his allotted fate in "the secret proportions of a heavenly scale." Only when he has exhausted that measure of pain which is his own *aeon* as a creature of mixed evil and good can he escape the wheel of suffering, consign his evil to eternal oblivion, and enter, by right of his anchorage in the divine good, into eternal participation in God's *aeon*.

Many of De Quincey's works have just this pattern of a descent deeper and deeper into hopeless darkness, followed at the last moment by a sudden ascent into light. This movement is the basic pattern of his narrative art, appearing in "Klosterheim," his longest story (XII, 5–156), in "The Daughter of Lebanon" (III, 450–456), in the "Dream-Fugue" attached to "The Vision of Sudden Death" (XIII, 318–327), in his essay on Joan of Arc (V, 384–416), and in "Revolt of the Tartars" (VII, 368–426). "Revolt of the Tartars" describes the crescendo of sufferings endured by a tribe during their epic journey across the wilderness of central Asia to the borders of China. As the Tartars are pursued and gradually decimated by the Russians, their experience is "one vast climax of anguish, towering upwards by regular gradations, as if constructed artificially for picturesque effect" (VII, 393). In the end, just when all seems about to be lost in a frenzy of carnage, they are saved by the Chinese army, and their hell is turned suddenly to heaven.

In the same way, the "Dream-Fugue" ends with this sentence: "A thousand times, amongst the phantoms of sleep, have I seen thee . . . followed by God's angel through storms, through desert seas, through the darkness of quicksands, through dreams and the dreadful revelations that are in dreams; only that at the last, with one sling of His victorious arm, He might snatch thee back from ruin, and might emblazon in thy deliverance the endless resurrections of His love!" (XIII, 326, 327). De Quincey interprets the central mysteries of Christianity as just this mixture of descent and ascent. Man could, through the crucifixion, rise victorious over death, but only because God himself had descended into the abyss of death. A divine height and an infernal depth were brought together on the cross: "There it was, indeed, that the human had risen on wings from the grave; but, for that reason, there also it was that the divine had been swallowed up by the abyss; the lesser star could not rise, before the greater should submit to eclipse" (I, 40).

Is death itself the liberation from suffering? That would contradict the assertion that "he shall rise again *before* he dies." And how can we reconcile the idea of an escape from the wheel of suffering with the experience, in opium dreams, of the *eternal* return of the same suffering?

It is not death which is the liberation — not death, but the moment before death. In this moment, and only in this moment, can a man rise again before he dies. The moment of dying has no earthly future. In another moment the evil of the life of the dying man will be consigned to oblivion, and the good will be joined to God. The last moment of life can never return to haunt the memory of the dying man in eternal resurrections, and it cannot be the first link in a causal chain which will reverberate down his future life to curse him with its consequences.

How can there be an end to what seems the eternal return of the past? The answer lies in De Quincey's recognition of the sham eternity which lies in a finite space of time. A few instants of time can stretch out interminably in the apprehension of the opium dreamer. These few instants can be infinitely divided, until it seems that there is room in them for perpetual repetitions of the past moment of loss, in Piranesi-like self-multiplication. This infinitude of the finite exists only in the mind of the dreamer. The moment passes in its own good time, though it seems eternal to the dreamer. So eventually pass all the allotted moments of a man's life, filled though they may be with the experience of what seems the eternal return of the same suffering. Each man has his *aeon*. The last moment of life comes at last, and that last moment is the final repetition of the Paradise of childhood and its loss. "But love," says De Quincey, "which is *altogether* holy, like that between two children, is privileged to revisit by glimpses the silence and the darkness of declining years; and, possibly, this final experience in my sister's bedroom, or some other in which her innocence was concerned, may rise again for me to illuminate the clouds of death" (I, 43).

Beyond the last moment, the last repetition of that which has bound the whole life into unity, lies — not God, but the solitude of the blue sky with its empty depths. God, we remember, has withdrawn to an infinite distance, and at the moment of dying each man is still a weary way from heaven. But the encounter with death shows, in a burst of revelation, that God has been present in the world all along. He has been present precisely where nothing else is, and the empty blue sky is the exact image of his presence in the world. God is present in all negative things: in emptiness, loss, solitude, and grief, in all those experiences which seem to a man to open gulfs in himself into which he might fall forever. In John Paul's "Dream upon the Universe," which entered so deeply into De Quincey's imagination, the angelic being takes the dreamer through astronomical distances until, after miraculous journeys, they have passed through all the nebulae, galaxies, and milky ways, and finally reach a place which is empty. The dreamer is horrified by this emptiness, but his conductor tells him that this vacuum is the very presence of God. He is granted a vision of "those unseen depths of the Universe which are emptied of all but the Supreme Reality" (XI, 293). God is the negative image of the creation, dwelling wherever the creation is not: "Then my heart comprehended that immortality dwelled in the spaces between the worlds, and death only amongst the worlds" (XI, 292). In the same way the culmination of De Quincey's experience of the death of his sister is a revelation of the proximity of solitude and grief to God. Just as the cloudless summer sky is an expression of the immanence of God experienced as an absence, so grief and solitude seem to cast a man into the depths, but actually raise him up into communion with God:

> Grief! thou art classed amongst the depressing passions. And true it is that thou humblest to the dust, but also thou exaltest to the clouds. . . . in solitude, above all things, . . . God holds with children "communion undisturbed." Solitude, though it may be silent as light, is, like light, the mightiest of agencies; for solitude is essential to man. All men come into this world *alone;* all leave it *alone.* . . . The solitude, therefore, which in this world appals or fascinates a child's heart, is but the echo of a far deeper solitude, through which already he has passed, and of another solitude, deeper still, through which he *has* to pass: reflex of one solitude — prefiguration of another. (I, 44, 48)

Solitude, with the grief that belongs to it, is man's way of experiencing the abyss which separates him from God. It is also his way of holding communion with God. Man knows God through the absence of God. Solitude broods over every heart, "like the Spirit of God moving upon the surface of the deeps," for solitude is "like the vast laboratory of the air, which, seeming to be nothing, or less than the shadow of a shade, hides within itself the

principles of all things" (I, 48). The solitude of childhood or mid-
life is really only a prefiguration of "the final solitude" which man
will face "within the gates of death" (I, 49). We must pass through
death, the ultimate solitude, in order to reach God. *This* is the
"mighty relation between God and death" which De Quincey
glimpsed in his vision of the eternal flight and pursuit of God's
throne in the far blue sky, for the empty air is a negative image of
God. At the moment of death, we shall experience a fathomless
solitude, but through it we shall also experience, by anticipation,
our reconciliation with God and with all we lost when we were
exiled from the Paradise of childhood. De Quincey, after his sister's
death, sees in the white clouds beyond the church windows a vision
of dying children rising slowly through the gulf between them and
God. Through that "dreadful chasm of separation" they "*must*
pass slowly*" (I, 47), for they cannot come instantaneously to God.
In another description of the moment of dying, De Quincey imagines that Joan of Arc, on the fiery scaffold, recaptures her happy
childhood, but this time without the dark foreknowledge of the
suffering that was to follow it. The last moment of life is the only
moment which cannot be shadowed by premonitions of loss: "By
special privilege for *her* might be created, in this farewell dream,
a second childhood, innocent as the first; but not, like *that,* sad
with the gloom of a fearful mission in the rear" (V, 414).

And so, finally, De Quincey's own last moments, strangely
enough, fulfill his prophecy that a reunion with his sister would
illuminate the clouds of his death. At the moment of dying he experiences for the last time a repetition of the pains of his life, and
then he enters anew, after the whole circular *aeon* of separation
from it, the Paradise of childhood. But now this Paradise is secure
forever. The evil dies, and the good is affirmed in its permanence.
The "eternal circle" is completed at last. De Quincey's penultimate speech is apparently a confession of the guilt he felt toward
his mother for his disobedient flight from school into a life of
wandering. The last words of all show, across the widening gulf
of death, that De Quincey found his sister again at the last moment of his life, and that he did indeed "rise again before he
died":

Twice only was the heavy breathing interrupted by words. He had for
hours ceased to recognise any of us, but we heard him murmur, though quite

distinctly, "My dear, dear mother. Then I was greatly mistaken." Then as the waves of death rolled faster and faster over him, suddenly out of the abyss we saw him throw up his arms, which to the last retained their strength, and say distinctly, and as if in great surprise, "Sister! sister! sister!" The loud breathing became slower and slower, and as the world of Edinburgh awoke to busy work and life, all that was mortal of my father fell asleep for ever.[17]

[17] Page, II, 305; the words are those of one of De Quincey's daughters.

✺§ III §✺

Robert Browning

The real way seemed made up of all the ways —
Mood after mood of the one mind in him;
Tokens of the existence, bright or dim,
Of a transcendent all-embracing sense
Demanding only outward influence,
A soul, in Palma's phrase, above his soul,
Power to uplift his power, — such moon's control
Over such sea-depths, — and their mass had swept
Onward from the beginning and still kept
Its course: but years and years the sky above
Held none, and so, untasked of any love,
His sensitiveness idled, now amort,
Alive now, and, to sullenness or sport
Given wholly up, disposed itself anew
At every passing instigation, grew
And dwindled at caprice . . .[1]

At the beginning Browning is a huge sea — massive, limitless, profound, but, at the same time, shapeless, fluid, and capricious. His surroundings crowd in from all directions with a suffocating pressure, like "lukewarm brine," "green-dense and dim-delicious, bred o' the sun" (IV, 293), or like "one warm rich mud-bath" (VII, 392). But it is not enough to say that Browning is pressed in on all sides by a great bulk of matter. He *is* that matter, that ocean, that "protoplasm" (IX, 180). His body is the whole mass of the ocean, and his mind is dispersed everywhere throughout that ocean, to its farthest depths. Browning can convey in his poetry an extraordinary sense of the way consciousness flows out through the senses, plunges into the secret substance of the surrounding world, knows it from the inside, as one's own viscera are known, and gradually

---

[1] F. G. Kenyon, ed., *The Works of Robert Browning*, Centenary Edition in Ten Volumes (London, 1912), I, 334. Numbers in parentheses after texts refer to volume and page numbers in this edition.

spreads to the farthest reaches of the universe — reaches which are
still intimately apprehended, even if only indistinctly. Or, it would
be equally true to say that the world invades and engulfs the self,
flowing in to fill every cranny of consciousness, until the mind is
no longer outside of anything, but has everything inside itself.
Consciousness permeates the world as heat and light irradiate molten metal, or "As if in pure water you dropped and let die/A
bruised black-blooded mulberry" (III, 358), or "As saffron tingeth
flesh, blood, bones and all!" (IV, 92).

Just as Browning has no separate individuality, so the universal
substance of the world has no form. It is as shapeless as the sea,
as the potter's clay, or as the primeval ooze from which all things
have yet to be made. It is "one blank mud-mixture" (VII, 313).
Just as Browning's language often seems about to collapse back
into an incoherent mutter, so the world itself, for him, is always
in danger of sinking back into shapelessness — for "the monstrous
wild" is "a-hungered to resume/Its ancient sway, suck back the
world into its womb" (IX, 235). Browning too, like the total world
which is his huge body, has an impulse to return to this primal
chaos, for he has "a need, a trust, a yearning after God" (I, 11),
and the original slime is closer to God than any finite object. Any
shaped thing betrays its failure to be everything. But the primal
chaos is potentially anything and everything. It is a negative image
of God.

This vast Browning-sea is full of motion, an indistinct trembling
and swelling. It moves because of its potency. Obscure "detona-
tions, fulgurations" (IX, 151) stir its "turbidity" (X, 157); an
"energy . . . streams/Flooding the universe" (X, 166). An apparently anarchic force breaks up every fixed state for the sake of
the creation of future forms. Exploding what is now out of stagnation, it is an organizing power sweeping through the universe, and
driving it onward toward ever more complicated forms of life. It
is:

> . . . that originative force
> Of nature, impulse stirring death to life,
> Which, underlying law, seems lawlessness,
> Yet is the outbreak which, ere order be,
> Must thrill creation through, warm stocks and stones,
> Phales Iacchos. (VIII, 75)

Browning's sea of matter is "a-shine,/Thick-steaming, all-alive" (I, 209). It bubbles and heaves with latent life, and holds in its pregnant depths the seeds of all possible forms. All is "a-seethe within the gulf" (X, 242), and this seething ocean is "stocked with germs of torpid life" (IX, 152). It squirms with vitality, like a corpse full of maggots, or like a stagnant pond full of "leeches quick,/And circling blood-worms, minnow, newt or loach" (I, 210): "From edge to edge/Of earth's round, strength and beauty everywhere/Pullulate . . ." (X, 187).

The whole viscous bulk of the world sways this way and that, taking first one form and then another, disposing itself anew "at every passing instigation." Each seed of potential life struggles to "wriggle clear of protoplasm" (IX, 180), and to establish itself as a separate life. Each is "an universe in germ — /The dormant passion needing but a look," or some other stimulus, "To burst into immense life!" (X, 305). But every tendency to form is frustrated by the anarchic swarming of "All that life and fun and romping,/All that frisking and twisting and coupling" (III, 123). Each seed of life is a *universe* in germ. It would sovereignly dominate the whole sea. This impulse is resisted by all the other equally imperious forces. The universe, for Browning, like the self which coincides with it, is a struggle of immense irreconcilable forces locked in elemental combat. It is "A teeming crust — /Air, flame, earth, wave at conflict!" (I, 318).

A recurrent image of molten rock imprisoned in the earth expresses Browning's sense of the violent impulse toward form which must fight its way through the restraining weight of the whole world. Only if it is stronger than this massive inertia can "the ore that grows in the mountain's womb" (III, 358) break forth into the open, wriggle clear, and realize the form it latently contains. So Diana, the perfection of human form, appears to have been "bred of liquid marble in the dark/Depths of the mountain's womb which ever teemed/With novel births of wonder . . ." (X, 228).

This latent impulse to take form exists in many ways throughout the universe. Sometimes Browning describes the power of stagnant salt-water to crystallize, sometimes the birth of volcanoes, sometimes the bursting into bloom of boughs in the spring, sometimes the sudden appearance of mushrooms on moss, sometimes the horrible spread of a parasitical growth on the human body, sometimes the creeping growth of a seaplant which will ultimately overwhelm great rocks with its remorseless proliferation (I, 340, 153, 161, 162; III, 203; I, 123, 138, 185, 186).

Massive substance, a seething diffused energy, a shaping force urging the shapeless bulk toward form — these make up the initial Browningesque self and Browningesque world. To say that the self is a bubbling cauldron of contradictory impulses is the same as to say that the world itself is a swarming of larvae all dwelling together, crisscrossing, teeming, crushing one another. But all these forms are possible, not actual. The soul is seething with an immense power of life, but so far it is not actually anything or anybody. As Charles Du Bos puts it in a brilliant phrase, Browning's personality is "tout ensemble la plus massive et la plus poreuse qui fut jamais." [2] Just as his soul is in an embryonic state, so the world is at the time of the primal swamp or pregnant mud, when the long evolutionary process leading to the creation of distinct forms has not yet taken place. "That mass man sprung from," says Browning in echo of the evolutionists, "was a jelly-lump/ Once on a time; he kept an after course/Through fish and insect, reptile, bird and beast" (VII, 124). This jelly-lump is the first stage in Browning's itinerary of creation, and the first stage in his own genesis.

Though this combination of great mass and great power seems capable of anything, the jelly-lump is paralyzed by a fundamental contradiction in its impulses. The problem is how to "shoot/ Liquidity into a mould" (X, 241). This solidifying of the liquid must be a fulfillment of all the potentialities of the sea, not a curtailment of them. To choose one form out of the infinite number of possible shapes is to relegate all the others to the limbo of torpid seeds, each "doomed to remain a germ/In unexpanded infancy" (I, 269). Back and forth Browning vacillates between the desire to become some one concrete thing, and the desire to remain permanently uncommitted, and therefore the only material mirror of the infinite richness of God. The intimate movement of his earliest poems, "Pauline," "Paracelsus," and "Sordello," is a repeated process of half-crystallization of the primitive bulk, followed by reliquefaction, and return to the viscous mass of pent-up

[2] *Études Anglaises*, VII (1954), 164.

energy. These poems move between the contrary motions of concentration and expansion, unable to choose between them. On the one hand, Browning cries, "My soul's spark/Expands" (I, 28); on the other he wishes "to circumscribe/And concentrate" himself (I, 200). With immense effort he "turns [his] whole energies to some one end" (I, 21), but scarcely has he done this than a kind of horror of limitation overcomes him. Like Cleon, he is painfully aware of the difference between his poor garden-fountain water-spout and "the great river" he would like to be. For "a man can use but a man's joy/While he sees God's" (IV, 167). When Aprile, in "Paracelsus," tries to limit himself to a single shape, he is assailed by "mist-like influences, thick films," like "whirling snow-drifts" (I, 83) — the irresistible appeal of the other possibilities he has abandoned for the sake of one among them. Unable to resist, he returns again to his original state of formless potency.

One could say that the most pervasive happening in Browning is crystallization leading to discovery of its inadequacy and a return to chaos. This process dominates his obscure inner life, at a deep vegetative level, where the profound organic rhythms of selfhood beat out their measured pulsations, untouched by surface changes, "As fathoms down some nameless ocean thing/[Takes] its silent course of quietness and joy" (I, 10). All the various forms this pattern can take in Browning's poetry are verbal expressions of an organizing form which is the ground swell of his being, and can never be fully expressed in any form. One mode of the relation between form and formlessness is just this irreconcilable opposition between "Soul, the unsounded sea," with its fathomless depths of feeling, and the attempt in art to "Arrest Soul's evanescent moods," "Give momentary feeling permanence," and fix in an unalterable form the "passions rise and fall,/Bursting, subsidence, intermixture" (X, 242,243). The almost insuperable problem is how to bring up from the deeps into the light of day "The abysmal bottom-growth, ambiguous thing/Unbroken of a branch, palpitating/With limbs' play and life's semblance!" (X, 242). Though the pulsation of passion can never be brought alive and intact from the depths, this shaping power governs the surface, and remains the same, whether it is expressed in the rhythmic alternation of solidification and dissolution in "Pauline,"

"Paracelsus," and "Sordello," or in the dominant images of the "Epilogue to Dramatis Personae," "Fifine at the Fair," "Red Cotton Night-Cap Country," "Numpholeptos," the "Parleying with Charles Avison," or "An Essay on Shelley." This pattern appears most pervasively and organically as the heartbeat of Browning's language, the unique tempo of his verse, and the intimate movement of his thought. The structure of "Pauline" and "Sordello" is an unpredictable alternation between conflicting impulses of the spirit. First one is expressed, then another, then the first in a new form, and so on. The rhythm of these poems, and their effect on the reader are well expressed by a passage in "Pauline":

> Thou knowest, dear, I could not think all calm,
> For fancies followed thought and bore me off,
> And left all indistinct; ere one was caught
> Another glanced; so, dazzled by my wealth,
> I knew not which to leave nor which to choose,
> For all so floated, nought was fixed and firm. (I, 29, 30)

These juxtapositions of contradictory impulses, these sudden illogical transitions, these failures to proceed in a straightforward, coherent fashion, by no means disappear from Browning's verse after "Sordello." Toward the end of his life, in particular, the old murkiness returned, for example in the "Parleyings with Certain People of Importance in Their Day." The heart of Browning remains a struggle of irreconcilable forces. In these late poems he begins again to express this struggle directly, and to go back toward the infinitely dense, wholly inexpressible chaos at the center. The true source of the obscurity of Browning's verse is his unwillingness to betray his apprehension of this center. For him the most important experiences are intuitions of indivisible wholes. These wholes can never be expressed in language, for words are the "mere presentment" "of the whole/By parts, the simultaneous and the sole/By the successive and the many," and therefore "perceptions whole . . . reject so pure a work of thought/As language." To express perceptions in words is like trying to make a suit of armor for Proteus (I, 226).

Since no garment of language can never be more than provisional, Browning must be ready at any moment to reconsider even the most basic questions. Even though a particular poem may come to a momentary equilibrium and triumphantly conclude:

"This, then, is established, and I shall hold to it," we know that the next poem will destroy this formulation and begin again. This habit of "Still beginning, ending never" (I, 75) is one of the central characteristics of Browning's thought. Even at the last minute of life he will still be moving, still rejecting the latest expression of the indivisible whole, and still starting over indefatigably to make another, which will only be rejected in its turn.

One way to deal with the incongruity of perception and language is the method of the internal dialogue, as in "Christmas Eve and Easter Day," "La Saisiaz," or the "Parleyings." Rather than speaking as one person, Browning divides himself up into two or more persons who battle with one another, and allow him to sway his thought now this way, now that. Many of his so-called dramatic monologues, such as "Bishop Blougram's Apology," "Prince Hohenstiel-Schwangau," or "Aristophanes' Apology," are really internal dialogues. They juxtapose or intermingle contradictory points of view. These poems are full of sudden shifts from one attitude to another, lappings this way and that, as of a viscous liquid which takes form only to lose it. Back and forth sloshes his thought, like half-frozen water in a bucket, now hopeful, now desponding: "Worst, best,/Change hues of a sudden: now here and now there/Flits the sign which decides: all about yet nowhere" (X, 154). The only thing certain is that the inner dialogue will go on indefinitely, only arbitrarily brought to a conclusion, and chopped off into a poem. At all costs he must keep open, remain in that state of "porous density" which, being nothing, is everything, as the primeval mud holds in germ all evolution. The "Parleyings" and the other inner dialogues, with their interminable garrulous ruminations, are closer to this original state than the dramatic monologues, for in the former he is not one person, one world, one point of view, not even for the duration of a single poem. To tarry too long in any one form would be to risk the "eternal petrifaction" (III, 169) of his spirit, its freezing into a single mold. So he oscillates within the poem back and forth between contradictory impulses, coming as close as he can to satisfying them all at once. Opposing points of view grapple with one another in a close embrace.

The linguistic mirror of these sudden shiftings of point of view is the breathless haste of Browning's language. His words come in bursts of half-coagulated syntax. He starts in the direction of one grammatical expression of thought, stops suddenly in the middle (for *that* way will not say it all), and then rushes off toward another syntactical form which, half complete, is broken again, and another tried, and so on. The dash, the exclamation point, and the colon are Browning's favorite marks of punctuation: full stops, but not complete breaks — the juxtaposition of related linguistic units which are syntactically incompatible:

> Law must be
> Active in earth or nowhere: earth you see, —
> Or there or not at all, Will, Power, and Love
> Admit discovery, — as below, above
> Seek next law's confirmation! (X, 188)

In such passages an immense linguistic energy is prevented from going wholeheartedly in any one direction. It bursts out irrepressibly in a violent splutter, only to be checked as soon as begun by an equally powerful force preventing it from spending all its energy in that one direction. Browning is a "semantic stutterer." [3] He has a great many things to say at once, and they all rush out simultaneously — producing a sentence all dashes and parentheses — a sentence which strives to exist all in a moment: all its parts in the same flash of time, not sequentially. A typical sentence in "La Saisiaz" begins with one metaphorical expression of the idea, stops suddenly, begins again with an entirely different metaphor, stops again, tries to pull itself together by adjuring itself to speak "Plainlier!," and then, far from clarifying, collapses into an incoherent coruscation of dashes, parentheses, broken phrases within phrases. Finally the sentence congeals, lamely and with evident difficulty, in a concluding phrase of characteristic stuttering staccato, grinding to a halt at last with a single word full of little dental and labial explosives:

> If the harsh throes of the prelude die not off into the swell
> Of that perfect piece they sting me to become a-strain for, — if
> Roughness of the long rock-clamber lead not to the last of cliff,
> First of level country where is sward my pilgrim-foot can prize, —
> Plainlier! if this life's conception new life fail to realize, —
> Though earth burst and proved a bubble glassing hues of hell, one huge

[3] See Stewart W. Holmes, "Browning: Semantic Stutterer," *PMLA*, LX (1945), 231–255.

Reflex of the devil's doings — God's work by no subterfuge —
(So death's kindly touch informed me as it broke the glamour, gave
Soul and body both release from life's long nightmare in the grave)
Still, — with no more Nature, no more Man as riddle to be read,
Only my own joys and sorrows now to reckon real instead, —
I must say — or choke in silence — "Howsoever came my fate,
Sorrow did and joy did nowise, — life well weighed, — preponderate."

This syntactical complexity is related to Browning's fondness for words and whole passages full of rough, clotted consonants. Such a love can be seen in his use of grotesque proper names, real or invented: "Bubb Dodington," "Hohenstiel-Schwangau," "Blougram," "Karshish," "Sludge," "Bluphocks," "Sibrandus Schafnaburgensis." He cannot resist the appeal of "some rich name,/Vowel-buds thorned about with consonants,/Fragrant, felicitous, rose-glow enriched/By the Isle's unguent" (VIII, 22). One reason for this appeal is the fact that a word full of bunched consonants, like the burly, muscular rhythm of Browning's verse, is nearer the original shapeless mud. Vowels are more rarefied and spiritual, the "rose-glow," but consonants share the density and viscosity of matter. They are the rose's thorns or "the Isle's unguent": "Rumble and tumble, sleek and rough,/Stinking and savory, smug and gruff . . ." (III, 385).

Browning's poetry is full of such visceral language, but "Sordello" is of course his most sustained effort in obscurity. Its language is a succession of half-solidifications of a heavy murk of words, momentary congealings which soon dissolve or burst, sprinkling us with fragments, like a magic tree which explodes in "bloom-flinders and fruit-sparkles and leaf-dust" (I, 258). Well might he plead with us to accept this strange incoherence, in a passage which describes it perfectly: "Nor slight too much my rhymes — that spring, dispread,/Dispart, disperse, lingering overhead/Like an escape of angels!" (I, 258). Just when the reader thinks the poem is going to come clear at last, opacity sets in again, in a series of phrases which are linguistic fragments, meaningful in themselves, but refusing to come together in a total pattern of meaning. This poem is close to the starting point of Browning's language: an incoherent speech which goes on interminably and refuses to leap into any particular form of language. This is another mode of the tension between form and formlessness. The central bulk is potentially any form of language, and is therefore closer than any single statement to the whole perceptions Browning seeks to express. Browning's language is often close to the inarticulate noise which is the source of all words. In that noise everything is said simultaneously and so not said at all. Such language is a stammering mutter which refuses to commit itself to comprehensible speech, and merely laps back and forth like a sea ungoverned by any moon. It is a kind of incessant murmuring which perhaps goes on even in dreams or in deepest sleep, a murmur which wants to put an end to itself by taking some definite form, but is forced always to reject whatever form it has attained.

There is a close relation between the metaphysical or psychological problems which are dominant in Browning and the specific form his language takes. The language of "Sordello" or the "Parleyings" suggests that Browning does not really want to be clear, precise, and comprehensible. The incoherent particulars of the historical background of "Sordello" are intentionally obscure. They are obscure because it is not the history which Browning seeks to express. Rather, using this, he wants to express, as he says, "the development of a soul," but, one should add, the development of a soul which does not develop, which remains close to the inexhaustible murmur of the language behind language, the formlessness prior to all form.

ॐ

The gigantic amalgam of Browning and the world is not really doomed to remain "mid the slush and ooze" (IX, 160), paralyzed by its inability to choose among possible configurations of its mass. Though Browning often sinks back to this apparently inescapable impasse, he finds even in his earliest work a way to leap beyond it. This leap is made by an act of spontaneous withdrawal from the mass of matter. At the center of all that weight, pressed in by it on all sides, but essentially different from it, is Browning himself, his separate individuality. Just as this self-consciousness isolates itself from the external world, so it even isolates itself from all the qualities and powers of the mind. All the rich affective life of consciousness is foreign to it. This central self is an empty, lucid self-awareness and nothing more:

> I am made up of an intensest life,
> Of a most clear idea of consciousness
> Of self, distinct from all its qualities,
> From all affections, passions, feelings, powers . . . (I, 11)

Browning is both diffused through his body and the world, as water is absorbed by a sponge, and at the same time he is withdrawn from them, an infinitesimal spark of distinct life at the middle point. He is like the center of a sphere, which remains separate, though its radii reach to every part of its volume, or like the sovereign sun, which sheds light uniformly in all directions, but stays an intense spot of fire in undiminished splendor. Browning's selfhood is separate from his body and his feelings, and yet "it exists, if tracked, in all" (I, 11). And in the same way his self-awareness can be tracked everywhere in the surrounding world, but still remains isolated. It exists "as a centre to all things,/Most potent to create and rule and call/Upon all things to minister to it . . ." (I, 11).

Along with self-awareness and the power to expand goes "a principle of restlessness/Which would be all, have, see, know, taste, feel, all—" (I, 11). No lines in Browning better express the expansive energy of his soul, the violent instinct of self-aggrandizement which would know all things, and, knowing them, become them. This process of assimilation is more than "having" or possession, and more than knowing things by that most abstract sense, eyesight. Browning can become only what he "tastes," and, by tasting, makes a part of his own body, so that he can "feel" it from the inside. "Have, see, know, taste, feel"— the line is not a mere series of synonyms for possession, but describes a process whereby what is outside is gradually absorbed, until finally the goal is reached: to be the object. Moreover, Browning's expansive energy is not satisfied with the assimilation of one object or even a great many. His restlessness will not be appeased until it has swallowed up "all" that is. The way this process of assimilative knowledge seems a matter of tasting, swallowing, and digesting is expressed in an extraordinary passage in "Mr. Sludge, the Medium." The senses, says Mr. Sludge, go out from the self like an anteater's long tongue, "soft, innocent, warm, moist, impassible" (IV, 333), and, adhering to the things of the world, make it possible for the self to swallow them up.

If possession of the world is only the result of a long process of "throwing out the sense," then it is not really an initial datum. And in the same moment in which we recognize that the world is other than ourselves, we see that it is not really, as it had appeared, still in a primitive stage of formlessness. The world is full of a great number of created forms, animate and inanimate, all of which have wriggled clear of protoplasm and established their right to exist. Here, as always in Browning, the principle governing the relation between self and world is what might be called a phenomenological one: the world and the self form one indivisible unit, and the way the world appears will depend on the powers of differentiation of the self, as well as on the nature of that world. Now that Browning has withdrawn into lucid self-consciousness he can see that the world is full of actualized germs, "fish and insect, reptile, bird and beast." The problem which in the interior of Browning seems insoluble has long since been solved for the outside world. The world's mass of matter turns out to be big enough to permit the simultaneous development of a multitude of distinct forms. Each quick seed is certainly a "universe in germ." This means, however, not that each seed must assimilate the whole universe, but that each realized form is a unique perspective on the universe. Each seed orders the primitive mud in a certain way, and only this gives rise to the fundamental distinction between the organism itself and what is not the organism. Organization takes place by exclusion as well as by inclusion. A certain part of the primitive stuff is appropriated and ordered in a certain way, but everything else remains alien to the new-formed organism. Each organism is related in its special way to what is outside it. It sees only so much, and from one point of view. As in the philosophy of Nicholas of Cusa, the world is full of centers of life, from each one of which the totality is viewed differently, but all of these can crisscross and intersect without conflict, so harmoniously is their interrelation balanced.

God himself is the shaping force, present everywhere in the universe in a thousand distinct forms, and delighting in the multitudinous variety of his creation. Browning affirms in his own way the doctrine of plenitude, and its corollary, the immanence of God. His God does not seem to be absent at all:

> The grass grows bright, the boughs are swoln with blooms
> Like chrysalids impatient for the air,
> The shining dorrs are busy, beetles run
> Along the furrows, ants make their ado;
> Above, birds fly in merry flocks, the lark
> Soars up and up, shivering for very joy;
> Afar the ocean sleeps; white fishing-gulls
> Flit where the strand is purple with its tribe
> Of nested limpets; savage creatures seek
> Their loves in wood and plain — and God renews
> His ancient rapture. Thus he dwells in all,
> From life's minute beginnings, up at last
> To man — the consummation of this scheme
> Of being, the completion of this sphere
> Of life . . . (I, 162)

God transcends the world, and yet he dwells within even the lowest forms of life. One can equally well say that God contains each form as a mouth contains what it tastes. The gustatory metaphor appears in Browning's definition of God as well as in his description of his own way of knowing the world. His God "tastes an infinite joy/In infinite ways" (I, 161). If God is the stream of energy flooding the universe, God also gives bounds to the flood, and says to each creature: "E'en so,/Not otherwise move or be motionless, — grow,/Decline, disappear!" (X, 273).

Having made the act of self-extrication Browning discovers that there is visible everywhere in the creation a divine power which not only endows brute matter with vitality, but gives each center of vitality a specific direction and limits. He has only to look within himself to find the interior law which will give bounds to his exuberance. To put it another way, all he needs do is to yield to his "out-soul" (I, 249), the moon which would organize his tides, exert "such . . . control/Over such sea-depths." This "out-soul" may be experienced as a direct inspiration from God, or it may exist incarnated in some human being, a mediator of God's will. In either case a direction is given to Browning's energy by a legitimate ruler exterior to the self.

When this strategy is tried, it fails. Though Browning turns both outside and inside, he finds to his dismay that though he is full of energy, this energy has no limiting form. He can discover neither any out-soul nor any inner instinct telling him to become one person rather than another. In vain does he cry out: "Yet, could one but possess, oneself, . . . some special office!" (I, 200), or: "I would have one joy,/But one in life, so it were wholly mine,/One rapture all my soul could fill" (I, 21). The inner self remains the same fluid sea, "untasked of any love." The sky remains empty. No moon troubles its bland vacancy.

Browning is forced by this crucial experience to assume that he is different from every other thing or person in the universe. Each other center of life has a given nature, which instinctively fulfills itself in a single way, as only cherry trees grow from cherry stones, and only pine trees from pine cones. *His* nature is a contradiction. His inner law seems to be a tumultuous need to "become all natures, yet retain/The law of [his] own nature" (I, 241). It is as absurd and unnatural, says Browning in a striking metaphor, as if a chestnut should wish also to be a larch and a pine tree (I, 241).

An important passage in "Sordello" (I, 244, 245) analyzes the sad consequences of this anomalous situation. Ordinary, healthy, limited people are like normal plants. Each has an intrinsic nature of his own, and this nature faces outward toward a world which is unequivocally alien. Life for such people is a benign process of assimilating what is other than themselves. They can safely "become what they behold" because their inner structure of selfhood is so secure. Everything they yield to will be made over in their own image and become "Native to the soul/Or body." But when Browning sets himself over against a world full of realized forms, he is, like Sordello, his spokesman, caught in a new impasse. He discovers that he, alone among God's creatures, has no inner law, or, rather, that his inner law is the need to be everything. At once he must say that nothing is alien to his soul, and that everything is alien. Nothing is alien to him because everything in the world is potentially present in his spirit. As a result, there is nothing other than his soul, nothing with which he can engage, as do all other creatures, in the benign "peace-in-strife,/ By transmutation." At the same time everything is utterly alien to him, for he altogether lacks the power to become in reality what he is potentially. Only if he could in a single leap identify himself all at once, soul and body, with all forms of life could he "begin to Be." He has no way to take that leap. He remains in a state of pure virtuality, torn to pieces by "multifarious sympathies" "he may neither renounce nor satisfy." [4] Potentially everything, he is actually nothing at all. This impotence turns every joy to dust, and makes death seem the only change to expect.

There is one other possibility. Could it be that he, unlike all other men, has been chosen by God for an unheard-of adventure? Browning's inner instinct drives him to realize all forms of life. But only God is, as Browning says in a significant formulation "the perfect poet,/Who in his person acts his own creations" (I, 85). Perhaps Browning, alone of all men, is destined to leap beyond finitude and identify himself with the infinite center of all things. Only the attainment of this goal would make possible the satisfaction of his Promethean urge to "be all, have, see, know, taste, feel, all." "Pauline," "Paracelsus," and "Sordello" are Browning's versions of a central adventure of romanticism — the attempt to identify oneself with God.

&

Heart and brain
Swelled; he expanded to himself again . . . (I, 237)

The beginning of this adventure is Browning's resolve to trust his inner ebullience. His heart and brain bubble with energy and multitudinous desires. If this power could be "hurled/Right from its heart" it would, literally, "encompass the world," so great is its expansive power (I, 334). Though there is no out-soul directing his sea, perhaps the inner energy is its own justification, and guarantees his right to leap beyond himself to the very throne of God. Such at least is Paracelsus' sense of his own mission, a sense that probably derives as much from Browning's own nonconformist background as from the historical Paracelsus. Browning foists on Paracelsus his own version of the Protestant doctrine of election. Paracelsus need only trust the promptings of "the restless irresistible force/That works within [him]" (I, 49). "Too intimate a tie/Connects [him] with our God" (I, 50) for him to

[4] Horace E. Scudder, ed., *The Complete Poetic and Dramatic Works of Robert Browning*, Student's Cambridge Edition (Boston, 1895), pp. 93, 94.

have any doubt of his calling. "What fairer seal," he asks, "/Shall I require to my authentic mission/Than this fierce energy?" (I, 49).

Paracelsus wants nothing less than to know "the secret of the world" (I, 47). For him " 't is all or nothing" (I, 71), and he cries: "I have made life consist of one idea," "one tyrant all-/Absorbing aim" (I, 69). He wants to "comprehend the works of God,/And God himself, and all God's intercourse/With the human mind" (I, 55). He must put himself in the place of God, and know the whole world from the point of view of God.

The image of fire or the sun runs through "Paracelsus." Paracelsus is called "Aureole," and describes himself as having been "from childhood . . . possessed/By a fire — by a true fire" (I, 52). The goal that lures him on is fire also, the central fire of the divine sun. He can liberate his inner fire only by making it coincide with God's fire. Like Prometheus or Phaeton, he wants to seize and control this sacred fire, and then in casual condescension to bestow its gifts on mankind. He will "Pluck out the angry thunder from its cloud,/That, all its gathered flame discharged on him,/No storm might threaten summer's azure sleep" (I, 53).

Paracelsus' "aspiration" is a single motion of the soul, but it has two elements, one of rejection, and one of appropriation. He repudiates other men and all their wisdom, all the past, and all partial truths. God's secret cannot be won by the gradual piling up of fragments of knowledge until at last a mountain is made which will scale heaven. He must make a single leap "out of this world," beyond all history, all other men, and all specific truths, in order to attain his transcendent goal. His quest, like that of the protagonist of "Pauline," is imaged as the unending journey of a mountain-climber who reaches one peak or plateau only to see from its height another still higher summit to climb, and so on forever.[5] Only if Paracelsus goes above and beyond everything, "elevates [himself] far, far above/The gorgeous spectacle" (I, 53)

---

[5] This image, so important for Browning's sense of his own inner spiritual movement, appears first in a footnote to "Pauline," written in French, strangely enough, and supposed to have been spoken by Pauline about her lover: "Je crois que dans ce qui suit il fait allusion à un certain examen qu'il fit autrefois de l'âme, ou plutôt de son âme, pour découvrir la suite des objets auxquels il lui serait possible d'atteindre, et dont chacun une fois obtenu devait former une espèce de plateau d'où l'on pouvait apercevoir d'autres buts, d'autres projets, d'autres jouissances qui, à leur tour, devaient être surmontés" (I, 27).

of the world, and reaches the top of the highest peak can he fulfill his Promethean boast: "I had . . . determined to become/The greatest and most glorious man on earth" (I, 69). It is no accident that Browning chooses to write a poem about Paracelsus, that Renaissance magician and alchemist who wanted to achieve a godlike completeness of power and knowledge. Browning's Paracelsus seeks in the philosopher's stone not only the power to turn base metals to gold, but also the transmutation of his own inert and mortal clay to angelic brilliance.[6]

The magic does not work. When Browning's early heroes try to escape from the "clay prisons" (I, 21) of themselves, and reach divine knowledge, they experience merely the dissipation of their powers into a murky emptiness. The expansiveness of Paracelsus, Sordello, and the protagonist of "Pauline," their attempts to know and be everything at once, leads not to an intensification of life, but rather to just the opposite, a rarefaction, a thinning out, an evaporation of immense energies into the intense inane. The dramatic climax of Browning's three earliest poems is the failure of romantic Prometheanism.

Sometimes this failure is expressed in an appropriate alchemical image. The golden sun fails to materialize in the crucible, and the mage is left with mere dead earth (I, 131). Sometimes the image is of the Titans or of Phaeton struck down by Jove's thunderous fist just when they are about to reach heaven (I, 145). The fullest description of the failure of Prometheanism shows Paracelsus pursuing the will-o'-the-wisp truth from valley to mountain and even deep underground. This pursuit is governed by the constant rejection of the sensible qualities of the world, its "beauty," as the mere robe of the one ubiquitous truth which is sought behind all the variety of natural forms:

> For some one truth would dimly beacon me
> From mountains rough with pines, and flit and wink
> O'er dazzling wastes of frozen snow, and tremble
> Into assured light in some branching mine

---

[6] Browning seized upon certain essential points in the life and doctrine of the real Paracelsus and remade them in the image of his own interior life, but his choice of hero is one more link with the tradition of romanticism. For that tradition had been initiated in part by a revival of the ideas of Paracelsus and other such Renaissance philosophers. See, on this point, Albert Béguin, *L'âme romantique et le rêve* (Paris, 1956), pp. 50–52.

Where ripens, swathed in fire, the liquid gold —
And all the beauty, all the wonder fell
On either side the truth, as its mere robe . . . (I, 70)

As Paracelsus carries this pursuit deeper and deeper, lured by the central fire, he does not get closer to his goal. He finds that the tantalizing light only leads him further across a trackless sea, and then disappears, leaving him becalmed over a "dead gulf" (I, 70). This gulf is the old fluid abyss of selfhood, filled now with a stagnant ocean, its great energy exhausted, illuminated not by the light of divine truth, but by the fitful gleams "from its own putrefying depths alone" (I, 70). His sense of divine mission is gone. The soul is returned to its old state of instability, yielding "sicklily" again to every passing instigation, and "all is alike at length . . ." (I, 70).

The failure of the strategy of Promethean expansion leads to a double discovery. Browning finds that his inner ebullience does not give him the right to overflow in all directions, "encompassing the world." Instead of reaching divine fullness he squanders his energies in the void. No grandiose mission calls him to an unexampled adventure. The failure of Prometheanism leads Browning to an "existential" discovery: the discovery of his own gratuitousness. No one but himself is responsible for his inner turmoil.

This discovery is related to another metaphysical one. He finds that God has withdrawn from the world, or at any rate from his own heart and mind. The two discoveries are really the same. He is entirely on his own *because* God is not present in his soul. God seems to be operating everywhere else in the world, as an immanent force directing the development of life and justifying it. But when Browning turns inside himself, where the presence of God should be most close and intimate, he finds — nothing but himself. When he tries to go outside, and to embrace the God who seems so manifest in the world, he sickens at last on the dead gulf of himself. This leads to a complete reversal of his original boisterous conviction that his "fierce energy" was the very presence of God working in his soul. Now he finds that he knows nothing whatsoever about God. He has nothing but the incomprehensible intelligence of his own suffering:

I know as much of any will of God
As knows some dumb and tortured brute what Man,

His stern lord, wills from the perplexing blows
That plague him every way . . . (I, 102)

This theme of the impossibility of a face-to-face confrontation
with God is one of the constants of Browning's poetry, reappearing not only in the dramatic monologues, but also in the poems
which seem to be more directly expressions of Browning's own
beliefs. The absence of God is one meaning of the celebrated
philosophy of incompleteness. Renan, in the "Epilogue to Dramatis Personae," describes the "dwindling into the distance" (IV,
369) of the star of God's presence on earth, and the poet, speaking as much in his own voice as he ever does, contrasts, in the "Parleying with Gerard de Lairesse," the blind De Lairesse's power to
see nature transfigured into myth, therefore linked with heaven,
and our latter-day matter-of-factness which sees in flowers merely
flowers. How did the change take place, he asks; "which was it
of the links/Snapt first, from out the chain which used to bind/
Our earth to heaven . . . ?" (X, 224). A late poem, "Fears and
Scruples," is a full expression of the anguish of God's unattainability. In this poem God is like an "unseen friend" who, though
loved and believed in, never makes himself manifest. And Browning cries out: "He keeps absent, — why, I cannot think" (IX, 42).

Though Browning's poetry is so different in atmosphere from,
say, Matthew Arnold's, though his world is a universe of plenitude
rather than of poverty, he is like Arnold and like many other
English writers of the nineteenth century in experiencing in his
own way the withdrawal of God and the consequent impoverish-
ment of man and his surroundings. Browning does not disbelieve
in God, but he finds it impossible to approach him directly. He
begins with the feeling that he contains everything in his vast
potentiality. The attempt to actualize that possibility leads him
to discover his inner nothingness, and his exclusion from the substance of being.

ε❧

Yet he is not nothing. It is true that in one sense he is nothing
yet, since he is only unrealized possibilities. If he tries to actualize
all these possibilities at once, he endures a sickening evaporation
and deadening of the spirit. When he comes back to himself after

his leap in the void he finds that he is still filled with the same seething desires. He is a congeries of tendencies and dynamic impulses, each one of which implies a complete human existence, taking a lifetime to fulfill. He can neither accept his imprisonment in himself, nor find any way to indulge his exuberant desires:

> I cannot chain my soul: it will not rest
> In its clay prison, this most narrow sphere:
> It has strange impulse, tendency, desire,
> Which nowise I account for nor explain,
> But cannot stifle, being bound to trust
> All feelings equally, to hear all sides:
> How can my life indulge them? yet they live,
> Referring to some state of life unknown. (I, 20, 21)

As Charles Du Bos saw, this passage is the center of Browning, and the key to his poetry, for the failure of romantic Prometheanism leads him to make a radical change in his poetry. After "Sordello," instead of writing poetry which is disguised autobiography, Browning writes poetry "always Dramatic in principle, and so many utterances of so many imaginary persons, not mine" (III, 107).

The dramatic monologue is not simply a technical discovery or adaptation, chosen because it makes possible vividness and immediacy, or some other objective value. The decision to write dramatic monologues is Browning's way of dealing with his own existential problem. Other men seem to have a single germ of life which can be fulfilled in a single mode of existence. He alone must find some way to indulge all feelings equally, to hear all sides of life. Like other men he is doomed to limitation, and must obey the natural law which says: ". . . beyond thee lies the infinite — /Back to thy circumscription!" (X, 216). Though Browning cannot ape God's infinitude, there is one way in which he can approach God's fullness, and that is through a certain kind of poetry. The direct way to God has failed. Now Browning must turn to the peripheral way, not the way up, but the way around. He must enter in patient humility the lives of the multitude of men and women who make up the world, and he must re-create these lives in his poems. Only by exhausting in this way the plenitude of the creation can he hope to reach the universality of the creator. There is not time to indulge in reality all the feelings which swarm within him. He must indulge them in imagination, in poetry.

Browning does not fool himself about the powers of poetry. Only God is the perfect poet, and enters completely into his poems. Only God can satisfy all his tendencies and impulses at once, for though the creation is temporal, all times are equally present to God. And only God is creatively autonomous. The earthly poet is dependent on the prior creation by God of the world, and can only imitate in his poems objects or people which already exist, have existed, or could conceivably exist. The mortal poet is bound to time. He cannot act all his creations at once, only one by one. Finally, he does not really enter, body and soul, into his creations. Each one of Browning's dramatic monologues is the playing of a role, the wearing of a mask. It is based on an "as if." Browning speaks for a time as if he were Mr. Sludge or Bishop Blougram. He is able to "enter each and all" of his "men and women,/Live or dead or fashioned by [his] fancy," and "use their service,/Speak from every mouth, — the speech, a poem" (IV, 177). But all along we know, and Browning knows, that his playing the role of Sludge is only temporary, that the monologue will soon come to an end, that he will soon be putting on another costume, and performing Caliban, Guido, or Cleon. The juxtaposition of a large number of dramatic monologues betrays the artificiality of any one of them. God actually *is* Guido, Sludge, and the rest (including Browning himself). Browning only pretends to be these men. The least, miserable, sordid gesture of a real flesh and blood man is in a way worth more than all the poems in the world, as a number of Browning's characters affirm. Cleon asks bitterly: ". . . if I paint,/Carve the young Phœbus, am I therefore young?" (IV, 168), and Norbert, in "In a Balcony," speaks with great disdain of poets and painters. It is far better to be himself than merely to watch from a distance the being of others (IV, 204). Bishop Blougram compares himself to Shakespeare, and boasts that what Shakespeare only enjoyed in fancy he has had in reality. Or at any rate he has had some of it, and that little is worth more than all the imagination in the world (IV, 143–145).

Browning, unlike Norbert or the Bishop, is nothing, nothing but unfulfilled desires. To be something in imagination is better than to be nothing at all. In his earliest poems the poet had expressed himself more or less directly. These poems had shocked and bewildered his readers by their morbid introspection and their obscurity. One remembers the reaction of John Stuart Mill to "Pauline." What these poems really express is Browning's failure to find a way to deal directly with his situation. After the description of his situation in "Pauline," he proceeds through the dramatization of the failure of Prometheanism in "Paracelsus" to the most obscure and murky poem of all, "Sordello," finished last of the three. In "Sordello" Browning's attempt to express himself directly and to live his life directly leads him further and more irrevocably back to the primal shapeless mud.

What better escape from this cul-de-sac than the poetry of role-playing? Such poetry, Browning sees, will allow him to organize his diffuse inner energy and give it a momentary plastic form. He will escape from the necessity of seeking an inner drive toward one particular shape. He can depend now on the imitation of forms which already exist or have existed. Since he commits himself only for a time to each life, he will not be petrifying himself in a false self, but will live in a constant process of temporary crystallization, followed by breakup, followed by reorganization in a different form. The difference now will be that the taking of form will be complete: the total patterning of the primitive magma in the shape of a single life. This taking of shape can be more complete precisely because it is based on an "as if." The fact that Browning remains uncommitted to any one of these forms will be evident only in the honesty and urgency of his constant disclaimer: "These are not my opinions or my experiences." In one sense this is unequivocally true, for these poems were written not by allowing his own unique germ of life to express itself, but by imagining what it is for Pompilia or Fra Lippo Lippi or Aristophanes to be themselves. They are not his opinions, not his experiences, not his life, because he has no opinions, no experiences, no life of his own. But in another way, all of these opinions, experiences, and lives *are* his, and W. C. DeVane is right to insist on the self-expressive side of Browning's poetry. They are all his because each one represents the fulfillment of one impulse of his spirit. Browning has no separate life of his own because he lives his life in his poetry.

Browning would probably have said that his Perseus-like saving of Elizabeth Barrett from her dragon of a father was the definitive private act of his life, the one act which fixed his nature for good, as he says of such an experience in "By The Fireside" (III, 201–211). In "One Word More" (IV, 173–180) he distinguishes between the public face he turns to the world in his poetry and the private self which is only for his wife, just as, in a very late poem, he says that he has done two things with his life: "verse-making" and "love-making" (X, 109). But the very fact that he made verse as well as love, and made verse so indefatigably and at such length, is proof that no single act or commitment, however intense, was enough to satisfy all the needs of his spirit. As he said in a letter to Isa Blagden, his real "object of life," his "root" in the strong earth, was poetry.[7] Only there could he assuage his desire to experience "all the ways" in which human beings have lived or might live.

In one sense Browning sets himself over against a world swarming with people. He is a neutral onlooker, observing what happens, and reproducing it in his verse, like the poet of "How It Strikes a Contemporary." He can do this so well because he has a latent possession of all possible forms of life. It is only a matter of letting one of his inner impulses flow out, take form, and he can become Sludge, Guido, or Caliban. Since Browning contains all these lives potentially in himself he can imitate them from the inside, marrying his mind and senses to theirs. This correspondence between what he is potentially and what the world is actually, is the basis of Browning's poetry, and of his intuitive method of comprehension. He knows other people as intimately as he knows himself, and excels in what Du Bos, in another brilliant phrase, called "the introspection of others," only because he contains the whole world and all its forms of life dormantly within himself. In a passage in "Sordello," Browning distinguishes between the passive, gentle souls, who yield themselves to external beauty, and the stronger men, the true poets, who see in what is outside themselves the objective revelation of a possibility of their own souls, "a twin/With a distinctest consciousness within" (I, 194). Browning is surely of the second sort.

[7] Edward C. McAleer, ed., *Dearest Isa: Robert Browning's Letters to Isabella Blagden* (Austin, Texas, 1951), p. 201.

If Browning has all forms of beauty "dormant within [his] nature all along" (I, 194), then he is a multivocal personality, and there is no way in which he can accede to Elizabeth Barrett's repeated request that, having written so much dramatically, he should now speak in his own person. "*Now* let us have your own voice speaking of yourself . . . ," she asks, "teach what you have learnt, in the directest and most impressive way, the mask thrown off however moist with the breath." [8] He cannot throw off the mask, for there is nothing behind it, or nothing but a face that is all faces at once, and so no face.

Can we not see another manifestation of this inner indistinction in Browning's constant insistence on his rights of privacy, his attempt to destroy his correspondence and his early poetry, and his bitter rejection, in several poems of the "Pacchiarotto" volume, of the idea that the public has any right to know the private life of a poet? Nowadays, in the epoch of Gide and Sartre, we are accustomed to the idea that a man may have no given "nature," as does a stone or a tree. But in Browning's day, and in England, the idea of the indeterminacy of selfhood was a scandalous notion, contrary to the traditional British conviction that each man has a substantial inner core of self. It was the wavering inner fluidity as well as the morbid self-consciousness of "Pauline" which so shocked Mill and other early readers. Browning's excessive desire for privacy, as well as his decision to write dramatic monologues, may be not so much an attempt to hide the positive facts of his private life as an attempt to keep hidden his secret failure to have the kind of definite, solid self he sees in other people, and feels it is normal to have. Henry James may be perfectly right, in "The Private Life," to sense a mystery in the disjunction between Browning's poetry and the public life of the man who went to so many dinner parties that people said he would die in his dinner jacket. The disjunction may not be where James saw it, in the contrast between the superficiality of the public life, and the creative depths of the hours when the poetry was written. The real secret may be the central formlessness which is hidden both by the poetry and by the life of party-going. Browning would then be another case of the insubstantiality of the histrionic person-

[8] *The Letters of Robert Browning and Elizabeth Barrett Browning: 1845–1846*, II (New York, 1899), 181, 180.

ality, that blankness behind the succession of roles which James ascribes, in *The Tragic Muse,* to the actress Miriam Rooth. If we turn to Browning's poetry to find a revelation of what he "really" believes we find ourselves bewildered by a profusion of apparently contradictory assertions, and Browning would affirm that even the poems which seem the most personal are just as dramatic and imaginary as any of the others. Many of the opinions and attitudes which seem most peculiarly Browning's own are put in the mouths of "villains" like Don Juan or Bishop Blougram.[9] The reader's imagination staggers, and he rushes to the letters to find the "real" Browning. There he finds, for the most part, Browning in a dinner jacket, the superficial, public Browning who could hardly have written "The Ring and the Book" or "Porphyria's Lover." Browning himself, the very pulse of his life and sound of his voice, is more present in the least of his poems, and we are forced to conclude that his "selfhood" must be defined as the failure to have any one definite self, and as the need to enact, in imagination, the roles of the most diverse people in order to satisfy all the impulses of his being. To be such a self was, in Victorian England, a shameful and reprehensible thing, and it is not surprising to find that Browning should hide it by various means — even, in part, from himself.

Though Browning's three earliest poems are clearly autobiographical, and though he tried his best to suppress "Pauline," with all the anxiety of a man who regrets an indiscreet self-revelation, nevertheless these poems too are the utterances of "dramatic persons." Paracelsus and Sordello are after all historical persons, and "Pauline" is a dramatic monologue, Browning's first. As he tells us, he conceived a plan of publishing anonymously, under different pseudonyms, plays, novels, operas, and poems. The public was not to know that all these works were by the same

[9] H. N. Fairchild's article ("Browning the Simple-Hearted Casuist," *University of Toronto Quarterly,* XVIII [1949], 234–240), though suggestive, does not really solve the problem. Not all the monologues have the giveaways Fairchild describes, and even then we are left with the problem of how to take statements in the body of the poem which, though dramatic, seem as if they might be Browning's "real" opinions. "Fifine at the Fair," for example, raises this problem in an acute form. Browning's devils all quote scripture, that is, they speak what seem to be, from the frequency of their reiteration, ideas close to Browning's own heart. The reader is driven to accept the notion that Browning did really want "to hear all sides," and that all these sides, Guido as much as Pompilia, were aspects of his own "nature."

person, and "Pauline" was supposed to be by the poet of the lot. Even this most personal poem was the expression of an assumed role, as Browning claimed in the preface of 1867 (I, xxi). His resistance to committing himself wholly to one voice was so great that at the age of twenty, before he had developed the theory of the dramatic monologue, he could not bring himself to "lay bare his heart" without persuading himself that he was only *pretending* to be a Shelleyan poet, full of anguish and nameless sin. Browning could not begin to speak at all unless he convinced himself that he was not speaking in his own voice. Only then would the inner ice melt, and the interminable flow of words begin, the garrulous rumble of his own inimitable voice.

Browning's inability to speak directly in his own voice, the neutrality and pliability of his spirit, link him to a certain aspect of the romantic tradition, an aspect visible not only in German romantic poetry and philosophy, but also in English romanticism. Browning carries just about as far as it can go the Keatsian notion of the chameleon poet who, having no nature of his own, is able to enter into the nature of things around him. One might say that Browning's distinctive contribution to romanticism is his extension of the idea of sympathetic imagination from natural objects to other people. Keats too had claimed to be able to be "with Achilles shouting in the trenches," as well as to enter into the life of the sparrow pecking the gravel, but in his poetry the sympathetic imagination of natural objects is paramount. Browning, like Keats, feels that he has the power to enter into natural things (I, 24), but clearly dominant in his poetry is the power of the introspection of other people. Both Browning and the romantics have "A need to blend with each external charm,/Bury themselves, the whole heart wide and warm, — /In something not themselves" (I, 194). Browning's special gift is his ability to "bury himself" not only in flower, bird, or tree, but also in the most diverse sorts of human beings.

This gift links Browning to another tradition: historicism. Historicism arises at the same time as romanticism, and has intimate connections with it. Both presuppose a breakdown of the traditional avenues of communication between man and the supernatural. A romantic poet like Hölderlin throws himself sacrificially into the void between man and God, and tries to make himself the vessel in which the divine fire is appeased and made benignant to man. Browning's earliest poems express his experience of the failure of this strategy. Beginning in the same place, with the absence of God, and its concomitant, the loss of selfhood, it is possible to go in another direction: to turn one's back resolutely on God, and to attempt to reach him, if at all, only through a complete inventory of all the diverse forms which human life has taken or could take. This is the strategy of historicism.

The attitude of historicism is humble and modest. It assumes that there is no way to create an absolute system of thought which will allow man to put himself in the place of God and see things *sub specie aeternitatis.* If a man tries to rise to such heights he will suffocate from lack of air, and his system, if he makes one, will lack pith and substance. Reality for man lies in the acceptance of a finite perspective on the world. The difficulty is that the historicist can find no reason to commit himself to any one point of view. He has the old hunger to know everything, but he cannot go directly toward the divine center, for that way is closed. Therefore he must go toward the periphery, the realm of eccentricity. He can approach an absolute vision only by attempting to relive, one by one, all the possible attitudes of the human spirit. He will go through history trying to reconstruct, from the inside, the intimate reasonableness of each age, each point of view, each great thinker or artist. He will try to find out what it would feel like to look at the world with the eyes of Aristophanes, Sordello, or Christopher Smart. Nor will he ignore the lesser people, the Balaustions, Bubb Dodingtons, and Sludges, for such people have also lived, and their unique mode of experience is part of the totality of what is or has been.

Such an attitude will not be sheer relativism, the cynical assumption that since all points of view are equally false, we might as well play capriciously at re-creating them. On the contrary, the historicist assumes that all points of view are true. If these perspectives contradict one another, so much the better, for that opaque, ambiguous, multiple thing, reality, exceeds any one pair of eyes. Only by making use of all historical perspectives, in all their diversity, can we hope to approach it. When we have exhausted history we shall go on into the future, and try to invent new ways of living and feeling, each one contributing its bit to

the endless task of the exhaustion of reality. The historicist wants
to have experienced all possible feelings, to have seen life from
all points of view. Such, in one way or another, is the project of
historicism, whether we find it flamboyantly, as in Nietzsche, with
the emphasis on the creation of new perspectives, or more soberly,
as in Dilthey or Groethuysen, with an emphasis on the comprehension of the historical past, or with a combination of the two, as in
Ortega y Gasset. It is to this tradition that Browning belongs. He
is England's most distinguished historicist, the one who explored
most deeply, in his own way, the implications of the historicist
attitude.

The dramatic monologue is par excellence the literary genre of
historicism. It presupposes a double awareness on the part of its
author, an awareness which is the very essence of historicism. The
dramatic monologuist is aware of the relativity, the arbitrariness,
of any single life or way of looking at the world. On the other
hand, Browning believes that value lies only in energy, vitality,
"life," intense engagement in a finite situation. As he says in "The
Statue and the Bust," "a crime will do/As well . . . to serve for
a test,/As a virtue golden through and through" (III, 401). The
only real evil, for man, is inaction, "the unlit lamp and the ungirt
loin" (III, 402). What exists for human beings is only the inexhaustible multitude of various lives which have been lived or can
be lived, and it is these which the modern poet, the poet of historicism, must attempt to re-create.

So we get the great gallery of idiosyncratic characters in Browning's most famous poems: scoundrels, quacks, hypocrites, cowards,
casuists, lovers, heroes, adulterers, artists, Bishop Blougram, Mr.
Sludge, Caliban, the Bishop ordering his tomb. Browning has committed himself, like Gide in some of his moods,[10] to the life of the
shape-changer, the life of the man who, nothing himself, borrows
with the utmost irresponsibility the life of others.

This description of Browning's poetic enterprise must be qualified by a recognition that behind the great crowd of grotesques
and idealists there is one constant factor linking them all together:

[10] Gide was much interested in Browning, and wrote perceptively about him in
his notebooks. See his *Journal, 1889–1939* (Paris, 1939), especially the entries for
May 30, 1930, and March 12, 1938. Unlike Browning, Gide only changes from one
sensual or emotional experience to another. He never places himself in a series of
other selves.

the consciousness of Browning himself. The multitude of eccentrics exists inside the poet as well as outside. In "Pauline" all these feelings and perspectives existed still within Browning himself, as "impulses," "tendencies," "desires," not yet projected into the lives of imaginary persons. Now all these forms of life, all these feelings, all these points of view, will be incarnated in the multitudinous variety of men and women who speak in his poems. The solution of the problem posed in "Pauline" is given in the speech of Aprile, the poet of "Paracelsus." Paracelsus has sought only knowledge and power. He has haughtily turned his back on his fellow human beings, and has attempted to leap, at once, over the gap separating man from God. But Aprile faces in loving patience toward the multiplicity of the world of time and space, and attempts to re-create all its forms in art. His description of his project in life is a perfect expression of the attitude of Browning himself as a writer of dramatic monologues. What Aprile will use all the arts to attain, Browning will attempt to achieve in a single medium:

> Every passion sprung from man, conceived by man,
> Would I express and clothe it in its right form,
> Or blend with others struggling in one form,
> Or show repressed by an ungainly form.
> . . . no thought which ever stirred
> A human breast should be untold; all passions,
> All soft emotions, from the turbulent stir
> Within a heart fed with desires like mine,
> To the last comfort shutting the tired lids
> Of him who sleeps the sultry noon away
> Beneath the tent-tree by the wayside well . . . (I, 78, 79)

ક

We have not yet exhausted Browning's theory of poetry. "Paracelsus" dramatizes two failures, the failure of Aprile the historicist as well as the failure of Paracelsus the Promethean. Only the poet who combines in himself both love and knowledge will succeed, for Aprile and Paracelsus are "halves of one dissevered world" (I, 84). What would this combination mean, and why is it necessary? The answer to these questions involves not only Browning's conception of the poet, but also his notion of the relations between God and the world.

God exists in two places in relation to the world. He is self-sufficient perfection of pure being, but he is also everywhere immanent in his creation. Between these two presences of God there is a vacancy. The transcendent God possesses in one moment, from all time, all his "everlasting bliss." The immanent God exists in his creation, and is bound, like that creation itself, to time and space. At the beginning of time there is God and his negative image, the fecund mass of the potential creation, bubbling and heaving with infinite latent life. Between them is an empty space, or rather an empty time, for it will require all of time for God's image to actualize itself in matter. On the one hand there is Protoplasm, on the other, the Protoplast. Between them is everything that exists (in the etymological sense of "standing out"), for the Protoplast, the divine potter, is both within his clay as an instinctive pushing vitality making for form, and outside things as a transcendent goal which pulls them as the moon pulls the tides. In both modes God is a vital energy, not a pure spirit. The medium in which his creative action takes place, the detachment from one absolute (the Protoplasm) and the yearning movement toward the other absolute (the Protoplast) is *time* — as we are told in the metaphor of potter and pot in "Rabbi Ben Ezra": "Ay, note that Potter's wheel,/That metaphor! and feel/Why time spins fast, why passive lies our clay, — " (IX, 267).

By the very fact that a thing exists in time and space and matter it is imperfect (since it is no longer the protoplasmic absolute and not yet the Protoplast), and, tormented by its imperfection, it strives toward ever higher reaches of being: "On the earth the broken arcs; in the heaven, a perfect round" (IV, 258). Time, for Browning as for the old Platonists, is a moving image of eternity, but it will take the entire span of time from the beginning to the end to realize gradually, in matter and space, the infinite riches of God. The whole creation forms a moving chain of being, with the higher forms growing out of the earlier and presupposing them, and the lower forms continuous with the higher and illuminated by them:

> . . . one stage of being complete,
> One scheme wound up: and from the grand result
> A supplementary reflux of light,
> Illustrates all the inferior grades, explains
> Each back step in the circle. (I, 163)

The creation is a circle, but it is an infinite circle, or, rather, an "eternal circle" (I, 165), for its most important dimension is the perpetual motion of time. The transcendent God is the perfect sun at the center, and the creation proceeds eternally onward in its ever-renewed approach toward God. At this moment of universal history man is "the completion of this sphere/Of life" (I, 162), but man has not yet achieved his full humanity, and, even when he does, he will only be a steppingstone to higher forms which will go still closer to God.

Browning rejects any notion of radical discontinuity in a person or in the universe as a whole. His model for both is organic growth. Though there may be startling changes, the flower and the fruit are already present in the seed, and any stage of the universe contains all its past and all its future too. Each stage grows out of all that have preceded and yet goes beyond them in complexity and fineness of development. Browning counsels us neither to reject the past, nor to dally with it, for progress is the law of life:

> What were life
> Did soul stand still therein, forego her strife
> Through the ambiguous Present to the goal
> Of some all-reconciling Future? Soul,
> Nothing has been which shall not bettered be
> Hereafter, — leave the root, by law's decree
> Whence springs the ultimate and perfect tree! (X, 232)

The creation slowly grows closer and closer to the goal which attracts it from the future: the divine perfection. The gap between the transcendent God and the immanent God will endure as long as time itself, for the creation is like an arrow aimed truly toward an infinitely distant goal, and each new stage in "that eternal circle life pursues" has a new "tendency to God" (I, 165).

Along its eternal circle life crawls from point to point. As in De Quincey's world, so in Browning's, it is impossible to leap over the intervening grades and reach God at once. This is bad enough, but in fact the situation is even worse, for Browning pictures God himself as continually going beyond his own infinity to reach an infinity of a higher power. Browning's universe is expanding, but his deity too is an expanding God, and makes a perpetual "progress through eternity" (IV, 69). There seems no chance for the creation ever to catch up. It is like an arrow speeding toward an infinitely distant target which is receding with infinite speed:

> . . . where dwells enjoyment there is [God]:
> With still a flying point of bliss remote,
> A happiness in store afar, a sphere
> Of distant glory in full view; thus climbs
> Pleasure its heights for ever and for ever. (I, 161)

Browning remains faithful to this intuition of the relation between the creator and the creation, and many years after "Paracelsus" devises a brilliant and definitive metaphor to describe it. In this figure the creation is seen not as an eternal circle, but rather as a curve, one of those mathematical lines, like the tangent curve, which approaches closer and closer to a straight line, its asymptote, which it will touch only at infinity. This is a better image than that of the eternal circle, for the eternal circle suggests an impossible attempt by the creation to return to its beginning after an infinite procession through time, while the image of the curve and asymptote is closer to Browning's idea of an indefinitely prolonged approach of the creation toward God:

> As still to its asymptote speedeth the curve,
>
> So approximates Man — Thee, who, reachable not,
> Hast formed him to yearningly follow Thy whole
> Sole and single omniscience! (X, 275)

The curve gets closer, but never touches the asymptote it yearningly follows. There is always a gap between the creation and God.

In that gap stands the poet.

The poet faces in two directions, upward toward the transcendent God, and downward toward God as incarnated in the creation. He must go through the whole universe with loving care, re-creating all its forms. He must also try to reach closer to God through this process. "A poet's affair," says Browning, "is with God, to whom he is accountable, and of whom is his reward." [11] What this means we can learn from "How It Strikes a Contemporary" (IV, 81–84), a charming poem in which Browning describes the true poet, a somewhat shabby man in a "scrutinizing hat" who walks through the town as a seemingly casual spectator. In reality he is "scenting the world, looking it full in face." His sharp eyes are ferreting out the heart-secrets of all its men and women. He is

[11] Quoted in W. C. De Vane, *A Browning Handbook* (New York, 1955), p. 237.

the town's "recording chief-inquisitor," and at night he goes home and reports everything he has seen to God. The poet, as God tells him in the poem, stands between God and man: "Too far above my people, — beneath me!" (IV, 83). Like David, in "Saul," the poet must be able to say:

> I have gone the whole round of creation: I saw and I spoke:
> I, a work of God's hand for that purpose, received in my brain
> And pronounced on the rest of his handwork — returned him again
> His creation's approval or censure: I spoke as I saw:
> I report, as a man may of God's work . . . (III, 193)

The poet must turn away from God, and set himself the task of making a complete inventory of God's creatures, plunging into their inner lives one by one and wresting their secrets. He must make clear the meaning of all these lives by reproducing them, for, as Fra Lippo Lippi boasts, we only begin to see the beauty and wonder of the world around us when it has been imitated in art (IV, 113). The poet can look at all possible lives from a point of view which is both detached and engaged. Therefore he is able to see the meaning which is hidden from people who are actually living their own narrow lives. This is valuable in part to other men, who are brought by art to see what is there all along but invisible to them. But the poet's ultimate responsibility is to God. Going through the whole world, he reports its nature to God. The poet is God's spy. Only because he has a commission from God has he the right and the power to go the whole round of the creation. He is the avenue by which the world is returned to its maker. The poet cannot go to heaven directly, but only with the whole creation. So Browning always affirmed the necessity of beginning at the bottom, recapitulating the whole ladder of creation, before trying to advance another rung:

> I at the bottom, Evolutionists,
> Advise beginning, rather. (X, 211)

> I say, o'erstep no least one of the rows
> That lead man from the bottom where he plants
> Foot first of all, to life's last ladder-top . . . (X, 187)

This is why both Paracelsus and Aprile fail. Aprile fails because he tries to limit himself to patient love of the creation. The artist must also have a relation to God. Paracelsus fails because he re-

jects the creation for the sake of an exclusive relation to the creator. He spurns all the prior points on the eternal circle life pursues,
and wants to leap in a moment to the goal: "I would have had
one day, one moment's space,/Change man's condition, push each
slumbering claim/Of mastery o'er the elemental world/At once
to full maturity . . ." (I, 166). Success comes only to those who
yield to time, accept the past, and submit to the necessity of reaching the future through toil and suffering. It is impossible to side-
step the long temporal process whereby the primal fecund mass
brings into being each of its potentialities, and gradually approaches to God and his infinite bliss. The creation's curse is that
it must "painfully attain to joy" (I, 166).

Paracelsus recognizes at last, just before his death, that only a
combination of power and love will make a successful poet, and
he expresses this insight in a variant of the image of the eternal
circle. The good poet must be like a planet which neither destroys
itself by plunging into the sun (Paracelsus-Phaeton), nor drifts too
far from God into outer darkness (like Aprile who wanted to love
only created things). Only the poet who is simultaneously related
in precarious equilibrium to both God and the creation can avoid
disaster, and be "a temperate and equidistant world" (I, 168).

Browning remains true to this conception of the task of the
poet, and makes it the basis of his fullest treatment of the subject
in his essay on Shelley.[12] In that essay he distinguishes between the
objective poet, like Shakespeare, who turns toward the world, to
imitate "the inexhaustible variety of existence," and the subjective
poet, like Shelley, who is "impelled to embody the thing he perceives, not so much with reference to the many below as to the one
above him, the supreme Intelligence which apprehends all things
in their absolute truth, — an ultimate view ever aspired to, if but
partially attained, by the poet's own soul." Browning imagines an
ideal poet who will perfectly fulfill both functions, though he ad-
mits that such a poet has not yet appeared. Both faculties operate
to some degree in all poets, for each poet must start with the material world and spiritualize that by lifting it one step higher toward God. Poets must face first toward the world, and then toward
the deity: "For it is with this world, as starting point and basis
alike, that we shall always have to concern ourselves: the world is

[12] Scudder, *Complete Works of Browning*, pp. 1008–1014.

not to be learned and thrown aside, but reverted to and relearned. The spiritual comprehension may be infinitely subtilized, but the raw material it operates upon must remain."

An eloquent passage in this essay gives Browning's definitive picture of the progress of poetry. The passage is another version of his fundamental image of successive crystallizations and dissolutions. There is one kind of poet who merely systematizes and makes generally comprehensible what is already known of the world. There comes a time when this view of the creation becomes stagnant and dead, "the shadow of a reality." Then will be the time for another sort of poet, a poet who is both destructive and constructive. First he will break the old picture of reality into pieces. This will allow him to get at new substance and see things no one else has seen. The new material will spontaneously take shape in the imagination of a later subjective poet. Finally, that new structure will reveal its resonance with God himself, its correspondence to the deity at a higher level than any so far achieved. The poets, working together, objective and subjective faculties alternating, will have gone with the whole creation one step closer to God, and "one more degree will be apparent for a poet to climb in that mighty ladder, of which, however cloud-involved and undefined may glimmer the topmost step, the world dares no longer doubt that its gradations ascend."

Browning's essay does not stop with definition. It implies that the poet secretly desires to combine in his own work objective and subjective poetry. "Nor is there," he writes, "any reason why these two modes of poetic faculty may not issue hereafter from the same poet in successive perfect works . . ."

But how can one poet fulfill both roles, and be himself the Archimedean lever which moves the world?

The first step in the fulfillment of this grandiose scheme is the imitation of all the multitudinous forms of life. The poet must seek in the world itself the new substance which will ultimately be recombined under a higher "harmonizing law" (Scudder, 1010). His first business is a patient investigation of this world, our perpetual "starting point and basis." What is the method of this vast inventory of creation?

Browning has the inexhaustible plenitude of created forms inside his own soul, but only in a latent state. He needs the outside world, where these forms, or some of them, already exist, in order to realize himself. This mirrorlike relation between Browning and the world is the basis of his theory of intuitive comprehension. There is no otherness, no mystery, in his world. Every person is immediately comprehensible to him because each man lives a life Browning himself might have lived. The validity of his poetry rests on his assumption that he can spontaneously put himself in the place of Guido, or Caponsacchi, or Miranda (in "Red Cotton Night-Cap Country"), or Chatterton (in the "Essay on Chatterton" [13]), and tell us how they felt and why they acted as they did. If someone should try to show him that he has misinterpreted the facts, Browning will reply that his inner sense cannot be wrong, that he knows Guido, Miranda, and the rest as well as he knows himself. Only because he contains all forms of life inside himself has he the power to go outside himself and enter into the life of all people and things.

There is another motive for Browning's passionate desire to place himself in the interior of other lives and find out their secrets. He assumes that God exists behind every thing or person, and delights himself in the unique flavor of each life. To reach the real truth behind a person, a flower, or an historical event is to reach not only the particular secret of a particular existence, but always and everywhere to encounter the divine truth itself.

This becomes in Browning a Pascalian or Blakean notion of the special closeness to God of the minuscule. We shall reach God best not by the hopeless attempt to expand ourselves to his size, like the frog imitating the ox, but rather by descending toward ever more minute particulars until below the smallest of the small, rather than beyond the largest of the large, we reach the splendor of God. Every grain of sand is not only irreplaceable and unique; at some moment it reflects the divine sun best of all created things, "returns his ray with jet/Of promptest praise, thanks God best in creation's name!" (VII, 184). So "A sphere is but a sphere;/

[13] Printed in Donald Smalley, ed., *Browning's Essay on Chatterton* (Cambridge, Mass., 1948).

Small, Great, are merely terms we bandy here;/Since to the spirit's absoluteness all/Are like," "The Small, a sphere as perfect as the Great" (I, 348), and "We find great things are made of little things,/And little things go lessening till at last/Comes God behind them" (IV, 351).

Every least object, and every least human being, carries a spark of the divine sun in his breast, and if we can really pierce to the center of any one of them we shall reach God himself. Fire under dead ashes, gold under dross, truth hidden behind a surface of lies — Browning devises numerous ways to express this notion. It first appears, appropriately enough, in "Paracelsus." The idea that God will be found at the center of the soul is an important part of the mystic tradition to which the Swiss alchemist belonged, and it was this tradition which was revived in the eighteenth century by writers like Saint-Martin, Hamann, Von Baader, and Steffens. From these writers it is only a step to Blake and Shelley, and so to Browning, who begins with the double tradition of Protestantism and romanticism, both of which contain this idea of the divine truth at the center of each soul, baffled and hidden by a carnal mesh of lies:

> Truth is within ourselves; it takes no rise
> From outward things, whate'er you may believe.
> There is an inmost centre in us all,
> Where truth abides in fulness; and around,
> Wall upon wall, the gross flesh hems it in,
> This perfect, clear perception — which is truth. (I, 61)

Browning cannot, in isolation, find the tiny point at the center of his own soul where he coincides with God. His only recourse is to bring into existence his inner potentialities one after another by plunging into the lives of other people, in hopes that he may reach the divine spark in that way. His task as poet is to reach and express the infinite enclosed in the finite: "From the given point evolve the infinite" (VIII, 272). He can free his own infinite depths if he can attain them in what is outside himself.

How does Browning take this plunge into the secret life of another man or woman?

There are two ways to know another thing or person: to make oneself passive and receptive, like an objective scientist, and let the thing reveal itself by displaying itself, or to fight one's way to its center, assaulting its secret places and taking it by storm. Browning's is the second way.

Browning repeatedly describes the poet's knowledge of others in terms of the physical penetration of some object which is hidden or closed in on itself, like a fruit or a shut-up flower (IX, 124; X, 224). The poet knows the world through his senses and his intuitive power, and these permit him to plunge "through rind to pith" (X, 184) of each thing he appropriates. Anything which presents a mysterious surface is an invitation to his insatiable curiosity, a curiosity both of the senses and of the soul. One suspects that part of the fascination for him of Elizabeth Barrett was her unavailability, the way she was immured in darkness and jealously guarded. Browning's Andromeda would be imprisoned in a cave, not naked on a promontory, and Browning, as Perseus, would have to fight his way through solid rock to reach her, as Caponsacchi breaks through all barriers to reach Pompilia.

Browning's problem is double. He has to batter his way to the secret center of the life of others, and he also has to express that experience in words. By naming things and people by the right words Browning breaks through rind to pith. His model is Christopher Smart, who penetrated from the surface to the center of each thing, and was thereby able to name things by their proper names, as did Adam. Adding "right language" to "real vision," he made it possible for us to see things with paradisiacal freshness, and to possess them wholly, until "all the life/That flies or swims or crawls, in peace or strife,/Above, below, — each had its note and name/For Man to know by . . ." (X, 184, 185).

The first principle of Browning's poetry is his attempt to make the words of the poem participate in the reality they describe, for he seeks to capture the "stuff/O' the very stuff, life of life, and self of self" (IV, 348). He wants his words to be thick and substantial, and to carry the solid stuff of reality. He wants, as he said in a striking phrase, "word pregnant with thing" (VIII, 294). To read a poem by Browning should be a powerful sensuous experience, a tasting and feeling, not a thinking. The poem should go down like thick strong raw wine, "strained, turbid still, from the viscous blood/Of the snaky bough" (IX, 104). It must make the same kind of assault on the reader that the poet has made on reality to seize its pith.

How does Browning manage to make his words pregnant with things?

Sometimes he achieves his goal by the plastic re-creation of the appearances of a scene, after the manner of Goethe or Keats, as in the deliberately classical frieze in the "Parleying with Gerard de Lairesse," where Browning is trying to show that he can, if he wants, be as lucid and sculptural as the Greek or Roman poets (X, 226–231). More often he is not satisfied with such a distant vision of a scene. He wants the reader to feel what he describes as if it were part of his own body, and to achieve this he must appeal to the more intimate senses of taste, smell, and touch, and to the kinesthetic sense whereby we make sympathetic muscular movements in response to the motion of things. All the ways in which Browning conveys his sense of being at the center of unformed matter are also used, with appropriate modifications, to express his experiences when he places himself at the interior of particular forms. The pervasive qualities of Browning's poetry are roughness and thickness. There are two opposite, yet related, causes for this texture. It expresses the shapeless bubbling chaos. It also expresses the substantial solidity of realized forms.

Browning wants to make the movement, sound, and texture of his verse an imitation of the vital matter of its subject, whether that subject is animate or inanimate, molten lava, flower, bird, beast, fish, or man. He thinks of matter, in whatever form, as something dense, heavy, rough, and strong-flavored, and there is for him a basic similarity between all forms of life — they are all strong solid substance inhabited by a vital energy. There are everywhere two things: the thick weight of matter, and within it an imprisoned vitality which seethes irresistibly out. The particular forms, however finely developed, are still rooted in the primal mud, and the means of expressing one are not unrelated to the means of expressing the other. It is by imitation of the roughness of a thing that one has most chance to get inside it. Things are not made of smooth appearances, but of the dense inner core which is best approached through heavy language.

Grotesque metaphors, ugly words heavy with consonants, stuttering alliteration, strong active verbs, breathless rhythms, onomatopoeia, images of rank smells, rough textures, and of things fleshy, viscous, sticky, nubbly, slimy, shaggy, sharp, crawling, thorny, or prickly — all these work together in Browning's verse to create an effect of unparalleled thickness, harshness, and roughness. These elements are so constantly combined that it is difficult to demonstrate one of them in isolation, but their simultaneous effect gives Browning's verse its special flavor, and could be said to be the most important thing about it. They are the chief means by which he expresses his sense of what reality is like. No other poetry can be at once so ugly, so "rough, rude, robustious" (X, 248), and so full of a joyous vitality.

Sometimes Browning achieves his effect by a direct appeal to the kinesthetic sense. The words invite us to imitate with our bodies what they describe, or to react to the poem as if it were a physical stimulus:

> As he uttered a kind of cough-preludious
> That woke my sympathetic spasm . . . (IV, 27)

> . . . the pig-of-lead-like pressure
> Of the preaching man's immense stupidity . . . (IV, 7)

> Aaron's asleep — shove hip to haunch,
> Or somebody deal him a dig in the paunch! (III, 386)

Sometimes the chief means is onomatopoeia — language at the level of interjection, exclamation, the sound of the word echoing the reality, often an affirmation of the body's organic life:

> Fee, faw, fum! bubble and squeak! (III, 385)

> . . . the thump-thump and shriek-shriek
> Of the train . . . (IV, 10)

> He blindly guzzles and guttles . . . (X, 321)

> . . . their blood gurgles and grumbles afresh . . . (X, 324)

Sometimes it is the use of words clotted with consonants, for bunched consonants seem to have power to express not only unformed chaos, but also the sharp texture of particular things:

> . . . slimy rubbish, odds and ends and orts . . . (X, 190)

> And one sharp tree — 't is a cypress — stands,
> By the many hundred years red-rusted,
> Rough iron-spiked, ripe fruit-o'ercrusted . . . (III, 175)

Sometimes, as in the last quotation, it is the use of verbs of violent action, whether in their primary form or in the form of participles which have become part of the substance of what they modify:

> Yataghan, kandjar, things that rend and rip,
> Gash rough, slash smooth, help hate so many ways . . . (IX, 72)

> If there pushed any ragged thistle-stalk
>   Above its mates, the head was chopped; the bents
>   Were jealous else. What made those holes and rents
> In the dock's harsh swarth leaves, bruised as to baulk
> All hope of greenness? 't is a brute must walk
>   Pashing their life out, with a brute's intents. (III, 408)

Sometimes the chief device giving strength and substance to the line is alliteration, often of explosive consonants:

> Here's John the Smith's rough-hammered head. Great eye,
> Gross jaw and griped lips do what granite can
> To give you the crown-grasper. What a man! (III, 392)

> First face a-splutter at me got such splotch
> Of prompt slab mud as, filling mouth to maw, . . .
> Immortally immerded . . . (VIII, 54)

> No, the balled fist broke brow like thunderbolt,
> Battered till brain flew! (VIII, 56)

> The barrel of blasphemy broached once, who bungs? (X, 277)

Sometimes the chief effect is produced by the quick heavy, often syncopated, rhythm, the heartbeat of the verse helping the reader to participate in the substance of the thing or person and the pace of its life. The rhythm of Browning's poems is internal, vegetative. It is not the mind speaking, but the depths of corporeal vitality, the organic pulsation of life. Browning manages, better than any other poet, to convey the bump, bump, bump of blood coursing through the veins, the breathless rush of excited bodily life, the vital pulse of the visceral level of existence, the sense of rapid motion. No other poetry is more robust in tempo:

> I sprang to the stirrup, and Joris, and he;
> I galloped, Dirck galloped, we galloped all three . . . (III, 112)

> Boh, here's Barnabas! Job, that's you?
> Up stumps Solomon — bustling too? (III, 385)

> Fife, trump, drum, sound! and singers then,
> Marching, say "Pym, the man of men!"

Up, heads, your proudest — out, throats, your loudest —
"Somerset's Pym!" (X, 248, 249)

Noon strikes, — here sweeps the procession! our Lady borne smiling and smart
With a pink gauze gown all spangles, and seven swords stuck in her heart!
Bang-whang-whang goes the drum, *tootle-te-tootle* the fife;
No keeping one's haunches still: it's the greatest pleasure in life. (III, 158)

Sometimes the effect is produced by a cascade of grotesque metaphors. In Browning's world anything can be a metaphor for anything else, and often he gets an effect of uncouth vitality by piling up a heap of idiosyncratic things, each living violently its imprisoned life:

Higgledy piggledy, packed we lie,
Rats in a hamper, swine in a stye,
Wasps in a bottle, frogs in a sieve,
Worms in a carcase, fleas in a sleeve. (III, 386)

Sometimes, however, it is a more subtle use of metaphor. Browning tends to qualify his description of external events with metaphors taken from the human body. This humanizing of dead objects is so pervasive in Browning's verse that it is easy not to notice it. His anthropomorphizing of the landscape is not achieved by a strenuous act of the imagination which transfers bodily processes to mountains or rivers. Everything in the world is already humanized for Browning, as soon as he sees it, and can be experienced as intimately as if it were his own body. The best proof of this is the casual and habitual way in which body-words are applied to the external world:

Oh, those mountains, their infinite movement!
    Still moving with you;
For, ever some new head and breast of them
    Thrust into view
To observe the intruder; you see it
    If quickly you turn
And, before they escape you, surprise them. (III, 305)

"Childe Roland to the Dark Tower Came" is a masterpiece of this kind of empathy. The effect of this weird poem comes not so much from the grotesque ugliness and scurfy "penury" of the landscape, as from the fact that the reader is continually coaxed by the language to experience this ghastly scene as if it were his own body which had got into this sad state:

> Now blotches rankling, coloured gay and grim,
>   Now patches where some leanness of the soil's
> Broke into moss or substances like boils;
> Then came some palsied oak, a cleft in him
> Like a distorted mouth that splits its rim
>   Gaping at death, and dies while it recoils. (III, 411)

Kinesthesia, onomatopoeia, "consonanted" (VIII, 296) words, verbs of violent action, alliteration, visceral rhythm, grotesque metaphors, pathetic fallacy — by whatever means, Browning's aim is to get to the inmost center of the other life, and working out from it, to express that life as it is lived, not as it appears from the outside to a detached spectator. This power of what Hazlitt called "gusto" is surely one of Browning's chief qualities as a poet. His ability to convey the "thingness" of things, in his own special apprehension of it, belongs not at all to the realm of ideas, and yet is at once the most obvious thing about his verse, and, it may be, the most profound. Certain of his very best poems are not at all complicated thematically, but they succeed magnificently in expressing Browning's strong feeling for the density, roughness, and vitality of matter. Such a poem is "Sibrandus Schafnaburgensis," with its extraordinary description of the adventures of a book he has pitched into the rain-filled crevice of a hollow plum-tree, and later fished up:

> Here you have it, dry in the sun,
>   With all the binding all of a blister,
> And great blue spots where the ink has run,
>   And reddish streaks that wink and glister
> O'er the page so beautifully yellow . . .
> How did he like it when the live creatures
>   Tickled and toused and browsed him all over,
> And worm, slug, eft, with serious features,
>   Came in, each one, for his right of trover?
> — When the water-beetle with great blind deaf face
>   Made of her eggs the stately deposit . . . ? (III, 122, 123)

Only Browning could have written such a poem, and only he could have written "The Englishman in Italy," with its admirable representation of an Italian landscape on a stormy autumn afternoon. Perhaps the best lines of all in this splendid poem are those describing the "sea-fruit." All the linguistic devices I have examined separately here work in concert, and, as in "Sibrandus Schafnaburgensis," word is indeed "pregnant with thing":

> — Our fisher [will] arrive,
> And pitch down his basket before us,
>   All trembling alive
> With pink and gray jellies, your sea-fruit;
>   You touch the strange lumps,
> And mouths gape there, eyes open, all manner
>   Of horns and of humps,
> Which only the fisher looks grave at,
>   While round him like imps
> Cling screaming the children as naked
>   And brown as his shrimps . . . (III, 301, 302)

ॐ

The methods of mimesis discussed so far work for both people and things. They are appropriate for imitating any matter informed by energy. Man is more than just these, however important they may be to even the most cerebral man. It is spiritual destinies which most fascinate Browning, and which he most wants to reproduce in his poems. For this more complicated task of imitation more complicated means are necessary.

The most obvious of these means is the dramatic monologue. Specific notions about human life lie behind this form of poetry and make it possible. Above all, Browning's monologuists are great talkers. An inexhaustible linguistic energy drives them to talk and talk and talk, and in talking to reveal themselves and the unique world they have built around themselves. Let any man, however clever and full of subterfuge, speak long enough, Browning believes, and he will expose his deepest secrets, allow us access all unwittingly to what is most inexpressible in his life — the very mark or note of his unique selfhood.

But we might be forced to wait a long time for this revelation. Browning, in spite of the length of many of his monologues, is anxious to reach the heart of each of his men and women as quickly as possible. Like a world-conqueror moving from city to city, he goes with the utmost rapidity from man to man, always hungry to make new conquests, for his aim is to possess the whole creation. Why does he assume that each town will soon fall to his blitzkrieg?

The assumption is made plausible by one all-important notion about human existence. Browning believes that each man, except perhaps the poet himself, has a permanent node or center of existence, and that this unchanging selfhood persists through all the vicissitudes of his life. If this is the case, then every action of a man, however insignificant, will reveal all of him, if we can understand it. This is another version of the idea that the small sphere is as perfect as the great. God is equally present in every part of the universe, from the fretful midge up to the greatest star; in the same way a man's permanent selfhood is equally present in his least gesture and in his most decisive acts. So Prince Hohenstiel-Schwangau, smoking his cigar in Leicester Square, tells his auditor that she will understand all his actions if she can understand why he connects two inkblots on a scrap of paper in just the way he does it (VII, 97). Browning did not need twentieth-century psychologists to tell him that the inkblot and the doodle reveal all! A man's life, says the Prince, is a strange kind of continuum, in which any point may be the center around which all the rest organizes itself into a pattern of converging rays: "Rays from all round converge to any point." This central point is just as complex in structure, has just as many parts, as the whole life from one end to the other. The smallest point is a complete image of the whole: "Understand one, you comprehend the rest." Each man lives in time, and must keep moving. But at any moment of time the whole world structures itself around the unchanging center of personality which persists through time, and sees the world always according to a unique perspective, just as the moon casts a uniform circle on the clouds it moves through (X, 120, 121).

If this is man's relation to what is around him, then the whole of a man's life is present in each moment of it, and we can begin anywhere in our attempt to understand him. Browning's dramatic monologues start suddenly in the midst of things. The reader is plunged abruptly into the midst of a consciousness, with its own assumptions and limitations, its own situation, and its own way of looking at things. The first lines of Browning's monologues are of special importance, and at their best they succeed in expressing the immediate pulse of a life, the unique flavor of an existence.

To read these monologues one after another is to be thrust suddenly into the thick of a life, then, when one poem is over, in another moment the reader finds himself in another personal world, radically different from the first, but just as real, just as inescapably *given* for the character himself.

Though it may be true that all a man's life is present in every moment of it, nevertheless certain moments express the life more dramatically than others, and make its meaning more manifest to the man himself or to others. Though Browning does not use the word "epiphany," he anticipates Joyce in his notion that there are certain moments which make the latent meaning of a life visible. Though a man has only one germ of life, that self is at first only an unrealized possibility. Only after a crucial decision, action, or experience does a man surround himself irrevocably with a tight net of circumstances. Then he becomes himself once and for all. Until now the man has been, in a sense, free, free as the shapeless sea. Henceforward he is fixed, trammeled in the results of his choice and act. Liquidity has been poured into a mold:

> How the world is made for each of us!
> How all we perceive and know in it
> Tends to some moment's product thus,
> When a soul declares itself — to wit,
> By its fruit, the thing it does! (III, 210)

Browning's aim is to get the whole meaning of a life into the most concentrated form. Sometimes this can best be done not by showing the crucial moment of decision itself, but by showing a much later time when a man looks back over his life, sees the pattern fall into place, and recognizes which was the best or most important event. A number of the monologues are like "Confessions" (IV, 302, 303), in which the speaker, on his deathbed, picks out one moment of his youth as the center of his life. Even "Porphyria's Lover," which seems so immediate, is written after the murder of Porphyria. This poem, like so many others by Browning, juxtaposes two moments: the present and some time in the past. Each man is always moving forward, and must change to some degree, even if it is only in the sense that each reaffirmation of his all-determining decision is different from all the others. It is impossible to fix life — which is the meaning of "Porphyria's Lover."

The best time to choose for a dramatic monologue may be neither the moment of death, nor the moment of repetitive reaffirmation, nor the original moment of choice. It may be simply a time when the character is thrown suddenly into a situation which brings him out strongly as he already is. The monologuist must talk, and to get him to talk it is only necessary to put him in a situation in which he will be stirred into speech to defend himself, and in defending reveal himself. The stimulus to volubility is the ticklish position. When Browning's characters, especially the so-called "casuists," are put in a situation of stress, a great burst of language rushes forth. So Aristophanes talks when, returning from a drunken party, he hears that his enemy Euripides is dead. So Sludge talks when he is found out in his knavery. So Fra Lippo Lippi talks when he is arrested in the street by the nightguard. So Guido talks in his cell, face to face with death.

Browning's magnificent exploitation of the potentialities of the dramatic monologue has tended to obscure the fact that he also used a great variety of other forms. The dramatic monologue is not appropriate in all cases. Browning is both "massive" and "porous," and can move at will in the realm of the opacity of unformed matter, in the realm of idiosyncratic form, and in the realm of the detached mind which surveys all life-forms from above. In some sense Browning is always in all three realms at once. Even in the most self-forgetful piece of role-playing the other situations are implicit. Only because he is withdrawn from his monologuists as well as engaged in their lives can he see the significance of those lives.

Historical perspective is one form of distancing. Browning often turns back on the past, as in "The Ring and the Book," and tries to discover its meaning. As historian he makes a basic assumption about the past: its continuity with the present. "What once lives never dies" (X, 233), and the past is therefore available not only to be understood, but to be brought back alive from the depths of the past. From one end of Browning's work to the other this notion of the poet as resuscitator of the past recurs:

> Confess now, poets know the dragnet's trick,
> Catching the dead, if fate denies the quick,
> And shaming her . . . (I, 180)

. . . Bring good antique stuff!
Was it alight once? Still lives spark enough
For breath to quicken, run the smouldering ash
Red right-through. (X, 244)

The historian-poet, turning back on the past from a distance, can bring the past back to life, recover its lost immediacy and vitality, and at the same time complete it, see it from the point of view of a later time as a whole life or destiny. He can pick out the moment which was crucial, show that as the pivot of the life, and, finally, he can see that life as part of a larger whole — human history or human life as an immense living organism, in its totality of seething life a gradual approach toward God. Each man lives his own life, but only the poet, standing as he does between the world and God, can glimpse the pattern made by all the lives together, and understand the way "each of the many helps to recruit /The life of the race by a general plan" (III, 211).

Browning's desire to express the living immediacy of each existence as well as its relation to the whole life of the race leads him to write many different kinds of poems. He is unwilling to let go any of the ways of getting at the infinite hidden in each finite thing. "One thing has many sides" (VII, 83). Any person or thing can be looked at and talked about in dozens of different ways, all equally legitimate.

Browning inherits the romantic notion that every impulse of his imagination may lead to ultimate truth and should be recorded just as it comes to him. There is a large measure of improvisation in his work. He wrote rapidly, sometimes with difficulty and much revision, but often straight on for long stretches of unbroken inspiration, so that in his later years his friends cautioned him against writing too much too fast. Like one of his own casuists, he needed to be impelled into speaking by something outside himself, and the exclamatory suddenness of the first words of his poems comes as much from Browning himself as from the role he plays with such gusto. It is as if the infinitely *disponible* mass of Browning has been stirred into life anew, given a direction and form by some violent provocation. If you push him hard he responds with equal energy, and will write you another huge poem, but he does not find in himself the strength or motivation to go in one direction rather than another.

There is something casual or accidental about Browning's poems. It is a matter of luck that we have these poems and not an entirely different set. All those other poems, the unwritten ones, were not called into existence by circumstances, and so remained unwritten. The subjects of his poems about historical persons or events are often not the great men, known to all, but obscure people who have hardly any place in history, and just happen to be known to Browning. He has a great fondness for the nooks and corners and backwaters of history. All people are interesting to Browning, and all are more or less equally interesting. He shares with his century and ours an inability to believe in the existence of the old kind of hero who stands head and shoulders above the multitude. With Dickens and Joyce he shares a sense of the complexity and depth of ordinary men and women. Few people have heard at all of some of the subjects of the "Parleyings": Bubb Dodington, Bartoli, Furini, De Lairesse, Avison. Before the nineteenth century one would not expect to find a poem about Mr. Sludge the medium, certainly not without such mock-heroic enhancements as we get in "The Rape of the Lock." Browning takes his men and women as he finds them, and does not need, as does even Joyce, to compare them to Ulysses or Penelope. Like other nineteenth-century writers, he must leap all the way from the trivial particular to the universal.

Just as the fact that the poem exists at all is accidental, since any number of other subjects would have done as well, so the order of the poem, the metaphors it uses, and its structure are also casual and fortuitous. The poem might have been written any number of different ways. It might have been longer or shorter. Its only justification is the fact that this is after all the way it came to Browning, as spontaneously and naturally as the pattern leaves make falling on a pond. There is throughout Browning a kind of anarchy of form and matter. He inherits nothing from the past, trusts every least instinct, and lets his poems grow like lawless sports in nature, unheard-of mutants directed by novel arrangements of chromosomes and efflorescing grotesquely — form, but unlike any other form. At any moment the whole direction of the poem may dynamically shift, and a huge new bubble outburst where was only flat latency before. He must not control any impulse to expression, and must give every possibility a chance to speak. Browning remains at the mercy of whim and the impulse of fortuitous circumstance, and his only consolation for this is his assumption that the world is a single continuous whole, like a tangle of yarn. Beginning anywhere, he is led everywhere. Just as each man is entirely revealed in a single gesture, so the whole life of the race is present in each man: "one page/Deciphered explains the whole/Of our common heritage" (X, 361). The only problem is to get started at all, for once started he is bound sooner or later to reach his goal. Hence he must cherish above all his sensitivity, his tendency to be shaken into form by the slightest external stimulus. Sometimes Browning reveals the triviality of the starting thrust of a poem, the "little fact/Which led [his] fancy forth" (X, 235). In the "Parleying with Charles Avison" he says that the sight of a blackcap stealing a cloth-shred for his nest in early March reminded him of a piece of music, a "bold-stepping 'March'" by Charles Avison. His memory, like the blackcap, snatched at random a rag of the past, and he was inspired to write a whole poem about Avison.

Browning ranges freely through the world, attacking reality in a great variety of ways, coaxing the truth out by indirection or assaulting it directly, treating all kinds of people and situations with all kinds of methods. He goes all the way from the absolute blind leap into a person in the dramatic monologues, to the halfway relation of the "Parleyings," to the meditative circling after the fashion of Henry James or Conrad in "Red Cotton Night-Cap Country," to the direct historical anecdote in the "Dramatic Idyls." He writes love poems, objective history, fragile lyrics, philosophical meditation with little basis in dramatic action, as in "La Saisiaz" and "Ferishtah's Fancies," plays, translations, a long poem with a fictional approach full of dialogue ("The Inn Album"), and so on.

All of these forms are like the dramatic monologues in that they seek the elusive truth hidden within individual human lives. For some subjects, however, an objective method is better than an introspective one. What men and women did and said, their manifest actions, are avenues to their secret centers. This exterior way, the way of the "Dramatic Idyls," is as valid as the interior method of the dramatic monologues. Browning did, after all, write a large number of plays. Like "Paracelsus" and "Sordello," the plays study the question of *power,* political rather than magical or poetical power, but still power. If "Paracelsus" shows the failure of the romantic Promethean to reach a universal truth, many of the plays have as their subject the opposite theme: the impossibility of embodying ideals in political reality. This theme is appropriately explored in a more objective form. Another objective genre which Browning treats in his own way is the historical novel. "Balaustion's Adventure" and "Aristophanes' Apology," taken together, represent, among other things, an extraordinary effort of historical reconstruction. Browning has used every means at his disposal, historical record and anecdote, biography, the scholia on the Greek plays, to find out and reproduce, as an immediate experience, what it would have been like to have lived in Athens at the time of the death of Euripides.

Two of Browning's modes of poetry represent more radical innovations, and deserve to be included among the characteristic creations of his genius. In the "Parleying with Gerard de Lairesse" Browning sets his vision of "earth's common surface, rough, smooth, dry or damp" (X, 223) against De Lairesse's vision of "Artistry's Ideal" (X, 221). He asks whether it would be good to have double vision, to see like himself and like De Lairesse at the same time: "Advantage would it prove or detriment/If I saw double?" (X, 223, 224). All the parleyings see double. In these poems Browning contrives to give two or more points of view at once, all overlapping, superimposed, transparent to one another. This is a great advantage to a man who believes that "one thing has many sides." Instead of being forced to accept one point of view in order to be able to speak at all, or, at best, being able to give diverse points of view only serially, Browning here contrives to see his subject from several points of view at once. For this reason these poems are at times very difficult reading. The "Parleying with George Bubb Dodington" is one of Browning's most bewilderingly obscure poems. It gives at once the views on political action of Bubb Dodington, Disraeli, and "Browning himself," if it is permissible to speak of Browning's own view — it might be better to say that the third view is simply that of the first speaker. There is in these poems no sovereign point of view. Only the various perspectives exist, the view and what is viewed inextricably bound up.

Finally, there is the method of "Red Cotton Night-Cap Country: or Turf and Towers." This poem can be classed, for technical virtuosity, with the most accomplished of the dramatic mono-logues. It is one of Browning's most grotesque poems. Like its title it is a huge, rough, awkward monstrosity, with its parts blown all out of size. It has a wild, disordered, undulating vitality, like the buildings of the Spanish architect Gaudí. "Red Cotton Night-Cap Country," to borrow a phrase from the poem itself, is "a heap grotesque/Of funguous flourishing excrescence" (VII, 392). Its subject, as contemporary readers complained, is dark, sordid, and Gothic. It is a tale of illicit love, self-maiming, religious fanaticism, mental instability, and suicide.

"Red Cotton Night-Cap Country" carries the method of indirection as far as it can go. Its technique is the reverse of the leap into the depths of another person in the dramatic monologues. Here, as in Conrad's fiction, the long-winded voice of the narrator intervenes between us and the story. The idea is to reach the depths by lingering on the surface, by just that "prolonged hovering flight of the subjective over the outstretched ground of the case supposed" for which James praised Conrad. Browning has here recognized that there are some human events whose truth cannot be reached directly. To leap directly at the story is to be repulsed and to be forced merely to retell superficial events, as does the newspaper. He must go around and around the story, seeing it from all sides, and gently coaxing the truth into displaying itself.

The movement of "Red Cotton Night-Cap Country" is a spiral one. The narrator circles very gradually and with infinite reticence from the falsely benign outside (the tower) toward the rotten center (the turf). The poem begins with a direct view of a pleasant country estate, and only very slowly, and by an elaborate building up in retrospect, as in Faulkner's novels, do we discover what ugly depths lie beneath this surface. Browning tantalizes the reader with hints and indirections. He has chosen the way to tell the story which takes the most telling, using, for example, an elaborate network of extended metaphors. These metaphors transfer the facts into another realm, where they can be played with and teased and turned this way and that. Such is the extended baroque metaphor comparing Miranda's religious faith to the tower and his sensuality to the turf inside. Only after a long series of these most elaborate spiraling circumlocutions does Browning enter at last inside the mind of Miranda as he stands on his tower, just before he leaps to his death, and looks back at "the life that rolls out ribbon-like/Its shot-silk length behind [him]" (VII, 379). In a way the whole poem is this moment blown out to its full dimensions, for a multitude of factors is involved in Miranda's leap and must be understood in order to understand the bare journalistic fact: a man leaped to his death from the tower of his estate. In another sense, the whole grotesque monstrosity of a poem is one "moment's flashing, amplified" (VII, 406), the moment when the poet pierced intuitively to the heart of the story, and saw all its circumstances in terms of that center. The moment of conception and the central moment of the action, the hero's suicide, are really the same moment. Only the fertilization of one by the other brings the poem to birth. In both cases "a minute's space" (VII, 378) expands to monstrous dimensions when its full contents and implications are expressed in words. "Red Cotton Night-Cap Country," born of the conjunction of these two moments, is like "one particle of ore" which "beats out such leaf" (VII, 378) when the poet puts it all in words, just as the lengthy speculations of "La Saisiaz" are born of the insight of one "pregnant hour" (IX, 152) when Browning climbed Mount Salève:

> Along with every act — and speech is act —
> There go, a multitude impalpable
> To ordinary human faculty,
> The thoughts which give the act significance.
> Who is a poet needs must apprehend
> Alike both speech and thoughts which prompt to speak.
> Part these, and thought withdraws to poetry:
> Speech is reported in the newspaper. (VII, 378)

"Speech is reported in the newspaper" — nothing could be a more forceful repudiation of the dramatic monologues, which consist entirely of a direct report of someone's words. Browning recognizes, in "Red Cotton Night-Cap Country" and in other poems, that there are some subjects which do not yield to the direct approach. If a subject will not yield to one approach he invents another, just as he invents new stanzaic forms with a kind of careless abandon.

෨

Does Browning find any laws which remain the same in all kinds of existence, or is he forced to conclude that each perspective on life is unique, and incompatible with all the others? After the failure of his Promethean assault on heaven, Browning starts out as a kind of nominalist, determined to explore the minute particulars of life in order to report exactly on their nature.

Like Don Juan, in "Fifine at the Fair," he wants to make generalizations if he can, and prove that the vast multiplicity of the creation is made up of special cases of certain universal laws. He will show how the complex and heterogeneous grows from the simple and homogeneous, how there is a single type of all life which manifests itself diversely throughout the world, "Not only in beast, bird, fish, reptile, insect, but/The very plants and earths and ores" (VII, 250). To understand inductively this type and its laws would also be to understand oneself, not only, as Don Juan says, "by contrast with the thing I am not," but also because one is oneself a version of the universal type, the "nude form" behind the "chequered robe" of life.

God is the universal type who has put "a spark/Of [his] spheric perfection" (X, 273) into each of his beings. Each created thing has, like the hero of "Pauline," "a need, a trust, a yearning after God" (I, 11). The aim of all creatures, not only of Browning in his Promethean youth, is to embody the infinite God within the bounds of their finitude. "A spark disturbs our clod" (IV, 262). If we allow that inner spark to express itself in a fit earthly form the goal will be reached — a life which is at once concrete and universal, God incarnate in a material reality.

Seeking infinity, the creation finds everywhere finitude. Each created thing is a seed, and that seed is endowed with a thrust of energy urging it to grow toward God, though it can achieve only the perfection of its own eccentricity. God is at the center of each created thing. God is its goal. All in between, the realm of time and space and material existence, is an area of falsehood, evil, lies, subterfuge, the million masks which disguise the divine seed:

> Truth inside, and outside, truth also; and between
> Each, falsehood that is change, as truth is permanence. (VII, 267)

Every individual thing is a point on the circumference of the eternal circle life pursues, and, though its spark of vitality comes

from God at the center, the radius of energy, by the time it goes
from center to circumference, endows the point on the periphery
not with its original "spheric perfection," but only with the energy to become something divergent, unlike any other thing. The
mystery of creation is the mystery of the transition whereby the
ray starting from the white light at the center gets gradually more
and more colored as it goes toward the circumference, until it
becomes an individual color, only one of the infinite ingredients
of white. The same finger of God touches clay again and again,
but one time it makes Adam, another time the tiger, then the
lamb, and so on, as unity inexplicably gives birth to multiplicity.
For "varied modes of creatureship abound,/Implying just as
varied intercourse/For each with the creator of them all," and
every man "has his own mind and no other's mode" (VII, 100).
Each creature bears the stamp of the deity, but the face is different each time, for God is protean:

> . . . a sense informs you — brute,
> Bird, worm, fly, great and small,
> Each with your attribute
> Or low or majestical! (X, 363)

> Never shall I believe any two souls were made
> Similar . . . (VII, 198)

Browning's term for this dissimilarity is "grotesque." The uncouth roughness of Browning's people and their speech, the way
each reveals himself as, like Caliban, a sport in nature, a kind of
wild monstrosity, is the outward and visible sign of their idiosyncrasy. In each creature there is "some deviation." No one is
made exactly in the image of God, and "in no one case there
[lacks]/The certain sign and mark, — say hint, say, trick of lip/
Or twist of nose, — that [proves] a fault in workmanship,/Change
in the prime design . . ." (VII, 247). Grotesque visible forms and
grotesque language are really the same, for both are the result of
the pushing out of a novel internal energy, an energy which may
express itself in appearance or in speech. Either is another example of "the wild grotesque" (VII, 201). So Don Juan dreams
of the carnival at Venice, where he sees a great crowd of men and
women all masked, each made monstrous by the grotesquerie of
his own penchant: "each soul a-strain/Some one way through the

flesh — the face, an evidence/O' the soul at work inside; and, all the more intense,/So much the more grotesque" (VII, 245).

Inside, the intense energy, the eccentric seed of life — outside, the grotesque visible form. Each person, by doing what comes naturally, becomes just that self God intended him to be, and in that process becomes grotesque. Every creature is surrounded on all sides by a swarming life which it must push out of the way or assimilate, or else it may end, like the newt in "Caliban upon Setebos," "turned to stone, shut up inside a stone" (IV, 298). This thickness may be material or social. All living things become themselves not only by growth from the inside, but by the transformation of what surrounds them. Everything in their neighborhood must be made over into their own image, as in "Andrea del Sarto" "a common greyness silvers everything" (IV, 118), or as in "Caliban Upon Setebos" everything is Calibanish. All Browning's characters can boast, with Prince Hohenstiel-Schwangau: ". . . no thing I know,/Feel or conceive, but I can make my own/Somehow, by use of hand or head or heart . . ." (VII, 112).

Browning repeatedly expresses his sense of the way a living thing does not stop with the bounds of its body, but creates around itself an aroma, an aura, a milieu, which is its habitation in the world. In itself the world "inert/Was, is, and would be ever, — stuff for transmuting, — null/And void until man's breath evoke the beautiful" (VII, 205, 206). But each strong life transforms the world until "an aura gird[s] the soul, wherein it seems/To float and move, a belt of all the glints and gleams/It struck from out that world, its weaklier fellows found/So dead and cold" (VII, 205). All things should fulfill the law which decrees "his own world for every mortal" (IX, 134). Browning finds something comfortable and cozy in the picture of a creature hidden safely away in its own appropriate milieu, as the "worm there in yon clod its tenement" (IX, 135), or "rose enmisted by that scent it makes" (VIII, 69). It is his very image of joy, and prime proof of God's goodness:

> There's the palm-aphis, minute miracle
> As wondrous every whit as thou or I:
> Well, and his world's the palm-frond, there he's born,
> Lives, breeds and dies in that circumference,
> An inch of green for cradle, pasture-ground,
> Purlieu and grave . . . (X, 122)

The lark's on the wing;
The snail's on the thorn:
God's in his heaven —
All's right with the world! (II, 114)

Browning's habitual image for the unit made of a live thing and its environment is the *sphere*. Each creature, from aphis to man, makes for himself a bubble-world, and within this "petty circle lotted out/Of infinite space" (I, 99), he lives. Each of these globules, from the smallest and simplest to the most inclusive and complex, is "perfect from centre to circumference," for "orbed to the full can be but fully orbed" (X, 239). The wisdom of God is manifest in the works of the creation not only in the cunning way each creature is made, but in the way each is surrounded by a circumambient milieu which fits it exactly:

His sprites created,
God grants to each a sphere to be its world,
Appointed with the various objects needed
To satisfy its own peculiar want . . . (I, 78)

Though this globed milieu is perfect in itself, and perfectly fitted to its tenant, it is only a "petty circle." Beyond its limits the inhabitant is absolutely forbidden to go. Each man, like any spider or aphis, surrounds himself with "*status, entourage,* worldly circumstance" (IV, 129), and he tends to be utterly blind to all else — "Limited every way, a perfect man/Within the bounds built up and up since birth/Breast-high about him" (VIII, 245). Browning has a strong sense of the abyss between "Man's impotency, God's omnipotence" (X, 124), and a strong sense also of the value of a humble acceptance of this limitation. Nothing but disaster befalls those who believe they are "equal to being all" (I, 195), and thereby make the mistake of "thrusting in time eternity's concern" (I, 195). Sheer blind ignorance is the best preventive of Prometheanism:

In such various degree, fly and worm, ore and plant,
All know, none is witless: around each, a wall
Encloses the portion, or ample or scant,
Of Knowledge: beyond which one hair's breadth, for all
Lies blank — not so much as a blackness . . . (X, 274)

Browning seems most to admire the man or beast who accepts limitation, seeks nothing beyond his own narrow sphere, and "turning in a circle on itself/Looks neither up nor down but keeps the spot,/Mere creature-like, and, for religion, works,/ Works only and works ever, makes and shapes/And changes" (VII, 115). Such a creature has best obeyed God. He has become and accomplished something tangible, has left "the handiwork, the act and deed,/Were it but house and land and wealth, to show/ Here was a creature perfect in the kind" (VII, 115). Such construction of the solid and real, a self and its entourage, seems to be its own justification, and it does not matter what is made, so long as it exists: "Whether as bee, beaver, or behemoth,/What's the importance?" (VII, 115). Browning's casuistical apologists defend themselves by saying that they have only fulfilled their natures as God has made them. In doing so they have brought a unique and irreplaceable self into the world, and can say: ". . . finally I have a life to show,/The thing I did, brought out in evidence" (IV, 147).

This matching of self and milieu is one of the constants of Browning's poetry. The triumph of "Caliban upon Setebos," for example, is the way it introduces us into a world where everything has been made over to fit the man. We are made vividly to feel what it would be like to see the world according to Caliban's unique perspective on it, for here there is no division between self and milieu. Caliban, lying in his mud bath like a dinosaur in the primeval ooze, participates intimately, through his touch and taste, in the life which surrounds him, and by an artful transfer of body-words to things in his milieu, and of milieu-words to his body, it becomes difficult to tell where his body stops and where the surrounding world begins. Even the distant sea and sky are, by the image of a spider-web (IV, 292), brought close and made part of the unity of body and world. The sky is no emptiness, but is a tangible substance crisscrossed by a network of palpable sunbeams which put every part of it in touch with every other part, the whole sky in touch with the sea, and both in touch with Caliban. This interpenetration of self and world is no longer that of the shapeless Browning in a shapeless ooze, but that of the formed creature in his fitting environment. "To each creature his own world" — this seems to be the most universal of truths, and the recognition of this truth is the sole prize of Browning's long journey through the creation.

ౖ

What has happened to the desire of created things to embody God in time and space, to express the infinite in the finite? In building a private world around themselves man and beast have gradually cut themselves off from God, until, in the end, they cannot even remember that there is anything but their own petty circle lotted out of infinite space. Within that narrow sphere they revolve endlessly, like animals in a cage, and ultimately their lives may stagnate for want of fresh air, as Andrea del Sarto suffocates in the circle of his own perfection. They may become fatally at ease, not in Zion, but in their own "nest-like little chamber" (X, 107). God seems to have condemned man to exclusion from God.

To remember Andrea del Sarto will remind us that this horrible stagnation takes place only in exceptional cases. Andrea del Sarto is tormented by the silver-gray passivity of his life, and is very much aware of what exists outside his sphere. All of Browning's people, from the hardly human Caliban up to St. John, are driven not only to speculate about the absolute, but to strive to possess it.

Browning makes a radical distinction between man and the rest of God's creatures. All creatures are limited to their own perspectives on the world, but man alone is aware of this limitation, and, in order to be aware of it, he must be aware that there is something outside his circle. On this "ignorance confirmed/By knowledge" (X, 58) all else depends. Especially in his later poems Browning keeps coming back to this starting point. Like a rush swept in the stream, man knows himself and that part of the stream where he is now, but where he has come from and where the stream is taking him he knows not: "Cause before, effect behind me — blanks! The midway point I am . . ." (IX, 131). This knowledge of ignorance and limitation is the only solid standing-ground in the incomprehensible flux.

Man is unable to stop with this sage acquiescence, and, in spite of its recurrence in Browning's late poems, it is not really the pinnacle of his wisdom. Once a man knows that there is something he does not know he cannot rest easy in his clay prison, but is driven to burst the bounds of his milieu in order to seek new knowledge. All Browning's characters are seeking some limitless satisfaction. Insects, plants, and animals are satisfied with the spheric perfection they can make within their limits. God already enjoys an infinite bliss in infinite ways. Only for men it is true that "what's come to perfection perishes" (III, 169). Man is unfinished and incomplete, and is constantly driven to go beyond himself in the hope that he may see God face to face. In one sense man is less than the merest starfish in his house of seaweed, since the starfish is perfect in his way, but "what's whole, can increase no more,/Is dwarfed and dies, since here's its sphere" (IV, 247), while man by his very incompleteness is moving toward what transcends both starfish and man. For "progress" is "man's distinctive mark alone,/Not God's, and not the beasts': God is, they are,/Man partly is and wholly hopes to be" (IV, 288).

Browning's chief objection to his casuistical villains is that they accept the status quo, and thereby turn themselves into beasts pacing in a closed circle. Unlike the frustrate lovers in "The Statue and the Bust," Bishop Blougram, Mr. Sludge, or Prince Hohenstiel-Schwangau can say with justice that they are as God has made them. But this is not enough, and the men who accept it are doomed to perish of their own smug self-satisfaction. Such people will become "finished and finite clods, untroubled by a spark" (IV, 261), and Browning condemns them without reservation: "That man has turned round on himself and stands,/Which in the course of nature is, to die" (IV, 285). For "a man's reach should exceed his grasp" (IV, 120), and only as long as men "go on moving" (III, 44) are they still alive. The people whom Browning admires, whether they are grammarians, lovers, adventurers, or mystics, are driven to "go on, go on" (IV, 74), and all guide their lives by their assumption that "man was made to grow, not stop" (IV, 283). As soon as we try to crystallize our lives, even in a good acquisition, we begin to dissolve, and quickly become nothing. This is one reason for the furious pace of Browning's poems. Though some of them are very long, they all move rapidly from one point to another, as if Browning fears the poem will evaporate and become mere fume of spirit, unless he keeps it moving fast enough to match the dynamic march of the world.

To live in the realm of imperfection and change, the intermediate area between beast and God, is to live in a place where all remains in doubt. This painful uncertainty is the very sign that one is still on the way toward God. If things become bland and comprehensible a man can be sure he is off the track, and has got stranded in some stagnant backwater. Browning's men and women, like Browning, accept eagerly the muddle of life, and fear slothful ease more than anything else. In a "ghastly smooth life" they would be "left in God's contempt apart" (IV, 75).

Browning frequently expresses the idea that life is a tangled mixture, "where wage/War, just for soul's instruction, pain with joy,/Folly with wisdom, all that works annoy/With all that quiets and contents, — in brief,/Good strives with evil" (X, 214). Man is a "medley" (X, 194); his life is "half female, half male — . . . ambiguous thing" (X, 154), "all halved and nothing whole" (IX, 141). In any man's life "false things [are] mingled with real,/Good with bad" (X, 149); "Joy, sorrow, — by precedence, subsequence — /Either on each, make fusion, mix in Life/That's both and neither wholly" (X, 120). Human existence, in short, is a "tohu-bohu" (X, 60), an inextricable confusion of "hopes which dive,/And fears which soar — faith, ruined through and through/By doubt, and doubt, faith treads to dust . . ."(X, 60).

Life *must* be so, for man could not stand to see God directly: "Our hutch/Lights up at the least chink: let roof be rent — / How inmates huddle, blinded at first spasm,/Cognizant of the sun's self through the chasm!" (IX, 176). The creation and its evil benignly hide God from us, until we are strong enough to look the sun in the eye, just as layers of falsehood protect the pure soul-drop in the profound deeps of each person. That "centre-drop" remains untouched by the thick coating of lies around it, "All unaffected by — quite alien to — what sealed/And saved it long ago" (VII, 249). The use of evil is "to environ us,/Our breath, our drop of dew, with shield enough/Against that sight till we can bear its stress" (IV, 149).

A world of falsehood and evil is good in still another way. Only such a world will keep man moving toward God. Life is a probation, and must remain cloudy, perplexed, and confused, for if any one of its laws is abrogated, especially the mixing of evil and good, the whole structure will tumble to the ground. "The good of goodness" will "vanish" when the "ill of evil" ceases, and "hope the arrowy," the testimony of our orientation toward God, will disappear if life becomes bland and unequivocal (IX, 148). We are not yet in heaven, and only if we suffer and are bewildered will we be driven to move step by step through the arduous struggle toward God: ". . . knowledge can but be/Of good by knowledge of good's opposite — /Evil" (X, 214). If we cannot even see good unless it is set against evil, so we can only hope to reach it through the beneficent struggle with evil, for "every growth of good/[Springs] consequent on evil's neighborhood" (X, 160), and "We must endure the false, no particle of which/Do we acquaint us with, but up we mount a pitch/Above it, find our head reach truth, while hands explore/The false below . . ." (VII, 215, 216). Man must immerse himself in the destructive element. On earth man "strives for good/Through evil" (X, 158), and it is "evil whereby good is brought about" (VII, 113).

Browning's vision of the ambiguous realm where man lives culminates in a conviction of the value of suffering and failure. Just as stagnation and complacency are the worst evils, so the best man is the one who tries for the most, suffers most, and fails most. The more acute our suffering and the more complete our failure the more surely we can promise ourselves ultimate joy. Knowledge wrung from suffering is the precious "balsam" from the "bruised" tree of life (IX, 138). At any moment the seemingly endless battle may end, and we may find ourselves suddenly and miraculously at our goal — but only if we fight on unflinchingly to the end:

> For sudden the worst turns the best to the brave,
>   The black minute's at end,
> And the elements' rage, the fiend-voices that rave,
>   Shall dwindle, shall blend,
> Shall change, shall become first a peace out of pain,
>   Then a light . . . (IV, 306)

ह॰

Never on earth can this happen. Peace remains future, something we have not yet reached. The soul's divine central drop seeks to express itself completely in an earthly form, but it always fails, and so it goes on indefinitely, seeking and never finding.

An eloquent passage in "Fifine at the Fair" describes this process in terms of magical transformations of buildings Don Juan sees in his dream. Each building lasts only for a time, and then "liquid change through artery and vein/O' the very marble [winds] its way" (VII, 253), it collapses gradually, and then another building shapes itself from the ruins, pushing its way from within. So the process goes on, like the "burgeoning" and decay of plants or of some other organic thing: ". . . temples . . . subdivide, collapse, /And tower again, transformed" (VII, 254). All this strange architectural "transfiguration" describes the endless change of the customs, science, philosophy, and religion man makes to screen his little round. Nature's endless proliferation of new forms out of the primitive mud is matched by similar transformations in society. The temporal progress of mankind is constant formation, followed by return to formlessness, followed by re-formation again, "shape re-shaped, till out of shapelessness/Come shape again as sure" (VII, 257). All human forms are modulations of a single inner germ of truth, and life is the same in its thousand different forms because the same truth remains behind the ever-changing "husk-like lies" which are "truth's corolla-safeguard" (X, 247). "Every lie [is]/Quick with a germ of truth" (IV, 357), but since "truth is forced/To manifest itself through falsehood" (VII, 267), truth is never fully expressed, though it always directs the expression.

The infinite variety of human lives has one universal meaning: the distance of all lives from God. The spark hidden under dead ashes, everywhere the same in every human heart, is just this universal law of the incompatibility between finite and infinite. As for Yeats, so for Browning, every least thing in time and space can be a center of the whole, the sun "glass-conglobed/Though to a pin-point circle" (X, 167), but for Browning the sun in the burning-glass is precisely *not* the true sun, but only another expression of the infinite distance of man from the deity. Everything, however small, is a center from which man can experience again his eccentricity, and the transcendence of God in relation to this misplaced center.

This theme of the failure of the finite to encompass the infinite is even present in the poems which celebrate the "infinite moment," the moment of musical, mystical, or amorous ecstasy when the screens between one person and another, or between man and God, are almost broken, in a time out of time which seems as long as eternity. Browning emphasizes the brevity of the infinite moment, the way it still involves incompleteness and dissatisfaction.

However close to God a man gets he must still say: "A film hides us from Thee — 'twixt inside and out,/A film" (X, 272). No finite moment, however intense, can have the full plenitude of God, or a complete possession of another person. Though in such poems as "By the Fireside" the lovers are, in the "moment, one and infinite," "mixed at last/In spite of the mortal screen" (III, 208, 210), the screen still remains, and the other side of Browning's experience of love is expressed in such a poem as "Two in the Campagna." The lover can almost place himself within the loved person, but not quite. All he gains is a poignant experience of a truth which he *almost* understands, and the wisdom born of this experience is the knowledge, once again, of the infinite dissatisfaction and yearning which is the fate of all finite hearts:

> Then the good minute goes. . . .
> Just when I seemed about to learn!
>   Where is the thread now? Off again!
> The old trick! Only I discern —
>   Infinite passion, and the pain
> Of finite hearts that yearn. (III, 220)

Man's tormenting failure ever to bring together the starting point, his heart, and its goal, the infinite, drives him onward in his characteristic motion from form to formlessness and back to form again. Browning discovers that this process is the universal rhythm of all human life everywhere. Scarcely has a man begun to enjoy the fruits of any accomplishment when he perceives its limitation, and breaks out again toward something beyond. Man is never really in one place, but is always, wherever he is, "halfway into the next" (IV, 153). This motif is expressed repeatedly in different ways, but perhaps the best version is in a very late poem, "Ixion." Man is, like Ixion, bound to a wheel of eternal suffering, and this suffering is his ever-frustrated attempt to burst through the bonds of his humanity and reach the "Not-Thou beyond it,/Fire elemental, free, frame unencumbered, the All" (X, 31). Man is limited, but only the "All" will satisfy him, so he keeps stubbornly trying again and again to break through to the elemental fire, only to find again and again that he is still surrounded by the "circumambient" (X, 32) flesh and its limitations.

"Ixion" demonstrates that there are curious analogies between Browning's thought and that of Franz Kafka. Their metaphysical experiences are in many ways the same, but the emotional tone and atmosphere are radically different. Browning is a very British and Victorian Kafka, a Kafka whose ebullient good cheer cannot be dashed by even the most disastrous failure. There is a little unintentional Kafkesque humor in the picture Browning gives of man hoping against hope, picking himself up after some incredible disaster, dusting himself off, and plodding indefatigably on. As in Kafka, the moment of illumination often coincides with the moment of death. Kafka would have understood "Childe Roland to the Dark Tower Came," and might have connected Roland's death with the fate of Joseph K., whose triumph, such as it is, coincides with his execution. Browning's characters, like Kafka's, remain "dauntless" (III, 413) to the last, always ready to try one more expedient, even when it might seem clear that all expedients are doomed to failure. Like Kafka's heroes, Browning's characters believe in God, and will be satisfied with nothing less than to "get to God" (IV, 99). Browning's characters too cannot reach their goal, and, as in *The Castle,* the chief testimony to God's existence is the continuation of the ever-renewed, ever-frustrated struggle to reach him. The difference is in Browning's robust acceptance of his Ixionlike situation, and in his earnest desire to believe that life is good and just:

> Strive, mankind, though strife endure through endless obstruction,
> Stage after stage, each rise marred by as certain a fall!
> Baffled forever — (X, 31)

This theme of failure is the best approach to the seeming contradictions of Browning's treatment of the problem of evil. There are two different problems of evil in Browning. Browning justifies the impersonal evil of sickness, cold, want, and natural disaster as part of the necessary economy of earthly existence. There is also personal evil, the malice in man's soul. Here there is an apparent contradiction in Browning's thought. He wants to judge people by an absolute standard, and to say that Guido is bad, Pompilia good. He also wants to say that every life, by the very fact that it exists, is good, an irreplaceable part of God's expression of himself in space and time. Though God enjoys an infinite bliss in infinite ways, it is through men, animals, insects, and plants that he does this. But the positive energy with which each creature fulfills its allotted role is the very act by which it affirms itself as evil.

Evil is ultimately imperfection, but imperfect substance. All things of time, space, and matter, by the very fact that they exist here, are less than God, therefore in a sense evil. The evil in Blougram, Sludge, or Guido derives in part from the fact that they are so intensely themselves, and are willing to be no more than themselves. Accepting their limitations, they become examples of grotesque and funguslike excrescence, deviation, idiosyncrasy. Affirming themselves as unique persons, they simultaneously affirm themselves as outside the truth.

The very sincerity toward themselves which Browning permits his monologuists forces them to go down layer after layer through falsehood until they reach the truth which is hidden in their hearts. This admission of their lie is truth, for it is their assertion of themselves as they do in fact exist. Moreover this true lie, when affirmed, permits them to recognize the special way in which they are related to the single great transcendent truth: by a "continual," however distant, "approximation to it" (Scudder, 1010).

Evil in Browning is not the terrifying nonentity of St. Thomas. It is the active reality of the color yellow or the color red. Such a color is not nothing, but it is not white either. It is part of white, and therefore related to the center from which it has rayed out. Any road is "one path to Heaven" (VII, 113), for "truth, displayed i' the point, flashes forth everywhere/I' the circle" (VII, 236). Standing anywhere we "Touch segment in the circle whence all lines/Lead to the centre equally, red lines/Or black lines, so they but produce themselves" (VII, 113). Each color is at once tormented by its failure to be white, and tantalized by the fact that it is somewhat white. The color red, or any other color, is torn in two directions: if it tries to become white it becomes nothing, for "an absolute vision is not for this world" (Scudder, 1010). In that direction it reaches only the emptiness of a realization that it is not white and cannot be so. Only as red is it anything at all, but to affirm its redness is to affirm its eccentricity, its evil, its grotesque failure to be white. The human situation in Browning's world reminds us of the sins of impatience and laziness in Kafka's parable. One must continually vibrate back and forth between two false and intolerable stances. The real sinners in Browning are those who acquiesce in being red or yellow, but even this is a form of relation to the white truth, and therefore a possession of it — as Browning's casuistical monologues show. Browning's dramatic poems rest on a double paradox: the white light shines in the heart of the blackest sinner, and even the best human being, even Pompilia herself, is imperfect.

Browning uses just this image of the relation of colored rays to unattainable white in an important poem, "Numpholeptos." Like so many of his poems it dramatizes man's relation to God in terms of the relation of one person to another. As the title suggests, the speaker is in love with an unattainable nymph, the white moon of his desire. Outward from this white node flow divergent rays of all colors in prismatic splendor, and the central white is "alike the source/And tomb of that prismatic glow" (IX, 50). Each color is related to the central white, and yet separated from it, in "divorce/Absolute, all-conclusive" (IX, 50). The nymph condemns her lover to a paradoxical and hopeless quest. He must seek the center by going away from it. He must traverse each ray to its limit, and, oh "absurd/As frightful" (IX, 52), must reach the moon unstained by it, reach white by the violent affirmation of yellow or red, as Browning tries to reach God by the technique of role-playing. The lover turns his back on the moon-nymph, and goes forth bravely on his absurd quest. Like Browning plunging himself into the subject of one of his monologues, he sinks into the yellow ray, and soaks himself in yellow. What is the result? Far from reaching white by the exploration of yellow, he becomes dyed through and through with yellow, and when he returns in his "sulphur-steeped disguise" (IX, 52) he "reek[s] suffused/With crocus, saffron, orange" (IX, 50), and all other possible shades of yellow. By following to its limit one of the colored rays going out from the center, he has only succeeded in becoming grotesque and eccentric himself, as Browning does when he dons the costume of Caliban or Mr. Sludge. He is "a man become/Monstrous in garb, nay — flesh disguised as well,/Through his adventure" (IX, 50). And of course the nymph rejects him with disdain when he presents himself before her. Then, in spite of momentary rebellion, he goes forth on another long walk for nothing, this time to explore the crimson ray to its limit. This submission to the periphery, followed by a return to the center and repulsion by it

can go on as long as eternity, just as Browning's life of role-playing could go on forever without getting him one step closer to his
goal.

Browning's attempt to fulfill himself and reach God by entering
into the lives of a great many men and women has led him inevitably toward his own special experience of the eternal return
— the infinitely prolonged repetition, life after life, of different
versions of the same failure to escape from finitude:

> . . . when this life is ended, begins
> New work for the soul in another state,
>   Where it strives and gets weary, loses and wins:
> Where the strong and the weak, this world's congeries,
>   Repeat in large what they practised in small,
> Through life after life in unlimited series . . . (III, 170)

ಶಿ

The strategy of role-playing seems to have been a total failure.
Nor do the other forms taken by Browning's poetry succeed in
reaching the central truth which is the ultimate source of each
eccentric surface. But Browning has, with the help of his alter
egos, seen more than any one of them can. Each one is one "facet-
flash of the revolving year," one ray of the "red, green and blue
that whirl into a white" (V, 44), one finite center from which the
universal truth can be experienced. That this *is* the universal
truth can best be seen by the poet who juxtaposes all these points
of view. Even so, to discover that failure is the law of human life
can scarcely be called a triumphant success, even though Browning insists that "The prize is in the process: knowledge means/
Ever-renewed assurance by defeat/That victory is somehow still to
reach . . ." (X, 113). Is this negative conclusion the upshot of all
Browning's prolonged attempt to live the lives of others?

Perhaps it will be possible to go even further, and use point
of view to transcend point of view. This is precisely the method
of "The Ring and the Book." It presents the Roman murder
case from the successive points of view of the people involved in
the events. To juxtapose different points of view on the same
events is very different from a series of poems presenting diverse
points of view on diverse events. "The Ring and the Book" im-

plies that there are as many different stories in any one story as there are people seeing the action. At the conclusion of the poem Browning affirms: "Here were the end, had anything an end" (VI, 296), as if to suggest that he could go on telling and retelling the story indefinitely, without ever exhausting it. There is no "Truth," only a large number of little subjective truths.

"The Ring and the Book" turns out to be precisely an heroic attempt to deny this implication of perspectivist art. It tries to escape the errors and falsifications of point of view. The philosophical and aesthetic moral of the poem is: "By multiplying points of view on the same event, you may transcend point of view, and reach at last God's own infinite perspective." How is it possible to use the veil of truth, man's ineradicable tendency to lie, to reach the truth itself?

"The Ring and the Book" assumes that the real truth exists hidden in any event or experience — God's own truth, the gold center behind the husk of lies. This truth is formless, invisible to man. While an event is taking place, the men and women engaged in it are too close to it to see the truth behind it. This truth can never be seen or expressed directly, or, if it can, this can happen only momentarily, as in Abt Vogler's extemporizing. Such an expression is private, incommunicable, and impermanent. The need, once again, is to discover a way to "pour liquidity into a mould," a way to give the formless gold a form which will remain and be available to other people. This problem is curiously like that faced by Mallarmé: art to be authentic must give expressive form to something which denies all form. The *néant* of Mallarmé is a negative version of the positive transcendence of Browning. All Browning's art is based on the paradoxical attempt to give form to the formless, and the central metaphor of "The Ring and the Book" is an attempt to express this paradox, just as the poem as a whole is an attempt to transcend it.

The metaphor itself is ambiguous and double. The pure truth of the gold which must be shaped into a ring by the addition of the alloy, Browning's imagination, is "fanciless fact" (V, 7), "pure crude fact" (V, 4), the brute disorganized material of the documents in the old yellow book, but at the same time it is the eternal truth of God hidden in the facts. The two are altogether distinct to the human eye. Yet when the final spurt of acid dissolves the alloy, the perfect ring remaining will be both kinds of gold made visible at once: the particular truth of history and God's unchanging truth. Only the sympathetic imagination of the poet can give a shape to the shapeless stuff of history, and at the same time make manifest the divine truth within it. So Browning answers the questioner who asks whether he has not made it all up, or whether the poem is really based on historical fact:

> Yes and no!
> From the book, yes; thence bit by bit I dug
> The lingot truth, that memorable day,
> Assayed and knew my piecemeal gain was gold, —
> Yes; but from something else surpassing that,
> Something of mine which, mixed up with the mass,
> Made it bear hammer and be firm to file.
> Fancy with fact is just one fact the more;
> To-wit, that fancy has informed, transpierced,
> Thridded and so thrown fast the facts else free,
> As right through ring and ring runs the djereed
> And binds the loose, one bar without a break.
> I fused my live soul and that inert stuff . . .
>   . . . so I wrought
> This arc, by furtherance of such alloy,
> And so, by one spirt, take away its trace
> Till, justifiably golden, rounds my ring. (V, 17, 44, 45)

But how can the formless truth be expressed in any form? Browning at times seems to think that music might be the answer. Music is specific sounds which make a sensible melody, but musical sounds are not limited by the fragmentary all-too-particular quality of language. The language of music, as Browning tells us in "Fifine at the Fair" and the "Parleying with Charles Avison," is a soul's language, and can best express the fluidity of the soul's deeps, as well as the oneness of the divine whole. But musical expressions of the truth pass and die, or give us only the pathos of the past, as Browning says in the "Parleying with Avison" and in "A Toccata of Galuppi's."

One final possibility remains, a possibility which is hinted at in the poems about music, and fulfilled magnificently in "The Ring and the Book." If we substitute the power of language to recover the past for what music can do in the present, perhaps we can, through an extravagant multiplication of perspectives on some past event, reach what was hidden behind that event when it was present. The advantage of the past is precisely the fact that it does not have the immediacy and engulfing intensity of the present. Since it was fact, and not the insubstantial stuff of music, it can fulfill, when recaptured by some supreme act of retrospective imagination and linguistic virtuosity, the double requirement of a perfect art: to be a concrete expression of universal truth. "The Ring and the Book" is essentially a gigantic act of resurrection, of imaginative memory. It is "mimic creation, galvanism for life" (V, 25). Browning can, he boasts, "commission forth/Half of [his] soul," and so, "by a special gift, an art of arts," "start the dead alive" (V, 25).

To revivify the past is also to "reach heaven," to liberate the gold truth which could not be reached through mere fancy acting on present fact. The puissant imagination of the poet needs the concrete task involved in resuscitating a specific past action in order to attain, by its means, a heaven otherwise unattainable. The historical imagination is a beanstalk leading to the magic country in the clouds, the "heaven [his] fancy lifts to, ladder-like" (V, 43). To the historical imagination must be added the presentation of numerous perspectives on the same events. As the Pope says, "Truth, nowhere, lies yet everywhere in these — /Not absolutely in a portion, yet/Evolvable from the whole" (VI, 166). The multiplication of narrators is the means of this "evolution."

This transcendence of point of view by yielding to point of view can best be seen in Browning's use of metaphor in "The Ring and the Book." Like the perspectives themselves, these metaphors always put something between the reader and the naked facts. Each time a part of the story is retold the new speaker uses a different metaphor. The metaphors look at the fact first one way and then another way. The personalities of the various speakers appear in the metaphors they use, for each metaphor is a new perspective on reality. It picks out one element or way of looking at the event and emphasizes it to the exclusion of all the others. To see the story over and over from different perspectives makes us very conscious of language, and of the way the necessity of using "barren words," "filthy rags of speech," "more than any deed, characterize[s]/Man as made subject to a curse" (VI, 169, 170). The truth cannot be expressed directly in language. One of the effects of reading "The Ring and the Book" is a sense of vertigo which results from seeing how plausible all these contradictory points of view can be made. How then can the poem reach the truth?

Indirection is the method of "The Ring and the Book," as of "Red Cotton Night-Cap Country." The very contradictions of the points of view are, like the diverse metaphors, so many "as if's" canceling one another out. Ultimately they give a glimpse of the real truth. Bit by bit the fictional versions of the facts, like the distancing of the facts in the depths of history, liberate those facts from being a "false show of things." The multiplication of points of view becomes a kind of elaborate oblique incantation which evokes the divine truth at the center of each finite person or event. The proliferation of perspectives on the story has as its goal by a kind of mutual negation to make something else appear, something which can never be faced directly or said directly in words. The "something" is at once the central truth of this particular story, the central truth of the human condition, and the transcendent truth which underlies all the particular facts which ever were or could be. At the end of "The Ring and the Book," Browning makes his great boast for the power of perspectivist art to go beyond the tragic situation of the unavailability of truth:

> . . . it is the glory and good of Art,
> That Art remains the one way possible
> Of speaking truth, to mouths like mine at least.
>   . . . Art may tell a truth
> Obliquely, do the thing shall breed the thought,
> Nor wrong the thought, missing the mediate word. (VI, 321, 322)

What is this great universal truth of which "The Ring and the Book" gives us a glimpse? It is the same old truth which his other poems express: the transcendence of God and the impossibility of joining finite and infinite. The sanctity of Pompilia and her pure love for Caponsacchi are incompatible with continued earthly existence. Her direct insight into God makes her too good for this world. "The Ring and the Book" is based on an opposition between the intuitionism of Caponsacchi and Pompilia, and the faith in law and reason of Guido and the lawyers. Guido bases his self-defense on his appeal to human law, and its claim to embody divine justice. In spite of the fact that Browning ironically allows Guido to use the metaphor of gold and alloy (V, 247), the whole purpose of "The Ring and the Book" is to deny every word of what Guido says in his defense: to deny that there is a chain linking man by successions to God; to deny that God's truth can be embodied in conventions, laws, manners, judgments, institutions. For Browning, as for Arnold, there is nothing "intermediate" between man and God, no "series" leading from one to the other and guaranteeing the truth of man's speech and law. Guido claims that every act of his, even the murder of Pompilia and her foster-parents, is justified by law, and therefore good. Here he is damnably wrong, and betrays his failure to know intuitively the truth which guides Pompilia and Caponsacchi, and is expressed "obliquely" by the poem.

Even this truth is only glimpsed for an instant. The huge complicated engine of the poem lifts the reader to this brilliant perception for a "breathless minute-space," and then he is plunged back into his usual darkness (VI, 296). "The Ring and the Book," like the frailest of Browning's lyrics, leads only to a momentary and evanescent perception. Like all his other poems, it expresses man's incapacity to understand or possess God. Browning has gone through the whole creation and developed the resources of his art to the utmost, but he has not advanced at all from his starting point, except to understand that starting point better, and to recognize that he cannot escape it. "God is it who transcends" (X, 284). Whatever Browning does, the sad gap between himself and God will still remain, as at the beginning, when he first found himself surrounded by the thick mass of the uncreated mud.

ھے

Does the gap really remain? At first it seems that Browning's constant lapping back and forth, forming and reforming himself, only keeps him at his starting point. Ultimately we see that this indefatigable movement is the very way in which man is most godlike. God too constantly transcends himself, and moves into ever-new spheres of being. What seems a sign that Browning cannot get started is actually a sign that he already possesses his goal. As long as he keeps moving he is in God's grace, and imitates in little the life of God. The form of Browning's poetry, in its internal contradictions, its uncouth, unfinished, rough-hewn quality, is the very image of the limitless perfection of God. On earth man is in a sense already in heaven, for in heaven he will pursue the same dynamic motion in a different sphere. Imperfection and incompleteness are closer to God than anything finished, for God himself is in a way incomplete. Though he is perfect, he is constantly adding new perfection to that perfection. God is not temporal, but the driving motion of time is a perfect image of his explosive eternity. The unfinished statues of Michelangelo best express the relation of earthly incompleteness to God:

> Aspire, break bounds! I say,
> Endeavour to be good, and better still,
> And best! Success is nought, endeavour's all.
> . . . there's the triumph! — there the incomplete,
> More than completion, matches the immense, —
> Then, Michelagnolo against the world! (VII, 399, 400; see also IV, 68 and VII, 202–204)

In a late poem, "Rephan," the speaker rejects a paradise of completeness, simplicity, and repose, where all things are "merged alike in a neutral Best" (X, 358). He stagnates there, and longs for a heaven of division, strife, incompletion, and "difference/ In thing and thing." "Oh, gain were indeed," he cries, "to see above/Supremacy ever — to move, remove,/Not reach — aspire yet never attain/To the object aimed at!" As a reward for such desires Rephan is sent to earth, for earth is like heaven, and a heaven of complete calm would be hell for man. Heaven will be a mixture of good and evil, not one "neutral best," for only in this way can it be full of energy and motion. A similar passage in "Prince Hohenstiel-Schwangau," surely describing Browning's own vision, foresees a heaven of process, in which man is constantly being granted a momentary possession of God's bliss, only to have God leap beyond him, whereupon the soul again expands to equal God in "new completion." In this way the joy of heaven is constantly being transcended by a greater joy:

> I suppose Heaven is, through Eternity,
> The equalizing, ever and anon,
> In momentary rapture, great with small,
> Omniscience with intelligency, God
> With man, — the thunder-glow from pole to pole
> Abolishing, a blissful moment-space,

Great cloud alike and small cloud, in one fire —
As sure to ebb as sure again to flow
When the new receptivity deserves
The new completion. There's the heaven for me. (VII, 112, 113)

It is from this point of view that the place of the doctrine of Christ's Incarnation in Browning's thought can best be understood. One of the constants of his poetry, it appears prominently, for example, in "Saul," "A Death in the Desert," and "Christmas-Eve and Easter-Day." A God of power might have made the universe and left it to its own fate. Only a loving God, a God who wishes the world and himself to remain bound together, would condescend to incarnate himself as a man, and to suffer and die as a man. "The evidence of divine power," says Browning, "is everywhere about us; not so the evidence of divine love. That love could only reveal itself to the human heart by some supreme act of *human* tenderness and devotion; the fact, or fancy, of Christ's cross and passion could alone supply such a revelation." [14] If it were not for the Incarnation, man would be doomed, as Browning fears at the end of "Christmas-Eve and Easter-Day," to a life of eternal striving short of God. But because God was what we are, we are already what he is, and share already, in every moment of our lives, the perfect life of God.

Ultimately the doctrine of Incarnation in Browning is the idea that each imperfect and limited man through whom the power of God swirls is a temporary incarnation of God, one of the infinitely varied ways in which God makes himself real in the world. Each individual life is a center around which the totality of the universe organizes itself and fulfills one of its infinite possibilities. Every life contains a unique element, something which is never repeated, but all lives contain the same invariant: the divine presence.

In the "Epilogue to Dramatis Personae" Browning describes the way the waters of the vast ocean form a momentary whirlpool around a single rock in their midst. In the same way the whirlpool of life around each self is God's face in the infinite waters, always the same yet always different, composed, decomposed, and recomposed anew in each man's private universe. Each whirlpool con-

---

[14] Mrs. Sutherland Orr, "The Religious Opinions of Robert Browning," *Contemporary Review* (December 1891), p. 879.

figuration of the ocean of life is an individual and vital thing, and yet universal. Even here Browning does not deny his assumption that only personal experience matters to man. We are returned once more to the situation in which Browning began: human consciousness surrounded by the great bulk of ocean, merged with that ocean. We find again the motif of successive crystallizations and dissolutions. But now at last the tension between form and formlessness has been appeased, appeased by the recognition that each momentary form in the shapeless waters is a new incarnation of God.

If each man possesses God so intimately, then there is no need for temples, priests, and the other trappings of organized religion, nor is it true to say, as even this poem earlier had said, that God is transcendent and unavailable to man. Each of us performs in every moment his own private sacrament of communion. In this communion God and man become one, for, as Browning said of the face in the waters in this poem, the face which belongs by turns to each one of us: "That face, is the face of Christ. That is how I feel him." [15] Browning finds that he, and every person whose role he may play, have, from the beginning and always, all that they want, and this recognition is the ultimate attainment of his long exploration of human existence. A man becomes universal not by the impossible attempt to live "all the ways," but by accepting wholeheartedly his limitation, for the particular *is* the universal, each man *is* Christ. Through this acceptance of limitation Browning, at last, both feels God and knows him:

> That one Face, far from vanish, rather grows,
> Or decomposes but to recompose,
> Become my universe that feels and knows. (IV, 372)

[15] De Vane, *Browning Handbook*, p. 315.

✑ IV ✑

Emily Brontë

When Emily Brontë began to write *Wuthering Heights* she did not leave the world of the Gondal poems. She transposed into fictional form the vision of things which her poems express. Just as there is no real distinction between the Gondal poems and those which are direct expressions of Emily Brontë's own inner experience, so the same moral and metaphysical laws prevail in the novel as in the poems.

Poems and novel share a quality which identifies them as belonging to the romantic tradition. Like the prophetic books of Blake they employ privately created personages and events to speak of things usually expressed in terms of collective religious myths. Heathcliff and Catherine Earnshaw in *Wuthering Heights,* Augusta Geraldine Almeda, Julius Brenzaida, and the other shadowy figures of the Gondal poems,[1] derive from no recognizable religious archetypes. They are creations of Emily Brontë's imagination, just as Urizen and Enitharmon are creations of the imagination of Blake, even though they may re-embody figures or concepts from various traditions. Yet Emily Brontë's characters, like the personages of Blake, are used to express general notions about the relations of God, man, and the universe.

If the writings of Emily Brontë confirm Blake's dictum that religion is another form of poetry, there is a sense in which they have the opposite meaning and are evidence of the irreconcilable difference between poetry and religion. A religious myth, to be valid, must become the form of a collective belief, and permeate the culture of a group. The validity of Emily Brontë's visions depends on their being kept private. Their purpose is to create an inner world excluding other people and the real world, as Emily Brontë affirms in a poem called "To Imagination":

[1] See "Dramatis Personae," pp. 43, 44 in Fannie E. Ratchford's recent reconstruction of the Gondal story: *Gondal's Queen: A Novel in Verse by Emily Jane Brontë* (Austin, Texas: University of Texas Press, 1955).

So hopeless is the world without,
The world within I doubly prize;
The world where guile and hate and doubt
And cold suspicion never rise;
Where thou and I and Liberty
Have undisputed sovereignty.[2]

If the sovereign realm of imagination derives from anything other than Emily Brontë's own spirit, it comes from supernatural visions, or from experiences of ecstatic fusion with nature — more from the "visions" which have encircled her, she says, "from careless childhood's sunny time" (P, 49), than from experiences of identification with nature, for one of the unsatisfactory things which imagination can replace is "Nature's sad reality" (P, 206). Music and poetry have the power to bring back summer in winter, good weather in a time of bad, just as they can bring back the remembered past, or replace grief with joy (P, 80, 90–92, 206).

Emily Brontë's willingness to submit to her "God of Visions" is equivocal. She wants as much to command her visions as to be commanded by them. The relation between the poet and her imagination is as much an ambiguous mixture of love and hate, of submission and rebellious defiance, as is the relation between Catherine Earnshaw and Heathcliff in *Wuthering Heights*. In both cases there is an attempt to reconcile two irreconcilable requirements: the need for a source of spiritual power outside oneself, and the need to be self-sufficient. In both cases the relation is a strange mixture of pleasure and pain. In a famous poem (P, 208, 209) Emily Brontë says that she has, against all "Reason," rejected everything that the real world has to offer: "Wealth," "Power," "Glory's wreath," and "Pleasure's flower." She has "cast the world away" for the sake of her allegiance to her "radiant angel," the God of Visions. Her relation to this angel of the imagination is not simply submission, for this "ever present, phantom thing" is "slave," "comrade," and "King," all three at once. The God of Visions must be a slave because Emily Brontë must control her visions and manipulate them at will. Only this control will make it possible for her "own soul to grant [her] prayer." She demands an omnipotent sovereignty within the realm of her imagination.

[2] C. W. Hatfield, *The Complete Poems of Emily Jane Brontë* (New York: Columbia University Press, 1941), pp. 205, 206. This volume will be cited hereafter as "P," followed by the appropriate page number.

The God of Visions must be "King" too, though a king against which she must "rebel," for only a power beyond the poet can guarantee the sovereignty of her visions. Most of all the God of Visions is an equal, bound to Emily in an intimate tie of love and hate, submission and domination, pain-giving and pleasure-giving. The inner world of imagination is no paradise of easy bliss. Its power to provide an escape from the dull "gloom" of "the common paths that others run" lies precisely in its ability to give pain! Emily therefore addresses her God of Visions as "a comrade," for, as she says:

> . . . by day and night
> Thou art my intimate delight —
>
> My Darling Pain that wounds and sears
> And wrings a blessing out from tears
> By deadening me to real cares . . . (P, 209)[3]

Emily Brontë's poems provide the best glimpse of the quality of her visionary world. After Emily and her sister Anne ceased to participate in collective literary games with Charlotte and Branwell they began their own game, the Gondal stories. The Gondal saga was apparently a shared daydream long before any part of it was written down, and it always remained in excess of the poems and lists of names or events which survive, and even, apparently, in excess of the extensive prose narratives which were written down but do not survive. The Gondal story was a long rambling narrative of melodramatic wars and love affairs, held together only by the centrality of one of its characters, Augusta Geraldine Almeda. But when Augusta died the narrative went on. The primary characteristic of the Gondal saga was its unfinished quality, its openness. Characters and events proliferated endlessly.[4] Gondal

---

[3] The ambiguity of imaginative or visionary experience appears in other poems too. See P, 48, 49, where the coming of imaginative vision, after the contemplation of a calm spring twilight, is spoken of as a kind of deliquescence of the spirit, in which the soul is overwhelmed by thoughts and feelings which gush from some inner spring, but give possession of the outer scene too. The same language is later used in a terrifying poem (P, 56, 57) in which a demon, who is perhaps a malign version of the God of Visions, declares its intention of carrying away the soul of the listener. This evil ecstasy will occur by an intensification of the "strange sensations" which "flood" their victim just as did the feelings of joy in the earlier poem

[4] See *Gondal's Queen*, p. 195, for a list of twenty-six Gondal characters in Anne's handwriting found on a tiny scrap of paper. Nothing at all is known of most of these characters.

seems to have existed as a full and substantial world replacing the real one, a world with its own chronology and progressive becoming. It was always there, ready to be entered at any time by Anne and Emily, together or separately, and going on even when they were not in it. Nothing is more curious or revealing than the way Anne and Emily in their various diary and birthday notes speak of the Gondal stories.[5] Notations of everyday happenings in the Brontë household, or historical events like Queen Victoria's ascent to the throne are juxtaposed against records of the Gondal world as if the two existed on exactly the same plane of reality. The Gondal events are spoken of in the present tense, as having reached at the moment a certain stage of happening. There is no assertion that the stories have been invented. Rather, Emily and Anne speak of their writing as the recording of events which have a prior and objective existence. They are historians or poets, not novelists.

The most striking evidence of the mode of existence of the Gondal saga is the fact that when Anne and Emily made a trip to York, their first long trip together by themselves, Emily wrote in her diary not of the events of the trip, but of their experience during that time of certain exciting events in the Gondal saga.[6] Emily was then only a month short of being twenty-seven years old! Perhaps in all literature there exists no stranger case of the invasion, domination, and destruction of the real world by an imaginary one.

The Gondal events did not become, like historical happenings, part of a vanished past after they had occurred. They functioned for Emily Brontë just as religious myths functioned for the Greek poets and tragedians. Transformed into a collection of eternal events, they were happening over and over again all the time, always there to be returned to and re-created in poetry. Emily often wrote poems about Gondal events several years after the narrative had, in the sisters' creation of it, reached that stage of its happening, and Miss Ratchford, in order to put the poems in what is apparently their proper sequence in Gondal history, must much alter the chronological order of their composition. In one sense

---

[5] See *Gondal's Queen*, pp. 185–194, for a convenient printing and discussion of these.

[6] See *Gondal's Queen*, p. 192.

the Gondal saga was a sequence of temporally related events, like history. In another sense it was the simultaneous existence of all its events in a perpetual present outside of time.

What is the significance of the fact that the Gondal saga was not the private creation of Emily alone, but was shared and lived in by Emily and Anne together? One piece of evidence suggests that, though the events of the Gondal stories were created by Anne and Emily together, and perhaps even revealed at times to Charlotte and Branwell, Emily's poems were kept secret even from Anne. "Emily is engaged in writing the Emperor Julius's life," writes Anne in her birthday note of 1845. "She has read some of it, and I want very much to hear the rest. She is writing some poetry, too. I wonder what it is about?" [7] But even if Anne was not permitted to read Emily's poems, or not permitted to read all of them, the Gondal realm itself must still be defined as a shared daydream, almost a collective mythology believed in by two people alone. Hence the objectivity and impersonality of the poems. Though the Gondal poems are full of the violence and passion of direct experience, these are dramatized in terms of the situation of some imaginary person. The poems have the impersonality of all authentic literature, for in them the experience of the author has been transposed to another plane, and the author herself has disappeared in her creation. The fact that the Gondal saga was jointly created by Anne and Emily is an important confirmation of this impersonality. The fact of double creation is nowhere evident in Emily's poems. So fully were Anne and Emily absorbed in their collective creation that all need to make the stories conscious affirmations of their own personalities seems to have disappeared.

The writing of *Wuthering Heights* was a brief but important interruption of this absorption in a world of imaginative vision. When, in the fall of 1846, *Poems by Currer, Ellis and Acton Bell* had failed and *Wuthering Heights* seemed unwanted by any publisher, Emily returned to Gondal, and wrote another poem about the Republican-Royalist war. After the publication and failure[8] of *Wuthering Heights,* she went back to this poem and was work-

---

[7] *Gondal's Queen*, p. 194.

[8] Not complete failure. See Jacques Blondel, *Emily Brontë: Expérience spirituelle et création poétique* (Paris, 1955), p. 17.

ing on it at the time of her death. *Wuthering Heights* was a treason against the visionary world. It exposed that world to the public gaze, and revealed its secret. In a way, though, the secret was still protected, since *Wuthering Heights* is a difficult and elusive work, a work with which no reader has felt altogether at ease.

Does not Emily's reluctance to let her work be known, and her simultaneous willingness to collaborate in Charlotte's plan to publish their work represent a contradiction which has meaning? Like Franz Kafka, who asked that his works be destroyed, and yet, significantly, did not destroy them himself, Emily Brontë wanted her vision of the world to remain private and at the same time wished it to be known. She wished it to remain private because it was valid for herself alone, and needed to remain private in order to be valid. At the same time she wished it to be known because only when it was read by others would it become real. This equivocation is already present in the fact that she expressed her visions in the language which she shared with millions of men. The publication of some of the poems in 1846 and the publication of *Wuthering Heights* in 1848 were an extension of this capitulation to the public world. In order to achieve authentic existence the poems and the novel had to take form in the minds of other people, and yet they needed to remain private too.

The fact that the novel and the poems were published under a pseudonym is a confirmation of this ambiguous attitude. Whereas Charlotte seems to have taken a pseudonym because it was proper for a lady writer to do so, Emily tried jealously to protect her real identity. When Charlotte went up to her London editors with Anne to put a stop to the rumor that all the Brontë novels were by a single person, Emily stayed home. She was apparently very angry when she learned that Charlotte had betrayed her identity as well as those of Anne and Charlotte.[9] To publish under a pseudonym was to gain for her works the sanction that only a reading of them by the public would give, and at the same time to protect her solitude and its visions.

The publication of the poems and the novel were an attempt by Emily Brontë to use other people for the affirmation of her own life while remaining safely hidden herself. If literature is, as

[9] Blondel, *Emily Brontë*, p. 84.

Mallarmé said, the creation of a "spectacle de soi," two persons at least are necessary to this creation: the writer and the reader. The brilliant stratagems which Emily Brontë devised in *Wuthering Heights* to persuade the reader to accept the world of her novel are striking and even pathetic proof of the powerful need which drove her to communicate her visions, even though that communication would in some sense destroy what was communicated by putting it at the mercy of the anonymous reading public.

So far I have spoken only of the mode of existence of Emily Brontë's writings, and hardly at all of their meaning. The origins of the latter are multiple. Emily Brontë's view of the world is derived in part from her readings in romantic literature and even more from the religious teachings she received in her childhood. But the meaning of her work was also influenced by the very conditions under which it developed. Her freedom from external restraints in her writing and her experience of the imagination as a dangerous, equivocal power may have contributed to the extremism of her work. Both poems and novel express themselves in hyperbole. They dramatize the clash of figures who embody elemental energies, and the special value of Emily Brontë's work lies in the way it explores the ultimate implications of certain traditional ideas and themes.

All creation is equally insane. There are those flies playing above the stream, swallows and fish diminishing their number each minute: these will become in their turn, the prey of some tyrant of air or water; and man for his amusement or for his needs will kill their murderers. Nature is an inexplicable puzzle, life exists on a principle of destruction; every creature must be the relentless instrument of death to the others, or himself cease to live.[10]

[10] "The Butterfly," *Five Essays Written in French*, trans. Lorine White Nagel, intro. Fannie E. Ratchford (Austin, Texas: University of Texas Press, 1948), p. 17. This essay was written by Emily Brontë as a devoir for her teacher M. Héger in Brussels. In its form it is a moralizing or theologizing of natural history in the manner of the famous *Meditations* of James Hervey, ardent Methodist and friend of John Wesley. But the moral which Emily Brontë derives from her butterfly has no parallel in Hervey's *Meditations*, in Wesley's *Compendium of Natural Philosophy*, or in eighteenth-century natural theology generally — which was dedicated to showing the wisdom and beneficence of God as manifested in the works of the creation. The transformation of the caterpillar into a butterfly is a traditional symbol of resurrection, or of the liberation of the soul. (Harvey makes the silk-

For Emily Brontë, created beings can only be related to one another destructively. The strongest and most implacable beings live the longest, for the life of each depends on the death of others, and if it does not relentlessly kill it will be killed, or die of inanition. The model of this relation is the consumption of one being by another. Nature is like a patternless maze created by a madman. Its insanity lies in the fact that the good of one part is the evil of another part. Therefore no coherent moral judgment can be made of any action or event. What is the worst evil for the flies, being eaten by the fish and swallows, is the highest good for the fish and swallows, since it is necessary to their life. Any attempt to make sense of life leads to inextricable confusion, and the creation can only be described, not understood. Viewed as a totality, nature is engaged in a constant act of suicide, tearing itself to pieces in the very effort to prolong its own life. Murder is the sole law of life, that is to say, life paradoxically depends upon death, and is impossible without it.

Emily Brontë's vision of the creation matches the traditional Christian description of the state of nature, the state after the fall and before the "new birth." John Wesley's sermon on "The Great Deliverance" is a good example of such a description.[11] Wesley, however, exempts from *his* tableau of ferocious destruc-

---

worm's change into a butterfly a type of Christ's resurrection and ascent into heaven, and hence of our own attainment of beatitude.) But in her treatment of the butterfly, as in other ways, Emily Brontë pours new allegory into old emblems.

[11] *Works*, VI (New York, 1826), 252–261. Wesley's picture of nature is strikingly like Emily Brontë's: ". . . what savage fierceness, what unrelenting cruelty, are invariably observed in thousands of creatures, yea, are inseparable from their natures! Is it only the lion, the tiger, the wolf, among the inhabitants of the forests and plains; the shark and a few more voracious monsters among the inhabitants of the waters; or the eagle among birds, that tears the flesh, sucks the blood, and crushes the bones of its helpless fellow-creatures? Nay, the harmless fly, the laborious ant, the painted butterfly, are treated in the same merciless manner even by the innocent songsters of the grove! The innumerable tribes of poor insects are continually devoured by them. . . . During this season of *vanity*, not only the feebler creatures are continually destroyed by the stronger; not only the strong are frequently destroyed by those that are of equal strength: but both the one and the other are exposed to the violence and cruelty of him that is now their common enemy, man. . . . And what a dreadful difference is there between what they suffer from their fellow-brutes, and what they suffer from the tyrant, man! The lion, the tiger, or the shark, gives them pain from mere necessity, in order to prolong their own life; and put them out of their pain at once. But the human shark, without any such necessity, torments them of his own free choice: and, perhaps, continues their lingering pain, till, after months or years, death signs their release" (pp. 256, 257).

tion the "Children of God," those who have been saved by grace
and by faith from the consequences of the fall. But for Emily
Brontë every man, to borrow Wesley's words, "does in effect dis-
claim the nature of man, and degrade himself into a beast." [12]
Man is as much a part of nature as flies, swallows, and fish. Like
the others he lives by murder and by murder alone. Or, rather,
man is worse than any other natural creature, for he kills wantonly,
"for his amusement," as well as "for his needs." The inexplicable
puzzle formed by the mixture of good and evil in any relation
between God's creatures is matched by the inexplicable puzzle of
man's own unique nature, for only he takes positive pleasure in
the useless infliction of mortal pain on other beings.

The darkest meaning of Emily Brontë's assertion that "all creation is equally insane" is the fact that no man can understand why
a good God should have chosen to create such a world at all. Each
man's life, like that of any other creature of nature, is merely a
sequence of violent acts done or suffered, and it ends in death.
". . . why was man created?" asks Emily Brontë. "He torments,
he kills, he devours; he suffers, dies, is devoured — that's his whole
story." [13]

Long centuries of civilization have created artificial barriers
between man and man, and between man and nature, barriers of
language, of custom, of moral restraint. Nevertheless, man's true
nature remains the same, ready to reappear at any moment if reason and morality are destroyed. The opening chapters of *Wuthering Heights* introduce the reader, through the intermediary of
the narrator, to a set of people living in the state of nature as it
is defined in "The Butterfly." This state also matches that of the
Gondal poems, with their wars and rebellions and sadistic cruel-
ties. In Gondal, as in the country of *Wuthering Heights,* every
man's hand is against his neighbor.

Lockwood's discovery of the nature of life at Wuthering Heights
coincides with his step-by-step progress into the house itself. On
his two visits he crosses various thresholds: the outer gate, the door
of the house, the door into the kitchen, the stairs and halls leading
to an upstairs room. Finally he enters the interior of the interior,
the oaken closet with a bed in it which stands in a corner of this

[12] *Works,* VI, 261.
[13] *Five Essays,* trans. Nagel, pp. 17, 18.

inner room. Wuthering Heights is presented as a kind of Chinese box of enclosures within enclosures. The house is like the novel itself, with its intricate structure of flashbacks, time shifts, multiple perspectives, and narrators within narrators. However far we penetrate toward the center of Wuthering Heights there are still further recesses within. When Lockwood finally gets inside the family sitting-room he can hear "a chatter of tongues, and a clatter of culinary utensils, deep within," [14] and Joseph can be heard mumbling indistinctly in the "depths of the cellar" (5). This domestic interior is, by subtle linguistic touches, identified with the interior of a human body, and therefore with another human spirit. Lockwood's progress toward the interior of Wuthering Heights matches his unwitting progress toward the spiritual secrets it hides. Just as the "narrow windows" of Wuthering Heights are "deeply set in the wall" (2), so Heathcliff's "black eyes withdraw . . . suspiciously under their brows" (1), and Lockwood's entrance into the house is his inspection of its "anatomy" (3).

The nature of human life within this "penetralium" (3) is precisely defined by the animals Lockwood finds there. The shadowy recesses of these strange rooms are alive with ferocious dogs: "In an arch, under the dresser, reposed a huge, liver-coloured bitch pointer surrounded by a swarm of squealing puppies; and other dogs, haunted other recesses" (3). Lockwood tries to pet this liver-colored bitch, but her lip is "curled up, and her white teeth watering for a snatch" (5), and later when, left alone, he makes faces at the dogs, they leap from their various hiding places and attack him in a pack. In a moment the hearth is "an absolute tempest of worrying and yelping" (6). The storm which blows at the exterior of the house and gives it its name (2) is echoed by the storm within the house, a tempest whose ultimate source, it may be, is the people living there. Lockwood's encounter with Heathcliff's dogs is really his first encounter with the true nature of their owner, as Heathcliff himself suggests when he says: "Guests are so exceedingly rare in this house that I and my dogs, I am willing to own, hardly know how to receive them" (6).

The animal imagery used throughout *Wuthering Heights* is

---

[14] *Wuthering Heights*, "The Shakespeare Head Brontë" (Boston and New York, 1931), p. 3. Numbers in parentheses after texts refer to page numbers in this edition.

one of the chief ways in which the spiritual strength of the characters is measured. Heathcliff is "a fierce, pitiless, wolfish man" (117), while Edgar Linton is a "sucking leveret" (131), and Linton Heathcliff is a "puling chicken" (237). Such figures are more than simple metaphors. They tell us that man in *Wuthering Heights,* as in the essay on the butterfly, is part of nature, and no different from other animals. Critics have commented on the prevalence of verbs of violent action in *Wuthering Heights,* verbs like "writhe, drag, crush, grind, struggle, yield, sink, recoil, outstrip, tear, drive asunder." [15] No other Victorian novel contains such scenes of inhuman brutality. No other novel so completely defines its characters in terms of the violence of their wills. In *Wuthering Heights* people go on living only if their wills remain powerful and direct, capable of action so immediate and unthinking that it can hardly be called the result of choice, but is a permanent and unceasing attitude of aggression. Continuation of life for such people depends on their continuing to will, for in this world destruction is the law of life. If such characters cease to will, or if their wills weaken, motion slows, things coagulate, time almost stops, and their lives begin to weaken and fade away. Unless they can find some way to recuperate their wills, their lives will cease altogether, or tend slowly in the direction of death. So Lockwood, after his terrifying dreams, says, as the hours crawl toward morning, ". . . time stagnates here" (30). So the second Catherine, at the low point of her life, when only her own action will save her, says, "Oh! I'm tired — I'm *stalled* . . ." (342). And so Isabella, one of the weak people in the novel, can only escape from the tyranny of Heathcliff by precipitating herself into the realm of violence inhabited by the other characters who survive. The description of her escape from Wuthering Heights is a condensed distillation of the quality of life in the novel: "In my flight through the kitchen I bid Joseph speed to his master; I knocked over Hareton, who was hanging a litter of puppies from a chairback in the doorway; and, blest as a soul escaped from purgatory, I bounded, leaped, and flew down the steep road: then, quitting its windings, shot direct across the moor, rolling over banks, and wading through marshes; precipitating myself, in fact, towards the beacon light of the Grange" (208).

[15] Mark Schorer's list. See his introduction to the Rinehart edition of *Wuthering Heights* (New York, 1950), p. xv.

Lockwood learns when he makes his second visit to Wuthering Heights what it means to say that the people there live like ferocious dogs, and can survive only through the strength of their wills. He finds that everyone at the Heights hates everyone else with a violence of unrestrained rage which is like that of wild animals. Anarchy prevails. Even that mild Christian, Nelly Dean, accepts this universal selfishness when she says, "Well, we *must* be for ourselves in the long run; the mild and generous are only more justly selfish than the domineering . . ." (105). At Wuthering Heights only force is recognized as an intermediary between people, and each person follows as well as he can his own whim. "I'll put my trash away," says Catherine Linton to Heathcliff, "because you can make me, if I refuse . . . But I'll not do anything, though you should swear your tongue out, except what I please!" (33). As in Lockwood's dream of Jabes Branderham's sermon, every moral or religious law has disappeared, or has been transformed into an instrument of aggression. The "pilgrim's staves" of the church congregation are changed, in Lockwood's dream, into war clubs, and the service, which should be the model of a peaceful community, collectively submitting to divine law, becomes a scene of savage violence, recalling the two times when Lockwood has been attacked by dogs, and giving an accurate dream projection of the relations among the inmates of Wuthering Heights (26).

This animality of the people at the Heights is caused by the loss of an earlier state of civilized restraint. For a human being to act like an animal means something very different from a similar action performed by the animal itself. There are no laws for an animal to break, and there is nothing immoral in the slaughter of one animal by another. The characters in *Wuthering Heights* have *returned* to an animal state. Such a return is reached only through the transgression of all human law. The inmates of Wuthering Heights have destroyed the meaning of the word "moral," so that it can be used, as Heathcliff uses it, to define the most inhuman acts of cruelty (174).

In civilized society man's needs are not satisfied immediately and selfishly, but are mediated by a complex system of cooperative action. Most social actions are for others, or for the sake of a future satisfaction. As a result, there is in civilized society little direct contact between men. Emily Brontë's example of civilized man is Lockwood, the foppish representative of fashionable society. Lockwood is mortally afraid of any close relation with another human being He is bored and weak, and has no idea what to do with himself. Ennui has brought him to Thrushcross Grange, and his attitude toward the country people is that of a condescending sophisticate who goes slumming in search of excitement.

Wuthering Heights is the opposite of this. There, people are open to one another. Nothing stands between them, and no law restrains them. Though this savagery puts people in extreme danger, it is, for Emily Brontë, better than Lockwood's artificiality and insincerity. Lockwood himself comes eventually to recognize this. "I perceive," he says, "that people in these regions acquire over people in towns the value that a spider in a dungeon does over a spider in a cottage, to their various occupants; and yet the deepened attraction is not entirely owing to the situation of the looker-on. They *do* live more in earnest, more in themselves, and less in surface change, and frivolous external things. I could fancy a love for life here almost possible; and I was a fixed unbeliever in any love of a year's standing . . ." (70). Unmediated relations to others may be a mortal danger to the self, but such relations are also a way of living a deeper and more authentic life. Lockwood has been a fixed unbeliever in any love of a year's standing. At Wuthering Heights he witnesses a love which has lasted beyond the grave.

There is one further reality to which Lockwood is introduced at the Heights. If civilized society keeps out the savagery of wild animals and northern tempests, it also keeps out the irrational tumult of supernatural forces. The latter, like the former, can never be reduced to man's measure. When Lockwood slides back the panels of the oaken bed and encloses himself in the innermost chamber of all he feels "secure against the vigilance of Heathcliff, and every one else" (20). But just here he is most in danger, not from human or natural violence, but from supernatural energies. This innermost room has a window to the outdoors, and through that window, in Lockwood's dream, the ghost of Catherine Earnshaw tries to come. The otherness of nature is replaced by the more frightening otherness of a ghost, and the stormy moors are established as the expressions of a supernatural as well as a natural violence. These spiritual powers are immanent in nature, and identified with its secret life. The expression of this double life in *Wuthering Heights,* as in Emily Brontë's poems, is an ancient and primitive symbol: the wind. There is a great storm on the night Mr. Earnshaw dies; another tempest when Heathcliff leaves the Heights splits a tree whose bough falls on the house; and there is a rainstorm on the night Heathcliff dies beside the very same window where Lockwood has seen Catherine's ghost. The immeasurable violence of occult forces matches the unrestrained violence of wild animals and of storms. All these terrifying forces have been released at Wuthering Heights, and people live there in close proximity to extreme danger. Inevitably they succumb to that danger. and the release of irrational passions from the depths of man's soul parallels the unchaining of energies outside man. In his dream the effete cosmopolitan Lockwood is brought, in spite of himself, to participate in the turbulence of Wuthering Heights. In a paroxysm of fear he rubs the wrist of the ghost-child to and fro on the broken pane until the blood runs down and soaks the bedclothes.

Why is it that things have reached this state at Wuthering Heights? Something has happened to break down all the barriers cutting man off from nature, from animals, and even from the supernatural realm. Man has been forced to participate in these as he did long ages ago before he became human by separating himself from them. Have nonhuman energies invaded the human world and succeeded in dominating it, as Lockwood is swept into the storm at Wuthering Heights, or have acts of man unleashed these energies outside of man by liberating them first from the untamed deeps of the human soul?

The violence of Emily Brontë's characters is a reaction to the loss of an earlier state of happiness. Heathcliff's situation at the beginning of *Wuthering Heights* is the same as the situation of many characters in Emily Brontë's poems, and the refrain of both poems and novel is "Never again" (P, 64).

This state of loss is dramatized in many of the poems as the longing in harshest wintertime for the vanished warmth of midsummer weather, or as the memory of an earlier time of happy love, ecstatic visions, or unity with nature. The sense of bereavement is often expressed as a condition of exile, imprisonment, or separation, or in terms of the grief of the living for the dead. The Gondal saga was apparently a species of prose epic, of which we possess only the lyric poems which were interspersed here and there in the narrative. These usually pick out some moment of special poignancy or significance, and dramatize it in the speech of the person who experiences it. Most often the moment chosen is not the time of joy, but the moment of sorrow, exile, or defeat. It seems as if all the elaborate machinery of the Gondal saga had been contrived as a means of expressing repeatedly, in different forms, one universal experience of absolute destitution:

> I know that tonight the wind is sighing,
> The soft August wind, over forest and moor;
> While I in a grave-like chill am lying
> On the damp black flags of my dungeon-floor. (P, 234, 235)

> Light up thy halls! 'Tis closing day;
> I'm drear and lone and far away —
> Cold blows on my breast the northwind's bitter sigh,
> And oh, my couch is bleak beneath the rainy sky! (P, 85)

Such people are suffering the anguish of irremediable loss. Their eyes are fixed backward in retrospective fascination on some past moment of sovereign joy. Only in that moment were they really alive, really themselves. Their present lives are determined by the loss of some past joy, and by the suffering caused by that loss. Such people live separated from themselves, and yearn with impotent violence to regain their lost happiness.

The fundamental dramatic situation of the poems reappears again in *Wuthering Heights*. Like a Gondal character, Isabella longs to be back at Thrushcross Grange after her elopement with Heathcliff, just as Heathcliff is tormented after Catherine's death, and just as Catherine suffers after her marriage to Edgar Linton. "But," she says, "supposing at twelve years old, I had been wrenched from the Heights, and every early association, and my all in all, as Heathcliff was at that time, and had been converted, at a stroke into Mrs. Linton, the lady of Thrushcross Grange, and the wife of a stranger; an exile, and outcast, thenceforth, from what had been my world — You may fancy a glimpse of the abyss where I grovelled!" (143). And Heathcliff cries out to the ghost of Cathy: "Be with me always — take any form — drive me mad! only *do* not leave me in this abyss, where I cannot find you! Oh, God! it is unutterable! I *cannot* live without my life! I *cannot* live without my soul!" (191, 192).

For Emily Brontë no human being is self-sufficient, and all suffering derives ultimately from isolation. A person is most himself when he participates most completely in the life of something outside himself. This self outside the self is the substance of a man's being, in both the literal and etymological senses of the word.[16] It is the intimate stuff of the self, and it is also that which "stands beneath" the self as its foundation and support. A man's real being is outside himself. Emily Brontë's writings are an exploration of the consequences of this strange situation.

The poems and the novel suggest three possible entities with which the self may be fused: nature, God, and another human being. Sometimes in the poems the first two of these are identified. The blending of earth and heaven in an intimate participation makes possible an ecstasy of the self and its escape from the prison of its finitude:

> High waving heather, 'neath stormy blasts bending,
> Midnight and moonlight and bright shining stars;
> Darkness and glory rejoicingly blending,
> Earth rising to heaven and heaven descending,
> Man's spirit away from its drear dongeon sending,
> Bursting the fetters and breaking the bars. (P, 31)

Sometimes, as in several passages in the novel and in a famous poem,[17] the foundation or substance of the self is God alone. Only after death will come fusion with the divine being and entry into a boundless realm of joy. God is more immanent than transcendent, more a ubiquitous presence than an external object. The deity is as intimate and pervasive as inner consciousness is to the self. But though God is present now in the depths of each human spirit, as well as everywhere in nature, the separateness of each person, as well as the opacity of his body and the world's body,

---

[16] See Kenneth Burke, "Paradox of Substance," *A Grammar of Motives* (New York, 1945), pp. 21–23, for a discussion of the notion of substance.
[17] "No coward soul is mine" (P, 243, 244).

prevent enjoyment of this identity. God "broods above" nature
and the self as well as "pervading" it (P, 243).

Existence after death will be radically different from life on
earth. In heaven there is no division into self and what is other
than the self. There each person is dissolved in an infinite subjectivity which is at last a full possession of the self. Heaven is the
place of a sympathetic participation of all beings, through God, in
each other's lives. This participation is the very definition of joy:
". . . I feel an assurance of the endless and shadowless hereafter
. . . where life is boundless in its duration, and love in its sympathy, and joy in its fulness" (189).

Though heaven is man's final goal, Emily Brontë's poems and
her novel are concerned initially with life on this earth, and the
chief example here of fusion with something outside the self is
the profound communion of children or lovers. The crucial sentence of *Wuthering Heights* is Catherine's bold expression of the
paradox of substance: "I *am* Heathcliff." Heathcliff, Cathy says, is
her being. Only so long as he exists will she continue to exist.
Cathy defines her relation to Heathcliff not only in her striking
formula, but also, in the surrounding sentences, in closely reasoned
language, the most logical and explicit in the novel. Her explanation describes her relation to Heathcliff in the same terms Emily
Brontë uses to define so lucidly the relation of the soul to God in
"No coward soul is mine." Just as God, in the poem, is both within
the soul and outside it, so, Cathy says, Heathcliff is at once within
her and beyond her. He is the part of her that exists outside herself, and that part is her true self, her essence, more herself than
she is. A created being entirely self-contained would have no use
or meaning. Without a self beyond the self, "an existence of yours
beyond you" (93), the self would be senseless and fragmentary.
Heathcliff is to Cathy as necessary as the very ground she stands
on, or, rather, as necessary as the eternal rocks beneath which support that ground. Heathcliff is both that which stands beneath her,
and that which she intimately is: ". . . he's more myself than I
am," cries Cathy. "Whatever our souls are made of, his and mine
are the same . . . Who is to separate us, pray? . . . My love for
Linton is like the foliage in the woods. Time will change it, I'm
well aware, as winter changes the trees — my love for Heathcliff

resembles the eternal rocks beneath — a source of little visible delight, but necessary. Nelly, I *am* Heathcliff — he's always, always in my mind — not as a pleasure, any more than I am always a pleasure to myself — but, as my own being . . ." (91, 92, 93).

Cathy affirms something more of her love for Heathcliff, something which has great importance for her life and his. In "No coward soul is mine" the essence of the soul is the God of whom one may say either that He is contained within the soul or that the soul is contained within Him, and in the same way the essence of every created thing is contained in God:

> Though Earth and moon were gone
> And suns and universes ceased to be
> And thou wert left alone
> Every Existence would exist in thee . . . (P, 243)

In the novel Cathy asserts exactly this of Heathcliff. Her relation to Heathcliff gives her possession not merely of Heathcliff, but of the entire universe through him, in an intimacy of possession which obliterates the boundaries of the self and makes it an integral part of the whole creation. "If all else perished," says Cathy, "and *he* remained, I should still continue to be; and if all else remained, and he were annihilated, the Universe would turn to a mighty stranger. I should not seem a part of it" (93).

Catherine's relation to Heathcliff differs in one important respect from the relation between the created soul and God as Emily Brontë defines it in the poem, or as it is defined traditionally in Christian theology. What Heathcliff is for Cathy, Cathy is also for Heathcliff. He speaks in exactly the same way about her as she speaks about him, and exactly the same relation is being dramatized, whether we see their love from the point of view of Cathy or from the point of view of Heathcliff. "Two words," cries Heathcliff, "would comprehend my future — *death* and *hell* — existence, after losing her, would be hell" (170). And in another place: " — oh God! would *you* like to live with your soul in the grave?" (185). If Heathcliff is the ground of Cathy's being, Cathy is the ground of Heathcliff's, whereas, though God's creatures could not exist without God, God is defined by His absolute self-sufficiency.

Cathy and Heathcliff are as inseparably joined as trunk and root of the living tree. Their relation to one another excludes or absorbs their relation to everything else. Each is related to the rest of the universe only through the other. Through Heathcliff, Cathy possesses all of nature. Through Cathy, Heathcliff possesses it. As in Donne's "The Sun Rising," the whole creation has organized itself around their relation, as around its center or source, and God in his heaven is ignored or dismissed. If the mystic says: "I am because I am God," or if Descartes says he is because he thinks, Cathy must say: "I am Heathcliff, therefore I exist." Her hyperbole is the climax and endpoint of the long tradition making love a private religion in which the loved one is God and there is a single worshipper and devotee. Emily Brontë, here as elsewhere, dramatizes in extremes, and carries the tradition of romantic love as far as it can go.

To remain happy Cathy need only maintain her identification with Heathcliff. That identification seems invulnerable, for, as Cathy affirms, it will survive every vicissitude of her relations to others. Her love guarantees its own permanence. If the lovers endure, their love will endure untouched. If either is annihilated, then the other will also disappear. The existence of each is altogether determined by the other.

ع

The love of Heathcliff and Cathy is not quite so simple as this. Between happy possession and annihilation stands a third dreadful possibility: the violent separation of the trunk from its root. If this happens the trunk may be forced to persist in a universe from which it has been dissevered. The intimate communion of all things with one another will perish with this disconnection. Then the universe will "turn to a mighty stranger," and the unwilling survivor will not seem a part of it.

Lockwood finds just such a situation when he first comes to Wuthering Heights. It is Heathcliff who has survived Cathy rather than the other way around. His anguish at being forced to live with his soul in the grave has turned Wuthering Heights into a kennel of hatred and aggression.

The passage in which Cathy explains to Nelly Dean her love for Heathcliff reveals in its form the fact that they have already been separated, even before Cathy's death. The profound communion of lovers can only be lived, not talked about, just as it can only exist at a time prior to the lovers' consciousness of themselves as separate persons. As soon as Cathy can say "I am I" she can no longer say "I am Heathcliff." Or rather, to be able to say it is implicitly to admit the loss of the identification it expresses. The sentence contains its own contradiction and denial, as do all sentences of the form "A is B." Cathy, in order to assert that she is identified with Heathcliff, must confess to their separateness, for is there not a different word for each? Though her language seems so clear and logical, it is tangled in contradictions.

Cathy's explanation of her love for Heathcliff mingles at least three different modes of relation. She says she *is* Heathcliff, that their souls are the same. This is the relation of identity or fusion. She says that her love for Heathcliff is like the eternal rocks beneath. This is the relation of substance. And she says Heathcliff is that which is beyond her and yet "contains" her, as, in traditional theology, all things are contained in God. This is the relation of container and thing contained. Each of these relations has its own appropriate dialectic, and the dialectic of each is different from those of the other two. It is impossible, logically, for two things to be related in all three of these ways at once. The proliferation of incompatible explanations in Cathy's speech testifies to the fact that she is talking about something which is beyond language and can never be pinned down in logical discourse. The three relations each in a different way express a paradoxical situation in which one person both is and is not another person. As soon as you begin to think about such a situation you realize its absurdity and impossibility, and to realize this is to have lost it for good. As in the Stendhalian analysis of happiness, so in Emily Brontë's dialectic of love: when you have it you cannot know that you have it, and to know it is to destroy it. It can only be known retrospectively, by exiles who look back in longing at the lost kingdom of joy. Cathy's explicit analysis of her relation to Heathcliff comes only after she has separated herself from him, and is about to marry Edgar Linton.

The love of Cathy and Heathcliff must be expressed in language which is concrete and symbolic rather than discursive. It must be described at a time before Cathy and Heathcliff are able to understand it or speak of it in abstract terms. Only then did it really exist. The diary which Lockwood reads during his terrifying night in the oak-paneled bed is the real inside of the inside, the secret center of the Chinese box of enclosures which makes up the novel. Through this diary Lockwood gets a glimpse of the past moment of exuberant joy which is the true origin of all the events of the novel. Cathy's description in her diary of her relation to Heathcliff is simple and direct. This simplicity shows their love as something lived rather than understood, something so much taken for granted that its extraordinary nature does not even appear. Clothes are ordinarily used to cover a single person's nakedness and to serve as a sign of his separateness. Like language, clothes are a symptom of the mediated nature of civilized relations. But Cathy and Heathcliff are so closely identified that clothes are for them a means of affirming their unity in opposition to society and all the world. The motif occurs twice in Cathy's diary:

> We made ourselves as snug as our means allowed in the arch of the dresser. I had just fastened our pinafores together, and hung them up for a curtain . . . (22)

> . . . my companion is impatient and proposes that we should appropriate the dairy woman's cloak, and have a scamper on the moors, under its shelter. (23)

Each of these passages implicitly identifies the union of Cathy and Heathcliff with one of the symbols of extrasocial violence in the novel. The recess under the dresser where Cathy and Heathcliff hide is also the place where, many years later, lurk the ferocious liver-colored bitch pointer and her swarm of puppies. The moors are a symbol of the wildness of nature as opposed to the restraint of indoor society. Childhood, like animal life or the windy moors, is outside civilization. Cathy and Heathcliff slept together in the same bed until old Mr. Earnshaw's death. Their relation was the profound consubstantiality of brother and sister in childhood, rather than the sexual union of lovers. The latter would presuppose a degree of separation which did not, for them, exist. Though Heathcliff has been found by Catherine's father wandering in the streets of Liverpool, "a dirty, ragged, black-haired child" (40), and brought home like a stray animal, he has been christened with the name of a brother of Cathy's who died in childhood. Heathcliff's mysterious origin and the fact that he re-

places a dead child identify him as an intruder from the dangerous
realm of occult or supernatural energies — an ambiguous realm,
perhaps benign, perhaps malign. "I was never so beaten with anything in my life," says Earnshaw as he takes Heathcliff out of his
greatcoat, "but you must e'en take it as a gift of God; though it's
as dark almost as if it came from the devil" (40). Heathcliff is the
outcast, the castaway, the Lascar or gypsy or disinherited prince
who, because nothing is known of his origin, must be identified
with the unknown, with all that is beyond the reasonable circle of
things which can be understood or clearly seen. Since he is initially
outside society he can only belong to it by disrupting it. For Cathy
to prefer Heathcliff to her real brother Hindley is a measure of
the attraction for her of the mysterious realm from which he
comes. Heathcliff is also her dead brother returned to life, and
their love is in a manner incestuous. Cathy and Heathcliff are
the same rather than different, whereas the souls of Cathy and
Edgar Linton are made of different substances.

The day described in Cathy's diary is also the last on which
Cathy and Heathcliff enjoy the full unconscious joy of their love.
Their scamper on the moors, on apparently that same Sunday,
leads them too close to Thrushcross Grange, and there they are
separated, never in this world to recover the naive perfection of
their union.

In the world of *Wuthering Heights* there are two extreme situations possible for man: the joy of a complete unconscious fusion
with another person, and the anguish of complete separation. The
second derives its peculiar bitterness from the fact that it is the
loss of the first. *Wuthering Heights* is written backwards, like a
detective story. First the reader encounters the corpse of a dead
community. Then the novel explains, by a process of retrospective
reconstruction, how things came to be as they are, and we get
glimpses, indirect and fragmentary, of the childhood love of
Heathcliff and Cathy, which stands at the origin of all that happens. The juxtaposition, in the early pages of *Wuthering Heights,*
of past and present, joy and suffering, communion and separation,
raises fundamental questions about the imaginative universe of
Emily Brontë. Is the separation of Cathy and Heathcliff simply
an unfortunate accident, or is it the dramatic expression of an
inevitable necessity, a law of life in the world of *Wuthering*

Heights? How does this loss of an earlier joy explain the return to a savage state of so many of the characters in the novel and in Emily Brontë's poems? The answers to these questions can be found in a consideration of the religious background of Emily Brontë's thought.

ह

I dreamt, once, that I was there . . . [H]eaven did not seem to be my home; and I broke my heart with weeping to come back to earth; and the angels were so angry that they flung me out, into the middle of the heath on the top of Wuthering Heights; where I woke sobbing for joy. (91)

Cathy's love for Heathcliff and existence in heaven seem to her mutually exclusive. To fulfill the former is to exclude herself from the latter. To be in heaven would be exile for her because it would separate her from Heathcliff. Either one goal may be reached or the other, not both. Cathy's love for Heathcliff is defiance of God and transgression of His law.

This opposition between love and religious duty has existed from the beginning of her relation to Heathcliff. The reader's first glimpse of this relation shows that their love exists as the repudiation of religious and moral obligation. "H. and I," writes Cathy in her diary, "are going to rebel" (21). They rebel against the coercion of religious and family authority. They rebel in the name of the anarchic freedom of their love. The diary entry describes events taking place on "an awful Sunday" after the death of Cathy's father, when her brother Hindley has become the tyrannical head of the household. Though the weather has been too bad to go to church, Joseph has conducted, for Cathy, Heathcliff, and the plowboy, a three-hour service in the garret. The tyranny of the foster-father (" 'You forget you have a master here,' says the tyrant. 'I'll demolish the first who puts me out of temper! I insist on perfect sobriety and silence' " [22].) is equated with the tyranny of a religion which requires that all pleasure be banished and every thought and act be directed to its service.

The symbol of this tyranny is books, the codified expression of an authority which demands to be obeyed. When Cathy and Heathcliff seek to escape from Sunday by hiding behind their pinafores in the arch of the dresser, Joseph sends them back to the good old Protestant Sunday occupation of reading pious tracts: "T' maister nobbut just buried, and Sabbath nut oe'red, und t' sahnd uh't gospel still i' yer lugs, and yah darr be laiking! shame on ye! sit ye dahn, ill childer! they's good books eneugh if ye'll read 'em; sit ye dahn, and think uh yer sowls!" (22). Reading is here opposed to "laiking." The former is directed to salvation, the latter is a vicious turning away from God for the sake of selfish pleasure. The Christian "either/or" is reaffirmed in the titles of the two tracts which Cathy and Heathcliff throw into the dog-kennel: "The Helmet of Salvation" and "The Broad Way to Destruction." There are only two possibilities open to these children: they may encase themselves within the rigid bounds of the helmet of salvation, or they may break through all barriers and go the broad way to destruction.

Joseph is of great importance in *Wuthering Heights.* He is "the wearisomest, self-righteous pharisee that ever ransacked a bible to rake the promises to himself, and fling the curses on his neighbours" (46). It is "his vocation to be where he [has] plenty of wickedness to reprove" (74). For Joseph the world divides it-self into two kinds of people, those who are, by God's grace, saved, and the much larger number who are irrevocably damned. Joseph considers himself one of the elect. As he says, in distorted echo of St. Paul (Rom. 8:28): "All warks togither for gooid tuh them as is chozzen, and piked aht froo' th' rubbidge!" (97). God, in Joseph's view of him, has established things for most people so that whatever they do they will be damned. Hence Joseph feels it his duty to serve as an avenue through which God's curses can be directed at the wicked, and through which information about the wickedness of mankind can be reported back to God: "O, Lord," he cries, "judge 'em, fur they's norther law nur justice amang wer rullers!" (352). Joseph's God is a God of wrath, a God who, like Joseph himself, judges everybody but himself as "nowt," to use one of Joseph's favorite words (see 15, 45, 99, 164, 352). Such a God is a sadist who takes pleasure in the suffering of his creatures, and joys in excluding them forever from joy.

Joseph's religion might seem of marginal interest in *Wuthering Heights,* a kind of foil for the gentler Christianity of Nelly Dean, if it were not for the fact that the central drama of the novel derives from the children's acceptance of Joseph's judgment of

them. Though they "rebel" against it, they nowhere deny its
validity. Their sense of their lives has been determined by the
influence of Joseph in the Earnshaw family. "By his knack of
sermonizing and pious discoursing," says Nelly Dean, "[Joseph]
contrived to make a great impression on Mr. Earnshaw, and, the
more feeble the master became, the more influence he gained. He
was relentless in worrying him about his soul's concerns, and about
ruling his children rigidly. He encouraged him to regard Hindley
as a reprobate; and, night after night, he regularly grumbled out
a long string of tales against Heathcliff and Catherine; always
minding to flatter Earnshaw's weakness by heaping the heaviest
blame on the last" (46).

Joseph makes articulate the view of the situation of man which
underlies *Wuthering Heights*. This view is a certain version of
Protestant Christianity. As is well known, Emily Brontë was influenced by two forms of Protestantism, the Evangelicalism of her
father, who was an Anglican clergyman, and the Methodism of
her Aunt Branwell and their servant Tabby. Mrs. Gaskell's biography of Charlotte Brontë gives one glimpse of these influences
at work. She shows the Reverend Brontë asking one of his daughters (Maria, the eldest, who died at eleven) "what was the best
mode of spending time," and being answered, "By laying it out
in preparation for a happy eternity." [18] The rejection of all pleasure now for the sake of eternal pleasure in heaven, the image of
the docile and submissive child, even the use of commercial language to describe the bargain of salvation — all these elements of
Protestantism are present in this vignette. It was perhaps Aunt
Branwell who most directly imposed on the Brontë children notions which might have been held at that time either by a Methodist or by an Anglican influenced by Evangelicalism: the concept
of the natural depravity of man, the need for a saving relation to
God, the relative unimportance of systematic theology, and the insistence on a few simple ideas, such as the view that all pleasure
is evil, the notion that all life here must be directed to the ultimate end of salvation, and the idea that only a life of restraint,
abnegation, and submission to duty will have any chance of reaching that end. The theory of child-raising shared by Methodism
and Evangelicalism, and enshrined in the children's books of

[18] Elizabeth Gaskell, *The Life of Charlotte Brontë* (London, 1879), p. 42.

the period, presupposes an absolute opposition between those thoughts and actions which are instinctive or natural, and those which can be approved. The former are all bad, for is not the child guilty of original sin, and therefore hellbent down the broad way to destruction? The only good acts are those done under co-ercion, whether that coercion is imposed from without or volun-tarily imposed from within. The moral life is a strenuous battle between the forces of good and the forces of evil, and if there is a moment of relaxation the forces of evil will win. So John Wesley, in his sermon "On the Education of Children," says: "To humour children is, as far as in us lies, to make their disease incurable. A wise parent, on the other hand, should begin to break their will, the first moment it appears. . . . [N]ever, on any account, give a child any thing that it cries for. . . . [T]each your children, as soon as possibly you can, that they are fallen spirits . . . Show them that, in pride, passion, and revenge, they are now like the Devil. And that in foolish desires and grovelling appetites, they are like the beasts of the field. . . . [A] wise and truly kind parent will take the utmost care, not to cherish in her children the desire of the flesh, their natural propensity to seek happiness in gratify-ing the outward senses." [19]

It is easy to see how a sensitive child subjected to these religious teachings might conclude that the battle is already lost before it begins, that the natural instincts for evil are too strong to be de-feated by any natural means, and that the terms of the conflict are established in such a way that victory is impossible. Just such a view of the relations between God and man is given in *Wuthering*

---

[19] *Works,* VII, 126–129. Further evidence that Emily Brontë was exposed to this attitude toward children may be found in Charlotte Brontë's portrait of the Evangelical schoolmaster Robert Brocklehurst in *Jane Eyre*. Brocklehurst is modeled on the Reverend William Carus Wilson, the proprietor of the Clergy Daughters' School which Emily Brontë attended with her sisters in 1824 and 1825, when she was seven years old. The real Carus Wilson was scarcely less unpleasant than the fictional Brocklehurst. He was the author of a great many children's books and periodicals, "spiritual penny dreadfuls," as Ford K. Brown calls them, all of which attempted to instill in children the fear of God and hell. "In the business of frightening little children into being Evangelical little children," says Brown, "he was a prodigious master; his relentless and righteously ferocious hands must have planted a religious terror in the minds of thousands of youthful Englishmen" (Ford K. Brown, *Fathers of the Victorians: The Age of Wilberforce* [Cambridge, 1961], p. 463). Brown's discussions of Brocklehurst and Wilson are on pp. 451–457, 463–473 of his book.

Heights and in Emily Brontë's poems. The situation in which Cathy, Heathcliff, and the characters of the Gondal poems find themselves is simple, unequivocal, and altogether reasonable. They have been taught that only two kinds of action exist. Those acts are good which are not an end in themselves, but are a means to the only good end: obeying God and getting to heaven. Bad acts are defined as all those which are pleasurable, a present good in themselves. This present life is to be defined as exile from heaven, an exile imposed by God, and any attempt to transcend it is disobedience of God's law.

For this reason the Methodists were opposed to mysticism, the most obvious expedient for crossing the empty space between a fallen world and God. If I can break through the heavy barriers of sinful flesh and enjoy here and now the measureless pleasure of union with God, then the irreconcilable opposition between the need to reach God and the impossibility of reaching him in this life will be broken. But the Methodists, like many other Christian sects, felt that union with God in mystic ecstasy is, even if authentic, only momentary, therefore simply a distraction from the main business of life, which is "to lay out time in preparation for a happy eternity." [20]

Emily Brontë also recognized the insufficiency of mysticism. One of her best poems contains a vivid description of the painful reawakening to this lower world after the ecstatic joy of mystic vision. The literal imprisonment of the Gondal character who speaks in the poem serves as an expression of the spiritual exile which Emily Brontë finds characteristic of human life. Mysticism is only a momentary escape from this pain:

> Then dawns the Invisible, the Unseen its truth reveals;
> My outward sense is gone, my inward essence feels —
> Its wings are almost free, its home, its harbour found;
> Measuring the gulf it stoops and dares the final bound!

[20] See Wesley's sermon on "The Nature of Enthusiasm" (*Works*, V, 390–399), and his preface to *Hymns and Sacred Poems* (1739) for his criticism of mysticism. "Trust not," says Wesley in the sermon, "in visions or dreams; in sudden impressions, or strong impulses of any kind" (p. 399), and in his journal for June 15, 1741 he criticizes Luther's commentary on Galatians for being "deeply tinctured with mysticism throughout, and hence often dangerously wrong." See Harald Lindström, *Wesley and Sanctification* (Uppsala and Stockholm, 1946), pp. 59, 76. There is a general discussion of mysticism in Emily Brontë in Blondel, *Emily Brontë*, pp. 189–223.

Oh, dreadful is the check — intense the agony
When the ear begins to hear and the eye begins to see;
When the pulse begins to throb, the brain to think again,
The soul to feel the flesh and the flesh to feel the chain! (P, 239)

Emily Brontë shared with the Methodists a recognition that every joy attained in this life, even the pleasure of mystic union with God, is temporary and fleeting, a pale image of the eternal joy of heaven. Only after death can man hope to attain everlasting and immeasurable joy: "A thoughtful Spirit taught me soon/ That we must long till life be done . . ." (P, 232). As long as we are alive our separation from God will persist. Therefore any experience in this world which is like union with God is another step down the broad way to destruction. It is to take an image of the only good end in place of that end itself. This is to commit the sin of idolatry, to put God's creature in the place of God, as when Heathcliff says of his imminent reunion with Cathy: "I tell you, I have nearly attained *my* heaven; and that of others is altogether unvalued, and uncoveted by me!" (381), or as when Emily Brontë writes of one of the Gondal characters: "His soul is glad to cast for her/Virtue and faith and Heaven away" (P, 140), or has another say to his lady: "For thee, through never-ending years,/I'd suffer endless pain . . ." (P, 152).

In order to be saved Heathcliff and Cathy apparently have only to choose the helmet of salvation rather than the broad way to destruction. There is only one difficulty: without God's grace, all human acts whatsoever, for Emily Brontë, are evil; they are all steps in the direction of hell. It is impossible to "lay out time in preparation for a happy eternity," for there is nothing a man can do with his time which will in any way bring him closer to God or ensure his being received in heaven after death. Whether he goes toward God, which means to seek here and now the pleasure of union with the deity, or whether he accepts his separation from God, all his acts increase the already infinite distance between his soul and God. Emily Brontë's world, like those of Kafka or Matthew Arnold, is a realm of the unavailability of God. For Emily Brontë, as for Kafka, man is doomed to commit one of two sins, the sin of impatience or the sin of laziness, the sin of trying to reach here and now, against God's interdict, union with Him, or the sin of accepting separation from God and seeking to establish a satisfactory world without Him. Emily Brontë would agree with Kafka that the sin most natural to man is not laziness but impatience. The difference is that Kafka's characters (K. in *The Castle* is a good example) always retain enough innocence to believe that they are just about to reach the goal of union with God, whereas Emily Brontë's characters do not hope to escape their situation in this life. In Emily Brontë's writings, all men are worthy of damnation, and there is no way to *choose* salvation. If it is attained it will come as a free gift from God to sinful man. As other critics have suggested, it may be that the Gondal poems in this owe something to Byron, as well as to the traditional doctrine of original sin. Augusta is a kind of female Manfred. She too is haunted by an inexpiable guilt, and whatever she does she is doomed. For Emily Brontë, as for Byron, all men are cursed, and no man deserves salvation, though all long to be virtuous: "All [are] doomed alike to sin and mourn/Yet all [live] with long gaze fixed afar,/Adoring virtue's distant star" (P, 122).

In this doctrine of the inevitability of sin Emily Brontë is more like the Calvinistic Methodist, George Whitefield, than like the Arminian Wesley. Wesley holds that God's grace is freely given to all; all men can be saved if they will accept this grace. But for Whitefield grace is offered only to the chosen few: ". . . God intends to give saving grace, through Jesus Christ, only to a certain number; and . . . the rest of mankind, after the fall of Adam, being justly left of God to continue in sin, will at last suffer that eternal death which is its proper wages." [21] Whitefield accepts the doctrines of election and reprobation. The free will of the individual has no real effect on his destiny, for a man's will is in the hands of God. Few are called and few are chosen, and some men, perhaps *most* men, are predestined to damnation, whatever they do. Emily Brontë, like Whitefield, emphasizes man's penchant for sin, and the seemingly Godforsaken situation of many men.

In the strange situation God has imposed on man, there are only two possible acts which man can perform, both of them evil, neither of them obedience to God's law. A man may go directly, in the present, toward the lost fusion with God, break down the

[21] See "A Letter from the Rev. George Whitefield to the Rev. John Wesley," in John Gillies, *Memoirs of Rev. George Whitefield* (New Haven, 1834), p. 632. The whole letter (pp. 628–644) is a succinct account of the doctrinal differences between Whitefield and Wesley.

walls cutting him off from what is around him, and seek to regain
the boundless joy of heaven. To do this is to reach only a false
and damnable image of communion. Taking the other course, a
man may accentuate the gap separating him from nature, from
other people, and from God. The expression of this choice is the
ordinary moral expediency of civilized society, represented in
Wuthering Heights by the Lintons. This selfish calculation is
obedience to God in one way at least: it makes the present moment not an end in itself, but only the means to some future end,
the conservation of one's property or the acquisition of more. But
though worldly prudence begins as fulfillment of God's law, it
ends as the establishment of a city of the world cut off from God,
dedicated to its own ends, and based on the calculating cooper-
ation of individuals, each intent on the perpetuation of his own
good. Historically the expression of this city of the world is the
commercial society of getting and spending which grew up within
Christendom, as if called into being by a profound contradiction
at the heart of its doctrine.[22]

Whether he seeks idolatrous fusion with some other person or
thing, in place of the impossible fusion with God, or whether he
seeks to perpetuate his own separateness, a man is, for Emily
Brontë, equally guilty. In her world the universal state of fallen
man is that described at the beginning of her last poem:

> Why ask to know the date — the clime?
> More than mere words they cannot be:
> Men knelt to God and worshipped crime,
> And crushed the helpless, even as we. (P, 244)

The condition of man in Emily Brontë's world is at once reasonable and unreasonable, and this contradiction derives from a contradiction in the nature of God himself. It seems perfectly reasonable that we should be required to obey God's law against actions
which do not have union with Him as their goal, but since no action here can have God as its goal, man's situation is unreasonable. God is at once the ordainer of separateness and the promise
of the ultimate joy of fusion with Him. The divine realm is uni-

---

[22] The classic studies of this process are Max Weber, "Die protestantische Ethik
und der Geist des Kapitalismus," *Archiv für Sozialwissenschaft und Sozialpolitik*,
XX, XXI (1904, 1905; English translation: London, 1930) and R. H. Tawney,
Religion and the Rise of Capitalism (London, 1926).

versal intimacy, the copresence of all things and persons in perfect possession of one another. The God of this heaven establishes reason, morality, and the isolation of objects and people in a spatialized world. To obey God in one way is to disobey him in another, and either way to merit damnation.

The fine line dividing a just and yet merciful God from an irrational tyrant is perfectly dramatized in the sermon Lockwood hears in his strange dream near the beginning of *Wuthering Heights*. Lockwood's dream suggests that Emily Brontë's God is at once a God of mercy, a God who will forgive man's sins, though they should number seventy times seven, and at the same time a God who dooms man to commit not only seventy times seven sins but also the unforgivable first of the seventy-first, "the sin that no Christian need pardon" (25).

The text of Jabes' sermon is Mat. 18:21, 22:[23] "Then came Peter to him, and said, Lord, how oft shall my brother sin against me, and I forgive him? till seven times? Jesus saith unto him, I say not unto thee, Until seven times: but, Until seventy times seven." The text bears first on the relations between neighbors, and expresses in striking form the Christian virtue of turning the other cheek. In the context of Christ's teaching the "seventy times seven" seems to suggest that we should go on forgiving our neighbor as often as he sins against us, even though he does so an outrageous number of times. But Jabes and his congregation are literalists, and read the text to mean that we should wait patiently through four hundred and ninety sins and then rise up and smite our neighbor down. So the congregation rushes on poor Lockwood at the end of the sermon, and so Lockwood demands the destruction of Jabes for having preached such an interminable sermon: "Fellow martyrs, have at him! Drag him down, and crush him to atoms, that the place which knows him may know him no more!" (26). This sounds not like the New Testament but like the Old Testament attitude echoed by Isabella later when she demands "an eye for an eye, a tooth for a tooth" (206) in her revenge on Heathcliff. Or we are reminded of Hindley's formulation of the moral law of the Heights: "Treachery and violence are a just return for

[23] Surely Ruth M. Adams is wrong when she says the text is Gen. 4:24. The phrase in Genesis is "seventy and sevenfold" not "seventy times seven," as in Mat. 18:22, and in the title of Jabes' sermon. (See her "Wuthering Heights: The Land East of Eden," *Nineteenth-Century Fiction*, XIII [1958], 58-62.)

treachery and violence!" (201). Jabes, Lockwood, and the congregation are interested not in the way Jesus' words are an admonishment to forgiveness, but in the way, to their perverted interpretation, they seem to justify, after a certain point, condign vengeance. The text is reversed in the same way that the pilgrim staves of the congregation are transformed into "heavy-headed cudgels."

The Reverend Jabes Branderham should have read further in his Bible, for in the verses following his text Jesus tells a parable which establishes a connection between the relations of man and man and the relations of man and God (Mat. 18:23–35). The parable is the familiar one of the Lord who forgives his servant a debt until he discovers that the servant has dealt without compassion with a fellow servant who owes him money. The Lord then turns the first servant over to the "tormentors," saying: "Shouldest not thou also have had compassion on thy fellowservant, even as I had pity on thee?" The verses assert that God will forgive us our sins if we forgive our neighbors' sins, but that he will punish us according to our deserts if we act without pity toward our neighbors. The God of *Wuthering Heights* is justified in treating his creatures cruelly. They are, for the most part, without pity or forgiveness for one another, and their conscious defiance of the law by which God reserves vengeance to himself echoes through the novel (see 69, 205, 206). Emily Brontë was fascinated by the moment when God, having forgiven man four hundred and ninety times, should be justified in replacing mercy with the most ferocious justice. Emily Brontë's God gives himself as unreservedly to vengeance as do Heathcliff, Hindley, or Isabella:

> The time of grace is past
> And mercy scorned and tried
> Forsakes to utter wrath at last
> The soul so steeled by pride.
>
> That wrath will never spare,
> Will never pity know,
> Will mock its victim's maddened prayer,
> Will triumph in his woe.
>
> Shut from his Maker's smile
> The accursed man shall be:
> Compassion reigns a little while,
> Revenge eternally. (P, 121)

In Jabes' sermon, as elsewhere in Emily Brontë's writings, both God and man are represented as waiting, with ill-concealed impatience, through the legally required time of mercy and forgiveness, until they can get down to the pleasant business of doing justified violence on one another to the limit of their powers. God is different only in that his power is infinite.

The sermon of the Reverend Jabes Branderham is a striking dramatization of the way Protestantism, in its attempt to recognize the uniqueness of each person and remove all intermediaries between the soul and God, can end by putting each man at an infinite distance from his neighbors and from God. Enmity and hatred are the only relations between man and man or between man and God which Jabes' sermon seems to allow. In the Christian society of *Wuthering Heights,* as in the state of nature in Emily Brontë's essay, destruction is the law of life, and God has condemned man to separateness. Never in this world will a man be able to enjoy with impunity anything which is like "the endless and shadowless hereafter," the eternity of Heaven where life is boundless in its duration, and love in its sympathy, and joy in its fulness.

Even more is implied by Jabes' sermon. Though the God of the sermon seems to be a deity whose ways can be understood by man, the mind overreaches itself in the attempt to comprehend him and attains at last the exasperation of a confrontation with infinite mystery. The Protestant tradition of "dividing" a text, in order to make more comprehensible to human reason the revelation of God to man, becomes, when it produces a sermon "divided into *four hundred and ninety* parts — each fully equal to an ordinary address from the pulpit" (25), an absurdity exceeding the patience and comprehension of man. If each of these four hundred and ninety parts must discuss "a separate sin," sins, as Lockwood says, "of the most curious character — odd transgressions that I never imagined previously" (25), another absurdity in the situation of man is revealed. Sinning can no longer be neatly compartmentalized into seven groups, easy to understand and remember. There are so many sins that their number seems to be infinite. The number of sins exceeds the grasp of reason, and each time a man sins he is doomed to commit a new and different sin: ". . . it seemed necessary the brother should sin different sins on every occasion" (25). Another corollary follows from this. Since there are so many different sins, it is unlikely that any two persons should commit the same sin. Though all men are sinners, each person is cut off from his fellows by his sins, just as the various moments of a man's life are divided from one another, since each new act is a new and different sin. The human condition imposed by the God of wrath leads to hatred, misunderstanding, and separation among people, for each man is isolated in the prison of his own odd transgressions, and cannot be measured by the standards which apply to others. It is no wonder that Jabes' sermon ends with a free-for-all among the members of the congregation, for if each man is unique it is natural that every man's hand should be against his neighbor.

In such a world the separation of Cathy and Heathcliff is inevitable, and their scamper on the moors leads them fatefully to the adventure which leaves Heathcliff outside the window of Thrushcross Grange looking in at a Cathy almost instantaneously changed, a Cathy with whom he is no longer consubstantial. Sooner or later, in their case as in all others, the isolation and discontinuity natural to human existence will be established. The separation of Cathy and Heathcliff happens as naturally and inevitably as growing up. Though Heathcliff can with some justice accuse Cathy of reaffirming their separation by marrying Edgar Linton, she is not the cause of its original occurrence. Its ultimate cause is the nature of human existence as God has established it.

The divine law making isolation follow escape from separateness operates repeatedly in Emily Brontë's poems. The characteristic dramatic sequence of the poems is the seizing of illicit sexual pleasure, followed by the inevitable sequel of separation, exile, imprisonment, and, eventually, death. The immediate causes of these sufferings are various, but their ultimate cause is always the same. The poems several times formulate this universal law of human existence. Gondal is a world where "future grief" is "entailed on present joy" (P, 187), a world where "Pleasure still will lead to wrong,/ . . . And Joy [is] the shortest path to Pain . . . !" (P, 185), a world where "bliss" is "bought by years/Dark with torment and with tears" (P, 121). Gondal is, finally, a world in which there are: "Relentless laws that disallow/True virtue and true joy below" (P, 122). No passage in Emily Brontë more perfectly expresses her grim view of the human condition. Both virtue and joy on earth are against God's law, and will inevitably be punished by the stern ruler who has established his irrevocable decree, as the childhood love of Heathcliff and Cathy is necessarily followed by their separation.

Once Cathy and Heathcliff are separated, what are they to do? What action is possible when the relentless laws have been enforced? Neither obedience of God nor defiance of him seem possible, for neither virtue nor joy is allowed in this lower world. In the reactions of Cathy and Heathcliff to their separation we can watch their apparently hopeless struggles against a God who seems, like his creation, to live on a principle of destruction.

ક~

True virtue and true joy are opposites. In *Wuthering Heights* Cathy seeks virtue in marrying Edgar Linton and in obeying the communal law of prudence, responsibility, and maturity. True joy lies only in her relation to Heathcliff. Both are impossible, disallowed by relentless law. Cathy's separation from Heathcliff occurs through the inevitable operation of God's law, but her mistake is not to recognize what has happened. She tries to have at once the two opposites which God has forbidden on earth. She marries Edgar Linton because it would "degrade" her to marry Heathcliff now that she has been transformed into a civilized young lady, but she does not believe that her marriage to Edgar will separate her from Heathcliff, for Heathcliff is "more herself than she is." She will use Edgar's money to "aid Heathcliff to rise, and place him out of [her] brother's power" (93). She apparently imagines a strange *ménage à trois* in which her relation to Edgar will satisfy the demands of virtue, and her relation to Heathcliff will bring her joy. She will evade God's relentless laws in the only way that it might be possible to do so — by achieving a state which is both virtuous and joyful. But this is impossible. God has established the human condition so that virtue and joy are incompatible, and therefore neither virtue nor joy is attainable in this world. The very definition of virtuous states is that they are not pleasant, and the very definition of joyous states is that they are achieved in reckless defiance of God's interdict against earthly pleasure.

Cathy recognizes this only when Heathcliff returns after his disappearance of three years, though she has already discovered the "very, very bitter misery" (113) of having virtue without joy, Edgar without Heathcliff. When Heathcliff returns she is forced at last to see that she cannot have both at once. "Will you give up Heathcliff hereafter," asks Edgar, "or will you give up me? It is impossible for you to be *my* friend, and *his* at the same time; and I absolutely *require* to know which you choose" (134). Cathy is unable to choose. Only the simultaneous possession of Edgar and Heathcliff would satisfy her. When she sees that she cannot have both she realizes at last that she is permanently separated from Heathcliff, that never again in this world can she enjoy the intimacy they have had as children. "I felt," she says, "that . . . we should all be driven asunder for nobody knows how long!" (133).

Cathy's reaction to this discovery is spontaneous and immediate. It is exactly analogous to the way Augusta, the heroine of the Gondal poems, reacts to similar situations. Cathy wills her own death. To will her own death is to will the consummation of her separation from Heathcliff. If the separation is inevitable, there is only one way she can retain sovereign control of her own life: to choose the separation and be herself the cause of it. "Well," she says, "if I cannot keep Heathcliff for my friend — if Edgar will be mean and jealous, I'll try to break their hearts by breaking my own. That will be a prompt way of finishing all, when I am pushed to extremity!" (133). And later: "Oh, I will die" (137).

In the same way Augusta recognizes that the sexual pleasure she has enjoyed with one or another of her lovers is doomed, by the fact that it is achieved through transgression of divine law, to come to an end. No such love can long continue, or even long continue to satisfy, for "every phase of earthly joy/Will always fade and always cloy" (P, 232). Augusta knows that she will sooner or later be rejected by her lovers if she does not reject them first, and so she betrays them, one after another, condemning Lord Elbë to death in battle, Amedeus to exile and death, Lord Alfred to exile and suicide, Fernando De Samara to imprisonment, madness, and suicide, and King Julius to assassination.[24] The cause of these betrayals is not unmotivated wickedness; it is Augusta's desire to maintain her autonomy. She recognizes that separation and suffering after joy are inevitable, and decides to be the cause of

[24] I am following the reconstruction in *Gondal's Queen*.

these rather than simply to endure them. The poems provide a
striking formulation of the law of love in the Gondal world: "I've
known a hundred kinds of love: /*All* made the loved one rue . . ."
(P, 152).

In Gondal not "lover" but "loved one" is the victim of love and
the one who most suffers. One after another Augusta implacably
destroys those whom she loves, as female spiders kill their mates.
Love in the poems is a form of destruction, part of the "principle
of destruction" on which life exists. Love is part of "earth's frenzied strife" that "makes destruction joy" (P, 198), and Augusta's
treatment of her lovers is only the most shocking example of the
law of nature which says that "every creature must be the relentless instrument of death to the others or himself cease to live."

Though love causes suffering and death in the novel as well as
in the poems, Cathy is very different from Augusta. Her way of re-
taining her sovereignty is to cause her own death, not Heathcliff's.
Cathy, like Augusta determined to remain in command even when
"pushed to extremity," takes the extreme step of starving herself
to death in order to punish Edgar and keep control of the situation.
"If I were only sure it would kill him," she says, "I'd kill myself
directly!" (139). Cathy's way of dealing with her plight is more
passive, more masochistic, than Augusta's way. Cathy is more like
Fernando, one of Augusta's betrayed lovers, who cries as he kills
himself: "O could I know thy soul with equal grief was torn, /This
fate might be endured — this anguish might be borne!" (P, 86). In
Wuthering Heights both lover and loved one regret love and suffer because of it.

In spite of Cathy's resolution in extremity, she does not reach
happiness in death. She reaches only the condition of absolute
division from the being who is more herself than she is. During her
death agony she expresses her desire to be in heaven: ". . . the
thing that irks me most is this shattered prison, after all. I'm tired,
tired of being enclosed here. I'm wearying to escape into that
glorious world, and to be always there; not seeing it dimly through
tears, and yearning for it through the walls of an aching heart; but
really with it, and in it" (183). Cathy makes it clear that she will
not be happy in heaven unless Heathcliff is there too. Heathcliff
remains alive, on this side of the barrier separating all earthly
creatures from the boundless realm of sympathy and joy which is

heaven, so she deludes herself with the notion that the Heathcliff of flesh and blood is not the real Heathcliff. She will take the real Heathcliff with her, the Heathcliff who is her own being: "That is not *my* Heathcliff. I shall love mine yet; and take him with me — he's in my soul" (183). The division between them is so complete that she sees two Heathcliffs, one an objective being separate from herself, the other existing in the depths of her own soul. She knows, nevertheless, that to be dead, and even in heaven, while Heathcliff is still alive, will only more irrevocably confirm her division from him. As she twice tells Heathcliff, she will not rest in the grave while he lives: "I'll not lie there by myself: they may bury me twelve feet deep, and throw the church down over me; but I won't rest till you are with me . . . I never will!" (144); "I shall not be at peace" (182).

By willing her own death Cathy retains control of her fate, but she does not transcend her separation from Heathcliff. Her way of dealing with her life, like Augusta's, leads to a more irrevocably confirmed isolation. Whether one waits passively for God to impose separateness, or whether one despairingly causes separation, whether one causes the death of others, or anticipates inevitable separation by choosing death for oneself, the result is the same — the "hopeless, endless mourning" of division from all that might bring joy.

ॐ

Heathcliff's situation after Cathy's death is different from hers while she lived, and his reaction to that situation is not the despairing acceptance of separateness, but the attempt to regain his lost fullness of being. The universal human desire is for union with something outside oneself. People differ from one another only in the intensity of their desire, and in the diversity of the ways they seek to assuage it.

After Cathy's death Heathcliff's whole life is concentrated on the suffering caused by his loss, and on the violence of his desire to get her back, for she is his soul, and without her he grovels in an abyss of nothingness. Why does Heathcliff spend so much of his time in an elaborate attempt to destroy Thrushcross Grange and Wuthering Heights, with all their inhabitants? Why does he take delight in torturing Hindley, Isabella, Hareton, the second Cathy, his son Linton? Why does he, both before Cathy's death and after, enter on a violent career of sadistic destruction? Is it because he is, as Cathy says, a "fierce, pitiless, wolfish man," or does his sadism have some further meaning?

During the violent scene of mutual recrimination between Heathcliff and Cathy which ends in the fight between Heathcliff and Edgar, Heathcliff tells Cathy that she has treated him "infernally" by betraying him and marrying Edgar. He will not, he says, "suffer unrevenged" (128). But, says Heathcliff, "I seek no revenge on you . . . The tyrant grinds down his slaves and they don't turn against him, they crush those beneath them — You are welcome to torture me to death for your amusement, only, allow me to amuse myself a little in the same style . . ." (128). Heathcliff's cruelty toward others is a mode of relation to Cathy. Though his appearance at Wuthering Heights in itself disrupts the Earnshaw family, Heathcliff's relation to Cathy forms the basis of his defiance of everyone else, and his destructive hatred attains its full development only after he is separated from her. His sadistic treatment of others is the only kind of revenge against Cathy he can take, for the person who most controls events in *Wuthering Heights* is not Heathcliff. It is Cathy herself.

Heathcliff's sadism is more than an attempt to take revenge indirectly on Cathy. It is also a strange and paradoxical attempt to regain his lost intimacy with her. If Cathy can say, "I *am* Heathcliff," Heathcliff could equally well say, "I *am* Cathy," for she is, as he says, his "soul." Possession of Heathcliff gives Cathy possession of the entire universe. If she were to lose Heathcliff, "the universe would turn to a mighty stranger," just as Heathcliff becomes an alien and outcast from all the world after he loses Cathy. If his childhood relation to Cathy gave him possession of the whole world through her, perhaps now that Cathy is lost he can get her back by appropriating the world. The sadistic infliction of pain on other people, like the destruction of inanimate objects, is a way of breaking down the barriers between oneself and the world. Now that he has lost Cathy, the only thing remaining to Heathcliff which is like the lost fusion with her is the destructive assimilation of other people or things. So he turns sadist, just as, in the Gondal poems, Julius Brenzaida turns on the world in war when he has been betrayed by Augusta. Heathcliff's violence against everyone but Cathy plays the same role in *Wuthering Heights* as does the theme of war in the poems. In both cases there is an implicit recognition that war or sadism is like love because love too is destructive, since it must break down the separateness of the loved one. Augusta too is a sadist. She moves quickly from inspiring her lovers to abandon honor for her sake to betraying them and causing them to suffer. Like love, sadism is a moment of communion, a moment when the barriers between person and person are broken down. The climax of sadistic joy is loss of the sense of separateness. It is as though the person who is forced to suffer had lost his limits and had melted into the whole universe. At the same moment the self of the sadist dissolves too, and self and universe become one. Heathcliff's relation to Cathy has been fusion with the whole world through her. He feels that he can reverse the process and regain her by assimilating the world, for his sole aim is to "dissolve with" Cathy and be happy at last (329). Now he proposes to do this by getting control of Wuthering Heights and Thrushcross Grange in order to destroy them both. "I wish," says Heathcliff of his property, "I could annihilate it from the face of the earth" (380). So he gives himself whole-heartedly to acts of sadistic destruction. No other figure in English literature takes so much pleasure in causing pain to others: "I have no pity! I have no pity!" he cries. "The more the worms writhe, the more I yearn to crush out their entrails! It is a moral teething, and I grind with greater energy, in proportion to the increase of pain" (174). In another place he tells Nelly his feelings about his son and the second Cathy: "It's odd what a savage feeling I have to anything that seems afraid of me! Had I been born where laws are less strict, and tastes less dainty, I should treat my-self to a slow vivifisection of those two, as an evening's amusement" (308).

Heathcliff's effort to regain Cathy through sadistic destruction fails, just as does Augusta's attempt to achieve through sadistic love a fusion with something outside herself, and just as does Cathy's decision to will her own death. Heathcliff's sadism fails because, as things or people are annihilated under the blows of the sadist, he is left with nothing. He reaches only an exacerbated sense of the absence of the longed-for intimacy rather than the intimacy itself. Augusta goes from lover to lover, destroying them one by one because she cannot reach what she wants through them. And Heathcliff finds that his career of sadistic revenge is a way of suffering the loss of Cathy more painfully rather than a way of reaching her again. "It is a poor conclusion, is it not," he asks. "An absurd termination to my violent exertions? I get levers, and mattocks to demolish the two houses, and train myself to be capable of working like Hercules, and when everything is ready, and in my power, I find the will to lift a slate off either roof has vanished! . . . I have lost the faculty of enjoying their destruction . . ." (369).

The reason Heathcliff gives for having lost the will to demolish the two houses is a confirmation of the fact that his relation to everything in the world is a relation to Cathy, and an admission of the defeat of his attempt to regain her by destroying the Grange and the Heights. He says that everything in the universe is a reminder that Cathy has existed and that he does not possess her. Through his destruction of others he has reached, in the wreckage left after his violence, the full realization of her absence: ". . . what is not connected with her to me?" he asks, "and what does not recall her? I cannot look down to this floor, but her features are shaped in the flags! In every cloud, in every tree — filling the air at night, and caught by glimpses in every object, by day I am surrounded with her image! The most ordinary faces of men, and women — my own features mock me with a resemblance. The entire world is a dreadful collection of memoranda that she did exist, and that I have lost her!" (370). The universe is identified not with Cathy, but with the absence of Cathy, and to possess the world through its destructive appropriation is not to possess Cathy, but to confront once more the vacant place where she is not. This is the hell in which Heathcliff lives after her death: "I could *almost* see her, and yet I *could not!* I ought to have sweat blood then, from the anguish of my yearning, from the fervour of my supplications to have but one glimpse! I had not one. She showed herself, as she often was in life, a devil to me! And, since then, sometimes more, and sometimes less, I've been the sport of that intolerable torture!" (331). Heathcliff's sadistic tormenting of others only leads him to be the more tormented, tormented by a Cathy whose strongest weapon is her invisibility.

ह‌≈ ،

There is no escape in this world from the suffering of isolation. Neither by passivity nor by willful action, neither by obeying God's law nor by transgressing it, will any living man or woman, for more than a delusory minute, cease to be bound by the suffocating walls of his own identity. The law dooming man to sin and suffer for his sins is irrevocably established. All creatures of God, both human and animal, are like the ugly caterpillar who hides in the flower and secretly destroys it, and it seems as if the whole creation were a mistake, a machine for creating evil, something which God should have annihilated the moment after the fall of man. Emily Brontë's vision of things leads her to reject and condemn the whole fabric of creation:

> I picked a flower at my side. It was pretty and newly opened, but an ugly caterpillar had hidden himself among the petals and already they were drawing up and withering. "Sad image of the earth and its inhabitants!" I exclaimed, "This worm lives only by destroying the plant which protects him; why was he created and why was man created?" . . . I threw the flower to the ground; at that moment the universe appeared to me a vast machine constructed only to bring forth evil: I almost doubted the goodness of God for not annihilating man on the day of his first sin. "The world should have been destroyed," I said, "crushed, just as I crush this reptile, which has done nothing during his life but make everything he touches as disgusting as himself." [25]

If the whole world is accursed, then man must seek death, not the death of others, but his own death. Much of Emily Brontë's work is an exploration of the various ways in which it seems man might attain, here in this world, something like the boundless sympathy and joy which are remembered from childhood or from some prenatal paradise. All the ways fail. Each leads only to a confirmation of the sin and suffering to which man is doomed. As a result, many of Emily Brontë's characters are led to the moment when, all else having failed, they expend their vitality to reach, as quickly as possible, the realm of death. Only in death can they find "endless bliss through endless years" (P, 185), the interpenetration of all things with one another which is heaven.

[25] *Five Essays,* trans. Nagel, pp. 17, 18.

Her characters do not seek death passively, through a relaxation
of the life force which will let death flow in as life slowly evapo-
rates. They are cursed with too much vitality for that. "So much
the worse for me, that I am strong," cries Heathcliff. "Do I want
to live?" (185). Death is the most violent act of will. It is the will
destroying itself by destroying the inner strength of the self, for
only when that strength is exhausted can death be reached.

What experience awaits man beyond the gates of death?

৵

> Shall these long, agonising years
> Be punished by eternal tears?
>
> No; *that* I feel can never be;
> A God of *hate* could hardly bear
> To watch through all eternity
> His own creations dread despair! (P, 138)

For Emily Brontë, if it is true to say that all men are worthy
of damnation, it is equally true to say that all men may be saved,
without exception. She does truly hold that doctrine of "universal
redemption" which Whitefield accuses Wesley of preaching.[26] Or
in any case she believes that all men have a chance to be saved.
If some men are to be saved, then all men may be saved, since no
man is any more worthy of salvation than his neighbor. It is as
though Emily Brontë had moved to the moment of death or to the
moment of the Last Judgment the time of the descent of God's
saving grace. She agrees with John Wesley that "God justifieth not
the godly, but the ungodly; not those that are holy already, but
the unholy." [27] For Wesley, God's grace operates on man in this
world and its acceptance is confirmed afterward in good works.
By these works a man will be assessed at the Last Judgment, for
good works are the sign of faith and of its supervening sanctification. Hence Wesley's opposition to antinomianism. Emily Brontë,
however, believes that some men can receive God's saving grace at
the moment of death.

This reversal of the law which seems to destine all men to
damnation is affirmed repeatedly in the poems. One Gondal char-

[26] "Letter to Wesley," *Memoirs of Rev. George Whitefield*, pp. 629, 634, 636.
[27] "Justification by Faith," *Works*, V, 50.

acter says: "If I have sinned, long, long ago/That sin was purified by woe" (P, 138). Augusta tells one of her lovers to "Call Death — yes, Death, he is thine own!" for though he has sinned in loving Augusta and is being punished for it by death, that death will be a liberation into eternal bliss. The dust of earthly sin never makes the soul impure:

> If thou hast sinned in this world of care,
> 'Twas but the dust of thy drear abode —
> Thy soul was pure when it entered here,
> And pure it will go again to God. (P, 71)

The most paradoxical consequence of Emily Brontë's view of the human condition is her belief that the suffering sin brings will be sufficient expiation for that sin. Each person is fated to commit a certain number of sins and to suffer a certain amount of pain before he can escape to heaven. The passive, obedient people, the Edgar Lintons of this world, do not really act within the law. They eke out over a longer period the necessary allotment of sin. Furthermore, the transfiguration of the world at the Last Judgment will be postponed until "Sin [has] spent its last drop of poison, [and] death [has] thrown its last dart." A certain number of sins are necessary to complete the great work of the exhaustion of evil which will make possible resurrection into the new life. The climax of Emily Brontë's drama of history is a universal holocaust in which all the sin and suffering of man and the animal world, through being endured and worked out to their bitter end, will be transfigured into the happiness of heaven: "God is the God of justice and mercy; then, assuredly, each pain that he inflicts on his creatures, be they human or animal, rational or irrational, each suffering of our unhappy nature is only a seed for that divine harvest which will be gathered when sin having spent its last drop of poison, death having thrown its last dart, both will expire on the funeral pyre of a universe in flame, and will leave their former victims to an eternal realm of happiness and glory." [28]

Since all are doomed alike to sin and mourn, all men quite properly should long for death, and the luckiest reach it soonest. In the same way the goal of the whole creation is its final flaming death, when all sin shall have been exhausted at last. One of the Gondal characters can cry, with perfect justification:

[28] *Five Essays*, trans. Nagel, pp. 18, 19.

Yet I would lose no sting, would wish no torture less;
The more that anguish racks the earlier it will bless;
And robed in fires of Hell, or bright with heavenly shine,
If it but herald Death, the vision is divine. (P, 239)

In the same way King Harold, in Emily's essay "King Harold on the Eve of the Battle of Hastings," is free from the smothering pleasures and intrigues of his court only when he faces death on the battlefield. Here, as in the Gondal poems, war leads to death, and the most heroic warrior is not the victor but the one who is killed in the fight. King Harold on the eve of the battle of Hastings is transfigured, sovereign, and free not only because he can now unleash all his instincts for cruelty and unrestrained violence (all good warriors are sadists), but because he is about to experience the truly liberating event of his life, his own death: "A soul divine, visible to his fellow men as to his Creator, gleams in his eyes; at the same time a multitude of human emotions awaken in him, but they are exalted, sanctified, made almost divine. His courage is not temerity, nor is his pride arrogance. His anger is justified, his assurance is free from presumption. He has an inner conviction that by no mortal power will he be defeated. Death alone can gain victory over his arms. To her he is ready to yield, for Death's touch is to the hero what the striking off his chains is to the slave." [29]

Anything which leads to death is divine, for death is an absolute transformation of our earthly state. The image which dominates Emily Brontë's description of this change is the transmutation of the ugly caterpillar into a beautiful butterfly, traditional image for the liberation of the soul. Between this life and the world to come there is no likeness, even though this life with all its horror and discord is a necessary prelude to the harmony of heaven. For this reason Emily Brontë, after describing the creation as "insane," can say, without irony: "Nevertheless, we celebrate the day of our birth, and we praise God that we entered such a world." [30] The signs that the sufferings of Cathy and Heathcliff have been transformed into the boundless peace of heaven are the "moths fluttering among the heath, and hare-bells" which Lockwood sees at the

[29] *Five Essays*, trans. Nagel, p. 12; see Roger Caillois, "War and the Sacred," in *Man and the Sacred*, trans. Meyer Barash (Glencoe, Ill., 1959), pp. 163–180 for an interpretation of the religious significance of war which matches Emily Brontë's.
[30] *Five Essays*, trans. Nagel, p. 17.

very end of the novel (385). In the same way, in the essay on the butterfly, the speaker has no sooner crushed the caterpillar (thus participating in the universal destruction of nature), than a beautiful butterfly springs forth and disappears into the sky.[31]

The fact that the caterpillar must be crushed in order to make possible the butterfly shows that even the most extreme example of radical change in nature is not adequate for Emily Brontë. The caterpillar has to die not "naturally" but violently, which is according to nature as Emily Brontë sees it. Life does not grow out of life, as butterfly from caterpillar, but only from death, as the butterfly rises from the crushed caterpillar. It is not a question of a flowing, however sudden the change of pace, but of an absolute break: life out of death, heavenly bliss out of earthly torment.

The image of the caterpillar transformed into a butterfly is not solely an expression of the change of sinful man into a blessed soul after death. It is also the proper image for the transformation of the whole world, at the last trump, into "a new heaven and a new earth." A recognition that this transformation is inevitable will answer all our presumptuous questions about the wisdom of God in permitting the creation to endure. Just as there can be no butterfly without a caterpillar, so there can be no "eternal realm of happiness and glory" without this insane world and its gradual exhaustion of the allotted measure of evil — down to the last drop. In the essay on the butterfly the speaker is moved by his vision of the miraculous change taking place before his eyes to exclaim: "Let not the creature judge his creator, here is a symbol of the world to come — just as the ugly caterpillar is the beginning of the splendid butterfly, this globe is the embryo of a new heaven and of a new earth whose meagerest beauty infinitely surpasses mortal imagination. When you see the glorious outcome of what now seems to you so mean, how you will despise your blind presumption in blaming Omniscience for not having destroyed nature in its infancy." [32]

In several of the poems the same double vision of the world appears. The world is at once the ugly sight it appears to mortal eyes, and at the same time those same elements glorified and transformed into their opposites. Every bit of suffering, violence, and

[31] *Five Essays*, trans. Nagel, p. 18.
[32] *Ibid.*

sin is necessary and good, for all are required by the ultimate trans-figuration. In one poem this transformation appears in the change of an "inky sea" to a brilliant ocean, "sparkl[ing] wide and bright," "white as the sun" (P, 221), and in another the speaker laments the inevitable destruction of the beautiful landscape of summer by the cold of winter. But suddenly the air seems kindled with "a thousand thousand glancing fires," and these "little glittering spirits" tell the visionary that the death of plants and animals in winter is necessary, like the evil of mankind, for it brings more quickly the "everlasting day." The song of the little glittering spirits is another expression of the idea that suffering is good, for the more intensely we suffer the sooner we shall reach death, and death is the one goal of life:

> O mortal, mortal, let them die;
> Let Time and Tears destroy,
> That we may overflow the sky
> With universal joy.
>
> Let Grief distract the sufferer's breast,
> And Night obscure his way;
> They hasten him to endless rest,
> And everlasting day.
>
> To Thee the World is like a tomb,
> A desert's naked shore;
> To us, in unimagined bloom,
> It brightens more and more.
>
> And could we lift the veil and give
> One brief glimpse to thine eye
> Thou would'st rejoice for those that live,
> Because they live to die. (P, 200)

If life is good only because it makes death possible, then Heath-cliff is perfectly justified in calling his career of sadism a "moral teething," and there is no doubt that he and Cathy reach again the joy of possessing one another only when they are "restored into the Deity" (P, 211), in spite of Heathcliff's defiant claim that he seeks only his own heaven. Death is the true goal of life, and death is most quickly reached by those who exhaust themselves in the futile attempt to deny the law of separateness imposed by God. In the poems and in the novel the two kinds of action which lead most directly to death are illicit love and physical violence. Though sadistic cruelty or illicit union with another person are not the same as death and the union with God which follows death, they are more like them than patient endurance of separateness. They break down the tough envelope of the self and prepare it for its dissolution into the boundless sympathy and love of heaven.

Cathy and Heathcliff reach in death what they possessed in this world when they were unself-conscious children, and did not know of their separateness. They reach peace not through obedient acceptance of isolation, but through the final exhaustion of all their forces in the attempt to reach union in this life. Their heroism is, in Georges Bataille's phrase, an "approbation of life to the point of death." [33] Cathy's death is caused by their embrace: "An instant they held asunder; and then how they met I hardly saw, but Catherine made a spring, and he caught her, and they were locked in an embrace from which I thought my mistress would never be released alive. In fact, to my eyes, she seemed directly insensible" (184). Heathcliff too reaches death through the exhaustion of his vitality. This exhaustion is brought about by his frantic attempt to reach Cathy's ghost: "I have to remind myself to breathe — almost to remind my heart to beat! And it is like bending back a stiff spring . . . it is by compulsion, that I do the slightest act, not prompted by one thought, and by compulsion, that I notice anything alive, or dead, which is not associated with one universal idea . . . I have a single wish, and my whole being, and faculties are yearning to attain it. They have yearned towards it so long, and so unwaveringly, that I'm convinced it *will* be reached — and *soon* — because it has devoured my existence — I am swallowed in the anticipation of its fulfilment" (371); ". . . you might as well bid a man struggling in the water, rest within arms-length of the shore! I must reach it first, and then I'll rest" (380).

At the end of *Wuthering Heights* Cathy and Heathcliff have reached the peace of union with one another through God, a God who is at once immanent and transcendent, utterly beyond this world, "brooding above" it, and within it as what "pervades" it everywhere, just as the soft breeze breathes over the moors in the last paragraph of the novel. One need not, as Lockwood says, "im-

---

[33] "L'érotisme est," writes Bataille in his excellent essay on Emily Brontë, ". . . l'approbation de la vie jusque dans la mort" (*La littérature et le mal* [Paris, 1957], p. 12).

agine unquiet slumbers, for the sleepers in that quiet earth," and "under that benign sky" (385). Only in death, the realm of absolute communion, can Heathcliff "dissolve with" Cathy and "be happy" at last. The final happiness of Cathy and Heathcliff, like their first union in childhood, can only be spoken of symbolically. The tremendous storm raised by the separation of the two lovers, a storm which has swirled out to engulf all the characters in the novel, has been appeased at last, and calm has returned. Heathcliff has broken through to the still point at the center of the whirlwind, the divine point where all opposites are reconciled and where he can possess Cathy again because he possesses all things in God. The calm he has reached has spread back into the world to be tangible in the soft wind breathing through the grass and blowing through the open windows at Wuthering Heights (350). Emanations from the center of peace have been liberated to flow out to the periphery of the circle, and to irradiate all the world with a benign and pervasive glow. The state of savagery in which Lockwood first found the people at Wuthering Heights has been transcended at last.

ઙૅ

What of the story of the second Cathy? The earthly happiness of Hareton and the second Cathy seems impossible, on principle, in Emily Brontë's world of suffering. Is the second story simply an example of a weak, delusory love set against the authentic love of Heathcliff and the first Cathy? It would seem so, for while the first lovers will be satisfied by nothing less than a complete fusion of their souls, Hareton and the second Cathy are content to remain separate and to communicate with one another by means of an intermediary. The symbols of their developing love are the books which Cathy teaches Hareton to read, the books which reclaim him from savagery and make him worthy to take possession of his inheritance.

The two kinds of love are related to time in radically different ways. Heathcliff and the first Cathy are willing to abandon all the earthly future and plunge into the eternal present of the life after death. Their love is a destructive holocaust which burns up time and sends it flaming out into the timelessness of infinity. The love of Hareton and Cathy is committed to duration. It brings about the re-establishment of civilization, a re-establishment which is objectified in Hareton's education, and in the garden which Cathy and Hareton cultivate together. Their love prepares itself a long future of calm love and rational communion.

The rhythm of separation and union in the two loves is also radically different. The first Cathy and Heathcliff are united in childhood, separated in adulthood, and reach union again only in the boundless realm of death. Their love moves through a process of union, separation, and reunion on a higher level which appears often in writings in the romantic tradition, and is like the dialectic of Hegel or like Novalis' vision of human life and history. The second Cathy begins her life alone, cut off from all experience of passion, separated by the walls of Thrushcross Grange from the physical and spiritual tumult at the Heights. Growing up for her is a process of crossing thresholds and barriers, and of breaking into the region of dangerous experiences — the experience of exploring Penistone Craggs and the Fairy cave with Hareton, the experience of Heathcliff's treachery and cruelty, the experience of marriage to Linton Heathcliff, and, most of all, the experience of her young husband's death. For the second Cathy, adulthood does not mean what it meant to her mother: separation from the one she loves most. It means rather the happiness of a moderate and civilized union with Hareton. She goes from separation to union rather than from union to separation, and there is no question of a third stage to come only after death. Her love is bound to this world and capable of being fulfilled here.

The love of the second Cathy pales beside the intensity of the first story, and the novel, in the very space and emphasis it gives to the first Cathy, seems to indicate that her kind of love is more valuable, more heroic. In spite of this, the presence of the two stories suggests that the meaning of the novel lies in some relation between them. One kind of man, the novel suggests, tends to ask from life more than it can give, an absolute union with another person. If he does this he will inevitably be driven toward death. Some men are willing to accept the limitations of earthly life and seek a love which is less complete. In such a relation language, civilized codes of action, all kinds of conventional barriers, will intervene between one person and another. If a man chooses this

kind of love he will substitute for the tragic grandeur of Heathcliff and the first Cathy the gentler affection of Hareton and the
second Cathy, but his love will not drive him irresistibly toward
death.

Is there no relation between the two stories but that of mere
juxtaposition?

A clue to a deeper connection between the two plots is given
by the fact that the first Cathy dies in giving birth to the second
Cathy. The sequence of generations is a striking example of the
universality of the "principle of destruction" by which every creature must be the relentless instrument of death to the others, or
himself cease to live. For reproduction is, in Joyce's phrase, "the
beginning of death." [34] The generations follow one another in endless propagation, and the sexual union of parents is an image of
death, in which each parent momentarily loses his separate identity
for the sake of the creation of a new individual. The connection
of reproduction and death in the sacrifice of one generation for
the next is much more immediate in the subhuman realm where
certain sea creatures are torn to pieces in the process of parturition, or, as in the case of certain fish, die soon after reproduction.
On the lowest level of life, the division of a single cell into two is
a perfect image of the way reproduction leads to death. When the
cell has divided there are two new cells, but the original cell has
disappeared altogether in the new life it has created.

If, in the human realm, reproduction is usually only the *beginning* of death, there is one occasion on which death and the
creation of new life are dramatically juxtaposed: the death of a
mother in giving birth to a child. The second Cathy is born in
just this way, and here, once more, death and life are seen to be
intimately related. Just as Augusta kills her lovers instead of willing her own death, so in her relation to her child she also reverses
Cathy. One of the most shocking events of the Gondal poems is
Augusta's infanticide. She recognizes that she must kill her child
in order to avoid the natural law by which the new generation
replaces the old one. The teeming proliferation of nature is a constant process of destruction out of which new life is constantly
born. The second Cathy's father commemorates every year not

[34] The phrase is from *A Portrait of the Artist as a Young Man*. See *The Portable
James Joyce*, ed. Harry Levin (New York, 1949), p. 499.

only the birthday of his daughter but the anniversary of the death of his wife. That Heathcliff and the first Cathy should not be the parents of the second Cathy is not only necessary to the plot, but also has meaning as a definition of their love. Their love can have no earthly fruits, but must lead unequivocally to death. The essence of their love is their unwillingness to sacrifice their oneness to anything else.

There is an even more fundamental way in which the two stories are related. Considered from a certain perspective *Wuthering Heights* has as its central theme the breakdown and reconstruction of civilization, and in this it transcends the Gondal poems, though without denying the picture of the world there presented. The final point toward which the novel aims is the moment when Hareton is worthy to reclaim his inheritance, the house with his name above the door and the date 1500 (3). Heathcliff is not the cause of the corruption of the civilization which flourished long ago, at a time just prior to the Reformation. When he comes to the sealed-in world of the Heights and the Grange that civilization is already corrupt. Its degradation consists in the fact that society in this region is cut off from God, living outside God's law and without His sustaining spirit. At the beginning of the novel there are only two ways to live, both bad because isolated from God. On the Heights every man's hand is against his neighbor, and the reigning religion is the perverted theology of Joseph, a religion of the absolute transcendence of God. This loss of contact between God and man is suggested by the fact that the local church, the Chapel of Gimmerton Slough, is without a pastor, and is already beginning to fall into rack and ruin. The obduracy and selfishness of the congregation have caused this decay, for they would rather let any clergyman starve than "increase the living by one penny from their own pockets" (25). Life at Thrushcross Grange is no better; it is weak, effete, and lacks even the malign vitality of the spiritual storm on the Heights. At the Grange society has set itself up as something reasonable and self-sufficient, dedicated to the getting and keeping of earthly belongings. We are given a savagely ironic glimpse of civilized love in the story of the way Lockwood made sheep's eyes at a pretty girl he met at a seacoast resort. He feared the communication of love, and shrank into himself "like a snail" (4), as soon as his hesitant overtures were returned. At the beginning of the novel a moderate love, such as that between Hareton and Cathy at the end of the novel, is apparently impossible, or bad if achieved. The symbol of the mediated communion of Hareton and Cathy, the printed page, is an expression of the weakness and self-enclosure of Edgar Linton. While the first Cathy is going through the great spiritual crisis of her life, her husband is alone in his room, reading.

What has intervened by the end of the novel to make possible the milder love of Hareton and the second Cathy?

What has intervened is the love affair of Heathcliff and the first Cathy. The love of Hareton and the second Cathy appears to be possible only because Heathcliff and the first Cathy have broken through life into death, and have liberated energies from the region of boundless sympathy into this world. *Wuthering Heights* is dominated by a sense of immense strain, the effort of longing and will necessary to pierce through to the supernatural world. The storm is greatest near the center. At the center is peace. When Heathcliff finally attains the shore toward which he has been straining, the reconciliation which he finds radiates back into the world he has left behind, and a moderate love is possible for Hareton and the second Cathy. Only through the violence of Heathcliff can calm love be other than the artificiality and self-enclosure of Lockwood or the Lintons.

In *Wuthering Heights* Emily Brontë shows that society, left to itself, gets more and more hollow and artificial, until finally the churches are all empty and God has disappeared. Only a recovery of God will make possible a renewal of society. Communication with the divine realm cannot be established calmly and beneficently. Someone must break religious and moral law and go into the forbidden space between man and God. To enter this space is to go into a region of terror and immorality, to be forced to bring this destructive power into the world, and to be torn to pieces by it. Cathy and Heathcliff have entered this dangerous area by attempting to prolong into adulthood the relation they have had as children.

The happiness of the second generation is made possible by the plunge into the divine storm of Cathy and Heathcliff, followed by its inevitable sequel: suffering and death. Only when the sin of the first lovers has "spent its last drop of poison," and they have paid for their pleasure with death — only then can the fierce wind of Wuthering Heights be transformed into the soft breeze which blows on Hareton and the second Cathy and through the open doors and windows at the end of the novel. The replacement of the first lovers by the second pair is the pre-enactment on earth of the transformation of earthly sin and sorrow into the joy of heaven which Emily Brontë speaks of in her essay on the butterfly. The peace of civilization and the irrational violence of Heathcliff's transgressions are not irreconcilable opposites. The destructive love of Heathcliff and Cathy is the necessary ground of the benign love of Hareton and the second Cathy.

This relation between the two stories is apparent concretely in the way the second Cathy's purgatorial suffering of the reality of death, as she sits alone by the bedside of her dying husband, is necessary to her growing-up and therefore to her eventual happiness with Hareton. She must suffer death vicariously, and reach the point when she can say, just after the death of Linton Heathcliff: "You have left me so long to struggle against death, alone, that I feel and see only death! I feel like death!" (335). Only when she has experienced death can she begin the slow process of educating Hareton and initiating the reconstruction of civilization. Her confrontation with death is caused by her unwilling involvement in Heathcliff's scheme to revenge himself on Cathy by destroying the Heights and the Grange. Here again the violence and suffering of the first lovers makes possible the goodness and happiness of the next generation. The individual experience of the second Cathy matches exactly the historical process dramatized in the whole action of the novel: from inauthentic isolation through terror, violence, and death to the establishment of a valid community based on mediated love.

But at the end of *Wuthering Heights,* though a good society has been created, the Chapel of Gimmerton Slough is still without a pastor, and its physical decay has proceeded apace. The dilapidation of the church is insisted upon, and a description of it is given at the very end of the novel, just before the final paragraphs describing the graves of Edgar, Heathcliff, and Catherine, the moths fluttering around the harebells, and the soft wind breathing through the grass. Why is the church not re-established along with the rest of civilization? The answer to this question will be a final formulation of the meaning of *Wuthering Heights*.

The church is still deserted because it is no longer necessary. God has been transformed from the transcendent deity of extreme Protestantism, enforcing in wrath his irrevocable laws, to an immanent God, pervading everything, like the soft wind blowing over the heath. This new God is an amiable power who can, through human love, be possessed here and now. The breakthrough into God's world of Heathcliff and Cathy has not only made possible the peaceful love of Hareton and the second Cathy; it has also made institutionalized religion unnecessary. The love of Heathcliff and Cathy has served as a new mediator between heaven and earth, and has made any other mediator for the time being superfluous. Their love has brought "the new heaven and the new earth" into this fallen world as a present reality.

৺ V ৵

Matthew Arnold

Hither and thither spins
The wind-borne, mirroring soul,
A thousand glimpses wins,
And never sees a whole . . . (415)[1]

For Arnold the soul, at the present time, is the casual locus of a succession of fragmentary experiences. Each man is able to see only a part of what is before him. He is forced to see it from a single perspective, and he is limited to a single instant of time. All man's experience is partial; therefore he cannot see the whole from a point of view which would escape the distortions of a limited perspective. Only this would make it possible for the soul to be a self. To be truly a self it is necessary also to possess the "immeasurable All" (423). Conversely, to be "true/To our own only true, deep-buried selves" is at the same time to be "one with the whole world" (440). For Arnold the soul, at this epoch of time, has no contact with the "deep-buried self." The self is as utterly beyond the reach of the soul, as the "All" or as God himself, and the soul has become a mirror forced to reflect, and therefore to be, whatever happens to come near it: "only the thoughts,/Raised by the objects he passes, are his" (252).

Like the *tabula rasa* of Locke and the sensationalists the passive mirror which makes up the soul is at the mercy of exterior stimuli. These stimuli define and redefine the soul behind the mirror as they succeed one another in random sequence, for each obliterates the last, as a mirror holds no memory of the objects it once reflected, or as a sponge takes on the qualities of each new fluid it absorbs. "Experience, like a sea," says Arnold, "soaks all-effacing in" (419). Just as Arnold's mirror-soul or sponge-soul has no mem-

[1] Numbers in parentheses refer to pages in C. B. Tinker and H. F. Lowry, eds., *The Poetical Works of Matthew Arnold* (London: Oxford University Press, 1957).

ory, even of the moment which has just passed, so also it has no way of anticipating the future: "But what was before us we know not,/And we know not what shall succeed" (253).

This mirror-soul is in aimless, fluctuating motion, "tossing continually" (39), or "eddying at large in blind uncertainty" (246). Man staggers, eddies, drifts, wavers, or wanders, upon "time's barren, stormy flow" (183), and his life is the aimless passage from one place to another: "A wanderer is man from his birth" (251).

This wandering takes place, in Arnold as in De Quincey, within a space without coordinates, center, or goal. Sometimes this milieu itself is in motion. It is then "a rolling flood" (424), or the "turbid ebb and flow" (211) of the "incognisable sea" (40). Sometimes it has the immobility of a desert waste or of the still, clear air of a summer evening. In either case it is without order. To be in one place in this uncharted space is the same as to be in any other place, for there are no paths or signposts by which the hapless wanderer might tell what origin he has left or what end he might seek. The soul is condemned to "fluctuate idly without term or scope" (260), driven by the aimless tides or by the random winds, himself "distracted as a homeless wind" (179).

Arnold is tormented by the impermanence of experiences, feelings, and thoughts. They are the passage of sensations, ideas, or actions which fill him, crowd the mirror, without really belonging to him. The elements of experience appear one by one in the mirror, apparently from nowhere, and disappear into the same void. One moment the mirror is empty, the next overfilled. There seems no way to put a stop to this "*alternation* of ennui and excitement," [2] this sequence of "mad delight, and frozen calms" (33). As soon as something is born within the soul, it dies, as snowflakes die on the warm earth, or as a wave holds one shape only a moment in the constant flux of the sea. "Our vaunted life," as a consequence, "is one long funeral" (44): "Joy comes and goes, hope ebbs and flows/Like the wave . . ." (44).

There is nothing, in the temporal flux forming the soul, which remains the same, no invariant tone or note, such as Maine de Biran or Valéry find, by which the soul might recognize its permanence. Nothing can be seized and held which might form an

[2] Howard Foster Lowry, ed., *The Letters of Matthew Arnold to Arthur Hugh Clough* (London: Oxford University Press, 1932), p. 106; hereafter cited as "CL."

"assiette" (CL, 130), a support for the soul. Arnold's description of "Montaigne's atmosphere and world" is a perfect definition of his own atmosphere and world. "It is," he says, "the world of man viewed as a being *ondoyant et divers,* balancing and indeterminate, the plaything of cross motives and shifting impulses, swayed by a thousand subtle influences, physiological and pathological." [3] The soul, in Arnold's world as in Montaigne's, is a plurality of fugitive, superficial selves, for consciousness does not adhere completely and permanently to anything but its own "elasticity" (CL, 138). The soul is aware in the midst of each experience that what is happening to it will endure only a moment and be succeeded by another unrelated event. There is not time enough to become identified with any experience and to bring into being the self it might determine. Man's existence is an endless sequence of half-lives, each one broken, truncated, unperfected. No one has been more aware than Arnold of the terrible fluidity of time, and of the discontinuity this flowing imposes on the soul which is forced constantly to begin again a life and a self it never has time to bring to perfection or finish:

> . . . each half lives a hundred different lives . . . (260)

> And we have been on many thousand lines,
> And we have shown, on each, spirit and power;
> But hardly have we, for one little hour,
> Been on our own line, have we been ourselves — (246)

Caught up, willynilly, in the ubiquitous flux and "whirl'd" "in action's dizzying eddy" (60), the soul is condemned to a fragmentation imposed by a triple motion. It is moving with an aimless spinning through a milieu which is itself in motion, swirling to and fro in random ebb and flow. This double eddying, an eddying within an eddying, determines the incoherent fluctuations within the soul, where "passions . . . for ever ebb and flow" (37), "Linking in a mad succession/Fits of joy and fits of pain" (33). The vertiginous wavering within the soul is the result of its double submission to the motion of things outside itself and to its own crazy motion through that motion:

---

[3] *The Works of Matthew Arnold in Fifteen Volumes,* IV (London, 1903, 1904), 274. Further references to Arnold's prose, unless otherwise noted, will be by volume and page numbers in this edition.

And on earth we wander, groping, reeling;
Powers stir in us, stir and disappear. (210)

Thoughts light, like gleams, my spirit's sky,
But they will not remain.
They light me once, they hurry by;
And never come again. (209)

ৡ

In such a world, "Who can stand still?" (194). Even the wise
Ulysses is a "wave-toss'd Wanderer" like everyone else, and it seems
that all men must, like the strayed reveler, yield to the drunken
motion of things and the self, and "Let the wild, thronging train,
/The bright procession/Of eddying forms,/Sweep through [his]
soul" (194).

Arnold's sense of the instability of man's present condition derives its poignancy from his opposing sense that things were not
always this way. Fortuitous circumstances — industrialism, science,
the rise of great cities — have combined to render the age "arid,"
"barren," "blank," and "unpoetical" (CL, 131, 126, 99), and to
deprive man of true selfhood. "My dearest Clough," cries Arnold,
"these are damned times — everything is against one — the height
to which knowledge is come, the spread of luxury, our physical
enervation, the absence of great *natures,* the unavoidable contact
with millions of small ones, newspapers, cities, light profligate
friends, moral desperadoes like Carlyle, our own selves, and the
sickening consciousness of our difficulties . . ." (CL, 111). If these
factors were changed things would be different. There was once
a time when man possessed himself and at the same time possessed
the whole world, a time when man, nature, and the gods were in
harmonious unity. What was that time, and what was it like?

The time of harmony is always past. To be able to describe it
rationally means no longer to have it, and to be forced to look
back at it with nostalgia, as to a lost paradise and its vanished
happiness. Nor can the poet reach this time by remounting the
temporal stream, for though it is the origin of the present, an unbridgeable space separates it from even the first of the broken,
evanescent moments leading up to the present time. It was a time

before times, for then time was not yet a tragically broken sequence. It was the unity of a perpetual present.

Whether this harmonious epoch is imaged as the childhood of
the race, or as a time even prior to that, the time of myth, its characteristics are the same. Essential to Arnold's definition of the
epoch of harmony, from whatever perspective he approaches it, is
the idea of fusion, of intimacy, of participation. Once, when the
green earth was close to the sources of time, the divine spirit was
the fluid principle of continuity in which each thing was melted
and lost its isolation without ceasing to be itself. Oppositions were
reconciled, not obliterated, by the divine spirit. That spirit was
the true foundation of selfhood. Possessing God, man possessed
also the true self which he has since lost. In these bad times things
and men are closed in upon themselves. The flowers have no per-
fumes, and each man is an island cut off from his fellows. But once
upon a time emanations and influences flowed back and forth between man, nature, and God binding them all in "one common
wave of thought and joy" (323). If God in the present time of suffering must be defined as transcendent, he was then immanent in
nature and in man's heart. As a result, man could read the depths
of his own spirit, down to the deep buried life, for that spirit was
irradiated by feeling, the best vehicle of communication and continuity. And man could read God and nature. All things earthly
and divine were revealed to him, and he was in intimate relation
to them all:

> Who can see the green earth any more
> As she was by the sources of Time?
>
> .   .   .
>
> What girl
> Now reads in her bosom as clear
> As Rebekah read, when she sate
> At eve by the palm-shaded well?
>
> .   .   .
>
> What bard,
> At the height of his vision, can deem
> Of God, of the world, of the soul,
> With a plainness as near,
> As flashing as Moses felt
> When he lay in the night by his flock
> On the starlit Arabian waste? (252, 253)

If man could then read in his own breast, and understand nature and God, he could also understand other people. Authentic community was possible, for "a current of fresh and true ideas" (III, 40) permeated the group, linking all its members in one cohesive culture, and true love was also possible.

The mind in these "damned times" operates by abstraction, definition, differentiation. In the good time the characteristic spiritual work was poetry, the act which mediates between God, nature, and man, binding them into one. True poetry describes such a unity, for the poet is a man who spontaneously possesses the joy of immediacy and expresses that joy in his poetry. The poet knows nature's secret, and is able, like Orpheus, his great ancestor, to breathe immortal air on the divine eminence where all times and places are to be seen, comprehended, and possessed at once. If the poet's feeling is deep, like that of Rebekah, who lived by the sources of time, his vision is not deep, but all-comprehensive, like God's:

> Deeply the Poet feels; but he
> Breathes, when he will, immortal air,
> Where Orpheus and where Homer are.
> In the day's life, whose iron round
> Hems us all in, he is not bound . . .
> He escapes thence, but we abide —
> Not deep the poet sees, but wide. (58)

In that far-off time when poetry was still possible, each poet, like the young Empedocles in Arnold's play, possessed a "self-sufficing fount of joy" (429), and, possessing this, could create the "lulling spell/Gods and the race of mortals love so well" (431). Poetry, in Empedocles' youth, was a magical charm which calmed opposition, and absorbed all things, earthly and divine, into its spell, as each separate note is absorbed into a melody without losing its individuality. Empedocles' anguished memory of the power he once possessed is Arnold's fullest description of the time of harmony. As always in Arnold there is a nostalgic reminiscence of something irrevocably lost rather than the celebration of something still present. Empedocles remembers a time when he was not yet exiled in an alien world, a time when he and Parmenides were part of a great band of philosopher-poets all striding together "on the road of truth" (436).[4] In that time Empedocles, like Parmenides, was not a wanderer in a trackless desert, but was moving on a path leading directly to the divine truth. In a sense he already possessed the truth, as an arrow possesses its target from the moment its trajectory begins. That the "truth" was divine rather than human is confirmed not only by the echoes of Parmenides,[5] but by the phrase "sacred load" a few lines further in Arnold's text (436). In that time, Empedocles says, "thought" and the "pure natural joy" of a spontaneous pleasure in nature were not incompatible. The "sacred load" of "mighty thoughts," thoughts such as come to someone on the way back to the sun of truth, was lightened by the simple sense pleasures of nature, and also by the pleasures of social intercourse. Empedocles was both philosopher and poet. He had the "thoughts" of the philosopher, the poet's unself-conscious joy in nature, and his plastic power to reproduce those forms. Like the Empedocles of Hölderlin's play, Arnold's Empedocles stood between man, nature, and the gods, and was able to "balance" between them, for these three realms were not yet separated, and could still be brought back into harmony.[6]

There are striking parallels between Arnold's *Empedocles on Etna* and Hölderlin's unfinished play on Empedocles. Hölderlin's play exists in three different versions, all incomplete. I know of no evidence that Arnold knew Hölderlin's play. The parallels seem to be the result of what Arnold called the *Zeitgeist*, which led poets in some ways very different, yet obsessed with the same cultural and personal problems, to write plays about the ancient

[4] "The road of truth" is Arnold's translation of the title of the first section of Parmenides' poem.

[5] The phrase which Arnold translates as "Sun-born Virgins" comes from the Proem of Parmenides' poem. The Proem is an allegorical description of Parmenides' escape from the darkness of falsehood into the light of truth. The form of this allegory, according to Kirk and Raven, is probably "borrowed from oracle- and mystery-literature" (G. S. Kirk and J. E. Raven, *The Presocratic Philosophers* [Cambridge, 1957], p. 268). Parmenides' guides are the "Sun-born Virgins," and the truth they lead him to is allegorically represented as a goddess. Like present-day scholars, Arnold seems to have interpreted the Proem as a religious statement, and to have transferred its framework to Empedocles' memories of his youthful aspirations.

[6] See Friedrich Hölderlin, *Sämtliche Werke,* ed. Norbert v. Hellingrath, Friedrich Seebass, and Ludwig v. Pigenot, III (Berlin, 1923), 220:

> Und milde wird in ihm der Streit der Welt,
> Die Menschen und die Götter söhnt er aus,
> Und näher wieder leben sie wie vormals.

philosopher-poet. Hölderlin was tormented by the partiality of time, the way it binds man "to the law of succession," and he saw history as cyclical, a sequence of good times and bad times determined by whether God is immanent in man, nature, and society, or transcendent. Like Arnold, Hölderlin longed to be able to reduce himself without loss to a simple, limited life, the life, say, of a peasant or a country preacher, a life which would possess the "All" through a complete absorption in an obscure part of the all. Hölderlin identified our epoch as a dark time when the gods have withdrawn from the world, and man is left "wandering between two worlds," waiting for the return of grace. The German poet was able in his poetry to express much more directly than Arnold the time of immediacy. He had experienced the intimacy of all things with one another, as well as the horror of their splitting apart, whereas for Arnold the age of harmony was from the beginning something he knew about only through hearsay and a kind of intuitive memory of a time he had never really known himself. The difference between the two poets might perhaps be summed up by saying that, whereas Hölderlin went mad, Arnold got saner and saner, more deliberate and reasonable, as time went on.

Arnold's Empedocles speaks with the English poet's own lucid awareness of loss. In the time of pastoral immediacy, he says, one could find an inexhaustible richness in each part of nature and in the circumscribed life of each unself-conscious countryman. Now any part of nature is a meaningless fragment reflected momentarily in the mirror of the soul. Then every part was a symbol or embodiment of the whole, for the divine vitality was concentrated in each part. Poetry could be what it always should be, a concrete universal, the expression of the whole in the form of something individual and physically real:

> The smallest thing could give us pleasure then—
> The sports of the country-people,
> A flute-note from the woods,
> Sunset over the sea;
> Seed-time and harvest,
> The reapers in the corn,
> The vinedresser in his vineyard,
> The village-girl at her wheel. (436)

The concept of poetry as a concrete universal is the basis of Arnold's aesthetic theory, and is behind all his critical judgments. The tragedy of our time and the source of its "poetrylessness" (CL, 126) is the fact that now concrete objects have no significance beyond themselves. The way man has transformed religion into a set of theological dogmas is further evidence of his separation from the divine life. Modern man is doomed to be frigid when dealing with the concrete, and can have energy and warmth only when dealing with abstractions. "If one loved what was beautiful and interesting in itself *passionately* enough," says Arnold, "one would produce what was excellent without troubling oneself with religious dogmas at all. As it is, we are *warm* only when dealing with these last — and what is frigid is always bad" (CL, 143). He complains of a "growing sense of the deficiency of the *beautiful* in [Clough's] poems" (CL, 66), and, later, puts it another way by saying that Clough's poems "are not *natural*" (CL, 98). Only poetry which flows as spontaneously from the poet as a flute-note from the woods, or the song of the village-girl at her wheel can be true poetry. Profundity of thought is of no help to the poet: ". . . the greatest wealth and depth of matter is merely a superfluity in the Poet *as such*" (CL, 99). Without the "Homeric qualities" of "out-of-doors freshness, life, naturalness, buoyant rapidity" (CL, 158) a poem is nothing. These qualities cannot be learned. They must be an instinctive expression of the constructive power of the poet: ". . . naturalness — i.e. — an absolute propriety — of form [is] the sole *necessary* of Poetry as such . . ." (CL, 98, 99). Whether Arnold finds these qualities in Homer, in the English romantic poets, in the Guérins, or in Senancour, or whether he tries to create it in his own poems, as in the songs of Callicles in *Empedocles on Etna,* naturalness and plastic form are Arnold's fundamental tests of authenticity in poetry.

Naturalness and plastic form are possible only in a time when the poet can participate in the life of nature. So Keats is praised for possessing "natural magic" and "naturalistic interpretation," and for seeing that beauty, truth, and joy are related (IV, 86). Senancour's Obermann "Heard accents of the eternal tongue/ Through the pine branches play" (310).[7] Wordsworth is the great-

---

[7] Compare the passage from *Obermann* which Arnold cites in his essay on Senancour: "I would fain hear what will go on subsisting; in the movement of

est of the romantic poets, for he is a poet of pastoral immediacy. He shares the life of nature, and is able to recreate the existence of country people who are not yet exiles in a divided world: "Wordsworth's poetry is great because of the extraordinary power with which Wordsworth feels the joy offered to us in nature, the joy offered to us in the simple primary affections and duties; and because of the extraordinary power with which, in case after case, he shows us this joy, and renders it so as to make us share it" (IV, 112). His poetry renews "the freshness of the early world" (272), the era when the green earth was close to the sources of time. In fact Wordsworth shared so completely nature's "bare, sheer, penetrating power" (IV, 116), and was, as a result, so spontaneous and natural in his poetry, that it seems as if his poetry were spoken directly by Nature herself (IV, 114). This naturalness and naïveté are what Arnold most admires in folk poetry or in poetry written at a time when there was a living literary tradition. He attempts to get this naïveté into his own poetry. "The use of the tradition, above everything else," he says in a note on "Sohrab and Rustum," "gives to a work that *naîveté*, that flavour of reality and truth, which is the very life of poetry" (493).

Arnold does not want poetry to be *about* its subject. He wants it to share in the vitality of that subject, and to be itself animating, a radiant source of joy. "It is demanded [of a poem]," says Arnold, "not only that it shall interest, but also that it shall inspirit and rejoice the reader: that it shall convey a charm, and infuse delight" (xviii). He distinguishes between two kinds of poetry. In authentic poetry the divine spirit, natural things, and the spirit of the poet are expressed simultaneously in one linguistic form. Modern poetry has suffered a four-fold split, and is by turns the expression of abstract dogma, mere description of objects, ornamental exuberances of language, and the "dialogue of the mind with itself" (xvii).

The apparent contradictions in Arnold's literary criticism disappear when it is seen that true poetry, for him, must be all four of these things at once. Sometimes he rejects modern poetry for being too cerebral, too subjective: "An allegory of the state of one's

---

the forest, in the murmur of the pines, I seek to catch some of the accents of the eternal tongue" (*Essays by Matthew Arnold* [London: Oxford University Press, 1914], p. 479).

own mind, the highest problem of an art which imitates actions! No assuredly, it is not, it never can be so: no great poetical work has ever been produced with such an aim" (xxiv). Sometimes he rejects poets like Keats and Shakespeare for writing poems which are merely "occasional bursts of fine writing" and "a shower of isolated thoughts and images" (xxiii): "More and more I feel that the difference between a mature and a youthful age of the world compels the poetry of the former to use great plainness of speech as compared with that of the latter: and that Keats and Shelley were on a false track when they set themselves to reproduce the exuberance of expression, the charm, the richness of images, and the felicity, of the Elizabethan poets" (CL, 124). Sometimes he repudiates description in poetry, what he calls "mere painting," as being "fatal . . . to its airy and rapidly moving life" (CL, 99). Such poetry would be a sequence of superficial images, like Tennyson's verse, which "dawdles" with the "painted shell" of the universe (CL, 63). Sometimes he criticizes poetry for being abstract thought, for "excit[ing] curiosity and reflexion" rather than attaining "the *beautiful*" and giving "PLEASURE" (CL, 99). In all these cases the basis of the criticism is the ideal of a poetry which will be a reconciliation of opposites, "airy and rapidly moving," and at the same time a "sensuous" "grouping" of "*objects*" (CL, 99); the concrete representation of an action, and at the same time an expression of fundamental and invariable truths about the human condition; impersonal,[8] not an "allegory of the state of the poet's mind," and yet an expression of the poet's character, for only the latter is the source of a great style, a style which will "compose and elevate the mind" (CL, 100): "Nay in Sophocles what is valuable is not so much his contributions to psychology and the anatomy of sentiment, as the grand moral effects produced by *style*. For the style is the expression of the nobility of the poet's character . . ." (CL, 101). This reconciliation of opposites could be attained even today, Arnold thinks, by an imitation of classical poetry. Greek and Roman poetry was based on a great mythical action, and therefore was marmoreal, concrete, but at the same time it expressed eternal truth. Nothing in Arnold's criticism is

---

[8] The poet, says Arnold, must permit the "inherent excellences" of a great action "to develop themselves, without interruption from the intrusion of his personal peculiarities"; he is "most fortunate, when he most entirely succeeds in effacing himself, and in enabling a noble action to subsist as it did in nature" (xxiii).

more striking than the way he forgets that poetry is written with words, and wants it to become as solid and sculptural, as detached from the mind and its "devouring flame of thought" (438), as a group of Greek statues: "The terrible old mythic story on which the drama was founded stood . . . in [the spectator's] memory, as a group of statuary, faintly seen, at the end of a long and dark vista: then came the Poet, embodying outlines, developing situations, not a word wasted, not a sentiment capriciously thrown in: stroke upon stroke, the drama proceeded: the light deepened upon the group; more and more it revealed itself to the rivetted gaze of the spectator: until at last, when the final words were spoken, it stood before him in broad sunlight, a model of immortal beauty" (xxii).

If true poetry must be the infinite embodied in the finite, its effect on the reader, in the "confusion of the present times" (xxiv), should be to give what joy gives: to transfer to the soul the consistency and permanence of the poem, to change the inner fluidity of the soul into something hard and durable, to raise it above the flux of life and give it something solid to stand on, to make it like a marble statue. This notion of a coagulation of the soul, giving it an "assiette" and transforming its dizzy motion into stillness, is often present as a buried metaphor in Arnold's descriptions of the effects of good poetry. To read the ancients has "a steadying and composing effect" (xxviii). They teach us "boundaries and wholesome regulative laws" (xxx), and offer "the only sure guidance, the only solid footing" (xxx). Elsewhere Arnold speaks of the "platform" of the classical (III, 66), and he rejects Chaucer because he lacks "high seriousness," and therefore does not give us "what we can rest upon" (IV, 25).

No one has struggled harder than Arnold to rescue himself and his readers from "the bewildering confusion of our times" by writing poetry which would be like the poetry of Homer or those other lucky bards who lived near the sources of time. If true poetry could be written now it would reintegrate the shattered world, and the poet would regain his primitive place as a mediator who prolongs and maintains the harmony of the "All."

The strongest evidence of our loss of the original harmony is the failure of poetry in our day. Poetry cannot create the joy it diffuses. The poet must possess joy before he can write his poem.

All Arnold's attempts to write poetry of action, poetry which is the solid grouping of beautiful objects, leads only to the lifelessness of *Merope,* of *Balder Dead,* even of *Sohrab and Rustum.* Arnold's most characteristic poetry, as he himself recognized, is not poetry at all by his definition. It expresses the melancholy of exile and fragmentation, rather than the joy of immediacy. "I am glad you like the Gipsy Scholar," he writes to Clough, " — but what does it *do* for you? Homer *animates* — Shakespeare *animates* — in its poor way I think Sohrab and Rustum *animates* — the Gipsy Scholar at best awakens a pleasing melancholy. But this is not what we want . . . what [we] want is something to *animate* and *ennoble* [us] — not merely to add zest to [our] melancholy or grace to [our] dreams. — I believe a feeling of this kind is the basis of my nature — and of my poetics. . . . My poems, however, viewed *absolutely,* are certainly little or nothing" (CL, 146). Authentic poetry breathes spiritual energy into its readers. Most of Arnold's poems do not inspire at all, and therefore are not true poetry.

Arnold's repudiation of *Empedocles on Etna* marks the climax of his recognition that joy must pre-exist poetry, and that true poetry, as a result, may be impossible in these damned times. *Empedocles,* he says, far from giving joy, is one of those poems "in which the suffering finds no vent in action; in which a continuous state of mental distress is prolonged, unrelieved by incident, hope, or resistance; in which there is everything to be endured, nothing to be done. In such situations there is inevitably something morbid, in the description of them something monotonous" (xviii). Poetry of this sort should not be published, for it adds to the confusion and degeneration of our times rather than stemming their black tide.

To look back in longing to the epoch of joy only makes man's present state all the darker by contrast. "That glow of central fire is done/Which with its fusing flame/Knit all [our] parts, and kept [us] one," and we are now nothing but the "poor fragments of a broken world" (320). The poetry of today, far from giving us aid in the bewildering confusion of our times, has itself succumbed to that confusion. Man today has one all-embracing problem: How can he re-enter his homeland, and, in the phrase from Édouard Reuss which Arnold quoted repeatedly in his notebooks, fulfill his basic task, which is the re-establishment of the kingdom of God on earth?[9] Only if that task were accomplished would authentic poetry again be possible, for only then would man possess his true life, and dwell once more "safe in the streets of the Celestial City" (III, 24).

ॐ

How can the kingdom of God be brought back to earth? Man now is "naked, eternally restless mind" (438). The joy of immediacy is his no longer. He must therefore seek something which will *mediate* between him and his lost home. Arnold's early poetry and his letters to Clough are the record of his search for some means to escape from the intolerable situation of detachment and aimless drifting. This testing of various forms of mediation continued all his life.

In the epoch of harmony there were no time and space in the usual sense, for the temporal and spatial dimensions of things bound them together rather than separating them, as all times and spaces are equally present to God. The disintegration which produced our world divided everything into fragments, with man isolated in the middle, able to turn toward each one separately, but never able to possess them all at once. It may be that the "world's multitudinousness" (CL, 97) is a prismatic diffraction of the original unity rather than a complete dispersal of broken pieces. Certainly Arnold rejects the division of *man's* nature into multiple faculties. Against this modern psychological theory he sets his notion that each man is inwardly and secretly one, as coral islands, separate on the surface, are joined in the deeps (4). If the world external to man is also a unity hidden behind apparent diversity then it would be possible to reach that unity by following any one of the separate elements far enough, with self-forgetful intensity. Only by experimentation could the poet discover which of the two grand alternatives is correct, whether the broken pieces

[9] "Voilà le but présenté par le Christianisme à l'humanité tout entière comme son but dernier et définitif: *le royaume de Dieu sur la terre*" (Édouard Reuss, *Histoire de la théologie chrétienne au siècle apostolique*, II [Strasbourg and Paris, 1860], 542, quoted in Howard Foster Lowry, Karl Young, and Waldo Hilary Dunn, eds., *The Note-Books of Matthew Arnold* [London: Oxford University Press, 1952], pp. 108, 141, 152, 176, 192, 229, 263, 366, 387, 544).

of the world are discontinuous with their origin, or whether the world, though multiple, is still connected, by however remote a series of gradations, with its source.

Just these alternatives and their consequences are balanced against one another in an important poem called "In Utrumque Paratus." Arnold at this time (the poem was first published in 1849) cannot commit himself to either possibility, but declares himself "ready for either." The two alternatives would lead to radically different conceptions of the human condition. If the present world of multiplicity is the result of a gradual "procession," a spherical expansion in all directions from an original and central "One all-pure," then, however far we have come from the moment of the primal birth of things, it would still be possible to "remount" the "colour'd dream/Of life" and reach, beyond all diverse colors, the white source of all (45). This remounting would mean isolation from the present fragmented times, but it would be an isolation and purity reached through these fragments, not by a discontinuous leap beyond them, for they still participate in their secret source, and are a means of reaching it.

On the other hand, it is possible that the multitudinous world has no divine origin or else has completely broken with that origin. If this is so, then the world must be defined materialistically, as the aimless combination and recombination of elements which have existed as an isolated brute mass from all time. The world is a "wild unfather'd mass," and has had "no birth/In divine seats" (45). If such is the situation, then no retrogressive remounting of the stream of life will ever reach anything essentially different from the present condition of things.

There is no way to tell which theory is correct, no way but by testing the various strands of this diversely colored life to see if any of them leads back to the One.[10] Like the hero of Browning's "Numpholeptos," Arnold must try first the red ray, then the green, and so on until the whole rainbow has been exhausted. Whereas Browning's nympholept goes out toward the periphery, Arnold

[10] In a new version of the last stanza of "In Utrumque Paratus" Arnold in 1869 proposed a third alternative, an evolutionist one. Man has grown from the earth, but earth and man with it are rising to ever-new heights of evolutionary splendor: "High as thy life be risen, 'tis from these;/And these, too, rise" (46). This idea of an autonomous development of matter was foreign to Arnold's need for a divine origin of history, and the variant stanza disappears in reprintings of the poem after 1869.

must try to reach directly the white light at the center which is the source of all color.

&

The most obvious reference of the image of "life's stream" in "In Utrumque Paratus" is to time. The image of time as a stream flowing from the high mountains of the past toward the distant sea of the future is one of the basic configurations of Arnold's imagination, appearing recurrently in his poetry, and, more covertly, in his prose, as in the famous definition of God as the "stream of tendency by which all things strive to fulfill the law of their being" (IX, 9). The image of the river of time pictures man's early history as taking place in the uplands or mountains near the source of the river, where the air is clear and pure. Now, in these latter days, we are flowing through the hot, flat plain, where the river is bordered by crowded cities, and our lives are determined by this heat and confusion, "changing and shot as the sights which we see" (253).

As Maurice Merleau-Ponty has shown,[11] the spatial representation of time as a river is full of ambiguities, however natural it may be to think of time in this way. Time is not the flowing river; it is a *relation* between the river and someone watching it. But the image changes bewilderingly depending on where we put the observer. If one imagines oneself standing on the bank watching time flow by, the past is not upstream, but downstream, where lie the waters which have already passed by. The ocean into which the river flows is not the mysterious future, but is the dumping ground of the past. The future lies upstream, where the waters are flowing which have not yet reached us. Only if we imagine ourselves as flowing with the river, as Arnold does in "The Future" and elsewhere, is the past upstream and the future downstream. In this case the river does not possess the contents of time. These already exist along the banks, in a spatial row, waiting to be passed by a point on the moving river. The river does not have any content, only the perpetual present of its motion past things. We do not move in relation to the river at all, but are a fixed point on an endless belt. Time is not a dimension

[11] *Phénoménologie de la perception* (Paris, 1945), pp. 470–472.

of things. They remain fixed eternally on the banks. Only the river moves, the river and the empty mind of man which is identified with a point on it. If we think of the river of time simultaneously from the points of view of the river and of the bank, as we are inclined to do, and as Arnold often does, then the ambiguity is complete. We are thinking of time at once as our motion past things, and as the motion of things past us. Time is both something moving and something still which we move past. In the same way past and future coincide in whichever direction we look, upstream or downstream. The image of time as a river, when examined, reveals itself as absurd and contradictory, but it is a rich absurdity, and a suggestive contradiction, as is proved by the many uses of the image, from Heraclitus' famous river, and the Platonic image of time as a moving image of eternity, to Yeats's river of time in "The Old Men Admiring Themselves in the Water" or "The Needle's Eye," and Eliot's use of the Mississippi in the "Four Quartets."

Though there is no evidence that Arnold was aware of the ambiguities of his image of time he manipulates them strategically, as in his constant suggestion that the origin and ending of time are the same. All man has lost by moving away from the "sources of time" he will recover when at last he reaches the sea. In "The Buried Life," one of Arnold's most important explorations of the image of the river, the poet affirms that to possess for a moment the "unregarded river of our life" (246) is to possess simultaneously "The hills where [our] life rose,/And the sea where it goes" (247). If the ending turns back on the beginning time is a circle, and every moment of time, though it seems isolated from the origin and end of time, is as close to God as the very first moment of creation. As in the old Plotinian or Augustinian theory of time, each moment, though part of an endless succession, partakes of the motionless plenitude of God:

> Thus yesterday, to-day, to-morrow come,
> They hustle one another and they pass;
> But all our hustling morrows only make
> The smooth to-day of God. (262)

Just as Arnold identifies beginning and ending, upstream and downstream on the river of time, so his use of the image also suggests that man is simultaneously flowing with the river and living in the bristling cities on the plain. If he is the isolated mind which runs with time and sees each object on the bank for only a moment, he is also the contents of the mind, and dwells, however fleetingly, in fixed abodes on the bank. Arnold's sense of his simultaneous detachment from life and enforced participation in it is perfectly expressed in the ambiguous relations between flowing water and fixed bank in the image of the river of time.

Does time, conceived of according to this image, permit any escape from the intolerable present? Though the image suggests the irresistible compulsion of time driving man from one moment to another, nevertheless, if time is a river, each moment is bound to the others in a succession so unbroken as to form a fluid continuity. If this is the case man might be able to "remount" the stream of time and reach the primal unity. Remount in what fashion? Arnold has been momentarily misled by his image. Time is not, like space, a fixed expanse which can be traversed in any direction by motion through it. Time is a one-way flow, and the moments which belong to the past can never be recaptured as present again. Arnold is truer to his experience of time when he describes his limitation to just the moment of time he is experiencing now, and even more true when he laments his inability even to hold on to the present. Time flows on remorselessly and tears him away from moments of pleasure or satisfied desire.

The most poignant versions of this theme have to do with Arnold's sense that the failure of love in these bad times is caused by the implacable flow of time. Time bears the lovers apart. "A Dream," for example, uses the image of the river of time to express the nightmare of an inability to reach the loved one. Though she beckons invitingly with her companion from the shore, "the river of Life,/Loud thundering, [bears him] by" (25).

Is there no power by which he may repossess the past? For other poets, for Arnold's much-admired Wordsworth, memory is the faculty which recaptures the past. What is Arnold's experience of memory?

His earliest poem about memory is the first of the Marguerite poems, "A Memory-Picture." Here, tormented by his premonition that the present happy hour with Marguerite will pass, he forces himself to fix the moment on his memory so that he may keep it always. If "Time's current strong/Leaves us fixt to noth-ing long" (24), perhaps we can cheat time by preserving the past indelibly in memory. Though the memory-picture is only a "dim remembrance" (24) of actuality, it is something at least preserved from time's obliterating power, and so the poet cries, "Quick, thy tablets, Memory!" (24).

The note of urgency in these lines betrays Arnold's lack of faith in the power of memory. He has no experience of involun-tary affective memory, the Proustian or Wordsworthian reminis-cence which brings back the past in all its freshness of sensible immediacy; he also lacks the power of a willed and rational memory, the memory which seizes violently on the present mo-ment and forces it to abide. Rather than enjoying the involuntary rising up of "spots of time" from the depths of the past, Arnold must suffer the involuntary disappearance of whatever once be-longed to him, but now belongs only to an unapproachable past: "And we forget because we must/And not because we will" (183).

In one poem Arnold is tormented by his knowledge that though the past cannot be recaptured in memory, nevertheless he will be able to remember that there is something which he cannot remember. If the "stedfast commandment of Nature/Wills that remembrance should always decay" (207), if mere ab-sence from the loved one means the gradual disappearance of her image from his heart, Arnold would prefer to forget Mar-guerite completely, as soon as he leaves her, so that if he were to meet her again she would appear as a stranger. Since total mem-ory is impossible Arnold asks for a total forgetting: "Me let no half-effaced memories cumber!/ . . . Dead be the past and its phantoms to me!" (207).

Arnold is able neither to forget nor to remember. He is con-demned to be visited by half-effaced memories of events he can neither escape nor repossess. The Marguerite poems are the ex-pression of this ambiguous relation to the past, a relation which offers no means of remounting the stream of life and reaching the "One."

The past is no pathway to the lost harmony, and its exploration only confirms Arnold in his isolation. What of the future? Since beginning and ending coincide in Arnold's theory of time, he might be able to reach what he has lost in the past by moving forward into the future.

Arnold finds a way to console himself for the way he is torn from pleasures as soon as he gets them, or is unable to reach them at all. Though it seems that he is eddying about in blind uncertainty, he is guided secretly by the unregarded river of his life. This "buried stream" is the inalienable law of his being, a law which is at once within him and outside him. It makes him break allegiances for which he is not destined, and drives him on toward a hidden goal (246). When he reaches this goal he will recover his "genuine self," and at the same time regain the intimacy with all things he has lost since the green sources of time. Man is forced by an "unknown Power" (310) to move on unceasingly with time, but since his life has a hidden direction and end, it is perhaps truer to say that he is drawn from the future by this goal than that he is driven by the past: "For this and that way swings/The flux of mortal things,/Though moving inly to one far-set goal" (448).

This view of time permits Arnold to assuage his sense of guilt for his unconquerable coldness and want of spontaneous feeling. It takes away his anguished feeling that it is *his* fault his love affair with Marguerite has been a failure. He cannot help it if he is "three parts iced over" (CL, 128). If the far-set goal is drawing him ceaselessly on, he is not responsible for being unable to love Marguerite as he wishes. It is the unknown God who drives him away from a love which is not destined to be his. It is possible to say that Arnold was hiding from himself his responsibility for his fiasco with Marguerite, but the motif appears often enough to show that it gave Arnold plausible solace:

> Who renders vain their deep desire? —
> A God, a God their severance ruled!
> And bade betwixt their shores to be
> The unplumb'd, salt, estranging sea. (182)

> Again I spring to make my choice;
> Again in tones of ire
> I hear a God's tremendous voice:
> 'Be counsell'd, and retire.' (174; see also 41)

In spite of the consolations of this idea, to believe that he is secretly moving toward a reconciliation with all he has lost does not change Arnold's experience of the present. It remains a directionless eddying, a "tedious tossing to and fro" (448), a wandering in the desert. In "Rugby Chapel," one of Arnold's most hopeful poems about the future, the poet opposes the "eddy of purposeless dust" of most men's lives to the sense of a clearly seen goal possessed by his father and others like him. As the poem proceeds it becomes clear that the goal is only an object of implicit faith. The actual present is a wandering in a rocky wasteland with no sight of the "bound of the waste":

> A God
> Marshall'd them, gave them their goal.
> Ah, but the way is so long!
> . . . Sole they shall stray; in the rocks
> Stagger for ever in vain,
> Die one by one in the waste. (291)

Arnold best expresses his experience of time in a much earlier poem, "Resignation." That poem begins by saying that all men need to propose to themselves a goal which they may reach before death and which, "gain'd, may give repose" (53). Our life does not fulfill this need. Arnold's temporal experience is here expressed in the description of a band of gypsies who, far from proceeding toward a goal, wander homelessly from one place to another, often returning by accident to a place where once before they had pitched their tents (55, 56). Time is not a progression at all, but a meaningless repetition, a repetition from moment to moment as long as life lasts of the same sense of deracination and infinite distance from the promised land. Whether Arnold looks toward the past or toward the future, time offers him no way out of the present sequence of moments each repeating the same suffering and isolation.

ॐ

If not time, then what of space, or the contents of space, the physical things which surround us in the present moment? If the image of the river of time is a misattribution of the traversability of space to the realm of time, will space offer that access to the center of reconciliation which time forbids? It can be crossed in any direction, and what dwells in space, nature, has often been seen as the earthly abiding place of an immanent spiritual force which is absent from man and his cities.

Arnold fluctuates in his doctrine of nature. Under the influence of the romantic poets, he tries to experience nature in the Wordsworthian way, and to feel that if he could only get outside himself he would find in nature a source of perennial vitality. In "The Youth of Nature" he praises Wordsworth for being "a priest to us all/Of the wonder and bloom of the world,/Which we saw with his eyes, and were glad" (229), and in his essay on Maurice de Guérin he defines the power of poetry as the ability to give us an intimate communication with nature and with the secret which nature contains: "The grand power of poetry is its interpretative power; by which I mean, not a power of drawing out in black and white an explanation of the mystery of the universe, but the power of so dealing with things as to awaken in us a wonderfully full, new, and intimate sense of them, and of our relations with them. When this sense is awakened in us, as to objects without us, we feel ourselves to be in contact with the essential nature of those objects, to be no longer bewildered and oppressed by them, but to have their secret, and to be in harmony with them; and this feeling calms and satisfies us as no other can" (III, 88). In "Lines Written in Kensington Gardens" Arnold speaks of the ever-new peace of nature, a peace which is a participation in the central One, the "calm soul of all things" (249), and he prays to share in this peace. Arnold envies nature's ability to act without feverish anxiety and hurry, her "toil unsever'd from tranquillity" (1).

Is it so certain that the peace of nature comes from a sharing in the divine life? It may be that nature is calm because isolation from God does not cause her to suffer as man does. Arnold sometimes reads in nature a lesson of grim endurance, the endurance of being just this bit of rock or turf here, untransfigured by any spiritual presence:

> . . . the mute turf we tread,
> The solemn hills around us spread,
> This stream which falls incessantly,
> The strange-scrawl'd rocks, the lonely sky,
> If I might lend their life a voice,
> Seem to bear rather than rejoice. (60)

Nature was once part of the divine order, and the stars were true sons of Heaven, imbued with a spiritual vitality, and possessors of a radiant joy. They "moved joyfully/Among august companions,/In an older world, peopled by Gods" (437). Now the stars, like man, are cut off from the divine joy, shine coldly with their own lonely light, and move in their courses by blind necessity. They are "unwilling lingerers" (437) in the wilderness of space, strangers both to heaven and to man, "without friend and without home" (438).

Such natural things are superior to man only in that they have been able to endure isolation from God without suffering. Nature, unlike man, has kept some remnants of "an immortal vigour" in its heart, and has "in solitude/Maintain'd courage and force" (438). But nature has this "free, light, cheerful air" (241) only because it has utterly forgotten its divine origin. Man is closer to God than nature is just because man knows of his distance from God and suffers because of it (241, 242). Arnold, in this mood, denies to the empty heavens any least memory of their suffering when they were separated from God: "I will not say that your mild deeps retain/A tinge, it may be, of their silent pain/Who have long'd deeply once, and long'd in vain" (244). The heavens have the calm and freedom of a corpse from which the spirit has fled, but it is better to be "untroubled and unpassionate" (244) than to suffer, as Arnoldian man must suffer, the continual torments of being separated from one's true self and knowing it.

In such passages Arnold proposes a very different picture of nature from Wordsworth's. Far from being, though apparently divided, actually one, a deep harmony in which man and nature share together in the inalienable presence of "something far more deeply interfused," Arnold's world has split apart. Nature is separated from man, and is a collection of unrelated fragments juxtaposed without order or form. Each rock, bird, tree, or cloud is self-enclosed and separate from all the others.

Arnold's inability to see nature in the romantic way is constantly betrayed by the landscapes in his poetry. All the complexity of romantic nature poetry is, for the most part, missing in Arnold, and his poetry is by comparison thin and two-dimensional. This flatness is of great significance, and reveals a new phase in the spiritual history of Western man. Not at all times can poets see in the meanest flower that blows a mysterious expression of the whole universe.

Arnold has no sense of a harmonizing power in nature, nor can he express the Coleridgean sense that each object, though unique, is at the same time a symbol of the totality. Each object means itself, and is not a symbol of anything further. Landscapes in his poetry are often a neutral backdrop before which the action takes place. The closest Arnold can come to the multi-dimensional symbolism of romantic poetry is the simple equation of allegory, in which some human meaning or value is attached from the outside to a natural object. This produces locutions in which a concrete thing and an abstraction are yoked by violence together, as in the "sea of life" (185), the "Sea of Faith" (211), the "vasty hall of death" (21), the "icebergs of the past" (322), and so on. Try as he will Arnold cannot often get depth and resonance in his landscapes, and his descriptive passages tend to become unorganized lists of natural objects. The disorder and flatness of these lists betray Arnold's sense that nature is just a collection of discrete things, all jumbled up together, with no pattern or hierarchy. Arnold's nature, like his own life, is repetitive, the repetition of more examples of the same objects, or of more views of the same disorder. In "Resignation," he describes his return with his sister to a scene he has visited ten years before. "Here sit we," he says, "and again unroll,/Though slowly, the familiar whole" (55). The scene is not really, it turns out, a "whole." There is no transfiguration of a revisited scene, as in "Tintern Abbey," and the suggestions of continuity in "unroll" are not supported by what follows:

> The solemn wastes of heathy hill
> Sleep in the July sunshine still;
> The self-same shadows now, as then,
> Play through this grassy upland glen;
> The loose dark stones on the green way
> Lie strewn, it seems, where then they lay;
> On this mild bank above the stream,
> (You crush them!) the blue gentians gleam.
> Still this wild brook, the rushes cool,
> The sailing foam, the shining pool! (55)

Hill, shadows, gentians; brook, rushes, foam, pool — the scene is a collection of the elements which happen by accident to be there, "strewn" about like the haphazard stones which lie in the center of the picture. There is no grouping, no inner force molding all to a unity, no "instress" such as Hopkins finds in nature, no interior tendency toward pattern or form. Everything is slack. The scene, if it expresses anything, expresses the disintegration of nature. When Arnold tries to be most like the romantic poets, as in the pastiche of Keats in "The Scholar-Gipsy," he is really least like them, in spite of his attempt to show the "interinanimation" of natural things. The esemplastic force sweeping through nature in the romantic vision has fled away and left dry isolated husks behind. In Arnold's hands nature poetry becomes like descriptions in a botanical handbook — accurate, but superficial:

> Through the thick corn the scarlet poppies peep,
> And round green roots and yellowing stalks I see
> Pale pink convolvulus in tendrils creep;
> And air-swept lindens yield
> Their scent, and rustle down their perfumed showers
> Of bloom on the bent grass where I am laid . ... (255, 256)

If nature is just a collection of things, it is hopeless to seek any spiritual presence there which might be a support for man. Imitating nature or seeking harmony with nature no longer means trying to plunge our roots, like nature's, in the ground of the absolute, or trying, through atunement with nature, to reach that ground. Each man must imitate nature in her mute acceptance of separation from God, and be like a stone, rounded in upon himself, with a stone's independence and persistence in being itself. Joy comes not from participation in the general life, but from a blind perseverance in performing the acts appropriate to our own natures. The stars and the sea are "Bounded by themselves, and unregardful/In what state God's other works may be" (240), and they "demand not that the things without them/Yield them love, amusement, sympathy" (240). Yet they perform their appointed tasks with joy. Each man must also learn to be a law unto himself: "To its own impulse every creature stirs;/Live by thy light, and earth will live by hers!" (8).

This lesson of nature is really a lesson of despair, for though nature is to be admired for her ability to endure isolation, this calm self-enclosure, the satisfied peace of a rock merely being a rock, is impossible for man. Man's trouble is that he finds in himself no given law to direct his being. He desperately needs help from outside, someone or something to tell him what to do and who to be. Can nature do no more than bid man attempt something impossible?

Sometimes Arnold proposes a third doctrine of nature. In this third theory nature does possess a secret life which is also the divine life. The trouble is that this life can only be reached with great difficulty, if at all. The fullest statement of this theory is in a poem which, like so many of Arnold's poems about nature, is an explicit consideration of the Wordsworthian doctrine of the Nature Spirit. "The Youth of Nature" is apparently another lament for the death of the great poet who could see into the heart of nature and communicate what he saw there. But as the poem progresses it gradually changes its tone and modulates into a questioning of Wordsworth's power to read the secret of nature. Though the divine pulse beats at Nature's heart, there is no Wordsworthian filial bond through which that blood can flow also through *our* hearts. The "loveliness, magic, and grace" (230) which Wordsworth saw in nature and expressed in his poetry were no illusion, no projection into nature of an idea of the mind, but even Wordsworth caught no more than an evanescent glimpse of them. Nature is the dwelling place of the divine spirit, but, as Nature tells the poet, man cannot reach and possess that spirit (231). There is also an ominous sentence in the essay on Maurice de Guérin, a sentence following the description of the power of poetry to give us the sense that we have nature's secret: "I will not now inquire whether this sense is illusive, whether it can be proved not to be illusive, whether it does absolutely make us possess the real nature of things . . ." (III, 88, 89). He will not ask, but in saying so he *does* ask, and radically puts in question the doctrine of poetry which he has just proposed. Nature possesses a hidden life, Arnold suggests, but poetry does not make us sharers in that life.

Accordingly, alongside the landscapes of mute objects, there is in Arnold's poetry another kind of landscape. This landscape expresses perfectly the notion that nature is the hiding place of an inner life which can only be guessed at or glimpsed momentarily.

This new kind of landscape represents neither a nature which is the dwelling place of an immanent spirit, nor a nature which is disintegrated and dead. God is present, but present as something fleeting and ungraspable, something which remains tantalizingly just beyond our ken. Arnold often presents a moonlight or twilight scene, a scene with no definite barrier to our sight. The diffused light seems to offer a principle of continuity which puts the spectator in touch with the most distant spot he can see. Space can be crossed, and even without crossing it man can see, hear, or smell things which he cannot touch or hold. Space is a conducting medium. But this space, which seems to offer all that time withholds, does not really give man access to the divine ground of things. Though space can be traversed by sight, seeing does not reach any goal, however far it goes. Space in these nocturnal scenes gradually fades away toward a horizon of obscurity which is not itself an end, but a penetrable distance which is proof that there is, beyond any place eyesight can reach, more space, and beyond that more space again. Space can be crossed, but this crossing does not reach anything different from the spot where the spectator stands:

> In the deserted, moon-blanch'd street,
> How lonely rings the echo of my feet!
>   . . . — but see!
> A break between the housetops shows
> The moon! and, lost behind her, fading dim
> Into the dewy dark obscurity
> Down at the far horizon's rim,
> Doth a whole tract of heaven disclose! (242)

> Coldly, sadly descends
> The autumn-evening. The field
> Strewn with its dank yellow drifts
> Of wither'd leaves, and the elms,
> Fade into dimness apace,
> Silent . . . (286)

> The sandy spits, the shore-lock'd lakes,
>   Melt into open, moonlit sea . . . (275)

> They stand and listen; they hear
> The children's shouts, and at times,
> Faintly, the bark of a dog
> From a distant farm in the hills.

Nothing besides! in front
The wide, wide valley outspreads
To the dim horizon, reposed
In the twilight, and bathed in dew,
Corn-field and hamlet and copse
Darkening fast . . . (234)

"Fading dim," "fade into dimness," "melt into," "outspreads to the dim horizon," "darkening fast" — these are the characteristic motifs of this third kind of landscape, and with them goes a constant sense of the precariousness of the moment of insight. Only by twilight or moonlight, when space is filled with a soft light, can man's senses move well enough through space to discover that this movement only takes him out into a dim obscurity or into the manifest barrenness of "a whole tract of heaven" or the "open, moonlit sea." The moment of twilight is only a moment, and just as space itself fades into obscurity or emptiness, so the moment when we can have this knowledge is ephemeral, and is fast darkening toward night, when space will no longer betray its nature to the spectator. It is as if the impenetrable obscurity into which space fades were closing in on the beholder, absorbing the clearer space around him in its blackness.

The central essence of nature is not blackness. The center is the all-inclusive One from which issued the multiplicity of the world. This center is everywhere in nature, and yet is revealed only evanescently. It is something which evades direct perception, and retreats beyond the farthest limit our senses can reach. Arnold most reminds us of Tennyson when he apprehends nature as full of melancholy, broken, fugitive things, things which are the covert revelation of a deity who remains a presence-absence, hidden as much as made manifest in things, never quite tangibly there, but glimpsed in the very moment of disappearing:

Like bright waves that fall
With a lifelike motion
On the lifeless margin of the sparkling Ocean;
A wild rose climbing up a mouldering wall —
A gush of sunbeams through a ruin'd hall —
Strains of glad music at a funeral . . . (36)

The waves, the rose, the sunbeams, and the music are images of something which has just emerged from occultation, and is about to return to its concealment.

Perhaps it is possible to pierce beyond these tantalizing appearances and reach what they momentarily reveal. In "Parting" Arnold rejects the lure of Marguerite, and chooses to follow the storm-winds of autumn which blow toward the mountains. If he can follow the winds he will reach the heart of nature. At that heart is the systole and diastole of forces, the expansion and contraction of the mists, which is the ever-repeated, ever-renewed process whereby space and time are born of what is beyond space and time, in "the stir of the forces/Whence issued the world" (177).

Though Arnold makes his choice for movement up the mountains toward the center of things, he remains static. The pulls in opposite directions, up and down, toward the mountains and toward Marguerite (who comes *down* the stairs), balance, and the poet remains fixed in an immobile equilibrium. In no one of Arnold's poems about space is any real movement made. Though these poems establish an orientation in terms of up and down which is the spatial version of the river of time, there is in them all an atmosphere of poise. It is not possible to make true progress through Arnoldian space, for whatever new place is reached is transformed into another version of the old places. Nor is it possible to embrace the totality of space by the addition of local spaces. Man is driven by a frenzied desire to know all and possess all at once: "Look, the world tempts our eye,/And we would know it all!" (423). But each man is limited to the spot where he is, and when he moves to a new place he loses possession of the place he has just left. As he progresses in his anxious attempt to reach totality by the addition of finite experiences he has a nightmarish sense that the sum of unexperienced things is growing larger rather than smaller: "But still, as we proceed/The mass swells more and more . . ." (423). Finally he must recognize the sad truth. Only God can know all the world at once. Man is limited to his own narrow perspective, and "Man's measures cannot mete the immeasurable All" (423). Though each man's state of mind seems all-important to him, it does not extend beyond his own being. When he is happy, and would have the moment stay, there are ten thousand other human beings who are in misery, and would have the moment pass (50–52). Neither thought nor

passion, however intense, can push out the barriers which limit
each man to one little area of space:

> . . . there's no mood,
> No meditation, no delight, no sorrow,
> Cas'd in one man's dimensions, can distil
> Such pregnant and infectious quality,
> Six yards round shall not ring it. — (50)

Arnold's exploration of space has been no more successful than
his exploration of time. Though man can move through space
freely, both actually and with his senses, as he cannot move in
time, it is impossible, however far he goes, to approach one inch
closer to the secret of nature. Arnold's deepest experience of
space is an anguished sense that he reaches, through space, all
he most desires, but that this communication is a brief echo of
something which remains infinitely distant, voices heard faintly
and fleetingly across great spaces, "like wanderers from the
world's extremity" (36). A scarcely perceptible sound, a "strain,/
From a far lonelier distance, like the wind" (238), is man's only
direct knowledge that something other than his present condition
exists, but this dim knowledge is enough to make him homesick
and melancholy, dissatisfied with his lot:

> Yet still, from time to time, vague and forlorn, . . .
> As from an infinitely distant land,
> Come airs, and floating echoes, and convey
> A melancholy into all our day. (247)

Neither space nor time offer a mediator between Arnoldian
man and what he seeks. His testing of these two fundamental dimensions of his existence has served only to confirm more hopelessly his isolation.

ह৵

Man is not only a creature of time and space, like a stone or
a tree. He is also a social being, and can form relations to his
fellows. Perhaps he can find in society or in the love of another
person what he cannot find in time or space. In the lost epoch of
harmony, love was still possible, and society was divinely ordered.

This lost harmony would be regained if we could re-establish love or discover a valid society.

Only a still genuine society could be depended on to mediate between man and God. Present society does not appear to be so when seen from the point of view of isolated, self-conscious man, though this may be an illusion. The only way to make certain would be to accept the role society would have us play. There is in Arnold's writings a recurrent suspicion that the fault is not with the times, but with himself. His coldness and detachment may be preventing him from discovering whether any of the ways of living offered to him are valid ones.

Arnold is attracted by his own version of the strategy of role-playing. At present he is "an aimless unallay'd Desire" (481). If he could act for a while as if one of the given ways of being were proper, he might find that the costume would become habitual dress. Arnold's copying in his notebooks of quotations of a courageous and morally stiffening sort was in one of its aspects an attempt to carry into practice this theory of role-playing. If he could go often enough through the act of writing down a solemn and constructive quotation from some wise man of the past, Bishop Wilson or Isaiah or Epictetus, he might come to believe in the quotation and be made over in its image. Then "the best that has been thought and said in the world" (VII, xxx) would be made current in Arnold's own life.

This method of role-playing never really works for Arnold, in spite of the bulk of his notebooks. He is never able to conquer his coldness. Arnold makes a bad actor, and his own anxious face is always present behind the mask of Bishop Wilson, Sophocles, or Spinoza. Arnold is never able to leap beyond the basic paradox of such a strategy. There is no way to be certain that a given course of imitative action will lead to its goal. But how, unless we are sure, can we give ourselves wholeheartedly to any path? There is an element of guesswork in any choice of a predetermined way toward an end. If we were certain the path would lead to the goal, we should already in some sense possess the goal, and should not need to go through any process to reach it. It is just this unpredictability which Arnold is unwilling to accept. He has to see the goal clearly before he takes the plunge. My "one natural craving," he says, is "a distinct seeing of my way as far as my own nature is concerned" (CL, 110). This is impossible. The goal stays hidden until it is reached. So Arnold remains permanently in his detachment, unable to accept any externally given code as the law of his being. At the crucial moment faith fails him, he throws down in disgust the mask of "duty self-denial etc.," and relaxes back into his usual inner slackness and anarchy: "What I must tell you," he writes to Clough, "is that I have never yet succeeded in any one great occasion in consciously mastering myself: I can go thro: the imaginary process of mastering myself and see the whole affair as it would then stand, but at the critical point I am too apt to hoist up the mainsail to the wind and let her drive. However as I get more awake to this it will I hope mend for I find that with me a clear almost palpable intuition (damn the logical senses of the word) is necessary before I get into prayer: unlike many people who set to work at their duty self-denial etc. like furies in the dark hoping to be gradually illuminated as they persist in this course" (CL, 110).

The key word here is "intuition," and the strain Arnold is putting on the word is revealed in his exclamation about it. He recognizes that he wants the word to express a contradiction: the possession of the goal before one has gone through the process necessary to reach it. The "intuition" of the goal which Arnold requires before he starts praying must not be a vague supposition. It must be "clear" and "almost palpable," or else he cannot be sure enough that the goal is there to get under way at all. The peculiarity of prayer, from the human point of view, is that it creates in its own act the goal which is sought. Prayer brings us into the realm where prayer is answered. The other acts which Arnold is considering here are of the same nature. The strategy of escaping inner emptiness by the playing of a role must accept the initial obscurity and uncertainty of the method, but Arnold is unwilling to work like a fury in the dark hoping for a gradual illumination. So he remains withdrawn from life, the disinter-ested critic of the institutions, the literature, the society, the re-ligion of his time. These present themselves to him never as something he has experienced from the inside, but as a spectacle to be regarded from a distance with a settled suspicion that the truth is not in them. As a critic of society he seeks rather to un-derstand than to sympathize. He wants to control society and to keep it at arm's length by a discovery of its laws. His attitude toward society is fundamentally defensive. The "demand for an intellectual deliverance," he writes, "arises, because the present age exhibits to the individual man who contemplates it the spectacle of a vast multitude of facts awaiting and inviting his comprehension. The deliverance consists in man's comprehension of this present and past. It begins when our mind begins to enter into possession of the general ideas which are the law of this vast multitude of facts. It is perfect when we have acquired that harmonious acquiescence of mind which we feel in contemplating a grand spectacle that is intelligible to us ·. . ." [12]

Arnold strives to understand the spectacle of life by looking at it with the scientist's cold, detached eye, by "see[ing] the object as in itself it really is" (III, 1). Another name for this disinterestedness is irony, the stylistic pose which separates itself from what it describes, and, holding it at a distance, hollows it out with subtle mockery. Arnold is a skillful ironist, but his irony is not, as with the greatest ironists, turned on himself. Irony, like the stance of disinterestedness, is for Arnold a way of not being swallowed up by the world. He fears more than anything else the possibility that he might plunge into the "immense, moving, confused spectacle" of life (Essays, 456), and be lost in its inauthenticity. Society is a dangerous whirlpool. "The rush and roar of practical life will always have a dizzying and attracting effect upon the most collected spectator, and tend to draw him into its vortex" (III, 27), and therefore man "must begin with an Idea of the world in order not to be prevailed over by the world's multitudinousness" (CL, 97).

Arnold always keeps himself erect and aloof, like a man fording a rapid, muddy river, holding his head high and walking on tiptoe. He never has the courage to try that mode of understanding which seeks to comprehend the rationale of an alien way of life by seeing how it would feel to accept it as one's own. Arnold recognizes that this mode of understanding is an important one, and even that it is the way of knowing most proper to the poet. The poet, in order to recreate in words the spectacle of life around him, must "become what [he] sing[s]" (193), but, whereas the Gods can with pleasure see and participate in the vast pano-

[12] Essays by Matthew Arnold, pp. 455, 456.

rama of life, the poet must pay the price of great pain for his
knowledge. Though the Gods cannot share human sorrows, the
poet must enter fully into the sufferings as well as the joys of
the heroes of his poem: " — such a price/The Gods exact for
song" (193). Being a poet seems to Arnold a matter of great suffering, the pain caused by breaking down the safe barriers of
cold solitude, going outside oneself, and entering into the warmth
and feeling of those who are engaged in life. Keats welcomes the
chance to be "with Achilles shouting in the trenches." The more
powerful the sensation the better. "Negative capability," sympathetic identification even with painful or melancholy things, is
for Keats the very source of joy, of truth, and of beauty. Arnold
fears such a loss of his self-possession, and goes out of himself
with great reluctance. He wants to make poetry as much as possible a matter of assimilation and control rather than of diffusion
and sympathy, though the process of taking the world into oneself
rather than going outward into the world also seems to him a
cause of suffering and effort: "For me you may often hear my
sinews cracking under the effort to unite matter . . ." (CL, 65).
Arnold fears that even this painful control over the world may
be impossible. The world may slip away, rise up against the soul,
and once more engulf it.

Arnold's fullest analysis of the danger of understanding through
sympathy is in a famous letter to Clough. As is so often the case
he projects into Clough as a *fait accompli* what he fears as a possibility for himself. Role-playing, he says, leads to a dispersal of
the self, its absorption by the chaotic multiplicity of all the ways
of living which society offers. "You ask me," he tells Clough, "in
what I think or have thought you going wrong: in this: that you
would never take your assiette as something determined final and
unchangeable for you and proceed to work away on the basis of
that: but were always poking and patching and cobbling at the
assiette itself — could never finally, as it seemed — 'resolve to be
thyself' — but were looking for this and that experience, and
doubting whether you ought not to adopt this or that mode of
being of persons qui ne vous valaient pas because it might possibly be nearer the truth than your own: you had no reason for
thinking it *was,* but it *might* be — and so you would try to adapt
yourself to it. You have I am convinced lost infinite time in this

way: it is what I call your morbid conscientiousness . . ." (CL,
130). Clough's conscientiousness is the tormenting awareness of
the possibility that the other fellow has found the secret of inner
certainty. Arnold's conscientiousness is that of the man who never
takes the plunge into life because he fears all given ways of living are imposture, and will contaminate him. He is not sure that
they are all false, but neither is he sure that any one of them is
true, and so he loses infinite time, just as Clough, in Arnold's
analysis of him, loses infinite time through being unable to take
one mode of life as permanently his. No man in these damned
times has a solid inner law and support for his being. In the
absence of this man can neither accept society nor do without it,
but must fluctuate between isolation and the halfhearted acceptance of a social role whose falseness he suspects from the start:

> Where shall [a man] fly then? back to men? —
> But they will gladly welcome him once more,
> And help him to unbend his too tense thought,
> And rid him of the presence of himself,
> And keep their friendly chatter at his ear,
> And haunt him, till the absence from himself,
> That other torment, grow unbearable;
> And he will fly to solitude again,
> And he will find its air too keen for him,
> And so change back; and many thousand times
> Be miserably bandied to and fro
> Like a sea-wave . . . (435, 436)

Arnold never really tries to reach the lost time of joy through
society. The basis of his attitude toward society is an inability to
believe that any social form embodies divine law, and his analysis
of society, in his poetry and in his prose, is an attempt to persuade
us of the truth of this presupposition. At one time society was in
God's hand, but an originally good society has drifted further
and further away from its holy beginning until mere empty husks
are left. In terms of these husks, shells from which the spiritual
vitality has departed, man in these days is forced to carry on his
collective life. Social forms no longer draw strength from God,
and, on the other hand, they are no longer appropriate to the life
man leads. An awareness of the artificiality, the hollowness, the
conventionality of present-day social forms characterizes the modern spirit: "Modern times find themselves with an immense sys-

tem of institutions, established facts, accredited dogmas, customs, rules, which have come to them from times not modern. In this system their life has to be carried forward; yet they have a sense that this system is not of their own creation, that it by no means corresponds exactly with the wants of their actual life, that, for them, it is customary, not rational. The awakening of this sense is the awakening of the modern spirit" (III, 174).

The forms of society are laws, institutions, religion, the arts, language. Most of Arnold's prose is "criticism" in the sense that it is dedicated to showing the emptiness of one or another of these social forms. *Culture and Anarchy* is based on the assumption that all classes of contemporary society, barbarians, philistines, and populace alike, are wrong in their claims to be divinely justified. England possesses "an aristocracy materialised and null, a middle-class purblind and hideous, a lower class crude and brutal" (IV, 148, 149). Rather than being "culture" in the sense of a viable human embodiment of divine truth, the three classes are, in one way or another, baseless anarchy, the anarchy, for example, of "doing as one likes," without any extrahuman justification. In the same way, at the heart of Arnold's several books on religion is the assumption that language cannot incarnate God's truth. *St. Paul and Protestantism* is an attempt to demolish the Puritan claim to speak "scientifically" about God in the language of the "covenant of redemption," "the covenant of works," "original sin," "free election," "effectual calling." The trouble with this kind of language is that it is "talking about God just as if he were a man in the next street" (IX, 8). We can never talk about God in this way. St. Paul had the secret of righteousness and lived in harmony with God's law, but Protestantism has reduced St. Paul to empty formulas, and lives outside the divine kingdom. In the chapter in *God and the Bible* called "The God of Metaphysics" Arnold attempts to demonstrate that the central words of metaphysics, "is," "being," "essence," "existence," "substance," and so on, are derived from words for physical nature. Since they all come from terms for earthly experience, they can tell us nothing whatever about God. "*Être*," says Arnold, "really means to breathe" (VIII, 90), and to say "God is," is simply to say "God operates, . . . the Eternal which makes for righteousness has operation" (VIII, 92, 93). Arnold assumes here that the origin of a

word permanently limits its meaning. Abstract words are metaphorical extensions of concrete terms. Therefore they can never
be anything but figurative. As abstractions they refer to nothing
at all. All we can honestly say about God and his heaven is: "We
know nothing about the matter, it is altogether beyond us" (VIII,
97).

This idea about the nature of language contains a theological
implication. It assumes that God transcends our speech. He can
only be defined negatively, as "not ourselves," that is, as unthink-
able, and therefore unspeakable. We cannot even speak of God
as "He," for that is to anthropomorphize God, to think of It after
the model of a "magnified and non-natural man" (IX, 19). "It,"
the "not ourselves," can only be known through Its operation,
as what "makes for righteousness," whatever *that* may mean.
Arnold wishes to show that all our language, even the most abstract and seemingly worthy of the transcendent character of the
deity, is a "throwing out" of figurative language toward something which it cannot name and has no hope of reaching. He
believes in God, but he does not believe that God can be spoken
about as we speak of the things of this world.

The "end and aim of all religion" is *"access to God,* — the
sense of harmony with the universal order — the partaking of the
divine nature . . ." (IX, 32), but if the language which a people
speaks cannot be an embodiment of divine truth, then society
itself is no mediator between man and the "universal order."
Language is one of the basic matrices of society, and no society
can transcend the limits of its speech.

Perhaps, Arnold sometimes feels, the divine order can be embodied in the actions of wise and just men, men who carry out
God's law even though that law cannot be formulated in a code.
Perhaps the course of human events is secretly ordered by a divine
Providence working immanently in things. Here, as elsewhere,
Arnold's ultimate experience is negative. Repeatedly in his first
book of poems he returns to the theme of divine law, and each
time he concludes that God's law either does not act at all in human life or acts in a way that makes God seem an unjust tyrant,
placing burdens on men too heavy to bear. "Mycerinus" is based
on a story in Herodotus about a wicked king who prospers while
his good and law-abiding son, Mycerinus, is condemned by the

inscrutable Gods to an early death. Mycerinus concludes that he was wrong to believe that "man's justice from the all-just Gods was given" (9). The Gods, if Gods there are, are either powerless, or care nothing for man. In any case man can know nothing of the divine realm. All our talk of God's law is merely "Stringing vain words of powers we cannot see,/Blind divinations of a will supreme" (10). So Mycerinus gives himself to revelry for the brief six years before he is fated to die. The "Fragment of an 'Antigone,' " in which Arnold wears the mask of Sophocles, picks out for imitation that part of the play which makes clearest the difficulties of obeying God's law. Both Antigone and Creon, though they act in opposite ways, think they are guided by divine law, and the result is suffering and death. Though the "order" of society is "heaven-ordain'd" (195), that order, when it is transformed into individual experience, is so baffling that it is as if man were left on his own, "unguided," and must make "his own welfare his unswerv'd-from law" (195). Arnold returns once again to the theme of law in "The Sick King in Bokhara." In that poem the anguish of the king who must unwillingly condemn a man to death in order to uphold the law is set against the desire of the criminal for punishment. The criminal would rather be stoned to death than remain unjustified. In these poems it is the ambiguity of divine law rather than its complete absence which is dramatized. God's command is either difficult to know, or condemns man to apparently unmerited suffering, or forces him to acts which are repugnant to his moral sense.

Later on Arnold will find it difficult to believe even in this flawed and unsatisfactory inherence of God's law in the world. "Merope," his most elaborate attempt to achieve the "platform" of the classical, once again has at its center the theme of law. The real protagonist is Polyphontes, the usurping ruler who has seized power because he has felt himself to be the man through whom God's law can be imposed on society. Man, the most important chorus tells us, can never be sure he acts under God's direction. God's law is never unequivocally present in any society or in any man's heart, and the man who acts as if he were divinely justified takes too great a responsibility and should be condemned: "Sternly condemn the too bold man, who dares/Elect himself Heaven's destined arm . . ." (353).

Law, like language, religion, or established customs, is no abiding place of the divine harmony, and the man who takes the role which society offers, far from approaching his goal, merely sacrifices his life to "some unmeaning taskwork" (243). There *is* a proper social order, but, though man would know it if he had it, he has no way to find out beforehand how to get it. It is as if man had a lock but no key, and were forced to make blindly key after key in the hope of getting the right one by accident, or, in the metaphor of "Revolutions" (239), it is as if he had a collection of letters, given to him by God, and could make the magic word by one and only one arrangement of those letters. Man is like a magician who has forgotten the talismanic formula, and tries desperately to find it by experimentation. Though he has tried permutation after permutation of the letters, and made of each of them a culture, he knows in his heart that no one of these words has been the right one. Man's sense of the unlawfulness of all he has yet made is the cause of the decay of civilizations. Each culture, at the height of its power, is undermined by a conviction of its wrongness. Then it "droop[s], and slowly die[s]" (239). The drive of history is a rage for order, a rage for order which becomes a rage for destruction when the right order is not found. Decades before Yeats or Valéry, Arnold has already their vision of history. He says his goodbye to Greece and Rome, and sees our own civilization as destined to go the way of the rest and become bits and pieces of archaeological debris.

Man as a social being is condemned to remain an outlaw, but once he could form an extrasocial relation to his fellows, the relation of love. In the epoch of harmony lovers could be transparent to one another, and see truly into one another's souls. This communion of lovers was the microcosm of the universal harmony in which it participated. Perhaps if true love could be re-established the cosmic background of love would also be recovered. Arnold in his own life seeks this way out of the sterility and "aridity" [13] of his existence. The record of this attempt is the Marguerite poems.

[13] Compare CL, 131: "God keep us . . . from aridity! *Arid* — that is what the times are."

These poems are dominated by nostalgia for an epoch when each person was not yet "enisled" (182) in the sea of life. Marguerite, on her Alpine heights, still belongs to the pastoral age, and if Arnold can love and be loved by her, he can return, through her, to the primal origin of things, for she is "a messenger from radiant climes" (208).

The poems express Arnold's discovery that love cannot be used in this way. Only someone who already participates in the divine life of nature would be a fit mate for Marguerite. Such a man would be himself an incarnation of the universal joy:

> His eyes be like the starry lights —
> His voice like sounds of summer nights —
> In all his lovely mien let pierce
> The magic of the universe! (202)

Unless Arnold already shares in the "magic of the universe," Marguerite will be opaque to him. Instead of permitting him access to her inner self, she will turn on him her "pure, unwavering, deep disdain" (202), the disdain of someone who has "look'd, and smiled, and [seen him] through" (202). Arnold is a hollow man, and because he needs from love the vitality which makes it possible to love, he is unable to love in Marguerite's way, the way of those who "bring more than they receive" (203). Marguerite is able to love because she contains her own springs of life and joy. She rejects disdainfully the modern sort of love, in which two people, as in "Dover Beach," need one another to fill up the void in their hearts. Such modern lovers plight their troth in the face of an awareness that there is no universal Love to guarantee particular acts of love. Aloneness is now man's real condition, and love is founded on its own despair. This is a modern "existentialist" kind of love, which says: "Since there is no 'Love,' in the sense of a power transcending man, let us create love out of nothing, in spite of the insecurity and even absurdity of such love." Marguerite has no need of this kind of love, and expects the same independence from her lover. She is one of those who "ask no love, [and] plight no faith,/For they are happy as they are" (203).

Just as Arnold must have a poet's nature first in order to write poetry, so he must participate in the universal harmony in order to create its miniature image in the intimacy of lovers. But Arnold is outside the timeless current of God's life, an island upon time's barren, stormy flow, and therefore love is impossible for him. He abandons Marguerite because he recognizes an essential lack in himself. He is "too strange, too restless, too untamed" (178), and she is right to reject him. He is right to leave her too, for rather than being a way to his true goal, the "establishment of God's kingdom on earth," love in these bad days leads man astray and diverts him from other possible ways out of the wilderness. Love tends to present itself to Arnold under the guise of passion, as a dangerous relaxation of moral stiffness, a "hoisting up of the main-sail and letting her drive." In "A Summer Night" the alternative to giving one's life to "some unmeaning taskwork" is the mad liberty of the "freed prisoner" who sails aimlessly across the tempestuous sea of life, "With anguish'd face and flying hair/Grasping the rudder hard,/Still bent to make some port he knows not where, /Still standing for some false impossible shore" (244). Against Clough's tendency to "welter to the parching wind," to *"fluctuate,"* Arnold feels it necessary to "stiffen [himself] — and hold fast [his] rudder" (CL, 146).

Along with this conviction that the only way to get through these bad times is aloofness and stiffness, the chin held high above the swirling waters, goes another attitude toward strong feeling. Arnold often feels guilty about his inability to abandon himself to passion: "I have had that desire of fulness without respect of the means, which may become almost maniacal: but nature had placed a bar thereto not only in the conscience (as with all men) but in a great numbness in that direction" (CL, 97); "I doubt whether I shall ever have heat and radiance enough to pierce the clouds that are massed round me" (CL, 126). It may be that his "coldness" and "invincible languor of spirit" (CL, 129) are not really good qualities at all. Though passion clouds intellectual clarity, this clarity may be the thing which is cutting him off from the divine vitality. If he could drown his lucidity in a current of powerful feeling he would find himself back in a realm where things blend in mutual interpenetration. While intellect coldly sets things against one another, and puts a void between them, feeling is a warm flow in which things lose their sharp edges, and the mind its separateness. Though speech belongs to surface life and is never authentic, the "nameless feelings that course through our breast" (246) come from the deep buried life and share its truth. In those rare moments when the buried life is liberated and "our eyes can in another's eyes read clear" (247) the vehicle of this possession of ourselves and of another person is not speech or intellect. It is the recovery of "a lost pulse of feeling" (247).

Religion, in Arnold's famous definition, is "morality touched with emotion." By itself morality is not strong enough to lead man to the good. Emotion comes, though distantly and obscurely, from God, and when morality is irradiated with this gracious element of feeling it is strong enough to guide man's steps toward heaven. Creeds and dogmas are not so important as the unspeakable feeling they express, and this feeling is the same whatever the creed. The fact that man is forced to use speech and concepts is merely proof of his separation from the fusing joy. In his religious books, as in his doctrine of poetry, Arnold wants to return to a time before abstract thought was necessary, a time when man lived his religion directly, in powerful feeling, without needing to think about it.

Arnold's theories of religion and love are strikingly similar, and he returns, in a religious context, to his notion that the loved one can serve as a mediator between man and God. In *St. Paul and Protestantism* he rejects the idea that Jesus is the Mediator either in the metaphysical sense of the divine Logos, or in the Old Testament sense of the Messiah. Science, he says, can neither prove nor disprove these ideas. They are something we can know nothing about. Arnold proposes as truly St. Paul's an analysis of the power of Jesus based on his own earlier theory of love between the sexes. Though there is a moral law which we should obey, by himself man is unable to know and follow this law. Jesus, alone of all men, was without sin, and He "lived to God" (IX, 59). Ordinary men are not strong enough to reach the kingdom of God by a cold performance of duty, but if they love Jesus, then the current of emotion and sympathy binding them to Him will allow them to reach God through Jesus. Only in this sense is Jesus the Mediator: "Every one knows how being in love changes for the time a man's spiritual atmosphere, and makes animation and buoyancy where before there was flatness and dulness. . . . [Being in love] also sensibly and powerfully increases our faculties of action." Wher. Paul loved Jesus, "appropriated" the power of Jesus, "the struggling stream of duty, which had not volume enough to bear him

to his goal, was suddenly reinforced by the immense tidal wave
of sympathy and emotion" (IX, 56, 65). What was possible for St.
Paul, reaching God through his love for Jesus, is by no means
necessarily possible for Arnold. Even for St. Paul this loving attach-
ment to Jesus was faith, the "power of holding on to the unseen"
(IX, 65). For the deity is an "unseen God" (IX, 67). In religion
as in love the ideas of separation, of unavailability, are essential
for Arnold. He uses here his basic metaphor of human life, the
stream. Religious life, like life in general, is a moving toward a
goal which transcends man, as the ocean transcends any point on
the river which flows toward it.

Nevertheless, if Arnold's analyses of love and religion are correct, perhaps by abandoning himself to passion man could win at
last to the promised land. In "The New Sirens" Arnold makes a
sustained attempt to consider the possibility of reaching the center
of reconciliation through passion. This poem, like "Parting," is
oriented in terms of a vertical axis. In "Parting" Arnold rejects the
downward pull of Marguerite for the sake of the "high mountain-
platforms" close to the origin of things. The protagonists of "The
New Sirens," on the other hand, are victims of the modern en-
chantresses. They have been lured away "From the watchers on
the mountains,/And the bright and morning star" (27). They have
left the high morning star of intellectual truth for the opposing
attraction of sexual passion. The new sirens promise to give the
poet all he has sought so arduously and unsuccessfully on the
mountains. Only through passion can man recover his lost proximity to God, for the heart "glean'd, when Gods were speaking,/
Rarer secrets than the toiling head," and the heart is still the best
avenue to divine truth: "Only, what we feel, we know" (28, 29).

The promise of the new sirens turns out to be false, and Arnold
has already, in this early poem, rejected the strategy of reaching
heaven through passion. Passion gives only a false semblance of
reconciliation and unity. It is a losing of oneself which is not a
finding of the new life. Even if the intoxicating sense of insight
which accompanies overwhelming feeling were a true glimpse of
God, it would be no more than a glimpse, for "on raptures follow
calms" (30). Passion is naturally evanescent. It cannot ever be consciously enjoyed, for to think of it destroys it. Man never realizes
the benefits of passion, for he is not himself when he abandons

himself to it. The life of passion, this alternation of ennui and excitement, is no way out of the sterility of these present times; "it cannot last: time will destroy it: the time will come, when the elasticity of the spirits will be worn out, and nothing left but weariness" (CL, 106). Weariness and ennui are the fruits of strong feeling, and man finds himself, after the expense of passion, still wandering in the desert, as far as ever from the promised land. Sensual ecstasy is no substitute for the "hard and solitary" "life of the spirit" (CL, 106). Arnold must bid his heart renounce passion forever, and return to his solitude:

> — and thou, thou lonely heart,
> Which never yet without remorse
> Even for a moment didst depart
> From thy remote and spheréd course
> To haunt the place where passions reign —
> Back to thy solitude again! (181)

ੈੈ

All the ways to escape from these damned times have failed. Not the exploration of time or space, not the acceptance of society, not love, not passion — no way will work, and whichever way Arnold turns he is thrown back on himself, and on his usual state of isolation and fluctuation.

Perhaps instead of struggling to get out of his situation man should accept his lot. A recurrent impulse of Arnold's spirit is the desire for calm, for immobility, for a total relaxation of effort. If all attempts to escape from his present state are hopeless, it might be possible to avoid pain by lying motionless like a stone. This would be the despairing resignation of the prisoner who, having struggled in vain against his chains, gives up trying to get free. It is this ability to accept coercion without anguish which Arnold envies in stones, trees, and stars. Nature is "mild and inscrutably calm" (232). Arnold also admires this ability to take what comes, not to ask anything from life, in Epictetus or Marcus Aurelius, and in such modern heroes as "Obermann." Man must, like the Stoics, "learn to wait, renounce, withdraw" (481). How can someone who is an "aimless unallay'd Desire" (481) achieve the calm endurance of a stone? It seems that only death will make him stone-like. Arnold does often "play dead" in his poems; he sets against a life of "turning, turning,/In mazes of heat and sound" (21) the calm immobility of a corpse, and he longs for the corpse's peace:

> Strew on her roses, roses,
> And never a spray of yew!
> In quiet she reposes;
> Ah, would that I did too! (21)

The dead, however, are out of life altogether. Arnold needs to find a way to achieve, in life, the peace of the dead. He sometimes thinks he has found a way in the notion of equilibrium, of distance, but not too great a distance, from the whirling world. If the full plunge into life puts a man at the mercy of the "mazes of heat and sound," and if a total withdrawal leads to the anguish of isolation, it might be possible to reach a point exactly in the middle, neither too close to life nor too far away from it. This strategy would be "not too near" "to men's business," but detachment would be used to comprehend that business, for through it one would "[win] room to see and hear" (59). What would be seen would be held at arm's length, and therefore understood and controlled by the "even-balanced soul" (2) of the spectator. This would not be as good as the true peace of a full engagement in a proper life. It would be "the second best" (49). But the second best is better than nothing, and if the poet could find the "quiet watershed/Whence, equally, the seas of life and death are fed" (59, 60), it might be possible to achieve a tolerable life by remaining poised there in precarious equilibrium. Having balanced himself in this way he would have found at last, in "sad lucidity of soul" (58), an assiette, a platform, a way to achieve fixity. From his "high station" (57) he could "[see] life steadily, and [see] it whole" (2).

Unfortunately, however hard he tries, Arnold cannot achieve the delicate equilibrium which has withdrawn from life to just the right distance. There is no secure platform at that spot. It is like suspending oneself in midair or balancing on a knife-edge. The pull to one side or the other is too great, and man plunges either into society or into solitude, either into life or into death. Immobility is impossible, and each man is condemned to "oscillation," to being miserably bandied to and fro like a sea-wave. The name for this perpetual wavering is "ennui . . . the disease of the most modern societies." [14] Arnold draws a classic description of ennui from Lucretius: "A man rushes abroad . . . because he is sick of being at home; and suddenly comes home again because he finds himself no whit easier abroad. He posts as fast as his horses can take him to his country-seat: when he has got there he hesitates what to do; or he throws himself down moodily to sleep, and seeks forgetfulness in that; or he makes the best of his way back to town again with the same speed as he fled from it. Thus every one flies from himself" (*Essays,* 468).

Though Arnold tries all the ways to fly from himself, his attempts to escape lead him inevitably back to his original state of ennui. His unsuccessful flights from himself are the very causes of that state.

The failure of every effort to reach peace leads Arnold to discover the essential nature of his situation. When man dwelt in the divine kingdom he could reconcile opposites, for all qualities existed together in harmonious tension. When the world exploded into multiplicity the opposites were divided from one another. Man hungers for unity, for totality. His exploration of the world leads to the discovery that this need must be frustrated. He can have any half of each of the pairs of opposites, never both at once. Fire, ice; height, depth; isolation, society; feeling, thought; clearness, force; aridity, fluidity; too much air or too little; freedom, law; self-possession, possession of the All — man can have only one member of each of these pairs. To have one quality without its opposite is loss of selfhood, not its recovery. The antinomies can never be reconciled, and man is condemned to the either/or of the exploded world. Arnold's thought, both in its imagery and in its conceptual axes, is dominated by the theme of irreconcilable opposites, and the constant appearance of this theme is evidence of his inability to experience the world as other than broken and disintegrated. He is either too hot or too cold, either oppressed by the stuffy air of great cities or suffocating in the thin air on the mountaintop, either tormented by solitude or poisoned by the "unavoidable contact with millions of small [natures]," either alienated from himself by submission to a false law, or driven mad by an empty freedom. He hurries everywhere, like a rat in a maze, trying to find some way of life which will bring together the op-

---

[14] *Essays by Matthew Arnold,* p. 468,

posites and allow him to have the plenitude of an undivided life. Everywhere he finds one extreme or the other, never the central harmony from which all opposites flow. Arnold's search for some power or mode of existence which will mediate between himself and God has failed in every direction. It has turned out to be impossible to remain poised in a calm equilibrium. In spite of himself he falls back into one or another of the opposites and begins again the miserable process of wavering. It seems as if "only death /Can cut his oscillations short, and so/Bring him to poise. There is no other way" (436).

è

One last strategy remains, self-dependence: "Resolve to be thyself; and know that he,/Who finds himself, loses his misery!" (240). Man must cut himself off from everything outside, and seek to reach the "only true, deep-buried [self],/Being one with which we are one with the whole world" (440). It may be that in his own vital depths man still encompasses the divine current. If he could withdraw from all superficial engagements in life he might find himself back in the streets of the celestial city. "Sink . . . in thy soul!" Arnold cries; "Rally the good in the depths of thyself!" (235).

This movement of withdrawal means, in one direction, a total rejection of the social world as it is. Arnold hopes that this self-purification will destroy the inauthentic, and permit the authentic to be revealed. By repudiating the false selves which have engulfed him in the rush and hurry of urban life, Arnold will allow to rise up and fill his inner emptiness the deep buried self which is his real identity. At the same time this will be a possession of the "general life," the soul of the world, the All. To possess the All is at the same moment to reach God. The "spark from heaven" will fall, and man will be the source of true and fresh ideas from God, a "bringer of heavenly light" (447). This light will illuminate human society. When man recovers his deep buried self he will himself become the mediator he has sought in vain.

The buried life is characterized by its individuality, and by the fact that to possess it coincides with possession of the totality of the world, therefore with possession of God. It is undifferentiated, like God himself, and yet it is *my* self, special to me alone. It is the self I recover when I escape from the successions of time and the divisions of space. The buried life dwells in the place where origin and ending are simultaneous. It comes from the depths of the soul in the form of floating, evanescent emotions which resist embodiment in words. It is truly a self — personal, and yet universal. To reach it would be to gain everything I lack.

In attempting to reach the buried life by cutting himself off from every contaminating influence Arnold makes his most frightening discovery, the discovery recorded in "Empedocles on Etna." At this moment the thin strand connecting the soul to the self and the self to God's joy is being cut, and the soul is being transformed into sheer emptiness. Whether by going down toward the deep buried self and finding it "infinitely distant" in the "unlit gulph of himself" (231), or by going up on the mountaintops toward the "unseen God," Arnold finds that by separation from everything external he gets not possession of himself, but the final loss of life and joy. Though he gets clearer and clearer, higher and higher above the turmoil of ordinary life, he does not get one inch closer to the buried self or to the divine spark. No revelation, no intuition, no presence of God is possible. What happens is a progressive evacuation of the soul, a progressive appearance of the true emptiness of consciousness. This emptiness is defined by its infinite distance from the buried self and from the divine transcendence. So Arnold writes, in "Stagirius," of the tragic situation,

> When the soul, growing clearer,
>   Sees God no nearer;
> When the soul, mounting higher,
>   To God comes no nigher . . . (38)

These lines, in their very banality of rhythm and expression, are of great importance to an understanding of Arnold. No other lines express so succinctly the pathos of his spiritual experience. The prosodic slackness of the verses, and the singsong of their feminine rhymes match the terrible spiritual slackness and despondency which is their meaning. In these lines is enacted that drama of the disappearance of God which makes the nineteenth century a turning point in the spiritual history of man. When every external way back to God has failed, the soul turns within, and hopes to reach the unseen self and the unseen God through rejection, simplification, clarification, the climb to the pure heights of the soul's solitude. Surely in its most secret places the soul is still bound to God. But clarity becomes vacuity, and the soul confronts at last the horror of its own nothingness. Though Arnold should climb forever he would not move a cubit closer to God, for no progress is possible along an infinite course, and he remains, however far he goes, an empty desire.[15]

In "Empedocles on Etna" the Greek philosopher-poet recognizes that there is still a thin strand connecting him to the universal life, a narrow channel through which he participates in the "immortal vigour" of earth, air, fire, and water. This "held-in joy" (438) of nature shares in God's life. Empedocles possesses God through nature, but at this very moment the fragile link to God is being broken. In a final attempt to save himself from isolation while there is yet time, Empedocles plunges into the crater. He sacrifices his separate existence for the sake of a total participation in the "All," the universal life which is diffused throughout nature (441).

Empedocles makes the extreme choice of suicide, and saves his soul, but Arnold only imagines this possibility. His rejection of suicide and his remorse for having considered it are clear enough in his repudiation of "Empedocles on Etna" in the "Preface" of 1853. Arnold chooses to remain behind as a survivor into those black times which Empedocles foresees. Empedocles kills himself at the moment he is about to become "Nothing but a devouring flame of thought — /But a naked, eternally restless mind!" (438). He knows that once a man is transformed into intelligence, he is doomed. His body will, after his death, find a home among the several elements from which it came, but mind can find no resting place in the universe. There is nothing it can blend with or find itself reflected in. The man who is all mind is condemned to wandering and solitude. He is irrevocably trapped in the prison of himself, and will remain one of "the strangers of the world" (439).

---

[15] "Stagirius" is also called, in some printings, "Desire." Stagirius, as Arnold explained in a note of 1877, was a young monk to whom St. John Chrysostom addressed "three books" (487). (See Migne, *P.G.*, 47:423–494, for Chrysostom's Πρὸς Σταγείριον.) It is appropriate that Arnold should in the title of this poem make a cryptic allusion to the fourth-century Church Father who inherited the tradition of negative theology and preached so eloquently on the transcendence and "incomprehensibility" of God. A manuscript variant of the crucial lines in Arnold's poem reads: "When the soul rising higher, to God comes no nigher — /When the mind waxing clearer sees God no nearer—" (38).

The last consequence of man's transformation into mind is the worst of all. A man who is wholly mind is unable to die. He is doomed, as in a passage from Eastern philosophy which Arnold recorded in his notebooks,[16] to the horror of the eternal return. His endless life will be a constant repetition of the same failure to escape from himself. He will be born again and again, and in each new reincarnation will seek frantically to be absorbed back into the general life. The elements will reject him as always, for mind is allied to none of them. He will be thrust back into life, again to seek unsuccessfully for death and its obliteration of self-hood. He will endure a perpetual transmigration, and move endlessly across the surface of existence, his "ineffable longing for the life of life/Baffled for ever" (439). As in Kafka's terrifying story of "The Hunter Gracchus," the worst suffering is that man should seek death, and yet be unable to find it. The discovery that man may be condemned to "be astray for ever" (440) is the climax not only of "Empedocles on Etna," but of all Arnold's experience.

The breaking of the unity of man, nature, and God which Empedocles experienced in his time, and which Arnold experiences in ours, is not an isolated event. The moment of Empedocles' death is a true turning point or pivot of history. It is the instant when God withdraws from the world. Only at such a time does man experience himself as complete emptiness. All Arnold's frustrated attempts to escape back to the epoch when man could participate in the divine life have led him inexorably to the discovery of the truth about man's present condition: vacuity and distance are what man, in these bad times, really is. And this vacuity and distance, "the void which in our breasts we bear" (424), can in no way be escaped.

ॐ

Though Arnold's explorations of the world seem to have led to an altogether negative revelation, the discovery that man is about

[16] See *Note-Books*, p. 10: "Let him reflect on the transmigrations of men caused by their sinful deeds, on their downfall into a region of darkness, and their torments in the mansion of Yama; . . . on their agonizing departure from this corporeal frame, their formation again in the womb, and the glidings of this vital spirit through ten thousand millions of passages . . ." (from the *Mānava Dharma Śāstra; or The Institutes of Menu,* tr. Sir William Jones, II [London, 1825], 180, 181).

to become a devouring flame of thought turns out to be an unexpected victory over wavering and vacillation. Arnold finds at last
an assiette and a positive course to pursue.

This reversal is the strange denouement of Arnold's spiritual
adventure. He discovers that true piety consists in accepting the
withdrawal of God. The responsibility of man in a time when
God is absent is to keep the void open for God's return. "I am
nothing," said Arnold in a passage which goes to the heart of his
sense of himself and of his time — "I am nothing and very probably never shall be anything — but there are characters which are
truest to themselves by never being anything, when circumstances
do not suit" (CL, 135).

After trying all the ways in which he might be something,
Arnold resigns himself to being nothing. His work thereby becomes one of the most important testimonies to the spiritual situation of the nineteenth century. Arnold's constant desire for rest,
for peace, is an attempt to refuse the situation in which he finds
himself. He is condemned to be inwardly a void, to be always in
motion, always an unsatisfied desire. He hates to be so "mobile,
inconstant" (III, 96), and tries to believe that it is not a meaningful situation, but a shameful failing, a directionless eddying from
one attitude or allegiance to another. His mobility is an endless
rejection of whatever has been reached for the sake of something
which has not yet been reached, a situation imposed by the disappearance of God and the consequent degradation of all human
values. Arnold's last and most characteristic posture is that of the
man who waits passively and in tranquil hope for the spark from
heaven to fall, "the leaven to work, the let to end" (449). He is
the man "Wandering between two worlds, one dead,/The other
powerless to be born . . ." (302), the man of the no longer and
not yet, a survivor who has persisted unwillingly into a time when
all he cares for is dead. Arnold is fascinated by those who, like
Obermann or the Scholar-Gipsy, withdraw from life and wait out
the interim, isolating themselves to keep their emptiness pure. He
sees in such figures an image of what he should be, of what he *is*,
in spite of all his superficial engagements in life.

The proper literary form for such a situation is the elegy, the
form of expression fitting for a man who sits by the body of a
loved one whose death is the death of a world. In his essay on

Emerson, Arnold quotes, with covert self-application, the Youths' dirge over Mignon from Carlyle's translation of *Wilhelm Meister*. In this passage Arnold's own situation is given in brief: "Well is our treasure now laid up, the fair image of the past. Here sleeps it in the marble, undecaying; in your hearts, also, it lives, it works. Travel, travel, back into life! Take along with you this holy earnestness, for earnestness alone makes life eternity" (IV, 352). Like Goethe's youth, Arnold is an elegist who mourns more than the death of the loved one in his dirge. There are a great many elegies among Arnold's poems. For him the truly poetic situation is the death of a great man or of someone deeply loved. In poem after poem, in "Thyrsis," "Rugby Chapel," "Balder Dead," "The Church of Brou," "Memorial Verses," "Haworth Churchyard," "Heine's Grave," and even in the several elegies for dead pets, Arnold dramatizes in the death of one individual the whole situation of his time. Though the past is dead, it is preserved undecaying in the tomb, and we must fare forth in a present life which draws its meaning from its relation to a treasure which lies in the tomb of the past. The earnestness of a reverent memory that the past joy once existed is all that connects the present to eternity. The mind preserves its relation to this joy by accepting nothing in the whirling quotidian world as a substitute for it. Man's inner emptiness holds the two realms, the authentic and the inauthentic, rigidly apart. In keeping the two realms separate Arnold obeys the divine decision, and participates, through suffering, in the mysterious withdrawal of God from the world. He becomes the void where that withdrawal is completed and maintained.

Arnold's notebooks and his social, literary, and religious criticism are like the elegies in that they too reject the present and embalm a dead wisdom. For "the best that has been thought and said in the world" is no longer current in society. It is kept alive, in these bad times, only by the effort of the critic to "learn and propagate" it, as a corpse might be kept alive by mesmerism. Though the tone of Arnold's prose is so different from that of his poetry, this difference testifies not to Arnold's escape from his earlier situation, but to the resigned acquiescence which he ultimately reaches. Arnold the critic can only say: "God exists, and I know it, but I do not know it directly, and I know too that He would be the only support of a civilization built on eternal values.

Unfortunately, at this particular moment I cannot tell you, and no man can tell you, what those values are. Believe no man now but the one who says, like the prophet crying in the wilderness before the coming of Christ, that the truth is, but not here, not yet." There is only one honest way for the man between two worlds to testify to a God who is no longer immanent. He must testify negatively: by denying truth to whatever is, and by formulas which are so general that though they assert the existence of the absolute do not pretend to contain it in words.

Certain modes of language keep their authenticity in a time when God is transcendent. All of these indicate somewhat vaguely a direction rather than claiming to participate in the reality they name. They are signposts which say: "God is somewhere over that way," rather than labels on a captured truth. In his essay on Spinoza, Arnold makes it clear that for him the value of Spinoza's philosophy lies not in what is expressed in rational language, but only in what that language is "driving at" (III, 364), in what its "tendencies" are. The value of a philosophical system lies not in what is contained in the system, for the trans-human truth can be contained in no system, but in the unspoken orientation of the system. Philosophy is the pursuit of an unattainable object: "A philosopher's real power over mankind resides not in his metaphysical formulas, but in the spirit and tendencies which have led him to adopt those formulas" (III, 363, 364). In the same way Arnold is extremely reluctant to limit the "sweet reasonableness of Jesus" to any dogmatic interpretation. The divine truth cannot be contained in concepts, nor in any maxims which can be extracted from Jesus' own words. The power of Jesus, his "secret," is something which is suggested by his sayings. It is transmitted indirectly and mysteriously, and to each man differently, as a pure inexhaustible well supplies fresh water to all who drink of it. "The very *secret* of Jesus," says Arnold, " 'He that loveth his life shall lose it, he that will lose his life shall save it,' does not give us a command to be taken and followed in the letter, but an idea to work in our mind and soul, and of inexhaustible value there. . . . Christianity cannot be packed into any set of commandments. . . . Christianity is a *source;* no one supply of water and refreshment that comes from it can be called the sum of Christianity. It is a mistake, and may lead to much error, to exhibit any series of maxims, even those of the Sermon on the Mount, as the ultimate sum and formula into which Christianity may be run up" (IV, 218, 216, 217).

In a similar fashion Arnold's expressions of the truths which are the center of his own system are left deliberately vague. They are scrupulously empty phrases. Their repetition empties them further of meaning, and testifies to the fact that though there is something to which the words refer, this something is not named by the words: "make reason and the will of God prevail" (VI, 8); "the best that has been thought and said in the world"; "high seriousness"; "the laws of poetic truth and poetic beauty" (IV, 36); the "Eternal, not ourselves, that makes for righteousness" (VIII, 26); the "stream of tendency by which all things strive to fulfil the law of their being"; "the absolute beauty and fitness of things" (III, 23). "Reason," "the will of God," "the best," "righteousness," "beauty," "fitness," "seriousness" — none of these terms is really given any definition by Arnold. They are the blank places in his discourse which testify to the fact that "we know nothing about the matter, it is altogether beyond us." The empty phrases repeated so often in Arnold's essays are a way of keeping the void open after the disappearance of God. Even when these phrases have a meaning, that meaning is negative. The definition of God as a "stream of tendency," besides using covertly Arnold's basic poetic landscape, is a perfect definition of a God who remains transcendent. Though God is the final end which pulls all things toward him, he is only what things "tend" toward, not what they possess already. Man tends to fulfill the law of his being in the same way as iron filings tend to orient themselves in a magnetic field — if the field is strong enough.

For Arnold the "Eternal not ourselves" at once is and is not the guarantee of human values. It is impossible to say exactly what human values are guaranteed. No one of them can at this time be put into words. Whenever Arnold asserts that he is naming the specific values which a given poet, philosopher, or religious thinker expresses, the reader is aware once again that the Eternal and man have not really been brought together through the words. Instead, their relation has been asserted in such a way as to preserve their separation.

ᢒᢏ

In spite of his penchant for elegy, Arnold faces toward the future as well as toward the lost past. The fact that such men as Wordsworth, Heine, Arthur Stanley, and Thomas Arnold once lived is proof that the joy which they possessed or believed in still exists. The signal-tree which Thyrsis longed to reach is still there as a goal toward which his monodist can direct his life. Thyrsis by dying leaped ahead to his goal, and his death is proof that "the light [they] sought is shining still" (269). In the same way the key phrases in Arnold's essays are witnesses to a truth which may someday return. In these empty linguistic shells a vacant place is kept intact, waiting to be filled, as the Scholar-Gipsy keeps himself uncommitted, waiting for the spark from heaven to strike him into life. In his essay on Falkland, Arnold praises those who "by their heroic and hopeless stand against the inadequate ideals dominant in their time, kept open their communications with the future, lived with the future" (X, 222). Like the Scholar-Gipsy, and like Falkland and his friends, Arnold the critic waits in a purity and emptiness which are carefully preserved by the rejection of falsehood. He waits for the return of God, the descent of the "fugitive and gracious light . . . ,/Shy to illumine" (268). Someday, he believes, "the harmony from which man swerved" will be "made his life's rule once more" (314).

Arnold does not see history as a gradual exhaustion of the original vitality of creation. History is cyclical, the alternation of periods of expansion and periods of concentration, periods of poetry and periods of criticism, times when God is within the world, and times when he inexplicably disappears. The river of time is a circle which returns on itself, so that the same moment of beginning is constantly repeated, as well as the same process of degradation and drying up. Or, rather, as in passages from Wordsworth and Goethe which Arnold knew,[17] time is a spiral. By a "progress en ligne spirale" (CL, 80) history returns at different levels to the same place, so that, though the same ideas, cultures, and epochs of history are repeated, perhaps time will eventually be fulfilled, and the promised land reached at last.

Arnold's conception of history as progress in spiral circlings reveals a fundamental contradiction in his thought. For the spiral

[17] See CL, 80. Lowry has identified the passages to which Arnold apparently refers (CL, 82).

both returns upon itself and does not return upon itself, and a new age of spiritual vitality both is and is not the repetition of an earlier current of true and fresh ideas. The new truths will be the same and yet different, and the dead age will never really return, for the new swing of the spiral is at a different height. Though Arnold recognizes that the old truths are dead, he can never quite bring himself to say that the new truth will be radically different from the old one. He often tries to suggest that it will be merely a reconstruction of the old, though elsewhere, for example in his language about the "spark from heaven," he recognizes clearly enough that the new dispensation will be novel and unpredictable, a bolt from the blue. "Bacchanalia; or, the New Age" (217–221) shows Arnold's horror of the new world he sees coming into being under his eyes — it seems to him a drunken brawl. He remains in the contradictory position of recognizing that the past is dead, without being willing to accept anything which is proposed as a reconstitution of culture. In this he is true to his fear of a premature attempt at reconstruction, and true also to his assumption that not in *his* time will the spark from heaven descend.

We must, Arnold believes, accept the absence of God, have faith in the return of better times, and do our best to beckon toward them. He concludes one of his most famous essays with a Biblical image for our plight. We are destined to wander in the wilderness and never to reach Canaan, but only the lucky live at a time when God is near. Our duty is to testify bravely to the existence of God in a time when our dwelling place is the desert: "It is no such common matter for a gifted nature to come into possession of a current of true and living ideas, and to produce amidst the inspiration of them, that we are likely to underrate it. . . . [T]here is the promised land, towards which criticism can only beckon. That promised land it will not be ours to enter, and we shall die in the wilderness: but to have desired to enter it, to have saluted it from afar, is already, perhaps, the best distinction among contemporaries; it will certainly be the best title to esteem with posterity" (III, 44).

To live in the present in terms of the future will be the best title to esteem with posterity because only through our faith in the future can we find strength to do the proper work of the present, a work of rejection, demolition, dissolution. Man "must be born again" (CL, 109), and in order to be reborn he must first die to the old man and the old world. Balder, in "Balder Dead," sees destruction of the old as necessary to the creation of the new. Only when "o'er this present earth and Heavens/The tempest of the latter days hath swept,/And they from sight have disappear'd, and sunk," shall we "see emerge/From the bright Ocean at our feet an earth/More fresh, more verdant than the last . . ." (128). As in the Yeatsian picture of history, the stages of civilization are, first, creation, then gradual decay, and finally dissolution, followed by a new creation. Only on the ruins of the old can the new be built. Arnold ends "A Comment on Christmas" with a prophetic vision of our time as, like the time of Jesus, " 'the end of *the age*,' 'the close of *the period*,' " and he urges his readers to accept destruction as the price of renovation. "Sometimes," he says, "we may almost be inclined to augur that from some such 'end of the age' we ourselves are not far distant now; that through dissolution, — dissolution peaceful if we have virtue enough, violent if we are vicious, but still dissolution, — we and our own age have to pass, according to the eternal law which makes dissolution the condition of renovation" (XI, 329).

After the failure of every attempt to escape from himself Arnold is left with only one thing to do. He must hover in the void, in one direction waiting for the lightning to strike, the dawn to come, and in the other direction sternly and implacably criticizing all present cultural forms as false. Through his strategy of withdrawal from practical involvement, he attains at last what he has sought from the beginning. Arnold's final platform is the absence of God.

"The Scholar-Gipsy" best expresses this stance. Arnold's gypsy lives in the rhythm of the perpetual round of the seasons. The ebb and flow of nature is his milieu. His constant alignment toward the spark which has not yet fallen gives him stability in the midst of movement, continuity in the midst of succession. Like the Scholar-Gipsy, Arnold postpones indefinitely the attempt to repossess the buried life, but he recognizes that an escape from fluctuation can be obtained by the rejection of every life less than the buried life, and by a permanent orientation toward the infinite distance where it lies.

In the end Arnold no longer faces toward the lost past, but toward the future return of the divine spirit, a return which he can almost see, as he waits in passive tension, renouncing everything here and now for the sake of something which never quite, while he lives, is actual and present. In "Obermann Once More" the ghost of the Swiss solitary tells Arnold that the dawn of the new world is about to come, and the poet, in what is perhaps the most hopeful passage in all his work, imagines that he sees the morning break — but over there, at a distance, high in the mountains where all things begin. The glimpse of this distant dawn, a dawn which still remains just in the future, is the final prize of Arnold's patient repudiation of everything else:

> And glorious there, without a sound,
> Across the glimmering lake,
> High in the Valais-depth profound,
> I saw the morning break. (324)

Gerard Manley Hopkins

Verily Thou art a God that hidest Thyself. (Isaiah, 45:15)[1]

Hopkins begins with a sense that he is isolated from other things by his higher degree of particularization. The stamp which has molded man is of a finer pattern than that which has shaped any other creature. "I find myself," he says, "both as man and as myself something most determined and distinctive, at pitch, more distinctive and higher pitched than anything else I see . . ."[2] It is as if the least differentiated creatures are most like one another and most in harmony with the rest of the universe. The closer man gets back to the "first slime" (P, 73) the more he shares with other things, just as a string which vibrates simultaneously on a whole gamut of notes is in tune with them all. But man is "life's pride and cared-for crown" (P, 73) because, in him, the "starting or stubborn elements" have been "forced forward" "to the one pitch required" (S, 123). Man is exquisitely tuned to oscillate at one frequency and one alone, with no blurring or slipping, no overtones or undertones. Man's shape is drawn with the finest pen. It is most exactly determined, given limits, and its intrinsic pattern is most distinctive.

This "unspeakable stress of pitch" (S, 123) is both a matter of my human nature, which I share with all other men, and a matter of my private selfhood, which I share with no man. But, "whether I speak of human nature or of my individuality, my selfbeing" (S, 122), I am isolated. As a man possessing the common human nature I share something with other men, but I am isolated from

---

[1] The passage from Isaiah is quoted by Hopkins as an epigraph to "Nondum," *Poems*, ed. W. H. Gardner, third edition (New York: Oxford University Press, 1948), p. 43; hereafter cited as "P."

[2] Christopher Devlin, ed., *The Sermons and Devotional Writings of Gerard Manley Hopkins* (London: Oxford University Press, 1959), p. 122; hereafter cited as "S."

all the rest of the creation, for human nature in itself is "more highly pitched, selved, and distinctive than anything [else] in the world" (S, 122). My real isolation, however, is my individuality, my selfbeing. I can find nothing anywhere in the world which bears the least resemblance to my sense of myself: ". . . when I compare my self, my being-myself, with anything else whatever, all things alike, all in the same degree, rebuff me with blank unlikeness; so that my knowledge of it, which is so intense, is from itself alone, they in no way help me to understand it" (S, 123).

Hopkins' expression for self-awareness is the most immediate and inward of the senses. The proof of selfhood is a matter of tasting, not thinking. His version of the Cartesian *Cogito* is: "I taste myself, therefore I am, and when I taste myself I find myself utterly different from everything else whatsoever." No one has expressed more eloquently the pathos of each man's imprisonment within the bounds of his own selfhood:

And this [my isolation] is much more true when we consider the mind; when I consider my selfbeing, my consciousness and feeling of myself, that taste of myself, of *I* and *me* above and in all things, which is more distinctive than the taste of ale or alum, more distinctive than the smell of walnutleaf or camphor, and is incommunicable by any means to another man (as when I was a child I used to ask myself: What must it be to be someone else?). Nothing else in nature comes near this unspeakable stress of pitch, distinctiveness, and selving, this selfbeing of my own. Nothing explains it or resembles it . . . searching nature I taste *self* but at one tankard, that of my own being. The development, refinement, condensation of nothing shews any sign of being able to match this to me or give me another taste of it, a taste even resembling it. (S, 123)

If it would be impossible to explain, to someone who had never tasted them, the taste of ale or alum or clove, so it is even more impossible to explain to another man how I taste to myself. My selftaste is, literally, "unspeakable." Words, those counters of shared experience, will not describe it. Only if another man could be in my skin could he know how it tastes to be me.

Since my selftaste is unlike anything I see outside myself I am led to ask: "From what then do I with all my being and above all that taste of self, that selfbeing, come?" (S, 123).

The proof of the existence of God, for Hopkins, comes not from the "world without," the manifest works of the creation, but from the "world within" (S, 122). Though my selftaste is so distinctive and determined it is for that very reason finite. It might be less or more or otherwise. But "nothing finite can determine its own being, I mean its being as a whole; nothing finite can determine what itself shall, in a world of being, be" (S, 124). Hopkins cannot accept the idea of a spontaneous tendency of brute matter to evolve toward higher forms. To him Darwinian evolutionism is an absurdity. Pattern must be imposed by a patterning force, and this patterning force must have a more highly developed pattern than the pattern it creates, for to create a pattern is a greater perfection than merely to possess that pattern. A differentiated form "can have been developed, evolved, condensed, from the vastness of the world not anyhow or by the working of common powers but only by one of finer or higher pitch and determination than itself" (S, 122, 123).

If man were one of the lesser creatures of the world, a stone or a kingfisher, he could see in the creation many things of higher determination than himself, and could imagine them to be his source. But man looks in vain throughout the creation for anything which could have made him: "And when I ask where does all this throng and stack of being, so rich, so distinctive, so important, come from/nothing I see can answer me" (S, 122). Therefore I must have been made by some being more highly pitched than I — some being outside the creation, who exists as an "extrinsic power" (S, 128). This being is God, the creator of all.

God is defined by Hopkins as a most "exquisite determining, selfmaking, power" (S, 125). Only such a power could have created man. God's infinity and his "selfexistence" (S, 128) consist not so much in his possession of some universal quality like "being," "power," or "will" (though he has these too), as in his possession of the most highly patterned self of all. His pattern is infinitely complex, and therefore he contains in himself the matrices for all possible and actual creatures, including man. God vibrates simultaneously at all possible pitches.

God does not exist as a manifest being, immanent in the works of the creation. When I ask where my throng and stack of being comes from, nothing I see can answer me. When I turn within I find only my own inimitable taste of self. Neither within nor without is God anywhere directly present to me. He exists only as a necessary deduction from my discovery of myself as the most highly pitched entity in the creation. Having created me and the rest of the world, he has apparently withdrawn from his handiwork, and lives somewhere above or beyond or outside, occupied with his own inscrutable activities. He is a God that hides himself. This is the religious situation in which many men of the nineteenth century find themselves, and it is the situation which is described in Hopkins' early poems.

ॐ

> God, though to Thee our psalm we raise
> No answering voice comes from the skies . . . (P, 43)

Hopkins' early poetry, the poetry he burned in the "slaughter of the innocents" after his conversion, expresses the suffering of a man who believes in God, but finds him unattainable, and who finds himself isolated in the midst of a universe which rebuffs him with blank unlikeness.

Such a universe has a double emptiness. There is nothing in it which shows any kinship to man himself, and there is nothing in it which reveals any sign of its creator. It is "like a lighted empty hall/Where stands no host at door or hearth" (P, 43). Distance, vacancy, silence — these are the keynotes of Hopkins' early poetry. To read it is to enter a universe of "abysses infinite," where we gaze in vain "On being's dread and vacant maze," where "Vacant creation's lamps appal," and where "Our prayer seems lost in desert ways,/Our hymn in the vast silence dies" (P, 44, 43).

Repeatedly in his early poems Hopkins dramatizes the situation of exile, self-enclosure, impotence, even of damnation. He writes "A Soliloquy of One of the Spies left in the Wilderness" (P, 25), a poem about Pilate (P, 117), and plans a poem about Judas (P, 278). His alchemist is powerless to change base metal into gold (P, 31, 32); in a startling anticipation of a very late poem he complains that "[His] sap is sealed,/[His] root is dry" (P, 144); and in another poem Hopkins laments that his "prayers must meet a brazen heaven/And fail or scatter all away" (P, 36). In these poems "world is wintering" (P, 40). Hopkins' only hope is escape from the waste land or a transformation of it. He wants to go to "Heaven-haven," where "no storms come" (P, 40), or he imagines, in a number of poems, the miraculous change of the desert into a land of plenty.

The miracle does not happen. The poet remains in a situation of painful immobility — and for a curious, but logical, reason. If man's starting place is his own self-consciousness or taste of himself, then he is doomed to see everything in relation to that self-taste. Wherever he goes he is the fixed point around which things organize themselves, as concentric circles around their center. He is the point of reference from which all things are measured, even the motion of things. He is the sun and node, the zero point, of the universe, and all things swirl in dynamic flux around him, watched from his vantage point of perpetual immobility:

> The earth and heaven, so little known,
> Are measured outwards from my breast.
> I am the midst of every zone
> And justify the East and West;

> The unchanging register of change
> My all-accepting fixèd eye,
> While all things else may stir and range
> All else may whirl or dive or fly. (P, 147)

Hopkins' awareness of his subjectivism is shown by the treatment in his early poems of the problems of perspective. In one poem he says his vision of Oxford is special to him, and declares that the harmony of her architecture is dependent on the point of view from which it is seen. The proportions of a chapel are "falsified/By visual compulsion" (P, 34). In another poem he asks whether the rainbow is subjective or objective, since it depends on the observer for its existence, moves with his motion, and yet after all is made by the sun shining on water (P, 129).

Hopkins' notion of the fixity of subjective consciousness within an evanescent flux of sensations recalls similar ideas in the writings of his tutor at Oxford, Walter Pater. The early Hopkins might well have agreed with what Pater says in the celebrated "Conclusion" to *The Renaissance*. For Hopkins too there is "no . . . permanence in the solid world" (P, 147), and that world seems to dissolve into a stream "of impressions, unstable, flickering, inconsistent, which burn and are extinguished with our consciousness of them." [3] Like Pater, Hopkins might have lamented that

---

[3] Walter Pater, *Works,* I (London, 1910), 235.

"every one of those impressions is the impression of the individual in his isolation, each mind keeping as a solitary prisoner its own dream of a world" (Pater, *Works*, I, 235).

It is not possible to say that Hopkins learned to see the world in this way exclusively from Pater, for Hopkins' most impressionistic or Paterian poem, "A Vision of the Mermaids," was written in 1862, before he went up to Oxford. This poem is an extraordinary swirl or blur of iridescent colors. Everything is in motion, caught up in a process of "swimming," "throbbing," "quivering," or "panting" "undulation" (P, 18, 19), and everything seems about to melt into something else. The poem sets up several sequences of imagery — colors, flowers, gems, sea-shells, music, parts of the body, the sunset, the mermaids — and defines them all in terms of one another, so that there is a bewildering vibration back and forth between one motif and another. This produces a coruscating surface of shimmering color in which all things are continuously transformed in the universal flux.

The meaning of the poem is a melancholy one. The mermaids appear on the surface of the water at sunset, and "in a half-circle watch the sun" (P, 22). They are a personification of the prismatic colors into which the white light of the sun is dispersed, and the sun is a symbol for the divine center, that absent God whose unattainability darkens Hopkins' early poetry. The Nereids, sea-nymphs who are periodically regenerated by plunging into the sun, leap up from the water, fly toward the sunset, and "Thro' crimson-golden floods pass swallow'd into fire" (P, 20). But the mermaids, like the alchemist in "The Alchemist in the City," can get no closer to the sun than "free long looking" (P, 33). The sun sinks beneath the horizon, the color vanishes from the west and from the irradiated waters, and the mermaids, their longing unassuaged, sink back into "the dusk depths of the ponderous sea" (P, 22).

"A Vision of the Mermaids" dramatizes the tragedy of an unsuccessful attempt to escape from the prison of Paterian phenomenalism. If Hopkins begins in a position near Pater's, unlike Pater he can see no way to make a viable philosophy out of it. The early poems do everything they can to transcend subjectivism. The mermaids long for the sun, and the alchemist in his central tower wants to reach "one spot" on the "horizon-round" (P, 32).

If he could reach the horizon he might be on the periphery of a circle around the divine gold sun rather than fixed in his subjective prison. The poet who finds himself the "unchanging register of change" looks with admiration on the "lovely ease in change of place" of the birds, clouds, and brooks which circle effortlessly around him (P, 147). He wants to pass beyond the situation of being always the center of the world. He would far rather circle around God. So, in another poem, the poet prays: "Let me be to Thee as the circling bird . . ." (P, 37).

How can this longing be transformed from prayer into reality? God has hidden himself, and the poet lives in a world where things are different from one another and from him. All is disharmony and dispersion.

ₔ

There is one possible mode of harmony and only one. By gradually extending the empire of this principle Hopkins puts the world together, escapes his isolation, and conquers that proximity to God for which he longs.

The poet's conversion to Catholicism does not give him overnight all that he wants. Even if he had permitted himself to write poetry just after his conversion the decade of slow construction recorded in the journals, letters, and early papers would have been necessary to the explosion of "The Wreck of the Deutschland" and the great nature poems. The putting together of the all-embracing harmony which makes these poems possible is like certain of Hopkins' meticulous landscape drawings.[4] In these it is not a question of sketching rapidly a composition which is filled in with details later. Hopkins can work only through the gradual ordering of minute details, each one of which is another tiny area conquered from chaos and blankness. This habit of microscopic vision is a basic characteristic of his mind, and exists in tense opposition to his desire to have a vision of the whole.[5] Not with universals but

---

[4] See Humphry House and Graham Storey, eds., *The Journals and Papers of Gerard Manley Hopkins* (London: Oxford University Press, 1959), Plates 19, 23, 24; hereafter cited as "J."

[5] See, for example, the memories of Hopkins of an old lay brother who had been with him at Stonyhurst: "One of Hopkins's special delights, said the brother, was the path from the Seminary to the College. After a shower, he would run and crouch down to gaze at the crushed quartz glittering as the sun came out again.

with individuals must he begin, for he is confronted at the beginning with a world of unrelated particulars. Only at the very end
will the harmony of the whole be revealed. In all realms this harmony is approached by the extension of a single sovereign principle.

This principle is *rhyme*. For Hopkins "any two things however
unlike are in something like" (S, 123), and insofar as any two
things are like one another they may be said to rhyme. In Hopkins' analysis of selfhood it seemed that any two things would
either be tuned to exactly the same pitch, and hence be in harmony, or would be so unlike one another that there could be no
relation between them. In a universe of unique particulars all
would be dissonance. But two strings not tuned to the same pitch
may still be in resonance, as are middle C and the octave above, or
as are C and G. Such notes are harmonic chimes of one another,
bound together by a subtle mathematical relation in their vibra-
tions. This relation may be found everywhere in the universe: in
words which resemble one another without being identical, in
trees or clouds which have similar but not identical patterns, and
so on. The universe, even though no two things in it are exactly
alike, is full of things which rhyme, and by extending the range of
observed rhymings who knows how many things may ultimately be
brought into harmony?

The principle of rhyme is first announced by Hopkins in an
undergraduate essay of 1864 ("On the Signs of Health and Decay
in the Arts" [J, 74–79]). There the comparison of two or more
things is said to "include the principles of Dualism, Plurality,
Repetition, Parallelism" (J, 74). In his dialogue "On the Origin
of Beauty" (1865) Hopkins shows that all forms of beauty, in nature and in art, are different versions of the relation which holds
between unlike things which are similar. This relation may be
defined in its most general form by saying: "Likeness therefore implies unlikeness . . . , and unlikeness likeness" (J, 105). Therefore, says Hopkins, "all beauty may by a metaphor be called rhyme
. . ." (J, 102).

Another motif recurs in Hopkins' undergraduate essays and in
the dialogue on beauty. This is the opposition between *diatonism*

'Ay, a strange yoong man,' said the old brother, 'crouching down that gate to
stare at some wet sand. A fair natural 'e seemed to us, that Mr. 'opkins' " (J, 408).

and *chromatism*. Diatonism is any change in things, any difference between part and part, which is abrupt. Chromatism is change or difference which is sliding or transitional (J, 76, 84, 104). At times it seems that this is a mere neutral principle. Things may shade into one another, or exist as nodes of pattern or hue separated by a gulf. Each kind of change leads to its own characteristic form of beauty, the chromatic style of Newman or the diatonic style of Carlyle (J, 76).

Elsewhere Hopkins shows a distinct preference for diatonic beauty. The reason for this is related to his rejection of the Paterian philosophy of flux. In an early essay on "The Probable Future of Metaphysics" (1867) Hopkins associates chromatism with the idea that the variety of beings in the world has developed spontaneously from the shapeless slime. In an evolutionary world species are not eternal types, like beads on a string. They are momentary and accidental coagulations of universal matter, developed without a break from the species below, and ready to flow at any time to a higher species in the perpetual stream of development. "To the prevalent philosophy and science," says Hopkins, "nature is a string all the differences in which are really chromatic but certain places in it have become accidentally fixed and the series of fixed points becomes an arbitrary scale" (J, 120). Such a view of nature is "a philosophy of flux," based on the ideas "of a continuity without fixed points, not to say *saltus* or breaks, of development in one chain of necessity, of species having no absolute types" (J, 120). Against this Hopkins puts his conviction that organization can only be imposed downward from a realm of predetermined types. He therefore opposes to evolutionary chromatism the diatonic philosophy which he calls in this essay "Platonism" or "Realism."

In Hopkins' choice of diatonism over chromatism more is at stake than the question of the direction from which the patterning force comes. In a chromatic world nature is a string, a series of infinitesimal points at all distances from one another. Each note, species, or color merges imperceptibly into its neighbor. All is "bleared, smeared" (P, 70), and "self in self" is "steepèd and pashed" (P, 104) in the perpetual flux. As a result, rhyming is impossible, and in a world where rhyme is impossible no principle of ordering remains. The individuals do not have sufficiently sharp or permanent patterns to have a relation of chiming with one another, and the intervals between species or individuals are not fixed enough to establish a regular system of harmony.

Against this "prevalent philosophy of continuity or flux" Hopkins sets his version of Platonic realism. It is a version which is calculated to preserve the possibility of rhyme. Against the floating species of evolutionism Hopkins proposes the existence of inalterable types at definite intervals, intervals which have a mathematical relation providing for a grand system of harmony. Hopkins' later doctrine of inscape, his feeling for pattern, and for the relation between patterns, is implicit in this early description of a world of imperishable forms at fixed distances from one another in the scale of being:

The new Realism will maintain that in musical strings the roots of chords, to use technical wording, are mathematically fixed and give a standard by which to fix all the notes of the appropriate scale: when points between these are sounded the ear is annoyed by a solecism, or to analyse deeper, the mind cannot grasp the notes of the scale and the intermediate sound in one conception; so also there are certain forms which have a great hold on the mind and are always reappearing and seem imperishable, such as the designs of Greek vases and lyres, the cone upon Indian shawls, the honeysuckle moulding, the fleur-de-lys, while every day we see designs both simple and elaborate which do not live and are at once forgotten . . . It may be maintainable then that species are fixed and to be fixed only at definite distances in the string and that the developing principle will only act when the precise conditions are fulfilled. (J, 120)

The principle of rhyme and a choice of diatonism over chromatism permit Hopkins to reconstruct the world. Diatonism guarantees the stability of patterns and of the intervals between patterns, and rhyme is the name for the relation between two patterns which chime like notes in a musical chord.

ॐ

The etymological speculations of Hopkins' early diaries are the first examples in his work of a reconstruction of the world through discovery of rhymes.

Words seem a perfect example of the disorder of the world. The universe is a collection of unrelated things, and words are a collection of unrelated names for those things, or for their qualities and actions. The best order that can be given to words is the arbitrary alphabetical sequence of the dictionary.

But some words sound like one another. The basis of Hopkins' etymological hypotheses is the idea that if words are similar in sound they will also be similar in meaning. Hopkins assumes that a group of words of similar sound are variations of some *ur*-word and root meaning. Among the earliest entries in his undergraduate diaries are lists of words of similar sounds with comments on their similarity of meaning. Hopkins already shows great virtuosity in finding out inner connections of word-sounds and meanings:

> *Grind, gride, gird, grit, groat, grate, greet,* κρούειν, *crush, crash,* κροτεῖν etc. Original meaning to *strike, rub,* particularly *together*. (J, 5)

> *Crook, crank, kranke, crick, cranky.* Original meaning crooked, not straight or right, wrong, awry. (J, 5)

> *Drill, trill, thrill, nostril, nese-thirl* (Wiclif etc.)
> Common idea piercing. (J, 10)

Each word for Hopkins is a node or pattern of linguistic energy. It has its own unique tone, but it is at a fixed interval from other similar words and is therefore able to chime with them, both in sound and in meaning. He notes that the sequence *"flick," "fleck," "flake"* is like a chord of variations on the same sound and meaning, each change in vowel producing a different tone in the chord and a new nuance in meaning (J, 11). Here the sequence is produced by a variation in the vowel, but a variation in consonant can produce the same kind of sequence, as in "the connection between *flag* and *flabby* . . . *flick* and *flip, flog* and *flap, flop*" (J, 12).

As Alan Ward observes (J, 499), such word lists are miniature poems, or poems in the rough. Though Hopkins may have been confirmed in his feelings for the interrelations of words by his study of Greek poetry, Old English alliterative verse, and Welsh *cynghanedd,* it is only a step from *"skim, scum, squama, scale, keel"* (J, 12) or *"spuere, spit, spuma, spume, spoom, spawn, spittle, spatter, spot, sputter"* (J, 16) to such characteristic passages of "vowelling" in his poetry as "bow or brooch or braid or brace, láce, latch or catch or key to keep/Back beauty" (P, 96), or "Earnest, earthless, equal, attuneable, ' vaulty, voluminous, . . stupendous/Evening" (P, 104).

The fundamental method of Hopkins' poetry is to carry as far as it will go, into every aspect of his verse, the principle of rhyme. His early diaries show him interested in words in themselves, without reference to the grasp they give of the external world. This develops into a view of poetry as a kind of music of words. What is important in poetry is neither the expression of the inner self of the poet, as some romantic poets had thought, nor the imitation of something in the external world, as Aristotle had said. Poetry, like music, is an autonomous art. Music makes patterns of sequences of tones. Poetry makes patterns of sequences of words. The notes in a piece of music tell us nothing about the external world, and the meaning of a word in poetry is also part of its substance, no more related to the outside world than its sound. Hopkins, in a famous letter to Bridges, affirms the similarity of music, painting, and poetry. Pattern is the one thing needful in all three: ". . . as air, melody, is what strikes me most of all in music and design in painting, so design, pattern or what I am in the habit of calling 'inscape' is what I above all aim at in poetry."[6]

It might seem, from the sentences which follow in the letter just quoted, that Hopkins means by "inscape" uniqueness of pattern, what Duns Scotus calls the *haecceitas* of a thing, its ultimate principle of individuality: "Now," says Hopkins, "it is the virtue of design, pattern, or inscape to be distinctive and it is the vice of distinctiveness to become queer. This vice I cannot have escaped" (L, I, 66). Poetry would seem to be a matter of making a pattern of words which is so highly pointed that it is unlike any other pattern of words. A poem should have the same unspeakable stress of pitch that a man's selftaste has.

This is not really the case, nor does inscape here mean anything like Scotus' *haecceitas*. The inscape of a poem, far from being a unique, unrepeatable pattern, is the design which different parts of the poem share, and which detaches itself from the chiming of these parts. Hopkins' theory of poetry is much like his theory of music.

In his experiments in musical composition Hopkins was most interested in melody and rhythm (see J, 457–497). The kinds of music which most fascinated him were those, like canon and fugue,

[6] Claude Colleer Abbott, ed., *The Letters of Gerard Manley Hopkins to Robert Bridges* (London: Oxford University Press, 1955), p. 66; hereafter cited as "L, I."

in which a basic pattern is stated and then developed in overlapping variations. In a late letter to Bridges, he made explicit the central idea of his theory of music: ". . . the air becomes a generic form which is specified newly in each verse" (L, I, 305). The inscape of a piece of music is that generic form, present in all specifications of itself, but usually visible only through our perception of their similarity or rhyming.

The inscape of poetry is analogous. Poetry is not distinguished from other uses of words by its intensity or complexity of meaning. The meaning is there only as a necessary support for the pattern. The design of a piece of verse would be just as visible, perhaps more visible, to someone who did not know the language in which it was written. Such a person would be better able to recognize the precise sound-shape of the words. The inscape is this shape of sound: "Poetry is speech framed for contemplation of the mind by the way of hearing or speech framed to be heard for its own sake and interest even over and above its interest of meaning. Some matter and meaning is essential to it but only as an element necessary to support and employ the shape which is contemplated for its own sake. . . . Poetry is in fact speech only employed to carry the inscape of speech for the inscape's sake — and therefore the inscape must be dwelt on" (J, 289). The inscape is a pattern of sound, and therefore "verse is . . . inscape of spoken sound, not spoken words, or speech employed to carry the inscape of spoken sound . . ." (J, 289). As in music the inscape is the generic form which recurs in varied forms throughout the composition, so the inscape of verse is a pattern of sound which may be repeated, and usually must be repeated in different specifications in order to detach it from its particular manifestations. The basic method of poetry as of music is repetition, the repetition of different forms of the same inscape. This inscape must echo and reverberate through the poem in order to become visible. The term "inscape," at least as Hopkins uses it in his theory of poetry and music, means just the opposite of the Scotist *haecceitas*. It means that which a number of particulars have in common rather than that which one particular shares with no other: "Now if this [the dwelling on the inscape for its own sake] can be done without repeating it *once* of the inscape will be enough for art and beauty and poetry but then at least the inscape must be understood as so standing by itself that it could be copied and repeated. If not/ repetition, *oftening, over-and-overing, aftering* of the inscape must take place in order to detach it to the mind and in this light poetry is speech which afters and oftens its inscape, speech couched in a repeating figure and verse is spoken sound having a repeating figure" (J, 289).

Hopkins begins in his early diaries with a fascination for the relations of word-sounds, and is led step by step to develop an intransigent theory of poetry. The letters to his fellow-poets, Bridges, Patmore, and Dixon, are full of professional discussions of the craft of poetry. He seems to be more interested in technical questions of rhythm, meter, and form than in questions of content. The striking peculiarities of his verse are ways of attaining the utmost refinement of inscape. There must be nothing flaccid or lax, no blurring or smudging of the pattern, but each part of the poem must be wound up to an intense stress or pitch of distinctiveness. Comprehensibility, grammar, and clear logical form may be sacrificed to the attainment of strongly marked pattern. Sprung rhythm, internal rhyme, consonant chiming, alliteration, "vowelling" — all the special characteristics of Hopkins' verse, all his "stress . . . on the naked thew and sinew of the English language" (L, I, 267, 268), are there to achieve the highest possible degree of what he called "brilliancy, starriness, quain, margaretting" (J, 290). These techniques of patterning work together to produce the extraordinarily sinewy and burly texture of Hopkins' poetry, its heavy substance and strongly marked inner structure, as of bones, veins, and tendons binding together a body and making it one. His description of "Harry Ploughman" might be taken as a description (and example) of the texture of his own poetry:

> Hard as hurdle arms, with a broth of goldish flue
> Breathed round; the rack of ribs; the scooped flank; lank
> Rope-over thigh; knee-nave; and barrelled shank —
>   Head and foot, shoulder and shank —
> By a grey eye's heed steered well, one crew, fall to;
> Stand at stress. (P, 108)

If Hopkins' poetry had substance without sinew it might be a loose heap of words turned things. The inner structure, the stress between word and word, makes the poem stand "as a beechbole firm" (P, 108). Each word or group of words is a stress of individualized sound. The poem is made up of the stresses between these stresses. It is "one crew" of parts all working together in harmonious unison. "Starriness" and "margaretting" are not attained through sharpness or crispness of pattern. They are attained only through the *repetition* of a crisp pattern which makes its inscape visible, as stars shine together against the dark field of the night sky, or as flowers bloom together in a meadow.

Hopkins' theory of poetry as the inscape of speech for the inscape's sake has organized and conquered the whole realm of words through an extension of the principle of rhyme. Different modes of echoing mean that all words taken together form an elaborate system of interrelated reverberations. Poetry is the exploration and exploitation of these possible "figures of sound" (J, 289). But in defining poetry in this way Hopkins has cut it off from the poet and from nature. He has reduced one kingdom to order only at the cost of isolating it as radically as a man's selftaste isolates him from the rest of creation. The figures of sound in poetry have an order and harmony of their own, but these are without relation to the poet. The poet is a skilled craftsman, coldly manipulating materials which remain external to him. His own personal distinctiveness remains untouched, unexpressed, uncommunicated.

ප්‍ව

Perhaps the principle of rhyme can be applied in other areas beside that of the sounds of words. It would be some satisfaction to find more order in the apparent chaos of the world, even if that order were to have no relation to the solitude of the self.

Alongside Hopkins' interest in the sounds of words there is an equally strong interest in the way words are a means of possessing nature. Hopkins knows that detached observation of nature is not a possession of it. There must be a strong grappling action on the part of the mind to go out and meet the powerful energy with which things are what they are. There must be what he calls a "stem of stress between us and things to bear us out and carry the mind over" (J, 127). This stem of stress is words.

If Hopkins makes the assumption that words of similar sound are derived from a common root, he also assumes that this root

word is often onomatopoeic. Though he knows that the onomatopoeic theory of the origin of language is somewhat discredited, he
is led by his feeling for words to reaffirm it. "In fact," he says, "I
think the onomatopoetic theory has not had a fair chance" (J, 5).
If words are arbitrary labels for things, they give no substantial
possession of the things they name, but are only signs pointing in
the direction of their meaning. An onompatopoeic word imitates
in its substance and inscape the substance and inscape of the thing
it names. Hopkins does not particularly like words which are a
superficial echo of the sound of a thing. The words which most
attract him are those which are a kinesthetic imitation of their
meaning, and give a deep bodily, muscular, or visceral possession
of the world. For him language originates in a kind of inner panto-
mime, in fundamental movements of the body and the mind by
which we take possession of the world through imitating it in ourselves. Words are the dynamic internalization of the world.

Browning, too, likes words which, as they are pronounced, give
a kinesthetic possession of the thing named. But Browning is most
interested in the rough, solid weight of matter which all things
share; consequently his onomatopoeic words are thick with harsh
consonants expressing the universal density of material substance.
Hopkins, on the other hand, has a strong sense of the variations in
texture, substance, and structure of the things of the world. He
likes the way a word, by the uniqueness of its inscape, is a perfect
match for one certain quality in the world and one only (though
this quality may of course be repeated in different phenomena).
Interspersed among the lists of words of similar sounds in Hopkins' early diaries are places where he experiments with the way
a single word opens up a precise area of the world, and gives him
a way to seize it: "Altogether *peak* is a good word. For sunlight
through shutter, locks of hair, rays in brass knobs etc. Meadows
peaked with flowers" (J, 47).

The inscape of words for the inscape's sake, words as a means
of grasping the things of the world — these two apparently incompatible orientations toward language exist side by side. Though
there does not seem to be any way in which they can be harmo-
nized, nature still seems worth studying and naming. What characterizes Hopkins' sense of nature and of the way nature may be
grasped in words?

At first it seems that there are no pervasive principles of organization. What pervades are principles of isolation.

The descriptions of nature in the journals are written from the point of view of scientific detachment. Even when it is a question of describing a subjective reaction to a scene this is given as objectively as the rest of the data: "I felt an instress and charm of Wales" (J, 258); "I felt a certain awe and instress . . ." (J, 249). Hopkins distinguishes his selftaste from the flavor of anything he sees, and this self-possession makes it possible for him to see things clearly. He remains himself; the cloud or waterfall remains itself, seen at a distance. Hopkins does not want to melt into the totality, to expand into vagueness, or to lose the sharp taste of himself in a possession of the "all." He will describe what is there to be seen, as completely and accurately as possible, and finds little difference in value between one phenomenon and another. He takes as much interest in analyzing the precise way in which steam rises from a cup of cocoa, as in describing the grandest sunset (J, 203, 204).

If the spectator remains spatially detached from what he sees, there is a temporal separation too. The journal entries were written up, sometimes more than a year after the experience, from notes taken at the time. There is always a more or less prolonged interval between the actual experience and its final crystallization in language.

A distance also exists between one item in the scene and another. The diaries and journals are made up of detached entries, each existing by itself and separated by a gap from those around it. There is no attempt to connect them together in some over-all pattern of meaning. The basic principle of the journals is the assumption that each cloud or tree or waterfall is unique, and must therefore be described in an individualized pattern of words.

Everywhere evident in the journals is an amazing linguistic virtuosity. Hopkins invents with effortless ease new combinations of words for each nuance of the appearances of nature. A respect for the idiosyncrasy of each thing is the law of this virtuosity. Hopkins views every item in nature as unique in pattern, texture, and inner structure, and it would seem that no more can be said about his journals than this. His celebrated terms, "inscape" and "instress," seem, when they apply to natural things at least, to refer, respectively, to the individual pattern of a thing and to the inner energy which upholds that pattern. The journals are the record of a long series of isolated encounters with unique inscapes. Each encounter already implies the insight into nature expressed in the octave of "As kingfishers catch fire," the idea that each thing in nature has its own distinctive note or tone, which it manifests in being itself, "doing" itself, "going" itself (P, 95). Nothing is like anything else, except in being "arch-especial" (P, 84).

੩੭

If this is Hopkins' nature and his relation to nature, disorder and isolation predominate. But certain motifs recur in the journals; there *are* principles of organization. Though for Hopkins no two clouds or trees repeat each other, certain qualities are characteristic of his apprehension of nature, and tend to be present in whatever he is describing.

Hopkins' nature, like Browning's, is solid and substantial, but unlike Browning's it is highly colored. Hopkins has a great sensitivity to the colors of things, and to nuances of colors within colors. Sometimes a journal entry will be chiefly an attempt to record exactly the colors of a scene: "Sunset over oaks a dapple of rosy clouds blotted with purple, sky round confused pale green and blue with faint horned rays, crimson sparkles through the leaves below" (J, 146).

Hopkins' nature is different from Browning's in still another way. Like Browning he has a powerful sense of the thick weight of matter, and can say of his view from a high place over a landscape to the sea: "I marked the bole, the burling and roundness of the world" (J, 251). For Browning, however, the burliness of matter is a more or less undifferentiated quality shared by all things alike. Hopkins sees the burliness of things as a manifestation of the inner energy of being which upholds things. This energy Hopkins calls "instress." "All things," he writes in his notes on Parmenides, "are upheld by instress and are meaningless without it" (J, 127). Though all things share the instress of being this intrinsic energy manifests itself differently in each thing. Each thing has its own kind of burliness.

This can be seen in several different ways. If Hopkins is sensitive to nuances of color he is equally sensitive to nuances of surface pattern. Each object has its own skin of rough or smooth, grainy, serrated, polished, or any one of a thousand other textures. Texture is one evidence of the inner energy of instress. Along with texture goes pattern. Each thing in Hopkins' world has the utmost freshness or sharpness of outline, and this distinctiveness of pattern is carried down to the tiniest detail. There is no blurring or softening of edges. Each thing stands out vividly as though it were surrounded by perfectly translucid air, and air can reach all the surfaces of even the smallest and most intricate object, so abrupt is the frontier between the object and its surroundings:

> Wild air, world-mothering air,
> Nestling me everywhere,
> That each eyelash or hair
> Girdles; goes home betwixt
> The fleeciest, frailest-flixed
> Snowflake . . . (P, 99)

Color, texture, pattern — all are evidence of the energy of instress which upholds the world. Perhaps even more important is Hopkins' sense of what might be called inner texture, the interior structure and grain of a thing. The inner quality of each thing is just as distinctive as is its exterior pattern or surface. Each object is held in being by a system of strands, ropes, or sinews, lines of force which reach everywhere from the center to the surface, organize the thing, and make it one. The unity of an object lies not so much in its exterior pattern or texture, as in the way every morsel of it is strung together and held in tension by an intertwined pattern of bones, muscles, and veins.

Hopkins sees even the most apparently slack and unstructured objects, like clouds or water, as roped and corded together by a tense network of lines of energy. The image of strands, wires, stems, or veins recurs in his work. He speaks of "wiry and whitefiery and whirlwind-swivellèd snow" (P, 59), or of a "skeinèd waterfall" and "veinèd . . . peá blossoms" (J, 50), or describes a cloud as "roped like a heavy cable being slowly paid and by its weight settling into gross coils" (J, 212), or tells of a lark's song which is a "rash-fresh re-winded new-skeinèd score" which "whirls" "off wild winch" in "crisps of curl" (P, 72). Even air, which seems so insubstantial and dispersed, is experienced as something which is woven together and falls in folds like a garment: "when I came out I seemed to put . . . on [the wind] like a gown . . . , I mean it rippled and fluttered like light linen, one could feel the folds and braids of it" (J, 233). When Hopkins wants to describe a state of mental slackness, an inertia of the spirit approaching despair, he falls naturally back on his sense of the way a thing should be strung together with lines of stress: "darkness and despair. In fact being unwell I was quite downcast: nature in all her parcels and faculties gaped and fell apart, *fatiscebat*, like a clod cleaving and holding only by strings of root" (J, 236).

Burliness and ropes of energy within, color, texture, and pattern without — these make up each created thing for Hopkins. If instress is the pervasive energy of being, upholding all things equally, inscape is the name for this energy as it manifests itself in the distinctive structure of things, both inner and outer. Hopkins was delighted to find in Jamieson's dictionary that "there *is* a word *scape* which is another form of *skep* or *skip* | basket or cage." [7] His own word inscape always implies the sense of a skeletonlike structure which captures and encloses an inner principle of life, as a basket or cage may imprison a wild bird of the air. The inner pressure of instress, permeating nature, is the true source of inscape, and brought into the open by it. The word is *in*-scape, the outer manifestation or "scape" of an inner energy or activity — not external pattern which is pleasing to the eye as design: "All the world is full of inscape and chance left free to act falls into an order as well as purpose: looking out of my window I caught it in the random clods and broken heaps of snow made by the cast of a broom" (J, 230); "Fineness, proportion, of feature comes from a moulding force which succeeds in asserting itself over the resistance of cumbersome or restraining matter" (L, III, 306). Inscape is the expression of a force which lives in change, and waterfalls which flow or clouds which are "moulded ever and melted across skies" (P, 74) as much possess inscape as a tree of distinctive pattern. Some of Hopkins' drawings are startlingly like Chinese paintings. Their swirling whirlpool patterns seem to manifest an organizing power sweeping through all things and bending them to shape. Similar expressions occur in his journals and poems:

[7] Claude Colleer Abbott, ed., *Further Letters of Gerard Manley Hopkins,* second edition (London: Oxford University Press, 1956), p. 286; hereafter cited as "L, III."

"whorlèd wave, whelkèd wave" (J, 56); "weeds, in wheels, shoot long and lovely and lush" (P, 71). Hopkins' nature, as much as Coleridge's or Whitehead's, is the locus of a vital process, the explosive meeting-point of a creative *élan* and the stubborn resistance of matter.

The offspring of this marriage of spirit and matter are all different from one another. The instress of being, though it is everywhere the same, has a mysterious tendency to express itself differently each time it subdues cumbersome and restraining matter to pattern. The physical conditions molding snowflakes are always similar, but no two snowflakes, among the untold billions which have fallen, have ever been exactly alike.

It is not altogether true to say that Hopkins sees nature as a collection of dissimilar particulars. All things, for him, share certain qualities: specificity of color and texture, sharpness of pattern, tenseness of inner structure, energy of being, and Hopkins' vision of nature is something "counter, original, spare, strange" (P, 74), something special to him. What all things share for Hopkins is precisely the fact that they are all different, each one unique in structure, shape, and color. Or, rather, things are alike in two ways: all possess the energy of being, "throughout one with itself" (J, 130), and all are distinctive in pattern. All things have instress and inscape. If instress makes things alike, the fact that all things are full of inscape means that things are alike in being unlike. But though this seems to permit nothing in nature analogous to the relation of rhyme in poetry and music, rhyming can actually be found everywhere in Hopkins' nature.

ત્ર

Hopkins rarely describes a single example of a natural phenomenon: not one tree, branch, cloud, flower, wave, or hill, but groups of similar ones together. Everything is multiple, and descriptions are most often in the plural:

Aspens blackened against the last light seem to throw their scarcer leaves into barbs or arrowheads of mackerel patterns. (J, 141)

As kingfishers catch fire, dragonflies dráw fláme,
As tumbled over rim in roundy wells
Stones ring . . . (P, 95)

Hopkins' nature is not made up of groups of the same thing side by side in helter-skelter disorder. Each thing is echoed by other examples of the same thing, and these exist not at random but in a patterned field, spaced at regular intervals, like notes on the diatonic scale.

Sometimes Hopkins sees this as a matter of nodes or beads of energy against a neutral background. Each node is a tiny whorl of power turning in on itself, but bound by lines of force to other nodes which exist around it, spaced at definite distances. Flowers growing in a field, stars shining in the sky — these are the most frequently recurring examples of this motif, but many other versions occur. Hopkins speaks, for example, of "the fields of heaven covered with eye-brights. — White-diapered with stars" (J, 17), of "reflection of stars in water. — Pointed golden drops. Gold tails" (J, 37), of "the flocks of villages/That bead the plain" (J, 39), of "grey cloud in knops" (J, 46), or in "a drift of spotty tufts or drops" (J, 138). Fields are "noted with primroses" (J, 55), or "pinned with daisies" (J, 134), and Hopkins tells of "round leaves of lime relieved on darkness within" (J, 140), or of elms "hung and beaded with round buds" (J, 230). Orchards are another example of patterned nodes of energy, and are "knopt/With green-white apples on the bough" (J, 68), and at night he sees the moon "roughing the lake with silver and dinting and tooling it with sparkling holes" (J, 184). Each such passage creates a characteristic space. Whether it is stars, villages, clouds, flowers, leaves, buds, or moondints, that space is an area full of a diffused material energy which has coagulated or crystallized into centers of organized force located at regular intervals. These centers stand in patterned order within the same field, and they all resemble one another. They are like a choir singing in unison.

There are other quite different ways in which Hopkins sees nature as a structured whole. Instress is a creative energy sweeping through the universe and manifesting itself in the inscapes of things. Inscape, however, may be not the pattern of particulars within a whole, but the structure of the whole. So Hopkins says of a nightscene in which moon, clouds, and trees are in harmony: "I read a broad careless inscape flowing throughout" (J, 218). Instress weaves nature together and makes it one, as the strands in a rope or web are one, or as the threads in a piece of cloth are unified. The woven cloth itself is inscape. To see nature as a web or cloth is still to see it as organized on a principle of recurrence or rhyme, but it is the crisscross threads or the repeated figures in the carpet which rhyme rather than self-enclosed spirals of force. There is more emphasis on the lines of energy joining things, as molecules are bound together in a magnetic field, than on the patterns of the isolated molecules themselves.

Hopkins' writings contain many descriptions of nature as a web or network of forces, or as contiguous forms repeated, like patterns on a quilt. He invents a bewildering variety of expressions for nuances of difference within this single intuition of the way nature is organized. He describes "lines of the fields" "like threads in a loom" (J, 23), or "moonlight hanging or dropping on tree-tops like blue cobweb" (J, 23), or clouds "like mesh'd and parted moss" (J. 66), or in "a white rack of two parallel spines, verte-brated" (J, 138), or in "long pelletted sticks" (J, 138), or in "oblique flake or thread" (J, 138), or in a "mesh of thready chalk-ing" (J, 151), or shaped "in leaf over leaf of wavy or eyebrow texture" (J, 184). He creates with inexhaustible fertility new phrases for clouds, each one catching a new shade of texture or shape, but all having in common a vision of clouds as organized like threads in a cloth or waves on the sea.

Leaves, branches, flowing water, and many other things are seen as patterned in the same way. Hills are " 'fledged' with larches which [hang] in them shaft after shaft like green-feathered arrows" (J, 183). Cornfields are "laid by the rain in curls like a lion's mane" (J, 183). Mountains "run like waves in the wind, ricked and sharply inscaped" (J, 180). A lawn shows "half-circle curves of the scythe in parallel ranks" (J, 143). Hopkins describes a sea "with little walking wavelets edged with fine eyebrow crispings, and later nothing but a netting or chain-work on the surface" (J, 184), or "just-corded near sides of the waves rising like fishes' backs" (J, 184), or "a webby space of foamy water" (J, 177), or a cascade "inscaped in fretted falling vandykes in each of which the frets or points, just like the startings of a just-lit lucifer match, keep shooting in races, one beyond the other, to the bottom" (J, 177).

"Parallel ribs" (J, 53), webs, nets, tucks, braids, meshes, "rows of loaves" (J, 189), "combs of fish-bones" (J, 147), "long flutings"

(J, 141) — the image of nature as woven in a crisscross pattern, or in parallel rows like waves permeates Hopkins' journals, and is the dominant motif in his vision of nature. The instress of being oscillates momentarily at a single frequency, and flows over a mountain, through the ocean, or through the shapeless water vapor which is the stuff of clouds. When it does this it leaves its mark behind in the form of rows of nearly identical trees, waves, or clouds in patterned repetition, like a textile design, or like a row of pots from the same mold. The random clods and broken heaps of snow made by the cast of a broom prove that all the world is full of inscape not because the snow falls into a single pattern, but because it falls spontaneously into a repeated pattern of parallel curves. The hand of the creator works in lavish abundance and produces an inexhaustible supply of any one species. All these examples rhyme.

If this is the case, what is inscape, and what becomes of the idea that everything in Hopkins' nature is unique? It may be true that each thing has its *haecceitas,* the individualizing form which distinguishes it from all other members of the same species, but this is not what most interests Hopkins, neither in his journals nor in his nature poems. What fascinates him is the inner law or pattern which any one oak tree, cloud, or flower shares with similar trees, clouds, or flowers. This is its inscape. Though any member of the species possesses its inscape, this pattern is most easily detached to the mind when we can see a large number of individuals side by side in echoing order. The inscapes of nature are in this exactly like the inscapes of rhythm and rhyme in poetry. Hopkins almost always speaks of more than one example of a thing whose inner law or inscape he is identifying: "The bluebells in your hand baffle you with their inscape, made to every sense" (J, 209); ". . . the curved type [of chestnut blossoms] is easily seen in multiplicity which in one might be unnoticed" (J, 136); "Found some daffodils wild but fading. You see the squareness of the scaping well when you have several in your hand" (J, 208). This process of comparison of similars by which inscape is detached to the mind is given succinctly in a curious description of a crowd of spectators in the Sheldonian theater: "Was happily able to see composition of the crowd in the area of the theatre, all the heads looking one way thrown up by their black coats relieved only by white shirt-fronts etc: the short strokes of eyes, nose, mouth, repeated hundreds of times I believe it is which gives the visible law: looked at in any one instance it flies" (J, 139).

Hopkins' experience of nature as inscaped leads to a vision of the universe as a great multitude of strongly patterned things. There are throngs of each kind, and all of each kind are alike, and rhyme, but each throng is apparently unrelated to any of the others. Nature is organized, but only partially.

৯০

There are further modes of rhyme which extend the echoing from the species to the whole, and show nature, in the end, as like a great chorus singing a harmonious composition of many voices.

Hopkins is interested not only in the inscapes of things but in the conditions which make those inscapes visible to a spectator. Only at certain times can he "catch" the windhover, or the "Greek rightness" of the beauty of the bluebells (J, 231). Most people never see inscape at all: "I thought," says Hopkins, "how sadly beauty of inscape was unknown and buried away from simple people and yet how near at hand it was if they had eyes to see it and it could be called out everywhere again" (J, 221). Inscapes are usually called out only to a man who is completely alone: "Even with one companion ecstasy is almost banished: you want to be alone and to feel that, and leisure — all pressure taken off" (J, 182); ". . . with a companion the eye and the ear are for the most part shut and instress cannot come" (J, 228). Even if he is alone inscapes may be hidden. A freshness and virginity of the mind, and a lack of preoccupation with past or future are necessary if he is to take in the true immediacy of sensation: "Unless you refresh the mind from time to time you cannot always remember or believe how deep the inscape in things is" (J, 205). Though the mind is fresh and undistracted inscapes still may not be caught. Certain seasonal changes bring into the open inscapes which have been there all along, but hidden. Spring, says Hopkins, "is the time to study inscape in the spraying of trees, for the swelling buds carry them to a pitch which the eye could not else gather" (J, 205). Both mind and nature must be poised to just the right pitch for the stem of stress to leap out and bear things over to the mind.

Even with the most ideal conditions the catching of inscapes is no "ecstasy," no merging of seer and thing seen in which all distinction is lost. Hopkins' description of the proper relation between self and world is another version of rhyming. The interior and exterior inscapes must echo one another, not merge. The stem of stress is not a current of force which unifies subject and object. It is the reverberation which shows that two separate things, the mind and what it knows, are in resonance.

This echoing of mind and world Hopkins calls a "canon of feeling." The mind and its object sing the same tune, but at a distance. The mind protects its integrity by taking a shape of feeling which is like the inscape it sees, and yet holds it at arm's length. If it cannot do this it may either be unable to feel the inscape, or, at the opposite extreme, the inscape may rush into the mind and carve out its own pattern there with painful precision, threatening the distinctiveness of the spectator's selftaste. The awareness of the need for a canon of feeling usually comes to Hopkins when there is a failure of correspondence between mind and world, a time when, like Coleridge in "Dejection: An Ode," he sees, not feels, how beautiful things are:

. . . the warm greyness of the day, the river, the spring green, and the cuckoo wanted a canon by which to harmonise and round them in — e.g. one of feeling. (J, 135)

To see the long forward-creeping curls of the newly-leaved trees, in sweeps and rows all lodged one with another down the meadow edge, beautiful, but distraction and the want of the canon only makes these graceful shapes in the keen unseasonable evening air to 'carve out' one's thought with painful definiteness. (J, 136)

When the canon of feeling exists there is a perfect echo in the mind for the inscape outside, and the empire of rhyme has been pushed one step further — from chiming of similar trees, clouds, or flowers to a chiming of the mind with what it beholds.

ॐ

A third form of chiming will complete the work of integration, and show all nature as one great chorus of voices echoed in canon by the shapes of feeling in the mind.

Hopkins has an extraordinary power to recapture the original strength with which a word can catch a certain reality and give an intimate possession of it. He wants words to be heavy with material substance, and speaks of "pregnant phrases" like "*putting the stone*" and "to *put* things, i.e. to represent them" (J, 19). For most men, a word like "put" flits airily through the mind, pale and abstract. Hopkins feels it, even in abstract uses, with all the force of the muscular action it suggests.

Along with this ability to make words a means of participating in the life and substance of the world goes another linguistic habit. Side by side with phrases like "putting the stone," there are, in the early diaries, such phrases as: "Thick-fleeced bushes like a heifer's ear. . . . Yew-trees, like ears, in hedges" (J, 38). With such phrases Hopkins begins to discover the power of simile and metaphor.

At first the transferred word seems to be simply an adjunct of the power to use words freshly. Metaphor, like the kinesthetic word, is a way of catching the perpetually renewed juice and joy of nature, and a way of expressing the uniqueness of each thing. Ordinary words have become dulled with much using, and when we say them we are like those that, having eyes, see not, and, having ears, neither hear nor understand. The metaphorical word breaks through the barrier of blunted words which hides reality. Suddenly we feel the unnamable sensation again, in all its vividness, as fresh as it was on the first day of creation.

A good part of Hopkins' genius with words lies in his command of metaphor. His mind spontaneously produces striking and original metaphors in lavish abundance. These metaphors transfer words from one area of reality to another and use the transferred term as a means of opening up an aspect of the world which would else remain hidden. To give two examples from hundreds in the journals, Hopkins makes the reader see again both "the tide that ramps against the shore" (P, 72), and that other almost indescribable element, "ethery flame of fire" (J, 130). Each time it is the brilliant metaphors which give a new hold on elemental reality:

I noticed from the cliff how the sea foots or toes the shore and the inlets, now with a push and flow, now slacking, returning to stress and pulling back. (J, 221)

Saw a lad burning bundles of dry honeysuckle: the flame . . . was brown and gold, brighter and glossier than glass or silk or water and ran reeling up to the right in one long handkerchief and curling like a cartwhip. (J, 219)

Sometimes Hopkins' metaphors are explicit and developed, as when he says the swollen river is "like ropes and hills of melting candy" (J, 212), or as when he describes clouds as "like the eggs in an opened ant-hill" (J, 219). Just as often, however, the metaphor is "buried." What appears at first to be merely an apt word draws its aptness from the fact that it is a metaphorical transfer. So Hopkins describes elms "hung and beaded with round buds" (J, 230), as if the elm twigs were strings on which the buds might be threaded like gems, or he speaks of the "gnarls of the water" (J, 223), as if the wave were the bole of a tree. Almost all the descriptions of clouds, which make up such a large part of the journals, are based on metaphors, and Hopkins has an admirable power to invent new metaphors for each new cloud shape or texture. Clouds are "honeycomb," "damask," "shuttles," "mealy," "lawn valences," "grassy tails," "mackerel," "spines," "lock-of-hair," "gauze," "curds and whey," "chains," "fleece-of-wool," "jointed sprigs," "scarf-ends," "blown-flix feather," "fish-pellets," "dolphin-backs," "white napkins," "sopped cake," "bats or rafts or racks," "puff-ball," "tossed pillows" (J, 27, 36, 67, 138, 139, 142, 148, 153, 165, 206, 207, 240, 260; P, 111) — the list could be extended almost indefinitely, and the same word or phrase rarely recurs.

Hopkins' use of metaphor seems part of that movement of his mind toward the expression of the absolute particularity of things. Each cloud is different from all other clouds, and this difference can best be expressed by a fresh importation of a word from another realm. But this respect for the idiosyncrasy of each cloud shape is only accomplished by confession that the cloud, though unlike all other clouds, is like something else — the cobweb, pillow, or meal to which it is compared. Metaphor is another form of rhyme!

If metaphor is rhyme the chiming of natural objects can be extended indefinitely. All unlike things are in something alike. Hopkins displays the linguistic implications of this fact in a strange passage in the early diaries. The passage begins with a series of phrases, each one of which is a single metaphor for a single thing. Each time Hopkins seeks the exact phrase to catch an inimitable reality. He is experimenting with the power of metaphor to pin down the object: "Pencil buds of the beech. Lobes of the trees. Cups of the eyes. . . . Bows of the eyelids. Pencil of eyelashes. Juices of the eyeball" (J, 72). Suddenly the passage reverses itself, and instead of one metaphor to catch the exact nuance of one thing, there follows a list of metaphors for a single thing, metaphors which get more and more fantastic, but which all have equal validity: "Eyelids like leaves, petals, caps, tufted hats, handkerchiefs, sleeves, gloves" (J, 72). If eyelids are like all these things, there seems no reason why the list could not be extended indefinitely. Anything can be metaphorically compared to anything else, and, if this is the case, then all things rhyme. The bewildering multiplicity of different metaphors for clouds or eyelids are examples of the way the possible rhymings of natural things can be extended to make all things metaphors of all things.

ε∾

Hopkins' vision of nature as organized and bound together in a universal harmony leads him to another definition of poetry. Poetry is not the inscapes of words for the inscapes' sake, but an attempt to catch in words the inscapes of things and their interrelation. The business of poetry is the "representing [of] real things" (J, 126), and the tense rhythm of Hopkins' poetry is not so much an attempt to make poetry musical as it is an attempt to echo in words the rhythm of instress as it sweeps through the cosmos, creating inscapes everywhere.

In the poem called "Pied Beauty" (P, 74) all the characteristics of Hopkins' poetry of imitation are present in great purity and concentration. An examination of this poem will show all the modes of rhyme working together to express a vision of the creation as harmonious multiplicity.

PIED BEAUTY

Glory be to God for dappled things —
  For skies of couple-colour as a brinded cow;
    For rose-moles all in stipple upon trout that swim;
Fresh-firecoal chestnut-falls; finches' wings;
  Landscape plotted and pieced — fold, fallow, and plough;
    And áll trádes, their gear and tackle and trim.

All things counter, original, spare, strange;
  Whatever is fickle, freckled (who knows how?)
    With swift, slow; sweet, sour; adazzle, dim;
He fathers-forth whose beauty is past change:
        Praise him.

Piedness, like beauty and like rhyme, is a relation between things which are similar without being identical. This relation organizes "Pied Beauty" at every level. Each individual thing, the poem says, is pied or dappled. Though it is all one thing, it is different from one place to another. A dappled or brinded cow is all the same cow, but in one place it is one color, in another another. This difference may exist in time or in space. A thing may be pied by having rose-moles, or by changing from swift to slow, from adazzle to dim.

Hopkins does not speak of individuals in "Pied Beauty." Each thing is given in the plural: skies, trout, chestnut-falls, finches' wings, fields, and trades. Only in the line: "All things counter, original, spare, strange" does Hopkins make explicit the notion that there is a "pied" relation among members of the same species. No two brinded cows are exactly alike, though they are all cows. So the rhymelike relation of pied beauty holds between all cows, skies, trout, and so on. But only groups of dappled things have visibly the relation of likeness in difference which makes them echo and chime, and therefore the poet says: "Glory be to God for dappled things."

Nature in "Pied Beauty" lives in movement and change. The sky's pattern of couple-color is only momentary; the trout are swimming; the chestnuts have fallen, and are like that evanescent and glowing thing, a fresh firecoal, perfect image of a dynamic energy which is spending itself by its very act of being itself. The finches fly; the landscape is plotted and pieced — what is fallow one year is "plough" or "fold" the text; and each trade, with its special gear and tackle and trim, is an activity of making and changing the world.

Though nature here lives in dynamic change it never repeats itself. Like the lark's song it "goes on . . . through all time, without ever losing its first freshness, being a thing both new and old" (L, I, 164). No two couple-colored skies, trout, or finches' wings are alike. They are counter to one another, original, "spare," in the sense that a spare part stands by itself, and strange, in the sense that they cannot be wholly known in terms of past experience. Though the poet can recognize that it is a cow, a trout, or a sky, to some degree it evades his categories and appears strange, a strangeness which makes him recognize that he does not understand how it is what it is. "Who knows how?" he asks, which may mean both: "How can I tell you all the ways in which things can be fickle or freckled?" and also: "It is impossible to understand how this comes about." This failure to understand the thing fully, though it registers on the senses, opens up the gap between sensation (or "simple apprehension") and perception (or "understanding") which is so important to Hopkins as a Scotist (see S, 174). When a thing appears strange, man becomes aware that to place it in a concept does not do justice to its uniqueness and originality. He comes to see the coarseness of such words as "cow," which must do duty for all cows, though each cow, as can be seen in the case of brinded cows, is in some sense original and strange. To name a thing rightly the poet must go beyond nouns, for the noun will tell how a thing is like other things of the same species, but not how it is different from them. Beauty lies in the copresence of the two, unlikeness with likeness, sameness with difference.

Words for the qualities of things, adjectives, are in one way more anonymous than nouns, since they can be applied indifferently to all things which share the quality in question. The Thomistic account of the way we know God in nature moves, as does "Pied Beauty," from perception of specific objects through perception of qualities which many species share to recognition of the God who fathers all. In another way qualities are closer to the true strangeness of sense-experience, for they exist at a level beneath that of concepts and a little closer to the immediacy of sensation. They are also more likely to suggest in their very sound the experience they name. "Freckled," "sweet," "sour," "brinded," "adazzle," "dim" — each of these seems to have been picked at least partly for the way its sound echoes its sense. Every quality-word names a special attribute of the sensible world, an attribute which may recur, but each time with its special "counterness" to other qualities. All words are general, but adjectives have a radically different form of generality from nouns.

What is the relation between qualities and pied beauty? Adjectives measure degrees of similiarity or difference within a certain category of experience. Qualities are a matter of more or less. Even colors are more or less intense, and other qualities are even more unequivocally a matter of degree. Something sweet is more or less sweet than other things, and sweetness exists only by comparison with its opposite, sourness, just as swiftness suggests slowness; brightness, dimness. Since sweetness and sourness can be measured by the same means (taste) they are in some sense the same. They are another case of sameness and difference. Adjectives are words by which we name the way all things are "counter, original, spare, strange," and so Hopkins is quite right to say "Glory be to God" for "Whatever is fickle, freckled, (who knows how?)/With swift, slow; sweet, sour; adazzle, dim."

His identification here of objective qualities (swift, slow) with qualities which much more depend on our senses for their existence (sweet, sour; adazzle, dim) shows his desire to bring spectator and scene together. The freckledness of a thing, its fickle disparity from itself in space or in time, is its way of having being, but this is immediately possessed through our sense-knowledge of the thing. Adjectives name qualities in things which are both subjective and objective at the same time.

Hopkins wants us to think that all words have this intimate participation in the nature of what they name. Reality has simultaneously the dynamic activity and instress of verbs, the solidity and substantiality of nouns, and the sensible vividness of adjectives. Signs of this are his fondness for participles, and his use of one part of speech in place of another. He likes to build up groups of words which form a single linguistic unit combining adjective (often as participle), verb, and noun. Sometimes nouns are turned into adjectives. The whole compound forms one word possessing the powers of all the major parts of speech. In "Pied Beauty" we have "landscape plotted and pieced" and "fresh-firecoal chestnut-falls." The phrases are dappled or pied and express in their structure the fact that the world is made up of groups of dissimilar things which are nevertheless similar and rhyme.

The rhymelike relation of beauty in the poem is more than that within individuals which are pied, or even among individuals of the same species which are the same and yet different. There is also a relation of piedness between different species, expressed here, as in the journals, by metaphor. The chestnut-falls are like fresh-firecoals, the skies are like a brinded cow, the moles on a trout are like roses, but likeness is not identity. We understand the chestnut-falls by means of the firecoals, but only by realizing that they are different as well as alike. Behind them both there is some general quality or qualities which they participate in, but each differently, just as all cows, however unique their pattern of color, participate in the species "cow."

All things are like one another in one way or another. All things rhyme. In this poem the things mentioned are, or can be, some shade of red or brown: skies, brinded cows, rose-moles on trout, firecoals, chestnuts, finches' wings, landscape, and even the gear and tackle of a trade such as shoemaking. The list of dappled things for which Hopkins says "Glory be to God" forms a "chord of colour" (J, 260). And all the things in the list share the quality of being pied; they are thus in yet another way rhymes of one another. Any two of the pied species taken together form a larger piedness enclosing the smaller one.

It is not an accident that two of the examples (sky and landscape) are universal in scope, for clearly the whole world, taken as a unit, is a case of pied beauty. The poem includes the four universal elements: earth, water, air, and fire. The fields, trout, skies, and firecoals are synecdoches, and the poem is cosmic in scope. Every piece of nature is in itself pied, and at the same time it is part of a larger and more inclusive piedness. The relation of sameness and difference, of the one and the many, of general and specific, pervades the whole universe.

The structure of the universe is echoed and imitated by the sound and structure of the poem. The relation of sound between the pairs of quality-words ("swift, slow"; "sweet, sour"; "adazzle, dim") is one of piedness. The pairs of words are opposite in meaning, and yet similar in sound, and this similarity in sound leads us to seek a relation of meaning. The poem's structure of sound, like its structure of meaning, and like the universe it imitates in little, is a complex network of relations of likeness in difference — pied beauty within pied beauty, and larger cases of pied beauty embracing smaller. There is an elaborate pattern of alliteration, assonance, and rhyme which creates a canon of sound repeating in another form the meaning of the poem. The relation between the two stanzas is pied. There is some carry-over in rhymes from stanza to stanza, but some of the rhymes are unique to their stanzas. The first three lines of the second stanza are like either half of the first stanza, but the last two lines are different. The poem is what Hopkins called a "curtal-sonnet" (P, 10). It is like an ordinary sonnet, but different, and so the relation of this sonnet to the usual sonnet is another case of pied beauty. The poem's structure of rhythm and sound seems to be all for the purpose of making the poem a model in little of the universe it names.

What of the first line of the poem and the last two? The poem describes the universe as a total harmony of pied beauty, but only as a way of praising God, its creator. What is the relation here between God and nature?

At first it appears that the first line of the poem and the last say much the same thing: a pious thanks to God for having provided this wonderful world of linked multiplicity: "Glory be to God for dappled things," and "Praise him." But at the end of the poem the statement relating the pied universe to God has a new meaning, for the poem has shown that the most inclusive case of the relation of sameness and difference is the relation of God to the universe. The creator and the creation rhyme.

God's beauty is "past change." He is single and eternal, not at all fickle or freckled, but this God of undifferentiated oneness has fathered forth the pied universe. Its seeds have lain in him, ready to flow forth and spring into material existence. God and the universe have the relation of pied beauty. The eternity, changelessness, and unity of God are set against the temporality, spatiality, self-division, and changefulness of the world, but one is the source of the other, and "like father, like son." The creation must somehow be made in the image of its progenitor.

Perhaps the ultimate case of piedness is God himself. If God is in one sense certainly "past change," beyond it altogether, and not pied beauty but the beauty of the One, in another sense God's perfection lies in the fact that he is the origin of difference, the meeting place of opposites. He may be past change not in the sense of transcending it, but in the sense of being beyond it toward the future as the goal of earthly changing beauty. All things flow from God and flow back to God. God is the most wonderful example of piedness, for in him the most radically different things, diversity and unity, are reconciled and made one.

If this is the case, we can see why Hopkins says "Glory be to God for dappled things" and "Praise him." The poem works from the first line back around to an apparent repetition of it through an exploration of the nature of pied beauty in the middle lines.

The last line is really repetition with a difference — it rhymes in meaning with the first line. At the end of the poem the reader knows that he should not simply say "Glory be to God for dappled things," blandly and neutrally. By understanding the dappled or pied nature of the universe he best understands the nature of God, though God's beauty is past change, and this knowledge makes it possible to praise God. The whole poem leads up to the two words which make up the final half line. These two monosyllables, in the sprung rhythm of the poem, take up as much time as seven syllables elsewhere in the poem. They are like two great concluding chords in a fugue: *Praise him.*

Why is it that God is best known through dappled things? The answer is double, epistemological and ontological at once. Man's only knowledge is through sensation. A single pure homogeneous sensation would be invisible, inaudible, without taste or feeling. The sensation would be there but man would not be aware of it. Man knows through comparison. Even the uniqueness of his self-taste can only be known by seeking similar tastes in the world. The need to set two different sensations against one another in order to know either one of them is the chief mark of man's epistemological limitation, and one reason he cannot know God directly. Piedness is necessary to knowledge of the world, and God cannot be known directly as the pure One.

There is more to the matter than this. In one sense the dappledness of things is a sign of their deficiency from the wholeness of God, for things which are fickle and freckled are differentiated in space and change in time, waver and are not consistent with themselves. In another sense pied things are the best earthly image of God's perfection. Something unpied is only one limited thing, one quality, one action, and that thing, quality, or action is a far cry from the infinite perfection of God in his fullness. But pied beauty is precisely a *concordia discors,* a unifying of diversity, and thereby a finite image of the infinite God. Hopkins may well say "Glory be to God for dappled things," for it is through fickle, freckled things, things which combine in themselves "swift, slow; sweet, sour; adazzle, dim," that limited mortals can best know God, and, by knowing, rightly "praise him."

Hopkins' long exploration of nature in his journals and poems begins with a respect for the integrity of concrete particulars. It culminates in the notion that "the world is charged with the grandeur of God" (P, 70). His vision of nature as pied beauty is balanced in tension between a strong sense of the uniqueness of each thing and a feeling of the omnipresence of God in all things. Inscapes, canons of feeling, metaphors, God as father of all — the principle of rhyme has been extended further and further until the whole universe, in itself and in its relation to its maker, is revealed as "like notes of a scale and a harmonic series" (S, 200). Poetry, to borrow further Hopkins' phrases for the angelic concord, is "like the playing on these notes, like the tune, the music" (S, 200). There are innumerable possible poems, but each of them is another exploration of the music of creation, another tune played on the scale and harmonic series of things.

࿋

How can the two theories of poetry in Hopkins be reconciled? A poetry which imitates the objective chiming of nature has nothing to do with a poetry which is the autonomous inscape of the sound of words. Neither of these two forms of poetry seems to have anything to do with the poet's distinctive selftaste. It was the painful isolation of that selftaste which drove the poet to his exploration of the way things rhyme. He can write word music of absolute beauty or poems of the most exquisite perfection imitating nature; he will still be as isolated as ever.

The case is even worse than this. There is in Hopkins a *third* theory of poetry, incompatible with the other two, and developed with the same fullness and cogency.

In a letter to Bridges, Hopkins affirms his belief that there is in the bee a specific shaping power which drives it to build naturally in hexagonal figures. This shaping power is like the instinct which makes birds of the same species sing the same song (L, I, 281). If the bee, the cuckoo, and the thrush express their inscapes in an outward form, so do all other natural things. The sharply patterned outward form which manifests inscape Hopkins calls the "sake," "that in the thing by virtue of which especially it has [its] being abroad, and that is something distinctive, marked . . ." (L, I, 83). All created things possess inscape. But this inscape manifests itself in what things *do,* as the bee makes honeycomb, as thrush and cuckoo sing their specific songs. Each mortal thing "deals out that being indoors each one dwells," and this is its way of being (P, 95).

The poet is a mortal thing too, and his way of existing is like that of any other created being. The bee builds honeycomb. The stone rings. The poet poets. In writing poetry the poet expresses the innate pattern of his inscape. Poetry, like other arts, is creative not in the sense that it makes something out of nothing, but in the sense that it imposes upon the raw material of its art, words, a distinctive and highly pitched pattern. This pattern is a copy or echo of the pattern of selfhood in the poet. The poet, like other creative men, sheds multiple replicas of himself, as a dandelion sows seeds on the wind: "But MEN OF GENIUS ARE SAID TO CREATE, a painting, a poem, a tale, a tune, a policy; not indeed the colours and the canvas, not the words or notes, but the design, the character, the air, the plan. How then? — from themselves, from their own minds" (S, 238).

Hopkins' discussions of music, poetry, and painting in his letters and journals presuppose the notion that a unifying inscape is necessary to make a work of art "beautiful to individuation" (L, I, 210). The source of this unifying inscape is the artist himself. The artist and his work are different versions of the same inscape. They rhyme. Like a man who leaves his fingerprints on everything he touches, the poet makes his poems, whether he wishes to do so or not, in such a way that they match the pattern of his individuality. The poet is like a stamp or mold which shapes everything according to its design.

In this third theory of poetry Hopkins commits himself to the notion that all authentic art is original and distinctive. "The effect of studying masterpieces," he wrote in a famous letter, "is to make me admire and do otherwise. So it must be on every original artist to some degree, on me to a marked degree. Perhaps then more reading would only *refine my singularity*" (L, I, 291). A true artist is not one example of a species, but "each poet is like a species in nature (*not* an *individuum genericum* or *specificum*) and can never recur" (L, III, 370). The individualized spirit in the artist is the cause of the individualized pattern or inscape which is the one thing necessary in art. In the sonnet to Henry Purcell, Hopkins praises Purcell's music because it is the direct expression of the composer's "arch-especial . . . spirit." Purcell's music is "none of your d — d subjective rot" (L, I, 84) because it expresses something deeper than subjective feelings. Just as a seabird opening his wings unintentionally reveals the "quaint moonmarks" on his under-plumage which stamp his species, "so Purcell, seemingly intent only on the thought or feeling he is to express or call out, incidentally lets you remark the individualising marks of his own genius" (L, I, 83). Hopkins likes inscape in art not for its own sake but because it is a revelation of the distinctive quality of the poet's soul. In Purcell's music it is "the forgèd feature" he likes best, and this distinctiveness of design is "the rehearsal/Of own, of abrúpt sélf" (P, 85). In another poem on music and architecture Hopkins says again that the harmony of art is an expression of the harmony of the artist's mind:

> Who shaped these walls has shewn
> The music of his mind,
> Made known, though thick through stone,
> What beauty beat behind. (P, 163)

This third view of poetry seems at last to have freed the self from isolation. The poet can make copies of his own selftaste which are comprehensible to others, and we can, through art, come to understand the "own, abrupt self" of a genius like Purcell. Those who are not artists may still remain imprisoned in themselves, but art is the liberating power which allows some men to go outside themselves, and even to find something which does not rebuff them with blank unlikeness. The artist has the pleasure of seeing himself mirrored everywhere in his own work. Like God, he has the power to emanate from himself in waves of creative instress which sweep through unformed matter and shape it in his own image. Whereas God possesses the molds of all possible created things, the poet oscillates at but one frequency, and can shape things in but one pattern. Each poem is the casting forth of a new "sake," a new expression of the inscape of the poet.

How can poetry do three things at once? There seems to be a contradiction at the heart of Hopkins' theory and practice of poetry. One kind of poetry permits an escape from the prison of selfhood, but this mode of poetry seems to have no relation to the other kinds. How could poetry express at once the inscapes of nature, the inscapes of words, and the inscape of the poet? Each of these realms has been organized in itself by an extension of the principle of rhyme, but there seems to be no rhyming between the three realms. Hopkins' exploration of language has led him to discover a division and disintegration of his world, for he finds that words can be used in three radically different and incompatible ways.

Hopkins' thinking so far has seemed like the gradual putting together from dispersed fragments of a great edifice, a bridge spanning the universe and binding its multiplicity into oneness. At the last moment the project has collapsed, and left three great towers standing in isolation from one another. Where is the power which will complete the construction of a unified world?

ટ&

The first hint of a principle of unification is given in Hopkins' undergraduate notes on Parmenides. The brief essay on words, which comes earlier in the same notebook (J, 125, 126), is an expression of Hopkins' insight into the three-faced nature of words. Each word expresses a subjective state, is a thing in itself, and names something in the objective world: "A word then has three terms belonging to it, ὅροι, or moments — its prepossession of feeling; its definition, abstraction, vocal expression or other utterance; and its application, 'extension,' the concrete things coming under it" (J, 125). The essay can offer no way of reconciling these three aspects of a word. It vibrates back and forth between the concepts of language which would be suggested by each one. The notes on Parmenides suggest the beginnings of an escape from this dilemma.

There is one thing, Parmenides assumes, which self, words, and nature all share: they have being, they exist, they *are*. If this is the case the fact that a thing, word, or thought *is* may be more important than what it is. Authentic thinking and authentic language are possible only if thought and words participate in the nature of what is thought or named. This participation may be in the fact that thoughts, words, and things all have being. "Being" here must be thought of as univocal, not equivocal; the word must mean the same thing when applied to each of the three realms. Hopkins quite rightly picks out the concept of the univocity of being as central in Parmenides. His notes are more than a partial translation and commentary. They contain at crucial points statements of Hopkins' own thought, statements whose importance is suggested by the fact that they are among his earliest uses of the terms "inscape" and "instress." Hopkins has an intuitive comprehension of Parmenides' vision of things, and he sees in that vision an escape from the conflict involved in his own triple view of words. His comments on Fragment Two of Parmenides' poem are an affirmation of his own sense of the univocity of being. Being, for Hopkins as for Parmenides, holds nature together, and makes language and our knowledge of nature possible. The instress and inscape of individual things and the drama of our intercourse with things are diverse manifestations of the universal power of being, and Hopkins, like Parmenides, has felt its permeating power. "But indeed," he says, "I have often felt when I have been in this mood and felt the depth of an instress or how fast the inscape holds a thing that nothing is so pregnant and straightforward to the truth as simple *yes* and *is*" (J, 127).

This passage is of great importance in Hopkins, for it marks the first step toward a final unification of his world. Being brings everything together, and is "throughout one with itself" (J, 130). Being must not be considered an abstraction, a passive condition of existing. Being is a vital force, a creative energy. It is spoken of repeatedly in Hopkins' notes on Parmenides as "the flush and foredrawn" (J, 127), as an energy which collects things together and gathers them into one. Being is instress, that which foredraws things and holds each thing fast in itself. Since this gathering power is the same everywhere, the most important characteristic of any individual thing is that which it shares with all other things, namely, the fact that it is. The best way of recognizing this is not by a description of the distinctive individuality of a thing but by a "simple *yes* and *is*." These are the fundamental words, the words on which the very possibility of language depends. Unless we can say: "Yes, there is something rather than nothing," or: "It is," we can say nothing at all, for all words are merely different ways of saying "yes" and "is." As the instress of being lies behind all the particularities of inscape, so the verb "to be" lies behind all words and makes them possible. The instress which foredraws all nature is the same as the "is" which gathers all language together, for language is a manifestation of thought, and thought, like external instress, is a foredrawing act. As Parmenides said: "Τὸ γὰρ αὐτὸ νοεῖν ἔστιν τε καὶ εἶναι: The same thing exists for thinking and for being." [8] The mind's act of thinking is one manifestation of the stress of being. The inscapes of nature are another. Language is the stem of stress which carries the mind over into things and things over into the mind. The same energy of being manifests itself in thinking, in language, and in things. Therefore all language is an expression of this ubiquitous being, and being and thought are the same: "To be and to know or Being and thought are the same. The truth in thought is Being, stress, and each word is one way of acknowledging Being and each sentence by its copula *is* (or its equivalent) the utterance and assertion of it" (J, 129).

The stress of being in the mind in answer to the stress of being in nature is necessary not only for universal statements but also for particular judgments. Unless there were being within and without, joined by the stem of stress of language, we could not even say "This blood is red," much less "Blood is red," for all speech is another way of expressing the "it is" which is the fundamental foredrawing act of the mind. What the mind knows is always and in every act of knowing the instress of being. All particularities are merely "husks and scapes" (J, 130) of this: ". . . the mind's grasp — νοεῖν, the foredrawing act — that this is blood or that blood is red is to be looked for in Being, the foredrawn, alone, not in the thing we named blood or in the blood we worded as being red. . . . Everything else is but a name . . . or disguise for it — coming to be or perishing, Yes and No . . . , change of place, change of colour" (J, 129).

Nature, language, and thought are seen by Parmenides as the same in being, and this concept of being suggests to Hopkins a way in which he can unify the realms which seemed destined to remain disparate. Nor is selfhood left out of this universal gathering. An individual inscape in nature is a mode in which the instress of being appears; the selfhood of a man is another scape or husk of being. Every created thing, man included, is an approach toward being, limited and baffled by its degree of nonbeing. The distinc-

[8] G. S. Kirk and J. E. Raven, *The Presocratic Philosophers* (Cambridge, 1957), p. 269.

tion between external objects and subjective selves is unimportant.
All things, including man, are modes of the one being: "For the
phenomenal world (and the distinction between men or subjects
and the things without them is unimportant in Parmenides: the
contrast is between the one and the many) is the brink, limbus,
lapping, run-and-mingle/of two principles which meet in the scape
of everything — probably Being, under its modification or siding of
particular oneness or [of?] Being, and Not-being, under its siding
of the Many" (J, 130).

In the Parmenidean fragments Hopkins as early as 1868 finds
a way to unify self, words, and world. This does not mean that he
is a Victorian Presocratic, depending for the very keystone of his
thought on Parmenides, although it is true that his reading of
Parmenides is a turning point in his thinking, and prepares him
for the decisive encounter some years later with Scotus and St.
Ignatius.

ॐ

The central principle of Catholicism, as Hopkins sees, is the
doctrine of the Incarnation. For him a basic difference between
Catholicism and Protestantism is their divergent interpretations of
the Sacrament of Communion. Protestantism has moved from the
doctrine of transubstantiation toward the idea that the communion service is a commemoration of the Last Supper. The bread
and wine are signs or symbols pointing toward something which
remains absent. The Zwinglian interpretation of the Eucharist
prepares the way for the situation in poetry and in life which is
characteristic of nineteenth-century man, and is experienced by
Hopkins before his conversion.[9] The thinning of the meaning of
the communion service spreads out to diminish the divine meaning
of the whole world. The heavens no longer declare the glory of
God. The deity retires to an infinite distance, and the universe
becomes drained of spiritual presence and meaning. The creation
becomes "a lighted empty hall," and poetry becomes the manipula-
tion of symbols which no longer participate in the reality they
name.

Hopkins' conversion is a rejection of three hundred and fifty

[9] See pp. 5, 6.

years of the spiritual history of the West, three hundred and fifty years which seem to be taking man inexorably toward the nihilism of Nietzsche's "Gott ist tot." Like the Catholic revival in Victorian England of which it is part, Hopkins' conversion can be seen as an attempt to avoid falling into the abyss of the absence of God. Hopkins, like other Catholic converts, is willing to sacrifice everything — family, academic career, even his poetic genius — in order to escape the poetic and personal destiny which paralyzes such men as Matthew Arnold, and leaves them hovering between two worlds, waiting in vain for the spark from heaven to fall.

In letters written at the time of his conversion and afterwards Hopkins emphasizes the doctrine of the Real Presence as the core of Catholicism. "The great aid to belief and object of belief," he writes in a letter, "is the doctrine of the Real Presence in the Blessed Sacrament of the Altar. Religion without that is sombre, dangerous, illogical, with that it is . . . *loveable*" (L, III, 17). The doctrine of the Real Presence is, as Hopkins says in the letter written to his father announcing his conversion, the only thing which keeps him from losing his faith in God: "This belief once got is the life of the soul and when I doubted it I shd. become an atheist the next day" (L, III, 92). Belief in the Incarnation and its repetition in the Eucharist offer the only escape from a world which has been rendered universally "sordid" by the disappearance of God (L, III, 226). Christ, in condescending to take upon himself not only the pains of manhood, but also its meannesses, transfigured these degrading characteristics of human life and made them radiant with spiritual significance. Belief in the Incarnation makes it possible to face the full triviality of human life, but at the same time it redeems this triviality and makes it part of the imitation of Christ: "I think that the trivialness of life is, and personally to each one, ought to be seen to be, done away with by the Incarnation . . ." (L, III, 19).

The doctrines of the Incarnation and the Real Presence are more than proof that there was and is some connection between the divine and human worlds. Ultimately, with the help of Scotus and other theologians, Hopkins broadens his theory of the Incarnation until he comes to see all things as created in Christ. This doctrine of Christ is a Catholic version of the Parmenidean theory of being, and it is the means by which Hopkins can at last unify nature, words, and selfhood.

To say that all things are created in Christ means seeing the second person of the Trinity as the model on which all things are made, nonhuman things as well as men. "We are his design," said St. Paul; "God has created us in Christ Jesus" (Eph., 2:10). To see things as created in Christ means seeing Christ as the Word, the Being from whom all words derive: "God's utterance of himself in himself is God the Word, outside himself is this world. This world then is word, expression, news of God. Therefore its end, its purpose, its purport, its meaning, is God and its life or work to name and praise him" (S, 129). Christ is the perfection of human nature, but he is also the perfection of birds, trees, stones, flowers, clouds, and waterfalls. He is, to give the Scotist term for this concept, the *natura communis,* the common nature who contains in himself all natures. He is the creative Word, the means by which God created all things. As Christopher Devlin puts it: "GMH thinks of Christ's created nature as the original pattern of creation, to a place in which all subsequent created being must attain in order to be complete" (S, 341). Each created thing is a version of Christ, and derives its being from the way it expresses Christ's nature in a unique way. All things rhyme in Christ.

This vision of Christ as the common nature is the culmination of Hopkins' gradual integration of the world. Christ is the model for all inscapes, and can vibrate simultaneously at all frequencies. He is the ultimate guarantee for the validity of metaphor. It is proper to say that one thing is like another only because all things are like Christ. The long exploration of nature in Hopkins' journals leads to certain key entries in which he comes to recognize that everything expresses the beauty of Christ:

I do not think I have ever seen anything more beautiful than the bluebell I have been looking at. I know the beauty of our Lord by it. (J, 199)

As we drove home the stars came out thick: I leant back to look at them and my heart opening more than usual praised our Lord to and in whom all that beauty comes home. (J, 254)

Such passages reveal what is distinctively Scotist about Hopkins' vision of nature, and demonstrate the significance of that journal entry where he says: "just then when I took in any inscape of the sky or sea I thought of Scotus" (J, 221). Scotus, like Parmenides, and unlike St. Thomas, affirms the doctrine of the univocity of being.[10] Scotus refers to Parmenides, and defends, against Aristotle's attempted refutation, Parmenides' proposition that all being is one. (See S, 284, and Duns Scotus, *Oxoniense*, I, iii, 2 and viii, 3.) If Parmenides is the Greek philosopher who comes closest to Hopkins' intuition of nature, Scotus is the theologian who seems to him "of realty the rarest-veinèd unraveller" (P, 84). Like Parmenides, Scotus believes that the term "being" means the same thing when we ascribe it to God and when we ascribe it to any creature.

The difference between Scotus and Aquinas on this point is a complex technical matter, and authorities tend to stress their ultimate agreement, or the verbal nature of their disagreement.[11] Even so, it would perhaps not be falsifying too much to say that Scotus and Aquinas represent opposing tendencies of thought, and that these tendencies, if carried to their extremes, would lead to two radically different concepts of nature and of poetry.

The concept of the analogy of being leads to an hierarchical view of nature. Each thing, in this view, possesses only a material and created equivalent of the immaterial and uncreated attributes of God. Things are *analogous* to the nature of God, and each thing in nature stands not for the whole nature of God, but for a particular attribute of the deity. The book of nature is a set of hieroglyphs or symbols, each one of which tells us something specific about God, the lion his strength, the honey his sweetness, the sun his brightness. In short, the concept of the analogy of being leads to something like the view of nature on which medieval and Renaissance poetry, with its horde of specific symbols, is based.

The idea of the univocity of being leads to a different view of nature, and therefore to a different kind of poetry. In this view natural things, instead of having a derived being, participate directly in the being of the creator. They are in the same way that

[10] See Cyril L. Shircel, *The Univocity of the Concept of Being in the Philosophy of John Duns Scotus* (Washington, 1942), Allan Bernard Wolter, *The Transcendentals and Their Function in the Metaphysics of Duns Scotus* (Washington, 1946), pp. 31–57, and Étienne Gilson, *Jean Duns Scot* (Paris, 1952). For the doctrine of analogy in Aquinas, see George P. Klubertanz, *St. Thomas Aquinas on Analogy* (Chicago, 1960).

[11] See, for example, Gilson, *Jean Duns Scot*, pp. 101–103.

he is. Each created thing, in its own special way, is the total image
of its creator. It expresses not some aspect of God, but his beauty
as a whole. Such a view of nature leads to a poetry in which things
are not specific symbols, but all mean one thing and the same: the
beauty of Christ, in whom they are created.

Hopkins sometimes speaks as if he believes in the analogy of
being, as when he says of created things: "They glorify God . . .
The birds sing to him, the thunder speaks of his terror, the lion
is like his strength, the sea is like his greatness, the honey like his
sweetness; they are something like him, they make him known,
they tell of him, they give him glory . . ." (S, 238). In spite of
such passages, and in spite of places in Hopkins' poetry where he
uses the specific symbolism of the Middle Ages and Renaissance,
the main tendency of his vision is toward seeing inscapes as versions
of the whole nature of Christ. Natural things are all, and all
equally, charged with the grandeur of God, and this overwhelming
fact is more important than anything specific about the nature of
God which may be learned from the special qualities of created
things: "All things therefore are charged with love, are charged
with God and if we know how to touch them give off sparks and
take fire, yield drops and flow, ring and tell of him" (S, 195). God's
beauty is like an ubiquitous fluid or electric energy molding
everything in the image of the Son.

This idea is the basic presupposition of Hopkins' nature poems.
In "The Starlight Night," the night sky, with its treasure of stars,
is like bright people or cities hovering in the air, like "dim woods"
with "diamond delves," like "grey lawns cold where gold, where
quickgold lies," like "wind-beat whitebeam," like "airy abeles set
on a flare," like a flock of doves flying in a barnyard, like May blossoms on orchard trees, and like "March-bloom . . . on mealed-
with-yellow sallows" (P, 70, 71). The poem, like so many of Hopkins' nature poems, is made up of a list of natural phenomena
set in apposition to one another. The poem says: "Look at this,
and this, and then this!" The things listed are all metaphors of the
night sky and of one another. They are parallel because they all
equally contain Christ. "The Starlight Night" ends with the affirmation that the night sky and the things with which it has been
compared are like barns which house the precious grain, Christ.
Christ is the treasure within all things.

The octave of "As kingfishers catch fire" is sustained by the same presupposition. The fact that all things cry, "Whát I dó is me: for that I came" is more than evidence that things express their inscapes by "doing" themselves. The echo here of the words of Jesus[12] tells us that in doing what they came for, in speaking themselves, nonhuman creatures are revealing their likeness to Christ and speaking his name. Like just men, kingfishers and dragonflies are of the truth, hear Christ's voice, and speak it again.

In the same way the basis of "The May Magnificat" is a comparison of the Blessed Virgin and nature. As Mary carried Christ within her and magnified him, all nature in May is quick with Christ, the universal instress which reveals itself in a thousand different inscapes: "This ecstasy all through mothering earth/Tells Mary her mirth till Christ's birth" (P, 82).

"Hurrahing in Harvest" is the most ecstatic expression of Hopkins' vision of the ubiquity of Christ in nature. The poem "was the outcome of half an hour of extreme enthusiasm" (L, I, 56). It was enthusiasm in the etymological sense, for the seeing of Christ everywhere in the earth and sky of this autumn scene was a supernatural harvest for the spectator. "Gleaning" Christ from the multitudinous spectacle, threshing him out from the husks which hid him, Hopkins took him as it were in the communion of love, and was himself lifted up into an inscape of Christ: "I walk, I lift up, I lift up heart, eyes,/Down all that glory in the heavens to glean our Saviour" (P, 74).

The doctrine of the common nature takes Hopkins one all-important step beyond the recognition that all things rhyme. The latter led to a sense that all nature is integrated, but is foreign to man. Hopkins' doctrine of Christ allows him to integrate man into the great chorus of created things. Man too is a scape of Christ, and reflects Christ's image back to Christ at the same time as he affirms his own selfhood. A man, like other created things, says "Christ" at the same time as he speaks his own name. All men are rhymes of Christ:

> . . . the just man justices;
> Kéeps gráce: that keeps all his goings graces;

---

[12] See John, 18:37: "Pilate therefore said to him: Art thou a king then? Jesus answered: Thou sayest that I am a king. For this was I born, and for this came I into the world; that I should give testimony to the truth. Everyone that is of the truth, heareth my voice."

Acts in God's eye what in God's eye he is —
Christ — (P, 95)

In imitating Christ man is also imitating natural things, and expressing his kinship with them. To know nature is also to know oneself, for the natural world is a mirror in which a man may see hints and reflections of his own selfhood. Hopkins' epistemology presupposes a new version of the Presocratic "theory of sensation by like and like" (J, 130). I am a "scape" of the common nature, Christ. Each natural thing is also a scape of Christ. Therefore I contain in myself and recapitulate in little all the variety of the creation, kingfishers, dragonflies, stones, trees, flowers — everything. To know them is to know myself, for they are rhymes for me, and for my model, Christ.

Hopkins has at last completed the edifice which seemed destined to remain in fragments. Everything has been brought under the aegis of rhyme. In doing this he has brought into harmony his three theories of poetry. Poetry can be at once self-expression, the inscape of words, and the imitation of nature. To imitate natural things is to express the self, for are not all natural things created in the image of man, since man too is in the image of Christ? To express the self is to imitate nature, for the best means of self-expression is those exterior things which so naturally and delightfully mirror the self. To express the inscape of the self in terms of the inscapes of nature is also to express the inscapes of words. Christ is himself the Word, the origin of all language. He is what "Heaven and earth are word of, worded by" (P, 65). The inscapes of nature flow from Christ the Word, and the inscapes of language flow from the same source. There is a natural harmony between the sounds of words and their meanings, and a poet seeking to express the harmonies of one will naturally express the harmonies of the other. Far from being the place where we are forced to confront the unbridgeable gulfs between world, words, and self, poetry is the medium through which man may best express the harmonious chiming of all three in Christ.

ह

Any definition of poetry, if pushed far enough, will lead back to Christ, for the ultimate origin and inspiration of poetry is the poet's love of God the Son. "Feeling, love in particular," says

Hopkins in a letter of 1879, "is the great moving power and spring of verse and the only person that I am in love with seldom, especially now, stirs my heart sensibly and when he does I cannot always 'make capital' of it, it would be a sacrilege to do so" (L, I, 66). Christ is the only person Hopkins is in love with. His power to write poetry is directly related to his religious life, and when there is a failure of grace there is a failure of poetry. Certain experiences of grace are too personal and too sacred to be made public in poetry. It would be a sacrilege to do so.

This connection between grace and poetic inspiration is behind Hopkins' accounts of the origin of his own poetic gift. He often uses imagery of flowing water to describe poetic inspiration: "Every impulse and spring of art seems to have died in me . . ." (L, I, 124); "Thinking over this matter my vein began to flow" (L, I, 136); " . . . my vein shews no signs of ever flowing again" (L, I, 178); "It is now years that I have had no inspiration of longer jet than makes a sonnet" (L, I, 270). Poetry is like a well or a spring which is usually dry, but suddenly and miraculously begins to flow.

Sometimes inspiration is described not as a spring or fountain, but as the descent of a tongue of flame, "sweet fire the sire of muse" (P, 114). This form of inspiration, like the other, is experienced subjectively as a rush of feelings which gives birth to creative thought. The flame of inspiration is like a fecundating jet of emotion which "leaves yet the mind a mother of immortal song" (P, 114).

Flowing water, flame, impregnation — these three images are precisely the ones which, for Hopkins, also define the descent of God's grace. In "The Wreck of the Deutschland," remembering the tongues of fire at Pentecost (Acts, 2:1 ff.), Hopkins describes his own experience of grace as being struck and burned with God's lightning, so that he was "laced with fire of stress," and "flash[ed] from the flame to the flame then, tower[ed] from the grace to the grace" (P, 56). The tongues of fire at Pentecost brought the gift of tongues to the apostles, and were themselves the breathing in both of grace and of the power to speak. In the same way stanza four of "The Wreck" associates grace, the Word, and the image of water (P, 56). The "gospel proffer" which constantly regenerates the soul and keeps it sweet is the "good news," the Word, Christ's gift.

In another stanza the nun's "conception" of Christ (P, 65) is described as the mental conception and uttering of the Word. Once more the descent of grace is associated with the miraculous bestowal of a verbal gift.

"The Wreck of the Deutschland" is about both poetic inspiration and grace. The poem is divided into two parts, the first recalling the time when Hopkins himself was touched by the finger of God, the second describing the wreck and the salvation of the nuns. Imagining the nuns' death has brought back vividly to Hopkins his own parallel experience. Remembering it, he has relived it again, and God's grace has descended once more into his heart. This experience of the renewal of grace is at the same time the renewal of poetic inspiration. Hopkins' poetic gift, artificially cut off at the time of his conversion, begins to flow irresistibly again, and, with the permission of his superiors, he writes the first of the great poems of his maturity.

Hopkins has put into the poem itself, in a stanza which is a hyperbaton or suspense in the midst of the storm, an account of its genesis. The poet pauses in his objective description of the wreck, returns to himself, and expresses, in a series of breathless ejaculations, his subjective response to the storm (P, 61, stanza 18). The tears which are the expression of his emotion at reading an account of the wreck are the signs of the flowing of poetic inspiration. This flowing melts his hardness of heart, makes words break from him, and generates the poem. The poem, consequently, is a "madrigal start"; it is like one voice, in a song of many parts, singing in canon a repetition of another voice. Another example of the principle of rhyme! The "new rhythm" whose "echo" had long been haunting Hopkins' ear, and which he first "realised on paper" in "The Wreck"[13] was not merely a new poetic device. Sprung rhythm is a reverberation, in the beat and tension of the lines, of the pulsation of grace which inspired the poem. The true theme of "The Wreck of the Deutschland" is not the heroic death of the nuns. It is Hopkins' response to hearing of the wreck — the father of grace and the father of poetry moving his heart simultaneously. For the two fathers are the same.

[13] Claude Colleer Abbott, ed., *The Correspondence of Gerard Manley Hopkins and Richard Watson Dixon* (London: Oxford University Press, 1955), p. 14; hereafter cited as "L, II."

This is so in a more subtle way yet. Christ operates as the immaterial cause of the "fine delight" which moves the heart and "fathers thought" (P, 114). He is also the motivating force behind a certain way of seeing nature which is necessary to the writing of poetry.

Here Hopkins' Scotism comes to the surface again. Following the subtle doctor, Hopkins distinguishes in a special way between three faculties of the mind: memory, understanding, and will. Will in this context is affective volition, "the faculty of fruition, by which we enjoy or dislike" (S, 174). The affective will moves toward a thing or repulses it after it has first been comprehended by the understanding. The understanding "applies to words; it is the faculty for grasping not the fact but the meaning of a thing. . . . This faculty not identifies but verifies; takes the measure of things, brings word of them; is called λόγος and reason" (S, 174). Before we can understand a thing we must apprehend it with our senses, and this first act of the mind is called "Memory." Memory, for Hopkins as for Scotus, applies to present and future as well as to past. Toward past things it is "Memory proper." Toward "things future or things unknown or imaginary" it is "Imagination." Toward present things memory is "Simple Apprehension," the "faculty of Identification." It is the primary direction of the mind toward a thing, a grasping of the bare fact that something is there before us rather than nothing: "When continued or kept on the strain the act of this faculty is attention, advertence, heed, the being *ware,* and its habit, knowledge, the being *aware.* Towards God it gives rise to *reverence,* it is the sense of the *presence* of God" (S, 174).

Ordinarily the mind moves rapidly from memory to understanding to will. Apprehending that there is something before it, the mind comprehends that thing with the reason, and then moves toward it or away from it, driven by the liking or disliking of the affective will. It is possible for the mind to prolong the stage of simple apprehension, and to remain hovering in that state in which it has grasped the fact that something is there, and may even have barely identified it, but has not yet gone on to analyze the thing with the understanding, and place it in a pre-existing concept. It is as if the mind were to remain at the stage of sensation, the awareness of color, texture, and form, rather than moving on to perception, the awareness that this is an ash tree, or a bluebell, or the moon rising. On awaking from sleep, says Scotus, sensation is likely to be particularly vivid, and simple apprehension may then be prolonged so that it can be identified as a separate experience. On awaking the mind is cut off from past and future, and in a daze of immediacy can concentrate on the present, distorting it neither with memory nor with expectation. The man waking from sleep apprehends what is really there before him, not the pre-existing structures of reason and will. Scotus calls this act of simple apprehension "confused knowing." It is *visio existentis ut existens,* a vision of the existing thing as existing. In such visionary sensation we see what Scotus called the *species specialissima,* nature in the very process of being created in the image of its model, Christ. In simple apprehension man is aware of the being of a thing, its beauty, its presence, what it shares with all other things, and with God.[14] Simple apprehension "keeps warm/Men's wits to the things that are" (P, 103).

This way of seeing things is the origin of poetry. Instead of seeing an object as an example of an abstract category the poet must see it as if it had just been created, and then the depths of his being opens up to receive, in a flood of emotion, the being of the thing he sees. Vivid sensation is a "prize" which pierces to the heart of the poet's being, and "wakes" him to another level of existence, a level closer to the heart of creation.

In "Moonrise," one of Hopkins' most exquisite poetic fragments, the poet tells how he "awoke in the Midsummer not to call night," and saw the waning moon just rising from the bulk of "dark Maenefa the mountain." His half-awake state made him vulnerable to the impact of sensation, and the scene plunged through the superficial layers of his consciousness to reach a level of perpetual vigilance. The rhythm of the lines and their syntax echo this process of an ever-so-delicate entry of reality deeper and deeper through the senses to the heart:

This was the prized, the desirable sight, ' unsought, presented so easily,
Parted me leaf and leaf, divided me, ' eyelid and eyelid of slumber. (P, 149)

To see things in terms of their existence is to see them at such a depth that it can be recognized that their creation is something

[14] See S, 298, and Christopher Devlin, "The Image and the Word," *Month,* N.S., III (1950), 114–27, 191–202, especially 196–199.

which goes on constantly. A vein of the Gospel proffer holds a man in being and keeps him from falling into nothingness, and natural things are kept in existence by a similar process of continuous creation. Since all things are perpetually renewed by God the poet knows that "There lives the dearest freshness deep down things" (P, 70). The first days of the creation are always being reenacted, and there is throughout nature, even now, "A strain of the earth's sweet being in the beginning/In Eden garden" (P, 71).

To see nature being created is to see things in terms of the common nature, the perfection toward which they all move. The *visio existentis ut existens* is the true source of poetry because only this way of seeing things can go behind mere intellectual recognition to a vision of all things as being continuously created in Christ.

A passage in "The Wreck of the Deutschland" makes clearer the importance of simple apprehension in the perception of Christ within nature:

> . . . tho' he is under the world's splendour and wonder,
> His mystery must be instressed, stressed;
> For I greet him the days I meet him, and bless when I understand. (P, 57)

These lines recapitulate the whole mental process from memory through understanding to will. "Instress" matches "greet": when I catch a glimpse of Christ in nature, "meet" him, I "greet" him. I respond to him, "kiss my hand" to him, instress my simple apprehension in answer to the stress felt from him (the "stroke and a stress that stars and storms deliver" in the next stanza). After the meeting of simple apprehension has been responded to by my kiss of greeting, this affirmation of my awareness leads me to "understand," and this understanding is finally ratified by an act of will going out, in desire, toward Christ in nature. This is the "blessing" of the last line, which matches the "stressed" of the line before. In this process the instress with which I prolong my simple apprehension and dwell on it is necessary to my comprehension of the presence of Christ under the world's splendor and wonder. His mystery must be instressed if nature is to be seen poetically.

The same assumptions lie behind another poem, in which Hopkins describes how ash-boughs "new-nestle at heaven most high." Such a scene is the most poetic thing he knows. As in "Moonrise," the initiation of the poetic act is spoken of as a deep and subtle penetration of the mind by natural objects. The mind must assimilate the world into its deepest recesses before the poetic *élan* is released:

> Not of áll my eyes see, wandering on the world,
> Is anything a milk to the mind so, so sighs deep
> Poetry tó it, as a tree whose boughs break in the sky. (P, 164)

Ash-boughs, which "touch heaven, tabour on it" (P, 165), are a supremely poetic sight because, in the yearning and reaching of the tiny new twigs and leaves toward the sky, the poet can see going on before his eyes the process of continuous creation. Earth is the mother of all things, but God is their father, and in the growth of the ash-boughs is visibly enacted the intercourse between heaven and earth. The moving toward heaven of the ash-boughs is their imitation of Christ. The incarnate God, mediator between heaven and earth, possessor of both a divine and a human nature, is the model for the double nature of all created things:

> . . . May
> Mells blue with snowwhite through their fringe and fray
> Of greenery and old earth gropes for, grasps at steep
> Heaven with it whom she childs things by. (P, 165)

The ash-boughs' imitation of Christ is also their imitation of us, for we too are fathered by heaven on mother earth in the image of Christ. A variant reading of the last two lines of "Ash-boughs" says just this: "it is old earth's groping towards the steep/Heaven whom she childs *us* by" (P, 165, my italics). Again Hopkins' doctrine of Christ binds together nature, poetry, and the poet.

Beginning with a sense of his own isolation and idiosyncrasy, Hopkins turns outside himself to nature, to poetry, and to God. Gradually he integrates all things into one chorus of many voices all singing, in their different ways, the name of Christ. Poetry is the imitation and echo of this chorus. Even the poet, by virtue of his share in the common nature, is assimilated into the melody of creation. The inscapes of words, the inscapes of nature, the inscape of the self can be expressed at once as the presence of Christ. The three ways of poetry are the same way, and the inspiration of poetry is always, in one way or another, the poet's affective response to the omnipresence of Christ.

The isolation of the poet in his selftaste has turned out to be apparent, not real, and Hopkins' early experience of the absence of God has been transformed into what is, in Victorian poetry, an almost unique sense of the immanence of God in nature and in the human soul. Neither Arnold, nor Tennyson, nor Browning is able to transcend so completely the spiritual condition of his age. Hopkins alone recovers a world like that of Eden before the fall, a world in which God, in the person of his Son, once more walks with man in the garden in the cool of the evening.

ε❧

Try as he may in his early nature poetry to see in man an "innocent mind and Mayday" (P, 71) and in nature an Edenic perfection, the "cheer and charm of earth's past prime" (P, 73), Hopkins is ultimately forced to recognize that both man and nature are fallen. This recognition explodes into discordant fragments the harmonious chorus of creation, leaving him once more in suffering and isolation. His integration of all things in Christ turns out to be not a description of what is, but a nostalgia for what would have been if Satan had not fallen, and if Adam and Eve, through their disobedience of God, had not followed Satan into the wilderness of separation.

The effects of the fall are visible first in nature. The creation lives in time, for "God gave things a forward and perpetual motion" (S, 198, 199). In an unfallen world things flow from God into material existence, and, having been created, fulfill themselves in time. They are sustained forever in immaculate perfection, continuously flowing to and from God in a rhythmic pulsation. When Satan fell he twisted things to match his own crookedness, "so wreathing nature and as it were constricting it to his purposes (as also he wreathed himself in the Garden round the Tree of Knowledge)" (S, 198). Interrupting the forward motion by which things fulfill their natures, Satan turned things in upon themselves. This inturned motion, like a coil winding tighter and tighter until finally it stops, is the very process of death. The devil brought death into the world, *Invidia autem diaboli mors intravit in mundum,* and therefore a "coil or spiral is . . . a type of the Devil, who is called the old (or original) serpent, and this I suppose because of its 'swale' or subtle and imperceptible drawing in towards its head or centre, and it is a type of death, of motion lessening and at last ceasing" (S, 198).

Hopkins' nature poems sometimes describe the world as a universal uncoiling, a perpetual springtime, but now he must recognize that there is a force in nature working against this and in the opposite direction: "In Nature is something that makes, builds up, and breeds, as vegetation, life in fact; and over against this, also in Nature, something that unmakes or pulls to pieces, what . . . is called Death and Strife" (L, II, 53). The devil has destroyed the harmony of nature, for he is "thrower of things off the track, upsetter, mischiefmaker," and "clashing one with another [he] brought in the law of decay and consumption in inanimate nature, death in the vegetable and animal world" (S, 199).

The Edenic world of poems like "God's Grandeur," "Spring," "Pied Beauty," and "Hurrahing in Harvest" gives way, in certain magnificent poems of Hopkins' last years, to a horrified vision of nature as a constant process of decay. The divine energy of instress which flows through nature and creates inscapes drives these inscapes to move on without stopping until they have exhausted and destroyed themselves. The clouds in "Hurrahing in Harvest" are continually made and unmade, "moulded ever and melted across skies" (P, 74). Only in some kind of movement can things radiate their inexhaustible energy, and keep their inscapes in being. The very force which creates things and sustains them in being transforms and destroys them. God permits Satan to wield the world, to turn it aside in imitation of his own depraved motion, spiraling in on itself.

As early as "The Wreck of the Deutschland" Hopkins recognizes the double nature of God, the way he is present in storms as well as in the "lovely-asunder/Starlight" (P, 57): "Thou art lightning and love, I found it, a winter and warm" (P, 58). (The alliteration here emphasizes the mystery of similarity and dissimilarity in the two aspects of God's nature.) In "Spelt from Sibyl's Leaves" and "That Nature is a Heraclitean Fire and of the comfort of the Resurrection," what had seemed, in "Hurrahing in Harvest," the simple perception that the inscapes of things are continually changing becomes an anguished recognition that the "forgèd features" of things are finally obliterated. As in Parmenides, "unmeaning (ἀδαῆ) night, thick and wedgèd body" (J, 130), which follows day and hides the perceptible forms of things, is taken as the symbol of that nonbeing which will overtake all mortal things:

. . . For earth ' her being has unbound, her dapple is at an end, astray or aswarm, all throughther, in throngs; ' self ín self steepèd and páshed —
    qúite
Disremembering, dísmémbering ' áll now. (P, 104)

At night things are as it were "dismembered," their inscapes
torn to pieces. They are "disremembered" too; it is no longer possible to recognize them, nor can the poet remember what they
were like in daylight. Memory, in Hopkins' Scotist scheme of
perception, means simple apprehension, visionary sensation. At
night man can no longer have that direct experience of the being
of things which opens up the depths of his own being and is the
source of poetry. Because Hopkins so much cherishes the "original
definiteness and piquant beauty" of things (L, III, 218) there is
great intensity of regret, of "pity and indignation" (P, 112), in the
image of "self ín self steepèd and páshed." It is a brilliant image of
the return of all individuated forms to the "thick and wedgèd
body" of formless chaos. In that chaos nature will be "all throughther." "Throughther," the dialect form of "through-other," sounds
like a telescoped form of a complete phrase such as: "each interpenetrated through and through with the others." It is a perfect
mimesis of the event described. The forms of the collapsed words
strain to differentiate themselves, just as the inscapes crushed into
chaos resist desperately the unbinding of their beings.

In "That Nature is a Heraclitean Fire" another of the Presocratic symbols is used, fire, the material manifestation of the
energy of being. In this poem the thousand forms in which this
energy manifests itself are seen to be as impermanent as clouds
or as straws in a bonfire. As Hopkins himself wittily said of the
poem, a great deal of early Greek philosophical thought is dis-
tilled in it, but the liquor of the distillation does not taste very
Greek (L, I, 291). The Heraclitean transformation of fire for all
things and all things for fire (Fr. 90) is present in the sunlight,
wind, clouds, rain, and earth of the scene. The fiery sun is never
directly mentioned, but it is the ultimate cause of all this activity,
and is present everywhere in derived form. The sun's heat generates the wind. The winds drives the clouds across the sky, and dries
the mud which is still viscous after rain. The elements live in a
constant interchange of energy.

Hopkins' equivalent of Heraclitus' "everlasting fire" (Fr. 30) is the Logos itself, Christ, the fiery breath which inflates the "cloud-puffballs," bends the trees, shines as sunlight, and rolls through nature as the universal instress of being. It is as if their failure to be more than an imperfect image of Christ's perfection drives things on in a frantic attempt to approach his fullness of being. But since the fall time has been twisted askew, and things move forward only to be consumed by the fire-wind of God. If "Spelt from Sibyl's Leaves" is a frightening vision of night as dismembering, the later poem is a hymn to day as destructive fire. The fiery energy of being, which seemed to inhere in things and sustain them in selfhood, impels things to an activity of selving which eventually unselves them. Only the "ethery flame of fire" remains constant, that and the activity of change itself, the ceaseless metamorphosis of one form into another:

> . . . Million-fuelèd, ' nature's bonfire burns on. (P, 112)

ชั

Perhaps man alone, life's pride and cared-for crown, has, in a fallen world, kept intact the image of Christ.

In the "Maidens' Song from St. Winefred's Well," Hopkins asks if there is any "bow or brooch or braid or brace, láce, latch or catch or key to keep/Back beauty, keep it, beauty, beauty, beauty, . . . from vanishing away?" (P, 96). The answer is categorical: "No there's none, there's none, O no there's none" (P, 97). In nonhuman nature the law is transformation, flux, the melting of clouds across the sky, but the law for man is absolute destruction, since his identity, though it is one of the inscapes of nature, is too subtle to retain its distinctness through even so many changes as a tree or flower will endure. Though man is nature's "bonniest, dearest ' to her, her clearest-selvèd spark," he too is "drowned" in the "enormous dark" of death (P, 112).

This means already the breakdown of Hopkins' unified theory of poetry. How can a poetry based on the rhyming of self and nature be used as a triumphant assertion of man's identity, if man and nature are as unstable as day which moves toward the tomb of night, as quick to change and as destructive as fire, and if it is to this universal flux that the poet must testify in his poems? Hopkins' three modes of poetry had been integrated by the theory of

Christ as the common nature. Such a poetry will be in the end a mere hymn to death.

The situation is worse yet. Man is different from animals and plants, as well as like them, and this difference makes his version of the common nature a thousand times more dangerous, more in jeopardy.

The inscapes of nature can die, but they cannot be evil, for "nature is incapable of producing beautiful evil" (L, III, 307). As long as natural things exist, they do what comes naturally: king-fishers catch fire, dragonflies draw flame, and stones ring. This spon-taneous expression of their inner natures is their way of praising God and speaking his name. Such praise is unintentional, and therefore neither right nor wrong, merely good. Nevertheless it never fails. Natural things can never fall short of that degree of perfection in which they are created: ". . . what they can *they always do*" (S, 239).

Unlike the rest of nature, man was created with self-conscious-ness and freedom. His reason for existing is exactly the same as that of the rest of the creation: "to give [God] glory" (S, 238). But right action, which reflects back to Christ his own image, does not come spontaneously to man. It is an act of choice: "man can know God, *can mean to give him glory*. This then was why he was made, to give God glory and to mean to give it; to praise God fréely, wíllingly to reverence him, gládly to serve him" (S, 239).

If man can mean to give God glory he can also mean *not* to. His freedom to rise to the image of Christ is also freedom to fall to the image of Satan. Before the fall man's nature and freedom were in harmony. Like the brute beasts man wanted to do what he was supposed to do. In Adam's fall we sinnèd all. Satan, the twisty old serpent, brought not only physical death in the natural world, but also "moral death and original sin in the world of man" (S, 199).

Moral death and original sin mean chiefly a splitting apart of the natural man and the spiritual man. As Christopher Devlin has said (S, 116-120), Hopkins' bifurcation of man, though based on orthodox Christian tradition, is carried to the brink of heter-odoxy. It derives from his Victorianism rather than from his Ca-tholicism. Like so many of his contemporaries, he was brought up in a strict Protestant family. This seems to have meant, for Hopkins as for Emily Brontë, being indoctrinated with the idea that whatever is done spontaneously is sinful, and must be prohibited. Hopkins as an undergraduate, before his conversion, went to extremes of ascetiscism, fasted and deprived himself. He seems even to have practiced self-flagellation, if one early poem can be taken as evidence: "You striped in secret with breath-taking whips" (P, 35). Hopkins is always overeager to punish himself, and carries his Lenten sacrifices to sometimes comic excess: "No pudding on Sundays. No tea except if to keep me awake and then without sugar. . . . Not to sit in armchair except can work in no other way" (J, 72).

This intransigent rejection of natural inclination appears in Hopkins' later writings as an extreme separation between nature and grace. Memory, understanding, and "affective will" taken together make up man's share in the common nature, his inscape. Hopkins often calls them simply man's "heart." On the other hand there is what he calls "elective will." This he identifies with the *haecceitas* of Scotus, man's individualizing form, his selftaste or pitch of selfhood. Often he calls man's selftaste his "personality," as opposed to his "nature." Since the fall, these two parts of the self, Hopkins tended to believe, are distinct. Following Scotus, St. Thomas, and Suarez, Hopkins summed up the difference between these two areas of the self in the distinction between two kinds of will: *voluntas ut arbitrium* (elective will) and *voluntas ut natura* (affective will).

Affective will, as its name implies, is man's natural tendency to move toward what the senses and emotions feel to be desirable. In a way it is not will at all, since it is not free: ". . . the affective will is well affected towards, likes, desires, chooses, whatever has the quality and look of good and *cannot choose but* so like and choose; so that the affective will, taken strictly as a faculty of the mind, is really no freer than the understanding or the imagination" (S, 152). Since it moves toward whatever is desirable the *voluntas ut natura* is perfectly satisfied with a finite object: "The memory, understanding and affective will are incapable themselves of an infinite object and do not tend towards it" (S, 138). If this is the case, then a man's inscape is without value in itself for his salvation. A man is saved only by going toward an infinite object, God, but "the tendency in the soul towards an infinite object comes from the *arbitrium*" (S, 138). Therefore the *arbitrium* is at the center of the drama of salvation, and the *voluntas ut natura* plays only a minor role.

The distinction between two kinds of volition will explain an apparent contradiction in Hopkins' thinking about the nature of human selfhood. This contradiction lies at the center of his thought, and is the reef on which is finally wrecked his integration of self, words, and world through Christ.

The contradiction about the self is also a contradiction about the nature of God. Individuality is sometimes seen as a matter of complexity and fineness of pattern. In this case the higher and more elaborate patterns recapitulate the lower ones, and God, the most complex pattern, contains in himself the archetypes of all things. God is the master key which opens all doors. Each thing repeats, not God's whole pattern, but some portion of it or simplified version of it. Man too, in this view of individuality, though he is not God, contains in himself the creatures below him on the scale of being, and he is created in the image of Christ. He need not feel alone in the universe, and can, if he is a poet, express his own inscape at the same time as he expresses the inscapes of nature.

At other times Hopkins thinks of individuality in a radically different way. Perfection of individuality is a matter of pitch, of taste, something so highly tuned and idiosyncratic that it is like nothing else in the world. The selftaste of Hopkins is what Scotus calls the *ultima solitudo* of man. At the deepest center of selfhood a man is alone. Each member of a group of such selves will be completely isolated from all the others. God must now be defined as the most individualized and unique person. As the most exquisitely tuned of all, God is the most isolated of all. God is the key which fits no finite lock.

The first of these concepts of individuality provides Hopkins with the basis for his gradual integration of all things into one great chorus of creation. It allows him to escape from the isolation to which his own selfhood at first seemed condemned. All the hopeful and "hurrahing" side of Hopkins' poetry derives from this idea about selfhood. A man can be saved by doing what comes naturally, because he is created naturally in the image of Christ. He can without qualms instress his own inscape.

The other definition of selfhood is no less integral to Hopkins' thought. It leads to the idea that a man has no kinship with anything, not even with God. All other things are in some way like one another, and this similarity in dissimilarity is the basis of rhyme. Man alone rhymes with nothing: "We say that any two things however unlike are in something like. This [a man's self-taste] is the one exception . . ." (S, 123). If this is so, a man can only hope for salvation if in some unimaginable way he is transformed into the image of Christ. This side of Hopkins' thought leads to the analysis of grace in the commentary on the *Spiritual Exercises* and to the somber poetry of his last years. It means a repudiation of the mood of "Hurrahing in Harvest."

If in one sense a man's selftaste is unlike God, since it is a taste peculiar to himself, in another sense it is more like God than is any other created thing. A man's affective will is brother to all things and, like them, will die in nature's bonfire. A man's *arbitrium* is, like God, absolute. As affective will or inscape a man actualizes only a tiny portion of the infinite riches of God. (God here is thought of as multiplicity.) As selftaste or *arbitrium* he is a replica in little of the whole nature of God. (God now is thought of as singularity.) It is in this way that a "man's personality or individuality . . . places him on a level of individuality in some sense with God" (S, 139).

In one way a man's selfhood is nothing at all; it is the empty power to taste in one way or another or to act in one way or another. Only if the self possesses a nature does it have a field in which to act and display itself: "Now a bare self, to which no nature has yet been added, which is not yet clothed in or overlaid with a nature, is indeed nothing, a zero, in the score or account of existence" (S, 146). In another way the bare self is freedom, elective will, and as such it is the created thing most like the infinite freedom and individuality of God.

The bare self is neither finite nor infinite. It is infinitesimal. Here extremes meet. The bare self of man is like a mathematical point. It has neither length nor breadth and yet it positively exists. Man's infinitesimal freedom, so weak that it can merely say yes or no to actions which its nature suggests, is his immortal and God-worthy part. The bare self or elective will has the power to fore-draw the freedom of play of its nature to a single point, and thereby give it an infinite intensity. Any positive number divided by zero is infinity, and even a small energy crowded in an infinitely small space will produce an infinite stress. Such quasi-mathematical terms are the best Hopkins can devise to express the relations between self and nature, self and God: "For a self is an absolute which stands to the absolute of God as the infinitesimal to the infinite. It is an infinitesimal in the scale of stress. And in some sense it is an infinite, if looked on as the foredrawing of its whole being" (S, 153).

Each man is both nature and bare self. In itself a man's nature is without individuality. Another man might conceivably have exactly the same nature. A man's individuality lies in his *arbitrium,* and therefore only what he does with his *arbitrium* determines his salvation or damnation: "Two eggs precisely alike, two birds precisely alike / will behave precisely alike: if they had been exchanged no difference would have been made. It is the self then that supplies the determination, the difference, but the nature that supplies the exercise, and in these two things freedom consists" (S, 147).

ᔰ

In spite of his love for nature, Hopkins has a permanent sense of guilt for this love. Nature is not evil. It is trivial: ". . . to admire the stars is in itself indifferent" (S, 166). But a man facing the possibility of an eternity of pain has no time for indifferent things. The lure of mortal beauty is Hopkins' way of experiencing the temptation of worldiness. His way of punishing himself for his sins is to deprive himself of the sweet distraction of natural beauty. The journals are punctuated with the records of these sacrifices, as when he says: "On this day by God's grace I resolved to give up all beauty until I had His leave for it . . ." (J, 71; see also J, 190, 249).

In spite of the fact that Hopkins can glimpse Christ in nature, this way to God is, in the end, of no use to him. Man can see God in nature but cannot possess him, and it is only possession that matters. In the same way, a poetry that imitates the inscapes of nature, even though it "catches" Christ in the windhover or in the azurous hung hills, is ultimately a distraction from the straight path. To reject nature is also to reject poetry about nature.

Poetry is an actualization of the poet's inscape as well as of the inscapes of nature. To actualize his inscape is to actualize his version of Christ, the common nature. Surely this is a step toward salvation! But no — even this is trivial. A man is saved by his free choice of God above all else. Only his *arbitrium* can make this choice. A man's inscape is in the image of Christ in exactly the same way as are the inscapes of kingfishers and clouds. For a man to affirm his nature is without significance one way or the other for his salvation. He can no more help being himself than can an egg. And poetry is the spontaneous expression of the poet's inscape or nature. It has nothing to do with his *ultima solitudo* and therefore nothing to do with his salvation.

Hopkins' doctrine on this point is obscure. The sonnet to Henry Purcell says that art is the expression "of own, of abrúpt sélf" (P, 85). This seems to mean that the artist can express in his art his *haecceitas,* but the headnote to the sonnet says that Purcell's music utters in notes "the very make and species of man as created both in him and in all men generally" (P, 84). This seems clearly enough to mean that Purcell's music expresses his own "arch-especial" version of the common nature, his inscape. It is difficult to believe that Hopkins meant the poem and its headnote to contradict one another. "Abrupt self" in the poem must therefore mean inscape, not *haecceitas.* This interpretation is reinforced by another poem in which Hopkins makes explicit the idea that the poet is not free to choose the individualizing pattern he will impose on his works. The artist is like a musical instrument which is tuned in a certain way and only capable of playing certain melodies. The source of the authenticity and vitality of his art is also the source of his limitation. The artist must obey the laws of his being:

> Not free in this because
> His powers seemed free to play:
> He swept what scope he was
> To sweep and must obey. (P, 163)

If the artist is bound by his being, art can hardly be the expression of the selftaste of the artist. For selftaste is elective will, radically free. Art must therefore be merely the expression of the artist's inscape. It has no more to do with right and wrong than does "sweet the golden glue/That's built for by the bee" (P, 164). Art is part of nature and therefore good, but it has nothing to do with a man's free will and its momentous choices.

If art is a part of nature's "growth in every thing" (P, 81) then art is indeed trivial, and Hopkins is right to have a sense of guilt about his penchant for poetry. If poetry is a hymn to beauty which must die and the expression of the mortal inscape of the poet, it is perfectly reasonable that Hopkins, as Devlin says, should treat his muse "as a Victorian husband might . . . a wife of whom he had cause to be ashamed" (S, 119). The writing of poetry seems to Hopkins neither right nor wrong; it is insignificant, like a talent for billiards or cricket.

This view of poetry explains why Hopkins burned his poems after his conversion, repudiated the writing of poetry as something which would "interfere with [his] state and vocation" (L, I, 24), and wrote poetry only after he could persuade himself that he had been ordered to do so by his superiors. He also tended to empha-size the undeliberate quality of poetic composition, as when he said, of those late poems, the "terrible" sonnets, that they "came like inspirations unbidden and against [his] will" (L, I, 221). The poems were not his responsibility, but were written spontaneously by his nature, or by some force moving his nature to express itself. Though writing poetry is what comes most easily and naturally to him, it must be rejected, and for that very reason, for the nat-ural man will never get to heaven. A letter to Dixon expresses unequivocally Hopkins' remorse for his poetry and the reasons for it: "The question then for me is not whether I am willing . . . to make a sacrifice of hopes of fame . . . , but whether I am not to undergo a severe judgment from God for the lothness I have shewn in making it, for the reserves I may have in my heart made, for the backward glances I have given with my hand upon the plough, for the waste of time the very compositions you ad-mire may have caused and their preoccupation of the mind which belonged to more sacred or more binding duties, for the disquiet and the thoughts of vainglory they have given rise to" (L, II, 88).

&

In the end Hopkins finds that poetry is not trivial or neutral, but, like other positive ways of affirming selfhood, a means to damnation.

A man can be saved only by becoming a perfect image of Christ. At first it seems that this means affirming with all his heart his Christscape. But the essential element in Christ is self-sacrifice, not self-affirmation. Only if a man imitates Christ in his sacrifice of himself is he worthy to return to God: ". . . the world, man, should after its own manner give God being in return for the being he has given it or should give him back that being he has given. This is done by the great sacrifice. To contribute then to that sacrifice is the end for which man was made . . ." (S, 129).

The self-sacrifice of Christ takes place on three different levels of eternity and time. The mystery of the procession of the Trinity is the mystery of sacrifice. The Trinity is at once three persons and one person. Christ is constantly proceeding from the bosom of God and bringing into existence the Holy Ghost as the relation of mutual love between himself and God. Just as constantly he is sacrificing himself out of love for God and being reabsorbed by the Father. This perpetual process of division and reunification is the intrinsic stress of selving in God.

The intrinsic procession of the Trinity is mirrored by an extrinsic procession which takes place in angelic or aeonian time. Christ so loves the Father that he chooses to go into the barren wilderness outside of God and repeat the sacrifice which he is perpetually enacting within the intrinsic procession of the Trinity. This first repetition of Christ's sacrifice, though it is the incarnation, is not yet the appearance of Christ as a man in our human world. Hopkins revives and turns to his own uses a curious distinction made by Apollinaris about A.D. 380. He understands a crucial text in St. John to describe two separate events: "The Word was made Flesh, and came to dwell among us." The first event Hopkins calls ἐνσάρκωσις (the taking a body), the second ἐνανθρώπευσις (the becoming a man). The incarnation takes place in angelic time. Christ's becoming a man takes place in human time. The two events are distinct (S, 171). Following Scotus once again, Hopkins believes that aeons before this world was created, or rather, on an entirely different level of time, that of the angels,

Christ went outside the Trinity, was incarnated, and offered himself in Eucharistic sacrifice. Hopkins' description of this process is an excellent example of the peculiar flavor and poetry of his theological writing:

> The first intention then of God outside himself or, as they say, *ad extra,* outwards, the first outstress of God's power, was Christ . . . Why did the Son of God go thus forth from the Father not only in the eternal and intrinsic procession of the Trinity but also by an extrinsic and less than eternal, let us say aeonian one? — To give God glory and that by sacrifice, sacrifice offered in the barren wilderness outside of God, as the children of Israel were led into the wilderness to offer sacrifice. This sacrifice and this outward procession is a consequence and shadow of the procession of the Trinity, from which mystery sacrifice takes its rise . . . It is as if the blissful agony or stress of selving in God had forced out drops of sweat or blood, which drops were the world, or as if the lights lit at the festival of the 'peaceful Trinity' through some little cranny striking out lit up into being one 'cleave' out of the world of possible creatures. The sacrifice would be the Eucharist, and that the victim might be truly victim like, like motionless, helpless, or lifeless, it must be in matter. (S, 197)

The repetition of Christ's self-sacrifice which takes place in angelic time does not occur in isolation. God creates the whole host of angels to bear Christ company and follow him back to God. If it had not been for the fall of Satan and the rebel angels this might have been the whole drama of creation — the fathering forth of the angels by God and their flowing back into God as followers of Christ's eucharistic sacrifice: "In going forth to do sacrifice Christ went not alone but created angels to be his company, lambs to follow him the Lamb, the flower of the flock, 'whithersoever he went,' that is to say, first to the hill of sacrifice, then after that back to God, to beatitude. They were to take part in the sacrifice and he was to redeem them all, that is to say / for the sake of the Lamb of God who was God himself God would accept the whole flock and for the sake of one ear or grape the whole sheaf or cluster . . ." (S, 197).

The rebel angels *did* fall. This necessitated the creation of man, and, ultimately, Christ's third enactment of his sacrifice, this time in the realm of human time. If the angels and man had not fallen "the sacrifice might have been unbloody; by the Fall it became a bloody one" (S, 257). The first two sacrifices are completed by a third, which re-enacts on earth once again the mystery of the death of God. On Corpus Christi, as Hopkins explains to Bridges, there is performed a sacred play which imitates the action of this third sacrifice. This play, says Hopkins, "represents the process of the Incarnation and the world's redemption. As Christ went forth from the bosom of the Father as the Lamb of God and eucharistic victim to die upon the altar of the cross for the world's ransom; then rising returned leading the procession of the flock redeemed / so in this ceremony his body *in statu victimali* is carried to the Altar of Repose as it is called and back to the tabernacle at the high altar, which will represent the bosom of the godhead" (L, I, 149).

In the secret procession of the Trinity, in the angelic *aevum*, and in Christ's redemption of the world is acted and re-enacted God's sacrifice of himself to himself. The world is "word, expression, news of God" because it is created in the image of the Word, Christ. The mystery of sacrifice must therefore be inscribed in the creation as well as in the creator, and especially in man, on whom all the rest of the creatures depend. As St. Paul said, in words Hopkins took as an epigraph for "Ribblesdale": ". . . the earnest expectation of the creature waiteth for the manifestation of the sons of God" (Rom., 8:19). Man is "Earth's eye, tongue, or heart" (P, 96), and only if man imitates Christ's sacrifice can the rest of the creation appeal to God through him.

Man has imitated not Christ but Satan. Before he was shown to man, Christ was presented by God to the angelic host as the leader they must follow in self-sacrifice. Lucifer refused to obey Christ. When he turned in upon himself and recognized his own beauty, he should have turned immediately to the source of that beauty, God. Instead, he prolonged his contemplation of his own beauty, and remained turned in on himself like a serpent. In this act he fell: "This song of Lucifer's was a dwelling on his own beauty, an instressing of his own inscape, and like a performance on the organ and instrument of his own being; it was a sounding, as they say, of his own trumpet and a hymn in his own praise" (S, 200, 201). By selving, singing himself, Satan exiled himself from heaven. Here once again Hopkins follows Scotus, for, as he says, "Scotus thinks that in Satan's contemplation of his own beauty was a sin of luxury" (S, 132). Hopkins' own splendid descriptions of the fall of Satan, magnificent examples of his theological imagination, are developed, so it seems, from this hint in Scotus. The image of the creation as a great "concert of music," in which "the ranks of the angelic hierarchies [are] like notes of a scale and a harmonic series" (S, 200), becomes a way of defining the damnation involved in any act of self-affirmation. Singing one's own note is Satanic. Through selving Satan worshipped himself as his own ultimate good, as if he were God, and for this he was cast out of heaven: "as a chorister who learns by use in the church itself the strength and beauty of his voice, he became aware in his very note of adoration of the riches of his nature; then when from that first note he should have gone on with the sacrificial service, prolonging the first note instead and ravished by his own sweetness and dazzled, the prophet says, by his beauty, he was involved in spiritual sloth ('nolendo se adjuvare') and spiritual luxury and vainglory . . ." (S, 179, 180).

Satan was not satisfied with his own refusal of the great sacrifice. He led the other bad angels to the same Satanic self-affirmation. The choir of angels, which should have been a collective act of self-abnegation, was thereby turned into a great chorus of dissonant voices, each angel singing his note at the top of his voice in self-absorbed self-worship. The chorus would have been harmonious if each angel had sacrificed himself and by so doing had transformed himself into an echo of Christ. Through arrogant self-singing it became a cacophony, "a counterpoint of dissonance and not of harmony" (S, 201). To be oneself is to be like Satan, to gather "closer and closer home under Lucifer's lead" (S, 201), for Lucifer is the center and prime model of self-adoration.

The musical metaphor here is not only a traditional image of the possible harmony of created things around God. In the context of Hopkins' thought it administers the final blow to his project of escaping isolation through artistic creation. Music and the other arts are the spontaneous expression of the inscape of the artist. This is bad not simply because a man's inscape is perishable and burns in nature's bonfire, nor because the spontaneity of art is neither right nor wrong and does not touch a man's *arbitrium*. Artistic selving is bad because it is devilish, an imitation of Satan rather than Christ. Like Satan's song, the artwork is a hymn in the artist's own honor and a sin of spiritual pride. The selving of the artist in his art, which at first seemed to make a man like the dumb creatures who in speaking themselves speak Christ, turns out to be an anticipation of the torment of the damned in hell: "Against these acts of its own the lost spirit dashes itself like a caged bear and is in prison, violently instresses them and burns, stares into them and is the deeper darkened" (S, 138). An inescapable logic seems to lead Hopkins from the nature poems, where poetry can simultaneously express nature, words, the self, and Christ, to the late sonnets, where self-affirmation forces a man to inflict upon himself, in self-mirroring anguish, a pain like that of the lost souls in hell:

> I see
> The lost are like this, and their scourge to be
> As I am mine, their sweating selves; but worse. (P, 110)

The delightful selftaste which is more distinctive than ale or alum has turned to the bitter taste of "gall" or "heartburn." Instead of being proof of man's Godlike self-sufficiency and independence, that selftaste is evidence of man's Satanic isolation. A man's *arbitrium,* the "selfyeast" of his spirit, as well as his nature, the self-stuff or "dull dough" which that yeast "sours" (P, 110), cannot be escaped, and each person seems doomed to remain his "sweating self." The poet in his poeting confirms his original depravity, and, instead of repairing the ravages of sin, allows himself to slip down the easy pathway toward the absolute isolation of hell. To become like Christ a man would need to give up both his inscape and his selftaste, cease to be the self and nature he has been created to be.

How can a man be brought to sacrifice himself?

Since the fall he has been "to his own selfbent so bound, so tied to his turn" (P, 96), that it seems impossible to imagine how he might uncoil the twisted spiral which turns him in on himself and toward Satan. Everywhere we see the spectacle of "wicked will, freedom of choice, abusing the beauty, the good of its nature" (L, III, 307), and abusing also the good of nature outside it. Man's power to destroy the inscapes of nature, "to thriftless reave . . . our rich round world bare" (P, 96), is repeatedly lamented in Hopkins' work. Far from being a creative force, the free will of man seems only able to express itself in destructive ways, whether by the corruption of his own nature or by the obliteration of the inscapes of nature outside. Now all is "bleared, smeared with toil;/ And wears man's smudge and shares man's smell" (P, 70; see also P, 83; J, 230).

A man can be saved neither by doing what comes naturally nor by the utmost efforts of his unaided will. Unless he gets help he will remain, after all his exploration of nature and art, still exiled within the bounds of his selftaste, still "Undenizened, beyond bound/Of earth's glory, earth's ease, all; no one, nowhere,/In wide the world's weal" (P, 107, 108). What force can transform him from what he is into an image of Christ?

ૐ

Grace is that force. The natural man is incapable of saving himself. Only God's grace makes him godworthy. Hopkins' concept of grace is the pivot of his thought.

Each man's selfhood has been an intention in the mind of God from all time, and a man's coming into existence on earth is the making actual of that divine intention. Man's creation is not finished with his first coming into existence. To God's eternal intention to create the man, and to his initial fulfillment of that intention, Hopkins, like so many theologians before him, adds the notion of God's continual creation of the self. Hopkins imagines this reiterated creation as a fluid stasis, in which the soul continually flows out from God and returns to God, only to be instantaneously recreated and held out again in separate existence. Like a fountain held erect by the pressure of its source, or like a mote suspended in a sunbeam, the soul is saved from annihilation by the continual pressure of God's creative action:

> Thee, God, I come from, to thee go,
> All day long I like fountain flow
> From thy hand out, swayed about
> Mote-like in thy mighty glow. (P, 167)

The forward and perpetual motion of things has, in a fallen world, become a tendency to drop or drift straight down into nothingness. No one has expressed more powerfully than Hopkins the sense of an internal hemorrhage of the soul, an innate propensity of the self to fall in on itself and disappear:

I am soft sift
In an hourglass — at the wall
Fast, but mined with a motion, a drift,
And it crowds and it combs to the fall . . . (P, 56)

Only the perpetually renewed gift of creative grace can counter-act this diabolical gravity of the soul. Like a well kept full by un-derground streams flowing down from the mountains, or like a mountain-climber suspended by a rope, the self is held poised over nothingness by a divine "pressure" which acts directly on the soul in every moment of its existence (P, 56). But though the source of the self is God, and though the self is always in touch with God, it is radically different from God. Having flowed out from God, the self tastes like nothing else whatsoever. The "strain of creating action as received in the creature," which "cannot cease without the creature's ceasing to be" (S, 137), is precisely its yearn-ing desire to move back toward God: ". . . the main stress or energy of the whole being . . . is its strain or tendency towards being, towards good, towards God . . ." (S, 137). Try as it will, the self cannot be other than itself. The mystery of selfhood is the mystery of how something can be wholly unlike its source, a source from which it is never separated. Having created the self, God holds it at arm's length and forces it to persist in its unlikeness to him: "God's most deep decree/Bitter would have me taste: my taste was me" (P, 110).

Just here, in the idea of the continual presence of God to the soul, forcing it to be one way rather than another, is the first glimpse of a way out of the impasse of selfhood. A man's self is not so much his taste as the power of tasting. If God can decree that the self should taste bitter, he can also decree that the self should taste sweet. Selfhood is the power of experiencing that taste which God wills I should taste.

The self at any one moment is both the power of tasting and what that power does in fact taste. The taste may be changed by God, or by a man's own free acts, for the self is *arbitrium*, elective will. A man's selftaste goes through all kinds of vicissitudes during his lifetime: "now he does well, now he sins, bids fair to be a sin-ner and becomes a saint or bids fair to be a saint and falls away, and indeed goes through vicissitudes of all sorts and changes times without number" (S, 148). The ability to taste persists during all these changes. It is *my* taste, *my* sin, *my* virtuous act, experienced by me and me alone, and this intimate relation between taste and the power which tastes it makes up the uniqueness of selfhood (S, 125). What Hopkins calls the "bare self" (S, 146) is the unique possibility of tasting which is the central dimensionless point of selfhood and becomes surrounded at different times by all the selftastes a man may have. Or the bare self is an empty shell which may be filled with an infinite number of different fluids, each with its own taste.

If selfhood is not unchangeable, what is grace? Grace is "any action, activity, on God's part by which, in creating or after creating, he carries the creature to or towards the end of its being, which is its selfsacrifice to God and its salvation" (S, 154).

Here at last is a way to escape the rehearsal of damnation involved in being unchangeably one particular taste of self. A man as sharer of the common nature may be in the image of Christ, but that image, like all created natures, is doomed to be burned in the bonfire of God's instress. Nature is no way back to God. A man's *arbitrium* or selfhood is so depraved that, even though it yearns to return to God, it can of itself do nothing to improve its selftaste. But God may graciously will to move the self to a better self and ultimately to that self which will correspond with Christ and be worthy of salvation.

ह➤

In his prose and poetry Hopkins uses a number of different metaphors to express the mystery of the action of grace. All these metaphors involve the idea that the self is not fixed and simple but multiple and capable of radical change.

In Matthew Arnold's thought the self is *ondoyant et divers*. A man is capable of being a hundred different selves and changing like the wind. Browning's poetry is based on the idea that the poet has a kind of negative capability, a power to become all men both historical and imaginary. In Hopkins there is a new version of the idea of the multiplicity of selves in a single person. For him the variability of the self is determined by God, rather than being an intrinsic tendency of the self to waver or alter, and this change is experienced as an act of the utmost violence.

Hopkins uses at least ten different metaphors, some traditional, some not, to explain the action of grace on the soul. Each one proposes a different model or scheme by which to think of the potential multiplicity of the soul and the action of grace. The abstract concept in each case is exactly the same.

Nothing could more emphatically suggest how far Hopkins has come from his vision of an interlocking harmony of nature in Christ. In the realm of inscapes all things are naturally metaphors of one another without ceasing to be themselves. The windhover is not a symbol. It is what it is. But it is also a figure of Christ. Its Christlikeness inheres in it as part of its being. The images of Hopkins' nature poetry belong to a realm of total immanence. Selfhood is a realm of dispersion, exclusion, the realm of the either/or. A man's selfhood, unlike his inscape, is not naturally Christlike. It is diabolically idiosyncratic. The self has no likeness to any natural thing. All things rebuff it with blank unlikeness. Language can describe it only indirectly, inadequately, for words describe species and inscapes, things which can be repeated and experienced by many men. Hopkins' use of language to describe the action of grace on the solitary soul is different, and necessarily so, from his use of language to describe the pied beauty of the world. In nature, words participate in the reality they name. To describe the soul, words must be literally metaphors, transfers from one realm to another. No words can describe directly what goes on in the ineffable regions of the soul's solitude. Excellent proof of this is the way Hopkins uses first one metaphor and then another to describe the action of grace. Each of these metaphors is appropriate not because they are all perfectly apt, but because no metaphor is really appropriate. The proliferation of metaphors is testimony to the incompatibility of words and the secret core of the self.

When, in Poem 65, Hopkins says he is "pitched past pitch of grief" (P, 106), two elaborately developed metaphors for the diversity of the self lie behind the word "pitch." [15] Pitch can be musical pitch, and, if so, this is the image of the self as like a string which vibrates at but one frequency. If the string can be tuned to one pitch it can also be tuned to others. Grace acts on the soul,

[15] There may be a third metaphor. The phrase can mean "*thrown* [by God] past the level of mere grief."

according to this metaphor, by tightening it up to a higher pitch, one more nearly in tune with Christ. To be pitched past pitch of grief is to be twisted to an exquisite pang of spiritual suffering, a pang beyond the pitch of mere grief.

Pitch may also mean angle of slope, as in the pitch of a roof. Hopkins develops this meaning of pitch in his commentary on the *Spiritual Exercises.* There is a "scale of natures" which is "infinite up towards the divine" (S, 147), and there is also an infinite scale of pitches of selfhood, from the perfectly erect and vertical pitch which coincides with Christ, on down through the neutral and horizontal pitch to a devilish pointing of the soul straight down toward hell in complete slackness (S, 147, 148). Points on the scale of natures are in themselves morally neutral, but pitch is "moral pitch, determination of right and wrong" (S, 148). The self as power of tasting is a kind of positive nothingness; in the same way the self as pitch is not so much the thing done or chosen as the fact that a unique person does or chooses in such a way. Pitch is "simple positiveness" (S, 151). To say "I go" and "I *do* go" is to say the same thing twice. Pitch is like that little auxiliary "do," which relates the action more emphatically to the doer, and tells us that it is not an anonymous going performed by anybody or everybody, but a particular going performed by me alone (S, 151).

The question arises: ". . . how can *each* self have all these pitches?" (S, 148). The answer is that pitch is elective will, freedom. The self has all these pitches in the sense that it is free to range from its present orientation toward God through the whole series from absolute right to absolute wrong.

But the self is *not* so free, or would only be so free in an unfallen world. Since the fall a man seems to be frozen or paralyzed in that pitch which has been given to him by God. He can alter it only in the direction of the droop toward hell. Grace is a direct action by God on the soul which lifts it from one pitch to a higher one closer to the vertical stem of the godhead. Grace may operate on the affective will of a man. This is a constraining action, which does not affect a man's freedom, for the affective will goes out automatically toward whatever good God proposes to it. The grace which moves a man toward his salvation is that which "shifts" him from one pitch or *arbitrium* to another more in "correspondence" to God (S, 148, 151). When God does this he changes the very selfhood of a man, and lifts it "through the gulf and void between pitch and pitch of being" (S, 156). This image of the operation of grace is another example of Hopkins' preference for diatonic over chromatic. Even if the number of pitches is infinite, there is always a space between adjacent pitches. The scale of pitches is established at fixed points with gaps between.

Hopkins' image suggests that the operation of grace changes not so much the self as the orientation of the self. But this interpretation is precluded by a passage in which Hopkins compares the mystery of grace to the mystery of transubstantiation. As the bread and wine are turned into the body and blood of Christ, so the profane self of a man is replaced by a new self which is more nearly Christlike. It is not a question of a change in substance, as in transubstantiation, but of a change in something even more precious, a man's immaterial selfhood. It is "God's finger touching the very vein of personality, which nothing else can reach and man can respond to by no play whatever" (S, 158). Grace is "an exchange of one whole for another whole, as they say in the mystery of Transubstantiation, a conversion of a whole substance into another whole substance, but here is not a question of substance; it is a lifting him from one self to another self, which is a most marvellous display of divine power" (S, 151).

If the image of the pitch of selfhood provides, in its working out, a coherent picture of Hopkins' theory of grace, there is another related, but significantly different, image. The image of pitch suggests that the self can have only one orientation of will at a time. The others exist in the realm of unrealized possibility. The new image suggests that those other pitches already exist and need only be liberated by God in order to reveal their pre-existence. In this new image the self is a three-dimensional solid, a pomegranate or tree-burl. The self existing at any moment is one cross-section or "cleave" of this solid. All the other cleaves are there waiting to be brought into existence. There are an infinite number of other worlds which could have been made of the virgin matter of chaos; in the same way there are an infinite number of other selves which I might be besides the one I am. Each man is "like a pomegranate in the round, which God sees whole but of which we see at best only one cleave" (S, 151). Seeing the whole, God can also move a man from one cleave of being to another "where the creature has consented, does consent, to God's will" (S, 154). The shift from one cross-section to another is, once again, grace, and once more Hopkins expresses the idea of a violence done to the self great enough to transform it completely.

❧

In the poems still other images are chosen to describe the action of grace, images which are more "subjective," in the sense that they describe grace not theoretically, but as it is experienced by the self. All these images tend to emphasize the terror of grace.

In "The Wreck of the Deutschland" grace comes as a flash of flame which laces the midriff with "fire of stress" (P, 56). Grace can also be felt, as in "Carrion Comfort," as an enormous force, the "wring-world right foot" of God which will, in its "heaven-han-dling," "untwist" a man's strands of being and rewind them in a new way (P, 106). Here the image of the pitch of a string is com-bined with the image of sinew or rope. The self is like a rope woven of many strands, and grace unweaves the self and reweaves it again according to another pattern.

The image of God as a power who can "wring [his] rebel" (P, 58) is related to another image in "Carrion Comfort." To receive the action of grace is like wrestling with God, as Jacob wrestled with the angel. So fiercely does the self, in spite of itself, resist the untwisting of its being in the "coil" of battle that it is as if it were fighting back against God with all its strength. Related to this, in Poem 65, is an even more violent image. Man is metal and God a blacksmith beating him into a new shape, so that his cries "on an age-old anvil wince and sing" (P, 107).

Along with these images there is yet another, a traditional one. The self is the unthreshed grain, and grace separates the wheat from the chaff. This image has connections with those of grace as fire, as wrestling, as untwisting, and as God's choice of one cleave in a man's burl of being. John the Baptist regenerated the soul with water, but Christ, as John said, baptizes with the Holy Ghost and with fire, for his "fan is in his hand, and he will throughly purge his floor, and will gather the wheat into his garner; but the chaff he will burn with fire unquenchable" (Luke, 3:16, 17). Hopkins in his commentary on these verses emphasizes the "vehemence" of the action of tossing souls in a winnowing fan, and he emphasizes also the absoluteness of the division which winnowing makes between the self worthy to be saved and those cleaves of being which must be discarded (S, 267, 268). In "Carrion Comfort," all the pain which the divine wrestler imposes is done so that "my chaff might fly; my grain lie, sheer and clear" (P, 106). In "The Wreck of the Deutschland" the storm which inflicts mortal suffering on the nuns and their companions is a threshing of souls, and Hopkins asks: ". . . is the shipwreck then a harvest, does tempest carry the grain for thee?" (P, 65).

The image of the grain threshed and harvested is related to the symbolism of the Eucharist and leads to another of Hopkins' images for grace. The taking of communion is an assimilation of the body of Christ which "makes of every Christian another Christ, an AfterChrist" (S, 100). Grace also transforms the self into an AfterChrist, and what more appropriate expression for this than the image of eating? In "Carrion Comfort" once again, where all these images are inextricably intertwined, the heart of the man who has been wrestled and threshed out by God "laps strength" and takes "cheer" from his transformation into Christ, as earlier he had refused to "feast" on the "carrion comfort, Despair" (P, 106). To feast on Despair would be to yield to the lure of a kind of self-cannibalism, to eat the dead body of one's loss of hope, to succumb to the diabolical pleasure of luxuriating in one's own bad selfhood. In place of this a man must endure the agony of being remade by God, and only then feast, but on Christ rather than on the carrion comfort.

The image of eating works in two ways. Not only does man become Christlike by assimilating Christ; he also is eaten by Christ, and thus, in another way, turned into Christ. In "Carrion Comfort" God, like a ferocious lion, views the "bruisèd bones" of his victim "with darksome devouring eyes," and when Hopkins asks who is cheered by the outcome of this battle, the devoured or the devourer ("O which one? is it each one?"), the answer is that both God and man are cheered by the sinner's transformation into Christ. Both are cheered because both are eater and eaten. Christ eats and is eaten by the self, and the self eats and is eaten by Christ. In the same way, in "The Wreck of the Deutschland," the "Feast of the one woman without stain," the Feast of the Immaculate

Conception which follows the death of the nuns, is another occasion on which Christ consumes and is consumed — as the ambiguity of the word "of" in the line just quoted suggests (P, 65).
Christ "has glory" of the nun, and the nun gives Christ glory by
sacrificing herself for him, as he sacrificed himself for her. The
"grain" is both Christ's body taken in the Eucharist and also, as
in "The Starlight Night," the harvest of just souls who are assimilated into heaven.

This leads to another equally ambiguous image, a sexual one.
Christ's "having glory" of the nun is also an image of sexual
possession. The salvation of the tall nun at the moment of her
death is described as a sexual act in which, like Mary before her,
she conceives and brings forth the Christ child:

> For so conceivèd, so to conceive thee is done;
>   But here was heart-throe, birth of a brain,
> Word, that heard and kept thee and uttered thee outright. (P, 65)

As Christ was conceived in purity, so must we conceive of him,
that is, come to know him. The tall nun is a repetition of Mary.
Christ the Word, *Logos,* is born in our brains when we understand him, and in our hearts when we become Christlike. To hear,
keep, and utter outright the name of Christ is like the conception,
gestation, and parturition of Christ by Mary. But the nun also
becomes Christ, through grace. The nun carries Christ within her
as Mary did, and therefore is in the image of Christ. Like Dante
and T. S. Eliot, Hopkins knows that Mary is the daughter of her
son, "la figlia del suo figlio." God is the lover who possesses her
and makes her pregnant with Christ. God is also the creating father
who makes sure that she herself is born in the image of Christ.
God and Christ, though two, are one in the unity of the Trinity.
God is father, bridegroom, and child, all three, and this multiple
and ambiguous sexual relation is repeated every time a sinful soul,
through grace, is reborn in the image of Christ. So, in "The
Blessed Virgin Compared to the Air We Breathe," Hopkins describes, in lines of exquisite beauty, the imitation of Christ by just
souls as a re-enactment of the bringing forth of Christ by Mary:

> Of her flesh he took flesh:
> He does take fresh and fresh,
> Though much the mystery how,

Not flesh but spirit now
And makes, O marvellous!
New Nazareths in us . . . (P, 101)

ॐ

Pitch, pomegranate or burl of being, rope-twisting, wrestling, threshing, eating, forging, sexual reproduction — Hopkins' images for the action of grace proliferate in baroque complexity, and betray in their diversity the impossibility of speaking unequivocally of events in the *ultima solitudo* of the soul. All these images describe a single conception of grace: grace operates not on the inscape of a man but on his individual selfhood; the activity of grace is exclusively on the part of God; there is no continuity between the old self and the new. God is a world-wringer, a wrestler, thresher, blacksmith, devouring lion, ravisher of the soul, and only if he kills me can he cure me. "Except a corn of wheat fall into the ground and die, it abideth alone: but if it die, it bringeth forth much fruit" (John, 12:24). Grace brings about the death and resurrection of the soul which it is powerless to bring about for itself.

To be reborn in the image of Christ means to accept a re-enactment of the passion of Christ, to offer oneself as a passive victim, to be sacrificed and suffer unto death as did our Lord. Hopkins distinguishes three kinds of grace, each coming from a different person of the Trinity, and imposing on the soul, in their sequential action, a repetition of Christ's crucifixion. There is first "creative grace, the grace which destined the victim for the sacrifice, and which belongs to God the Father" (S, 158). Then there is Christ's grace, which is "a purifying and a mortifying grace, bringing the victim to the altar and sacrificing it" (S, 158). Last there is the "elevating grace" of the Holy Ghost, which is "the acceptance and assumption of the victim of the sacrifice" (S, 158).

One final image for the action of grace, perhaps the most important of all, emphasizes the neutrality of the "positive infinitesimal" (S, 146) which remains the same through all the changes of the self. In this image the self is the contents of a hollow vessel. One moment the shell is filled with bitter selfstuff, and the next moment it is filled miraculously with Christ. As in the image of eating, of which this motif is a variant, the consumer becomes what he consumes, so that container and thing contained can no longer be distinguished: "it is Christ in his member on the one side, his member in Christ on the other. It is as if a man said: That is Christ playing at me and me playing at Christ, only that it is no play but truth; That is Christ *being me* and me being Christ" (S, 154). In this image as in the others the self seems powerless to resist or aid the action of grace. The influx of grace is, in one of Hopkins' most powerfully sensual images, like the tasting of something so powerful in tang that it fills the whole being to the exclusion of anything else. I am all in a moment overwhelmed and engulfed by a single all-pervasive taste, "brim, in a flash, full!" (P, 58). Every corner of my being is instantaneously occupied by Christ.

Could this really be Hopkins' doctrine of grace? Though the very core of man's freedom is changed by grace, that freedom seems to have no power to respond to grace. All seems to be done by God alone. This would be heresy, the Jansenistic extreme of saying that man has no influence on his eternal fate.

Hopkins is not saying this. He believes that "there must be something which shall be truly the creature's in the work of corresponding with grace: this is the *arbitrium*, the verdict on God's side, the saying Yes, the 'doing-agree' . . ." (S, 154). The elevating grace of the Holy Ghost can come only if man accepts the afflictive grace of Christ. Only "the aspiration in answer to his inspiration" (S, 158) can complete the work of sacrifice and transform the self into Christ. In "The Wreck of the Deutschland," when the tall nun, in the extremity of her suffering, cries out "O Christ, Christ, come quickly" (P, 63), this cry of aspiration is an invocation to the "arch and original Breath," the inspiration of the Holy Ghost which crowns the process of grace. In what Hopkins calls the "least sigh of desire" (S, 155), the "bare acknowledgment," the "counter stress which God alone can feel" (S, 158), there is a tiny corner left for man's free will.

It is only a tiny corner, for "even the sigh or aspiration itself is in answer to an inspiration of God's spirit" (S, 156). Man cannot initiate the movement toward salvation. "Correspondence" is the key word in Hopkins' theory of grace. A man's salvation is won by achieving a correspondence with Christ, and the only action on man's part which makes this happen is the minute movement of volition whereby he wills to correspond with God's grace: "And by this infinitesimal act the creature does what in it lies to bridge the gulf fixed between its present actual and worser pitch of will and its future better one" (S, 155). This "correspondence with grace and seconding of God's designs" (S, 197) is man's mite contributed toward the creation of his own best self.

All Hopkins' speculations about grace circle around an inexpressible mystery, a mystery parallel to that of the Trinity, in which the Persons are one and yet three. Here it is the mystery of how the self can be altogether changed and yet remain the same self. Ultimately this mystery can best be expressed by the image of a vessel which is conformed to what fills it. Container and thing contained are both ultimately in the image of Christ, and it is only because Christ fits perfectly into the self that the self can ever come to contain him. Hopkins' last word on the mystery of grace is a series of images of man as a hollow shell everywhere inhabited by Christ and brought into its own perfect shape by Christ. This is possible only if the man chooses to be his own proper self, which means consenting to his self-sacrifice to God:

. . . God rests in man as in a place, a *locus,* bed, vessel, expressly made to receive him as a jewel in a case hollowed to fit it, as the hand in the glove or the milk in the breast . . . And God *in forma servi* rests *in servo,*[16] that is / Christ as a solid in his member as a hollow or shell, both things being the image of God; which can only be pertectly when the member is in all things conformed to Christ. This too best brings out the nature of the man himself, as the lettering on a sail or device upon a flag are best seen when it fills. (S, 195)

> ຂໍ

Hopkins has finally escaped from his isolation. Through grace he can lose the bad self which seemed doomed to eternal solitude,

[16] This is a reference to that passage in Philippians (2:5–11) which is of capital importance for Hopkins' understanding of the Incarnation, and which is commented on in an eloquent letter to Bridges: "This mind he says, was in Christ Jesus — he means as man: being in the form of God — that is, finding, as in the first instant of his incarnation he did, his human nature informed by the godhead — he thought it nevertheless no snatching-matter for him to be equal with God, but annihilated himself, taking the form of servant . . ." (L, I, 175). Christ's humbling of himself in this way, says Hopkins, is "the root of all his holiness and the imitation of this the root of all moral good in other men" (L, I, 175).

and he can find the good self which is worthy to ascend to heaven and join the eternal choir around God. By imitating, with the help of grace, the great sacrifice of Christ he can get back to God.

All Hopkins need do is abnegate his selfwill, abandon his self-bent, and "empty or exhaust himself so far as that is possible" (L, I, 175). He must give up all attempts to reach God through his affective will. His efforts must be concentrated on his elective will, and on making that elective will a perfect servant of God. If he does this the affective will is sure to follow in its time: "Facere nos indifferentes — with the elective will, not the affective essentially; but the affective will will follow" (S, 256). Hopkins has chosen the negative way, the way of perfect obedience through the elective will. Now he need only wait, in patience and hope, for grace to descend.

This is just what does *not* happen. Though Hopkins has isolated experiences of grace, such as those recorded in "The Wreck of the Deutschland" and "Carrion Comfort," the central religious experience of his last years is the prolonged anguish of spiritual paralysis, dryness of soul, the absence of God and the failure of grace. The descent of grace in "The Wreck" and "Carrion Comfort" was painful enough. It was like being struck by lightning or threshed out by the divine reaper. This pain testified to the immediate presence of God in the soul, and was accepted willingly. All that disappears. It seems as if God has withdrawn from the soul and from the world, leaving Hopkins in a situation strangely like that recorded in his early poems — a situation of abandonment and impotent suffering.

Let there be no misunderstanding of this. Hopkins wavers neither in his faith nor in his vocation. His experience is not incompatible with Catholicism. It is spiritual desolation, a vanishing of God from the soul which, as St. Ignatius said, is God's way of testing the soul, and showing it how powerless it is by itself. But though the inner experience of Hopkins' last years is perfectly compatible with Catholic tradition, it is also to be understood in the context of the spiritual history of the nineteenth century. The experience recorded in the "terrible" sonnets, and in the late letters and retreat notes, is a striking example of the way the nineteenth century was, for many writers, a time of the no longer and not yet, a time of the absence of God. Hopkins has, beyond all his contemporaries, the most shattering experience of the disappearance of God.

Spiritual desolation as Hopkins knows it means first of all an isolation like that the poet suffered at the time of his early poems. The self is cut off from everything outside and shrinks into the impenetrable enclosure of itself. To find oneself in this imprisonment is like being suddenly awakened in the middle of a night so dark that the darkness seems to press in on all sides like the fell of some furry beast (P, 109). This darkness is both natural and transnatural, a dark night both of the soul and of the body. The self is cut off from God's sustaining power and dries up like a choked well or fountain. No vein of the gospel proffer feeds it. The self also ceases to participate in the on-going vitality of nature. Affective will and elective will have split apart, and from the point of view of the *arbitrium,* it seems as if there were no natural self at all. Cut off from its own inscape, the self no longer shares in the pied beauty of the inscapes of nature. In Hopkins' last poems natural images appear only as indirect metaphors for an experience which is transnatural. It is as if the poet were blind and dying of thirst, but it is a spiritual blindness and a spiritual thirst, for which physical blindness and thirst are mere figures (P, 111). The basis of these last poems is no longer an experience of nature, as in "The Windhover," but an experience taking place in the *ultima solitudo* of the self.

This isolation of the self from nature and God generates an acutely negative experience of space and time. In place of the constructive natural time of "Hurrahing in Harvest," or the fiercely disintegrative time of nature's bonfire, the sonnets of desolation describe time as a vertical fall. There is a complete absence of any sustaining pressure, and time is experienced as the plunge of the unsupported self into the chasm of its own nothingness. Each moment reproduces the nonentity of the one before, and since there are no distinguishable surroundings it is as if the self were pitching with infinite speed into an unfathomable gulf:

> O the mind, mind has mountains; cliffs of fall
> Frightful, sheer, no-man-fathomed. (P, 107)

Insomnia is a direct experience of time as a fall. The man who is pitched past pitch of grief into the abysses of the mind has but one comfort in the whirlwind: each day ends in a rehearsal of death, sleep. But suppose sleep will not come? Then the "black hours" of the night lengthen out until the sufferer is left at an infinite distance from the daylight time in which nature is visible, and in which the moments are a measure of change and growth. The moments of insomnia measure nothing, nothing but the repeating nothingness of the self in its endless fall. According to clock-time only a few hours have passed, but they have seemed years long, or more. A lifetime of suffering has passed in a single night. As in the opium dreams of De Quincey, Hopkins' time of desolation is elastic, and a brief span of it can stretch out toward infinite length. "With witness I speak this," cries Hopkins. "But where I say/ Hours I mean years, mean life" (P, 109).

This experience of the infinity of finite human time is matched by an experience of the infinity of space. The fall in time is also a fall in space, and one is the expression of the other. The desolate self, abandoned of all support, dwells in a space which is entirely without contents. Just as a small time, deprived of natural measure, stretches out to an infinite duration, so the confined space of the isolated self expands to infinite size. One could travel through this dark space forever without reaching either nature or God.

The most painful characteristic of this infinite space and time is the breakdown of language. Words are the meeting-place of self, nature, and God the Word. These three have split apart, and as a result language loses its efficacy. Words, instead of reaching out to touch things and give them over to man, no longer have strength enough to leave the self at all. Thwarted by some mysterious decree of heaven or hell, words become the opaque walls of the poet's interior prison. His speech becomes a stuttering staccato of alliterative monosyllables, each word thrown out despairingly in a brief spasm of energy, and each word closing in on itself with explosive or hissing consonants, as if to express, in its isolation from the words around it, the poet's failure to escape from his solitude:

> Only what word
> Wisest my heart breeds dark heaven's baffling ban
> Bars or hell's spell thwarts. (P, 109)

Cast outward by the mind to reach nature or God, words fall endlessly through a shadowy void and touch neither things nor the God who made them. Abandoned by God, Hopkins cries out for grace, but his words have lost their virtue and cannot reach their destination. No human words can reach a God who has withdrawn to an infinite distance:

> And my lament
> Is cries countless, cries like dead letters sent
> To dearest him that lives alas! away. (P, 109)

Language, nature, space, time — with the failure of grace all the ways fail in which the self can escape from itself and establish connections with nature or with God. As a result Hopkins, in his deprivation, experiences a horrible parody of the reflexive relation of God to himself. Instead of enjoying his own perfection of being, he lives in an endless circle of self-punishment, "this tormented mind/With this tormented mind tormenting yet" (P, 110).

The consequences of the failure of grace are not only evident in a few poems, those sonnets which were "written in blood" (L, I, 219). Spiritual dryness is Hopkins' almost constant state during his last years. So cruel has been his elective will to his affective nature that it has almost been able to destroy it. The result is a state of spiritual paralysis for which Hopkins has a striking image: sexual impotence. The power of sexual reproduction is perhaps the most important way in which man shares in the teeming growth of nature, but Hopkins' "go is gone" (L, III, 251). He is unable to beget anything, and as a result "time's eunuch." All around him there are creatures for whom time is a means of breeding and reproduction. Only for him is time experienced as an endlessly repeated impotent straining. Perhaps Hopkins' most poignant lines are those in "Thou art indeed just, Lord," in which the poet, from the enclosure of his desolation, looks out at the abundance of nature and measures the fearful extent of his sterility. The lines have truly that "terrible pathos" for which Dixon praised Hopkins (L, II, 80):

> See, banks and brakes
> Now, leavèd how thick! lacèd they are again
> With fretty chervil, look, and fresh wind shakes
> Them; birds build — but not I build; no, but strain,
> Time's eunuch, and not breed one work that wakes. (P, 113)

This passage is no mere poetic imagery. It is an exact description of Hopkins' almost constant condition during his later years. During this time he lies in a "coffin of weakness and dejection

. . . , without even the hope of change" (L, I, 214, 215). The feeling of impotence is with him always, and is expressed again and again in his letters to Bridges. His poetic inspiration, except for rare bursts, fails and dries up, for though the source of poetry is God's grace, it is a natural grace, acting on the heart or affective will and making it fecund. Hopkins' heart is lifeless, even though he pleads to his self to "more have pity on" his heart (P, 110).

Not only poetry fails. Hopkins' last years are strewn with half-finished projects, ambitious schemes which are planned, begun, and then abandoned when they are still in the state of "scaffolding" (L, I, 229), so that he cries in despair: ". . . and there they lie and my old notebooks and beginnings of things, ever so many, which it seems to me might well have been done, ruins and wrecks . . ." (L, III, 255). In his state of "melancholy" (L, III, 256) and "nervous weakness" (L, I, 193) he strikes out in all directions, hoping to find some channel which is still open and in which he can freely act. He studies the theory of music, and begins many compositions. He hopes to finish his commentary on the *Spiritual Exercises,* and plans a treatise on sacrifice, an essay on Pindar and Greek metrics, a work on statistics and free will, and various studies in classical philology. He thinks he understands the inner connections of meter and music and hopes to "set . . . them on a scientific footing which will be final like the law of gravitation" (L, III, 377). He plans "to write almost a philosophy of art and illustrate that by the Dorian Measure" (L, I, 247). He studies Welsh. He studies mathematics. He studies Egyptian mythology and hopes to show its relation to the Greek pantheon. He develops a brilliant theory of what he calls the "underthought" in Greek tragedy and Christian scripture (L, III, 252, 253). All fails. Nothing is finished. Nothing is published. He remains "a lonely began" (P, 109), and he is tormented by his professional failure as a Jesuit scholar and professor of classics. Far from escaping his spiritual paralysis, he merely succumbs to that worst fate of a man of genius: the scattering of his talents. His letters are a crescendo of laments bewailing his inability to finish anything he begins: "Every impulse and spring of art seems to have died in me"; "I am always jaded, I cannot tell why, and my vein shews no signs of ever flowing again"; "I am always tired, always jaded, though work is not heavy, and the impulse to do anything fails me or has in it no continuance"; "if in any leisure I try to do anything I make no way — nor with my work, alas!"; "it kills me to be time's eunuch and never to beget"; "Unhappily I cannot produce anything at all, not only the luxuries like poetry, but the duties almost of my position, its natural outcome — like scientific works. . . . All impulse fails me: I can give myself no sufficient reason for going on. Nothing comes: I am a eunuch — but it is for the kingdom of heaven's sake" (L, I, 124, 178, 183, 221, 222, 270).

The climax of Hopkins' spiritual experience is certain terrifying entries in the retreat notes of 1888. Here he yields to the carrion comfort of despair and self-loathing, and once again the image of the eunuch returns. Though it can be said that these notes are only a normal stage in the making of the spiritual exercises, and though they are followed a few days later by calm and objective discussions of biblical texts, they stand as cries from the depths of spiritual dereliction, and they are never afterwards qualified by testimony to the Pascalian tears of joy which might have accompanied a rain of grace. These notes can be said to form, on the basis of the evidence we have, the endpoint of Hopkins' spiritual adventure:

> . . . I began to enter on that course of loathing and hopelessness which I have so often felt before, which made me fear madness and led me to give up the practice of meditation except, as now, in retreat and here it is again. . . . what is life without aim, without spur, without help? All my undertakings miscarry: I am like a straining eunuch. . . . O my God, look down on me . . . Helpless loathing. (S, 262, 263)

ह

There is one last movement: hope in the "comfort of the Resurrection."

Hopkins has sought to find happiness in a sense of God's presence here and now, in this life. Turn where he may he finds another proof that for this life there is no hope. The only hope lies beyond the grave, at the Last Judgment, when man may be permanently transformed, body and soul, into Christ. In his last retreat notes Hopkins longs for death (S, 262), and his last words ("I am so happy") indicate joyful acceptance of the fact that he was escaping from this sad life at last. The ending beyond the ending and the last stage in Hopkins' spiritual journey, is the conclusion of "That Nature is a Heraclitean Fire and of the comfort of the Resurrection." Here he imagines the miraculous transformation of man into Christ as accomplished, once and for all. Man becomes the one cleave of his being which coincides with God, and inscape and self are joined in one. Only if this happens can he escape the crucifying contradictions of nature and grace, and be happy at last:

> In a flash, at a trumpet crash,
> I am all at once what Christ is, ' since he was what I am, and
> This Jack, joke, poor potsherd, ' patch, matchwood, immortal diamond,
> Is immortal diamond. (P, 112)

In this poem Hopkins expresses the extremity of his despair and hope, and stands aghast at the sight of a world visibly disintegrating and being consumed, as at the last trump. He is sustained by nothing but the comfort of the Resurrection, the hope of that miracle of transubstantiation which will change him from the impure carbon of matchwood, into diamond, change him from one allotropic form of himself to another so different that if there is any secret continuity between the two it is only that the same neutral possibility of being is, in each case, made real by God, made real in forms which are as far apart as the whole distance from hell to heaven.

As long as Hopkins is alive the change remains future, and this is the anticipation of happiness, not happiness itself: "It is as if one were dazzled by a spark or star in the dark, seeing it but not seeing by it: we want a light shed on our way and a happiness spread over our life" (S, 262). The image of a star, seen at a distance but not irradiating this present life, is a perfect expression for a God who is transcendent, not immanent. God has reappeared, but at a distance, across an unbridgeable space. He can never be reached in this life, and does not sustain Hopkins in what he is now.

There is a strange similarity between the final stance of Hopkins and that of Matthew Arnold. Hopkins has given up everything positive, everything natural, and lives without growth or productivity, except for brief spasms of poetic creation. He is nothing, a positive infinitesimal, and is waiting, so far fruitlessly, for the spark from heaven to fall. In the end, after a lifetime spent in God's service, he has not gone beyond his beginning, which was to know God as the deity of Isaiah, the God who hides himself.

Hopkins, who seems so different from other nineteenth-century writers who suffered the absence of God, in reality ends in a similar place. Like so many of his contemporaries, he believes in God, but is unable to reach him. Deserted by his nature, he is left with a blind violence of will toward a God who keeps himself absent. The saving power can come, for him at least, only beyond the gates of death, as De Quincey can rise again only at the moment of death, as Arnold waits in the vacuum between two worlds, and as Cathy and Heathcliff, in *Wuthering Heights,* must die to be reunited.

Only in Browning, of the writers studied here, are there hints and anticipations of that recovery of immanence which was to be the inner drama of twentieth-century literature. Browning alone seems to have glimpsed the fact that the sad alternatives of nihilism and escape beyond the world could be evaded if man would only reject twenty-five hundred years of belief in the dualism of heaven and earth. If man could do this he might come to see that being and value lie in *this* world, in what is immediate, tangible, present to man, in earth, sun, sea, in the stars in their courses, and in what Yeats was to call "the foul rag-and-bone shop of the heart." But Browning, like De Quincey, Arnold, Hopkins, and Emily Brontë, was stretched on the rack of a fading transcendentalism, and could reach a precarious unity only by the most extravagant stratagems of the spirit.

Index